W9-DCL-813

The Lorette Wilmot Library
and Media Center
Nazareth College of Rochester

DEMCO

THE CLASSICS
OF **WESTERN
SPIRITUALITY**

THE CLASSICS OF WESTERN SPIRITUALITY
A Library of the Great Spiritual Masters

President and Publisher
Lawrence Boadt, CSP

EDITORIAL BOARD

Editor-in-Chief
Bernard McGinn—Naomi Shenstone Donnelly Professor of Historical Theology and the History of Christianity, Divinity School, University of Chicago, Chicago, IL

Editorial Consultant
Ewert H. Cousins—Professor of Theology, Fordham University, Bronx, NY

John E. Booty—Professor of Anglican Studies, School of Theology, University of the South, Sewanee, TN

Joseph Dan—Professor of Kabbalah, Department of Jewish Thought, Hebrew University, Jerusalem, Israel.

Louis Dupré—T. L. Riggs Professor of Philosophy of Religion, Yale University, New Haven, CT

Rozanne Elder—Executive Vice-President, Cistercian Publications, Kalamazoo, MI

Michael Fishbane—Nathan Cummings Professor, Divinity School, University of Chicago, Chicago, IL

Karlfried Froehlich—Professor of the History of the Early and Medieval Church, Princeton Theological Seminary, Princeton, NJ

Arthur Green—Professor of Jewish Thought, Brandeis University, Waltham, MA

Stanley S. Harakas—Archbishop Iakovos Professor of Orthodox Theology, Holy Cross Greek Orthodox Seminary, Brookline, MA

Moshe Idel—Professor of Jewish Thought, Department of Jewish Thought, Hebrew University, Jerusalem, Israel.

Bishop Kallistos of Diokleia—Fellow of Pembroke College, Oxford, Spalding Lecturer in Eastern Orthodox Studies, Oxford University, England.

Azim Nanji—Director, The Institute of Ismaili Studies, London, England.

Seyyed Hossein Nasr—Professor of Islamic Studies, George Washington University, Washington, DC

Raimon Panikkar—Professor Emeritus, Department of Religious Studies, University of California at Santa Barbara, CA

Jaroslav Pelikan—Sterling Professor of History and Religious Studies, Yale University, New Haven, CT

Sandra M. Schneiders—Professor of New Testament Studies and Spirituality, Jesuit School of Theology, Berkeley, CA

Michael A. Sells—Emily Judson Baugh and John Marshall Gest Professor of Comparative Religions, Haverford College, Haverford, PA

Huston Smith—Thomas J. Watson Professor of Religion Emeritus, Syracuse University, Syracuse, NY

John R. Sommerfeldt—Professor of History, University of Dallas, Irving, TX

David Steindl-Rast—Spiritual Author, Benedictine Grange, West Redding, CT

David Tracy—Greeley Professor of Roman Catholic Studies, Divinity School, University of Chicago, Chicago, IL

The Most Rev. and Rt. Hon. Rowan D. Williams—Archbishop of Canterbury.

Norbert and Early Norbertine Spirituality

SELECTED AND INTRODUCED BY
THEODORE J. ANTRY, O.PRAEM., AND CAROL NEEL
PREFACE BY
ANDREW D. CIFERNI, O.PRAEM.

PAULIST PRESS
NEW YORK • MAHWAH

DISCARDED

LORETTE WILMOT LIBRARY
NAZARETH COLLEGE

Cover Art: St. Norbert in Orvieto, reproduction of an anonymous thirteenth-century painting. Courtesy of Abbot Gary Neville, O.Praem., St. Norbert Abbey, Green Bay, Wisconsin.

Cover design by A. Michael Velthaus
Book design by Lynn Else

Copyright © 2007 Daylesford Abbey and Carol Neel

All rights reserved. No part of this book may be reproduced or transmitted in any form or by any means, electronic or mechanical, including photocopying, recording, or by any information storage and retrieval system without permission in writing from the Publisher.

Library of Congress Cataloging-in-Publication Data

Norbert and early norbertine spirituality : selected and introduced by Theodore J. Antry and Carol Neel ; preface by Andrew D. Ciferni.
    p.   cm.—(The classics of western spirituality)
    Includes bibliographical references and index.
    ISBN 978-0-8091-4468-6 (alk. paper)—ISBN 978-0-8091-0577-9 (alk. paper)
    1. Premonstratensians. 2. Spirituality—Catholic Church. 3. Norbert, of Xanten, Saint, ca. 1080–1134. I. Antry, Theodore James. II. Neel, Carol.
BX3902.3.N67 2007
271'.19—dc22

                                                                    2007011342

Published by Paulist Press
997 Macarthur Boulevard
Mahwah, New Jersey 07430

www.paulistpress.com

Printed and bound in the
United States of America

CONTENTS

Preface   xi

Abbreviations   xiii

Foreword   xv

Introduction   1

Anselm of Havelberg, *Apologetic Letter*   29
    Introduction   29
    Text   38

Herman of Tournai, *Miracles of St. Mary of Laon*   63
    Introduction   63
    Text (excerpts)   69

Life of Godfrey of Cappenberg   85
    Introduction   85
    Text   92

The Hagiography of Norbert, the A and B *Lives*—
    Introduction   121

Version A: *Life of Norbert, Archbishop of Magdeburg*   126

Version B: *Life of Norbert* (excerpts)   175

Philip of Harvengt, "On the Knowledge of Clerics"   193
    Introduction   193
    Text   201

CONTENTS

Philip of Harvengt, *Life of Oda*   219
 Introduction   219
 Text   224

Notes   243

Bibliography   281

Index   301

Contributors to This Volume

THEODORE J. ANTRY, O.PRAEM., entered the Norbertine Order in 1957 and was ordained to the priesthood in 1966. He holds an MA in Latin from Marquette University and a PhD in medieval studies from the University of Notre Dame. He is currently the archivist for Daylesford Abbey in Paoli, Pennsylvania. He is a member of the order's international Spirituality Commission and an associate member of its Historical Commission. Antry's published work includes an edition of the medical work of the fourteenth-century Premonstratensian Thomas of Sarepta.

CAROL NEEL is professor of history at Colorado College in Colorado Springs, Colorado, where she has taught since 1980. She holds a BA in Latin from Bryn Mawr College and a PhD in history from Cornell University. She has written about the history of women and the family in the Middle Ages as well as about the medieval Premonstratensians. Among her prior publications is a translation of the *Handbook* of the ninth-century noblewoman Dhuoda. She lives with her husband and four children on a mountainside in Colorado Springs.

ANDREW D. CIFERNI, O.PRAEM., has been a member of Daylesford Abbey in Paoli, Pennsylvania, since 1959 and was ordained to the priesthood in 1968. He holds an STL from the Gregorian University (Rome) and a PhD in liturgical studies from the University of Notre Dame. He is a founding member of the North American Academy of Liturgy and the Catholic Academy of Liturgy and has taught at Catholic University of America and at Washington Theological Union, where he was academic dean. Ciferni is president of the international Norbertine Commission on Canonical Life and Spirit of the Order.

PREFACE

The work of the Second Vatican Council (1962–65) rested in many ways on the *ressourcement* theology that preceded it. The "return to the sources" demanded by the council was already in progress in many communities of consecrated life. The discovery of lost or neglected foundational texts, translation of ancient sources, and research made available in publications dedicated to the spiritual heritage of religious orders facilitated this renewal of the vowed life and continues in our own times.

In the United States the availability of texts and studies on the origins of the Canons Regular of Prémontré (Premonstratensians or Norbertines) has been minimal. The existence of canons regular is little known outside Europe; Vatican documents on consecrated life generally omit any mention of this group of men and women who are not monks, mendicants, or modern societies of apostolic life. This American lacuna has been in the process of being filled in the last several decades by the work—both individual and collaborative—of Rev. Theodore J. Antry, O.Praem., archivist at Daylesford Abbey in Paoli, Pennsylvania, and Professor Carol Neel of Colorado College in Colorado Springs, Colorado. In their translations of twelfth-century Premonstratensian sources, their writing and their teaching, they have been bringing to English-speaking Norbertines and to the larger academic community a vision of early Premonstratensian spirituality that both rests upon and challenges earlier interpretations of Norbert and his first men and women disciples.

Both the freshness of their translations and the new information they offer about our history aid the international Premonstratensian family in responding more faithfully to the council's other call, namely, to *aggiornamento* or legitimate adaptation to the times. The contemporary tension between return to the sources and legitimate adaptation to the times will be seen, in these works' contents, to have been prefigured in the primary sources presented and interpreted here. For this insight alone we stand in debt to the work of Father Antry and Professor Neel. A larger ecclesiastical and academic audience will benefit from what it may learn of this ancient *ordo vivendi Praemonstratensis* that in its origins adapted an earlier tradition and simultaneously helped set the stage for the religious movements of the thirteenth century.

Andrew D. Ciferni, O.Praem.
President
Praemonstratensian Commission on Canonical Life
and Spirit of the Order

Daylesford Abbey, Paoli, Pennsylvania
June 6, 2005

ABBREVIATIONS

AASS   Acta sanctorum quotquot toto orbe coluntur, ed. Society of Bollandists. 68 vols. Brussels, 1643–present.

AP   *Analecta Praemonstratensia*

BHL   *Bibliotheca hagiographica latina antiquae et mediae aetatis*, ed. Society of Bollandists. Subsidia hagiographica 6. Rev. ed. Brussels: Société des Bollandistes, 1909.

CC   Corpus Christianorum, series latina

CCCM   Corpus Christianorum Continuatio Medievalis

CSEL   Corpus scriptorum ecclesiasticorum latinorum

MGH   Monumenta Germaniae Historica, Scriptores, ed. Georg Pertz et al. 30 vols. Hannover: Hahn, 1826–92.

PL   Patrologiae cursus completus, series latina, ed. Jacques-Paul Migne. 221 vols. Paris: Migne, 1841–64.

FOREWORD

In 1984, Premonstratensians—or, as most English-speaking moderns call them, Norbertines—throughout the world celebrated the 850th anniversary of the death of their founder, St. Norbert. This man stood tall among his twelfth-century contemporaries, yet today scholars puzzle over the motivations behind his complex actions and his influence on his many followers. The place of Norbert's birth is in dispute; his entry into the canon of the saints was delayed for almost 450 years; he left no writings. His disciples, however, and others who knew him left an abundance of literature about his life and the early Premonstratensians' role in medieval religious reform. This volume aims, through their words, to convey a better understanding of the nature and influence of this important and multifaceted figure—itinerant preacher, reformer of canonical life, founder of an order, archbishop, and adviser to the imperial court. In turn, its contents suggest how St. Norbert's model shaped the goals and experience of his immediate disciples, as well as their successors in subsequent centuries.

Norbert and Early Norbertine Spirituality is intended for the use and edification not only of those interested in the Order of Prémontré and the European Middle Ages, but for those exploring the Christian spiritual tradition more broadly. Although it represents the collaboration of two translators, it would not have come to be without the support of colleagues, families, and friends—among them several Norbertine communities—who share our belief that this material deserves a wide audience. Professors John Van Engen and Bernard McGinn, Mohan Sawhney, O.Praem., Peter Stiglich, O.Praem., Leo Van Dyck, O.Praem., and Michiel Meeusen, O.Praem., have in various ways assisted our work. The interest of young Norbertines and students at Colorado College, especially Ambrose Criste, O.Praem., a Colorado College alumnus, has sustained our enthusiasm for this project. The research programs and reference staffs of the Newberry Library in Chicago, Illinois, have provided invaluable professional assistance. Andrew Ciferni, O.Praem., initially brought us together to work on this volume and, as his preface here evidences, has continued to participate in our discussions of these texts and the shaping of our translations. In all, our enterprise has been fostered by the efforts of, on the one hand, persons and institutions seeking to advance historical scholarship and, on the other, individuals and communities living in and reflecting on the tradition framed by these medieval texts.

We dedicate this book to the young people of the Norbertine Order in the hope that it may foster their vocations. We hope that the spirit of St. Norbert, who comes to life in the writings of his followers, may inspire them also to greater dedication and holiness of life, thereby rekindling for the modern world the vibrancy of his and his disciples' twelfth-century spirituality.

June 6, 2005
Feast of St. Norbert

Theodore Antry, O.Praem., and Carol Neel

INTRODUCTION

Among the new religious movements of the great twelfth-century reform of European Christianity, the Premonstratensians—the followers of Norbert of Xanten—are conspicuously under-represented in modern scholarship. Abundant recent attention to the cultural poetics and social history of medieval religion has yielded no monograph on the Order of Prémontré,[1] its founder Norbert has received no full scholarly biography,[2] and works on twelfth-century spirituality in general give little attention to the several important twelfth-century authors personally summoned by Norbert to his canonical reform.[3] At the same time, however, scholarly consensus acknowledges that the white canons of Prémontré were among the most prolific and influential of the period's regular religious groups, second only to the white monks of Cîteaux in the rapidity and extent of their growth after their foundation in France in 1120.[4] In their embrace of the Rule of St. Augustine, their advocacy of preaching and poverty for a revitalized clergy, and their high level of spiritual affect especially in relation to the Virgin, the Premonstratensians at once stood at the forefront of contemporary religious change and prefigured the mendicant movements of the 1200s. Ironically, the friars' effective eclipse of the white canons' growth in the course of the thirteenth century, rather than their twelfth-century prominence, is mirrored in Norbert's followers' relative obscurity among modern students of medieval culture and the historical development of Christian spirituality.

Twelfth-century accounts of Norbert and the white canons, however, their view untrammeled by this long historical perspective, affirmed the explosive proliferation of the white canons and celebrated the rigor of their commitment to imitation of Christ and his first apostles. Herman of Tournai, the Benedictine whose account of Norbert's first foundation at Prémontré formed part of his record

1

of events in the diocese of Laon, represented his and his confreres' astonishment at the almost preternatural instauration of a full-grown religious community at Prémontré within its first thirty years. Herman focused on two extraordinary aspects of this canonical foundation: first, the identity of its founder, Norbert, who left Prémontré after its establishment to continue his prior career as wandering preacher and was in 1126 elected archbishop of Magdeburg; and second, the extreme fervor of his followers' piety, which extended even to the women his community welcomed. For Herman, the great enthusiasm of the early Premonstratensians was predicated on Norbert's own. The historian of Tournai compared the canonical reformer favorably to Bernard of Clairvaux. The great white monk, Herman asserted, was indeed a fine preacher, but no better than Norbert. And Norbert had founded an order, while Bernard had only expanded one established by his predecessors.[5]

Bernard himself had an analogously lofty impression of his friend and contemporary Norbert. As he wrote in a letter to Geoffrey of Chartres in 1124: "As for what you have asked me about Norbert, whether he is going on pilgrimage to Jerusalem, I don't know. I saw him just a few days ago face to face, and I was then privileged to drink as from a stream from heaven, that is from what he said."[6] Bernard's description is extraordinary testimony on Norbert's charisma from the most charismatic figure of the age, but like much medieval testimony on Norbert of Xanten and the white canons of Prémontré it begs the question of the reformer's and his followers' charism. What spiritual goals motivated this "stream from heaven"? How did his personal model shape the spirituality of the white canons whom he established in France and across Europe? Did the Premonstratensians articulate or maintain a distinctive spirituality during their twelfth-century efflorescence, as their houses came to be linked by general chapters and statutes?

The identity and character of Norbert and the canons in his regular religious tradition are alike complicated by the central problematic condition of their historical representation: that Norbert himself left no written word. Robert of Molesme and Stephen Harding, the earliest organizers of Cîteaux, are similarly elusive, indeed still less clearly known in primary accounts, but quickly the voice of Cîteaux becomes Bernard's, and rich modern scholarship on the twelfth-century Cistercians homes and centers on the prolific oeuvre of the abbot of Clairvaux. Norbert's successors—some eminent, none dominant—present a dispersion and diversity more challenging to modern interpreters in terms of attending to their voices' community. Few modern studies assemble the major texts about Norbert from his immediate followers' hands.[7]

The translations gathered here represent some of the more important Premonstratensian works of the early decades and provide material for such synoptic consideration of their twelfth-century movement. Including the major representations of Norbert's life and work as well as central texts in the early Premonstratensians' definition of their own communities in the context of great contemporary spiritual dynamism, they suggest how the white canons whom Herman of Tournai observed from his Benedictine vantage interpreted and focused their own novelty as a religious form, and in turn how awareness of their novelty shaped their spiritual lives. Modern readers will be supported in their attention to these texts by preliminary review here of the place of regular canons such as the Premonstratensians in the pan-European reformation of the twelfth century.

Apostolic Life, Wandering Preachers, and New Foundations

Norbert's career and the communities he founded were at once typical and radical in their historical context. The great central theme of twelfth-century spiritual renewal, from the Gregorian reform of the eleventh century forward, was the revival of apostolic tradition. Much that was genuinely new was understood as imitation of the practices and principles of the early church.[8] Among the most prominent advocates of such paradoxically conservative innovation were wandering preachers like Gilbert of Sempringham, Robert of Arbrissel, and Norbert of Xanten. All three would plant religious communities, and, while none except Norbert closed his ecclesiastical career far from his first foundation, all became founders more to establish a home and refuge for the many enthusiastic converts won

3

by their preaching than because their initial intent had been to found monastic or canonical orders.[9]

More than either Gilbert, founder of the Gilbertines, or Robert, founder of Fontevrault, however, Norbert of Xanten seems to have focused on preaching the imminence of the apocalypse. To an extent this emphasis was circumstantial. Much fame was accorded Norbert for his successful extirpation of the heresy initiated by Tanchelm in Antwerp in the late 1110s. This anticlerical preacher, whose thought is obscured in the extant polemic against him but who seems to have shared with the ancient Donatists the belief that sacraments were vitiated by priestly corruption, was himself an extreme exponent of principles of ecclesiastical reform. But in Norbert's interpretation Tanchelm figured the Antichrist, and the champion of orthodoxy called his followers then to understand that their own times approached the end.[10] As Bernard of Clairvaux continued in his epistolary praise of a "stream from heaven," "I asked him what he thought about the Antichrist, and he asserted most emphatically that he was sure that Antichrist would be revealed while the world we know still lasts, in our own generation."[11] The huge audiences summoned by Norbert's preaching were called to believe that their age was coming to a close. Many who credited Norbert's assertion then followed him into religious life.

The clearest connection between Norbert's famous apocalyptic preaching and his foundation of what would, in the next decades, become the illustrious Order of Prémontré lies in his choice of a strict interpretation of the Rule of St. Augustine for his followers. As his later followers believed, Augustine himself had counseled Norbert in a dream that his Rule would serve them well at the last judgment;[12] the Premonstratensians would be regular canons rather than monks, recurring to a tradition of legislation for community life purporting greater antiquity even than that of the Benedictines. Adoption of this rigorous pattern of life, the so-called *Ordo novus*, girded Norbert's followers as securely as he thought possible in preparation for the end time. Before his conversion he himself had been a secular canon, and canonical tradition was again an important spiritual and institutional context for his own preaching and his followers' developing charism. Of the authors whose work is included in this volume, all assume readers' basic awareness of a distinction between monastic and canonical traditions; Anselm of Havelberg in particular takes that distinction as paramount in his apology for the dignity of his confreres. Further, Anselm and his confreres whose works are translated here all experienced religious community as directly shaped by Norbert, whose canonical way of life and biography therefore demand summary exposition.

Canonical Tradition and the Twelfth-Century Reform

The origin of canons, clerics living in community, lay in the fourth century, in the households of bishops. Augustine himself lived in such a "monastery of clerics" and wrote about its governance.[13] In late antiquity and the earlier Middle Ages, especially in urban communities, clergy sometimes lived together near a cathedral or at a collegiate church. Although they were not bound by a rule, as were, for instance, Benedictine monks, they lived according to *canones*, canons or directives of the church fathers and ecclesiastical synods. In the eighth century, however, Chrodegang, bishop of Metz, wrote a rule *(Regula canonicorum)* for the clergy of his cathedral church.[14] This rule was based on that of Benedict and included common formation, dormitory, meals, penitential practices, and prayer. Individual patrimony nevertheless remained private. The Synod of Aachen, held in 816 during the reign of Charlemagne's son, Louis the Pious, bound all clergy living in common to a rule known as the *Institutio canonicorum*. This pattern for community life was based on the Rule of Chrodegang and once again permitted individual patrimony. The Rule of Aachen continued to be an important influence into the central Middle Ages, remaining in force among secular canons such at the community of St. Victor in Xanten, where the Premonstratensian founder, Norbert, began his ecclesiastical career.[15]

During the later eleventh century, however, private ownership by the clergy became a burning issue as Gregorian reform sought a church cleansed of secular involvement. Inheritance and wealth were viewed as basic evils from which the church in general, including many communities of canons, suffered.[16] In the same period, the seven-hundred-year-old Rule of St. Augustine, in fact a group of related texts composed by the African father for clerics living in community, was recognized and copied. Since this Rule required holding all things in common, it was greeted with enthusiasm by reformers dedicated to revival of apostolic life. It began gradually to replace the Rule of Aachen for communities of clerics.[17] In 1059 an important reform synod required canons living together to hold the income of their churches in common, reflecting the influence of the revival of Augustinian notions of canonical life.[18] For the most part reform eliminating private property was undertaken by individual houses of canons, but it was occasionally carried forward by a bishop throughout his diocese.[19] In some areas individual houses, although there was no legal bond among them, formed a sort of union for support and shared customaries. Notable among these leading centers were Rottenbuch in Bavaria, Marbach in Alsace, Springiersbach in the Archdiocese of Trier, and Klosterrath near Aachen.[20] The revival of the Augustinian Rule encouraged the development of a distinction between "secular canons" and "regular canons," that is, between canons who continued to hold individual property and those who held property in common.

Hence the separation between those who continued to follow the Rule of Aachen, the secular canons, and those who began to follow the Augustinian Rule, now regular canons. Meanwhile, the latter group itself divided. The Rule of St. Augustine had been written down in two forms, the *Praeceptum* (also called *Regula ad servos Dei* or *Regula tertia*) and the *Ordo monasterii* (also called the *Disciplina monasterii* or sometimes *Regula secunda*). The latter was the stricter form.[21] Sometimes, adding still more complexity, further writings of Augustine pertaining to life in common were added.

The *Ordo monasterii* is a short Rule-text but, because of its unusual ordering of the daily liturgical schedule and its commitment to manual labor, fasting, and strict silence, was extremely restrictive for a house of canons with obligations outside its own community.[22] The *Praeceptum* or *Regula ad servos Dei* is longer and less strict, but additional statutes are required to make it useful for common life. Twelfth-century communities following the milder observance of the *Praeceptum* were known as the *Ordo antiquus;* those following the *Ordo monasterii* were known as the *Ordo novus.*

In founding Prémontré in 1120, with his characteristically rigorous spiritual discipline, Norbert would adopt the stricter Rule, allying his foundation with the *Ordo novus*.[23]

Norbert of Xanten as Preacher and Reformer

Only the basic outline of Norbert's personal history before his conversion is known. He was a noble Rhinelander born sometime between 1080 and 1085, perhaps at his family's castle in Gennep (modern Netherlands) or in Xanten (western Germany). As a youth he was offered to the church in Xanten as a secular canon, whence he became a chaplain in archiepiscopal and imperial circles. Converted around age thirty-five, he first astounded those who had known him earlier by wandering in rags and preaching to huge crowds. He then undertook the reform of the clergy by strict interpretation of the Rule of St. Augustine in the establishment of houses of regular canons. Finally, as archbishop of Magdeburg from 1126 to his death in 1134, he carried on his work of reform and then returned to imperial service as courtier and councilor of the Saxon emperor Lothair of Supplinburg. Throughout this wide-flung activity, Norbert's goal—like that of many spiritual leaders of his time—centered on reform according to the ideal of the primitive church as found in the Acts of the Apostles.[24] Yet moderns have had difficulty discerning more profound or distinctive coherence behind his multiple roles, as did some medievals. While many contemporaries praised his sanctity, others charged him with inconsistency and fickleness. The monk Idung of Prüfening, in his dialogue on the proliferation of patterns of religious life written about 1155, blasts the regular canons in Norbert's person: "Their founder, Dom Norbert, defected and went from being a barefoot donkey rider to being a well-heeled and well-dressed rider of caparisoned horses, from being a hermit he became a courtier in the court of Emperor Lothair, from black bread and lowly pottage he went on to royal and sumptuous banquets, from greatly despising the world to greatly manipulating worldly affairs."[25] Idung's assessment was thus radically different from that of his famous contemporary Bernard. Apostate or "stream from heaven"—Norbert himself stands behind

7

his followers' effort to define his and their charism, and readers of their works will find a summary of his career useful as background to all this volume's translations, especially his hagiographies, whose narratives of events are interspersed with edifying digressions important for understanding Norbert's followers' mentality but difficult to set in chronological order.

Most information about Norbert's activities and their contemporary reception comes from three major sources: two early hagiographies, labeled *A* and *B*, and a digression concerning him in a Benedictine abbey history, the *Restoration of the Monastery of St. Martin of Tournai*, written by the same Herman of Tournai whose *Miracles of St. Mary of Laon*, noted above, praised the Premonstratensians' astounding proliferation.[26] The two twelfth-century lives describe Norbert's conversion in a conventional account of an interrupted journey modeled on the apostle Paul's; the monk Herman takes up the story about four years earlier. When Norbert's hagiographers begin their respective accounts of their protagonist in 1115, they identify him as a subdeacon of the collegiate church of St. Victor in Xanten. In addition to serving as a secular canon there, as the lives make clear, Norbert was also a chaplain to the court of Frederick, archbishop of Cologne, thus familiar as well with the court of the Salian emperor Henry V. Less than a decade before the Concordat of Worms in 1122 the nobleman and courtier Norbert was thus a close witness to church-state conflict as the Roman papacy pursued ecclesiastical reform and growing royal power sought control of the German church.

The twelfth-century hagiographies record that Norbert, accompanied by a single servant, was in 1115 traveling toward a place called Freden when a storm came up, lightning struck, and he was thrown from his horse. Emotionally shaken, Norbert thought he heard a voice rebuking him, and he began to reflect on the words of the Psalmist, *Turn from evil and do good* (Ps 33:15; 36:27).[27] The *B* hagiographer then represents Norbert as asking, "Lord, what do you want me to do?" In response he heard not only *Turn from evil and do good*, but the second half of this psalm verse as well: *Seek peace and pursue it.*[28] As both medieval lives then relate, Norbert began to reform his hitherto worldly life after returning to Xanten from this conversion experience, visiting the Benedictine abbey of Siegburg and placing himself under the spiritual direction of its abbot, Cuno. The monk Herman gives a different but not incompatible view of Norbert's conversion in his *Restoration of the Monastery of St. Martin of Tournai*. In a short passage about Norbert and the foundation of Prémontré, Herman attributes the secular canon's conversion not to a heavenly voice out of a thunderstorm but to Norbert's direct experience of Henry V's mistreatment of Pope Paschal II in Rome in 1110/11, when the future reformer traveled there in Frederick of Cologne's retinue.[29] Perhaps Norbert's eyes were opened to the harshness of the world as seen in the abuse leveled against the pope and that these two descriptions of his conversion are the beginning and end points of the same event.

In any case, as the hagiographers attest, in the aftermath of his spiritual crisis Norbert approached Archbishop Frederick with the request that he be ordained to the diaconate and priesthood on the same day. Although such an expedited ordination was contrary to canon law, the prelate granted Norbert's request. Afterward Norbert went back to Siegburg and remained there for forty days preparing for the exercise of his priestly duties. He then returned to Xanten, where he attempted to reform his fellow canons living laxly according to the Rule of Aachen. They were loath to give up private ownership, and he eventually abandoned his efforts. Norbert then left Xanten, spending three years in prayer and study at a small, privately held church at Fürstenberg.[30] During this time he also went about preaching, evidently gaining widespread notoriety both for the content of his message and because priests did not typically preach outside their own churches; in 1118 he was summoned before an ecclesiastical council at Fritzlar to explain why he was preaching without permission, dressing like a monk although he was a cleric, and still living by his own financial means. Norbert responded by divesting himself of all his benefices and selling whatever he owned. Keeping only what he needed to celebrate the Eucharist and a little money, he then set out with two companions to St. Gilles in the south of France. On the way he gave away even the small funds he had kept. At St. Gilles he met with Pope Gelasius II, who absolved him of the canonical irregularity of receiving both diaconate and priesthood on the same day and gave him written permission to preach anywhere. So privileged, Norbert now returned to the north, where he was eager to preach in his own Germanic tongue. When he and his companions arrived at Orléans a third man, a subdeacon, joined them. All four continued on to Valenciennes, but the three companions there fell ill and died.

Valenciennes was, according to the medieval lives, a turning point for Norbert because there he met an old friend, Burchard, now bishop of Cambrai. Burchard's secretary, Hugh of Fosses, was attracted to Norbert's model and joined him on his preaching tour. At a time when feuds among local overlords harmed many innocents, Norbert chose peace as the theme of his preaching. As the *A* hagiography represents, he journeyed with his companion from village to village, "preaching and reconciling those at odds with one another and reducing old hatreds and wars to peace." Norbert's *A* hagiographer again writes, "People flocked to him in droves and during Mass heard words of exhortation from him about doing penance or about the hope of eternal salvation promised to everyone who calls on the Lord's name." He sought no contributions, and anything that was offered he distributed to the poor and lepers. He amazed contemporaries with his new style of life, "namely to live on earth and seek nothing from the earth."[31] The *B* hagiographer writes that, as their fame spread, Norbert and Hugh not only spoke to rural and urban crowds but were invited into clerical communities. After they preached, they were asked "many questions about orders, rules, habit, and diverse institutions of the holy fathers, about the life and customs of prelates...about the heavenly sacraments and heavenly life."[32] Thus Norbert's preaching, now supported by Hugh, found multiple audiences among clergy and laity.

Eventually, on hearing of the death of Gelasius II, Norbert went to Reims, where his papal successor, Callixtus II, was holding a council. The reformer's goal was to obtain a renewal of his permission to preach. At Reims he met Bartholomew, bishop of Laon, who introduced him to the pope. There, portentously, the pope entrusted Norbert to Bartholomew's oversight.[33] The bishop then convinced Norbert to settle in his diocese. At first Bartholomew asked the canons of St. Martin just outside the city to elect the reformer their abbot. Norbert himself was hesitant. The canons, when they learned more of Norbert's rigorous reform program, bluntly refused his prelacy: "We do not want this man over us."[34]

Norbert and the Premonstratensians

In the spring of 1120, as the medieval lives and Herman the monk's writings alike record, Bartholomew of Laon took Norbert around his diocese in the hope of finding a place for him to establish a community according to his ideals. After being shown various likely sites, Norbert chose Prémontré. As both hagiographies assert, "Here he pledged to remain if God would allow him to gather companions."[35] Herman the monk quotes Norbert: "I will remain here, father, because I know that God has destined this place for me."[36] Norbert spent the year preaching and attracting companions to build up his new community. Women were from the beginning participants in the Premonstratensian enterprise; at Prémontré, Herman of Tournai points out, and indeed at its daughter houses, sisters lived close by. In 1121, Norbert chose the Rule of St. Augustine for the governance of his community, many of whose members were already canons like him; reformist discussion, legislation, and textual recovery of the past half-century must have rendered this document of governance for clerical life a logical choice. The men of Prémontré made their profession as Augustinians at Christmas in 1121, but Norbert did not consistently remain among them, instead continuing his itinerant preaching during temperate months. Three years later Norbert was invited by Burchard of Cambrai to preach in Antwerp against Tanchelm's eucharistic heresy. Tanchelm was already dead when Norbert arrived, but the heresy was still thriving. The reformer quickly recovered the heretic's followers to orthodoxy, and his presence in Antwerp resulted in the foundation of another Premonstratensian house there.

In 1126, however, as the medieval sources affirm, Norbert went still further afield. In Speyer, in the presence of the German king and papal legate, he was elected archbishop of Magdeburg, where he served on the eastern frontier of the Christian empire from 1126 until his death in 1134. The first four years were spent in reforming the archdiocese. The latter four were primarily given over to the support of Innocent II in the aftermath of the disputed papal election of 1130. In 1133 Norbert journeyed to Rome with Bernard of Clairvaux in the company of the German king, Lothair III, for the twofold purpose of ousting the antipope, Anacletus II, and crowning Lothair emperor. The archbishop fell ill on the return trip, probably infected with malaria, and died the following year on June 6.

The later development of Norbert's foundations must be traced in a variety of charters, capitularies, and abbey histories. When Norbert was elected archbishop in 1126, he had left the community he had established at Prémontré in the care of Hugh of Fosses. By this time, in addition to Prémontré, Norbert had founded more communities: at least Floreffe, Cappenberg, Varlar, Ilbenstadt, Antwerp, and Vivières. He was himself never abbot or provost of these houses but functioned rather as overseer holding the properties in his own name.[37] He had appointed superiors in each house to function in his stead, just as he had appointed Hugh at Prémontré. When Norbert became archbishop in 1126 he was, however, no longer able to care for houses multiplying so quickly, from which he was now far away. In 1128, when a delegation was sent from Prémontré asking about his intentions regarding these houses, he instructed them to hold an election at his first foundation. Norbert recommended Hugh, and the latter was unanimously chosen abbot. Hugh was with Norbert at Magdeburg when his election at Prémontré took place. When Hugh returned to France, he in turn appointed abbots in the other houses founded by Norbert.[38]

Until Hugh's abbacy and for some time thereafter, the eventual Order of Prémontré was as yet not a formal network of religious communities but a group of independently established houses, each recognizing Norbert as founder. For his part, Norbert evidently had no intention of founding an order in the later sense of the term, rather intending a renewal of the canonical institute through the original Rule of Augustine.[39] The preacher-archbishop was himself the human thread of unity connecting these houses. Twice he sought and received approbation for the communities he was founding, first from a papal legate and then from the pope himself, but he requested these privileges for his houses as individual communities, not as a network of affiliated institutions. What he therefore received was endorsement for the way of life that was lived in the various houses that he founded.[40]

Norbert's activity as a founder of religious communities took place alongside two important related developments in the shape and organization of religious life. On the one hand was the reform movement of the canons, of which he and his followers were a part and which extended beyond ministry and preaching to ideas about reform according to the pattern of the early church. On the other hand was a sharp increase in the power of the bishops. Since Norbert was establishing houses of clerics and was the sole authority over these houses, he was in a sense assuming the position of a bishop, who is normally the superior of clergy, so countering the contemporary trend to aggrandizement of episcopal authority.[41] The maturation of Prémontré and Norbert's later foundations was thus conditioned by potentially orthogonal pressures: spiritually driven canonical reform and politically driven development of the ecclesiastical hierarchy.

At the beginning of his abbatial administration, Hugh of Fosses decided to gather the prelates of Norbert's foundations annually "for the reparation of any decline of the order, for eradicating excesses and for the healthy restoration of anything necessary."[42] In so ordaining he followed the model of the Cistercians. Eventually the meetings summoned by Hugh developed into annual general chapters, whose first statutes were drawn up in the 1130s;[43] these were revised and expanded around 1174.[44] In 1143 Pope Celestine II made it obligatory for all abbots and provosts following the customary of Prémontré to attend the annual general chapter.[45] By creating a general chapter and eliciting papally supported statutes, Hugh was able to alleviate some of the objections of diocesan bishops to independent houses of clerics in their territory. The place of Norbert's followers in the increasingly articulate organization of Latin Christendom was now defined.

Further rapid administrative development occurred in the later twelfth century, after the last of the texts included in this volume were written in the 1150s; because these circumstances are sometimes imputed to the earlier Premonstratensians, they may usefully be rehearsed here as a reminder of their anachronism relative to this volume's translations. Twelfth-century papal-imperial conflict and resulting ecclesiastical schism in 1160–77 seriously threatened the unity of the order. While Prémontré and the houses of Western Europe remained faithful to Alexander III, the houses belonging to the empire followed the antipope Hadrian IV. Consequently, after the schism the Eastern houses of the order no longer felt obligated to send their prelates to general chapters, presumably because the statutes had been altered during the schism,[46] but foundations of new houses continued apace across Europe. These new establishments were arranged in a system of filiation; that is, each founding or mother abbey had certain rights of visitation and control over the daughter abbey, as was the case among the Cistericans. During the schism of 1160–77 efforts at centralization reached a high point. In 1177 Alexander III decreed that the abbot of Prémontré was the father abbot of all Premonstratensian houses.[47] Around the same time individual houses were assigned to particular groups called circaries, first mentioned in the statutes of 1174. With this change the annual visitation of daughter houses by the abbot of Prémontré lost meaning. The general chapter annually appointed two visitators for each of the houses of a circary; these reported to the general chapter.[48] The Premonstratensians had thus by the end of the twelfth century become an internationally directed network of religious houses; their foundations extended from Wales to beyond the Elbe.[49] At mid-century, however, neither their organization in circaries nor their secure position as a great religious order can have been evident to authors drawn by Norbert's charism to its earliest communities.

Nor can East-West division among the Premonstratensians have seemed problematic. Although Norbert had directly founded Prémontré and, as archbishop, himself brought his followers to Magdeburg, Premonstratensian foundations in the East and West indeed manifested some differences. Almost all the houses west of the Rhine adopted the title abbot for their superior in the style of the French canons. On the other hand, the German houses, especially those in eastern Germany, called their prelates provost.[50] German houses sometimes resisted efforts toward uniformity and centralization, instead clustering around the canonical community in Magdeburg where Norbert first installed his followers about three years after his archiepiscopal election; canons from Magdeburg and its daughter houses were influential in spreading Christianity among the pagan Wends east of the Elbe.[51] But among his religious foundations, in the first decades after Norbert's death, unity was sufficiently loose that its potential breakage can hardly have threatened. So the Premonstratensians of mid-century, in their hagiographical and theological works, are concerned to define their historical role and spiritual goals rather than to maintain uniformity of practice.

Contents of This Volume

The seven texts from six authors translated in this Classics of Western Spirituality volume represent the Premonstratensians of the generation who knew the founder, Norbert. The first is excerpted from the *Miracles of St. Mary of Laon* of the Benedictine Herman and represents a perspective on his preaching and his new religious community among local, long-established monasteries. All other works included here were written by Norbert's immediate followers to establish models of sanctity for the men and women in their religious houses or to define fundamental features of the reform they lived. With the exception of the *B* life of Norbert, whose major addenda to the earlier *A* life are included here instead of the entire text because repetition of the whole would add too greatly to this volume's length, all are complete works—or at least as complete as manuscript evidence attests. Like the *Miracles* recorded by the Benedictine, these six texts from the hands of canons drawn by Norbert to his canonical reform were written in the middle decades of the twelfth century, within twenty or thirty years of his death.[52] They express his successors' perspective on his legacy and their relationship with his model as preacher, founder, and bishop, as well as their sense of his communities' role as sites of specifically Augustinian canonical life among a contemporary proliferation of patterns of regular religious obedience. Later Premonstratensian authors, like the famous late-twelfth-century mystic Adam of Dryburgh, who eventually became a Carthusian,[53] might indeed have been included here. They have not been because the tighter limit of this group of six authors' direct personal knowledge of Norbert or his immediate circle enables a more rigorous consideration of the character of the movement he founded in its early days. If a distinctive Premonstratensian charism can be seen to have existed in the twelfth century, then the community of ideas,

15

images, and affect among those whose written records most fully attest Norbert's influence is the context in which it is best explored.

Do, then, these texts define the historical role and self-understanding of the Premonstratensians with a clarity later confreres, their contemporaries in other religious or secular callings, or moderns interested in the development of medieval spirituality can discern? That these followers of Norbert and their Premonstratensian communities understood themselves as distinctive or believed that they participated in a distinctive spirituality is not a given in scholarly discussion of twelfth-century religious life. From the nineteenth century until recently, some scholars have argued that the coherence of the twelfth-century Premonstratensians as a network of religious houses was weak; there might seem to be little purpose in characterizing spiritual life in a Europe-wide affiliation so loosely bonded. So, for instance, various historians have argued that the Saxon circary, whose region's political and ecclesiastical center was Norbert's eventual archiepiscopal see and where his most famous follower, Anselm of Havelberg, wrote his great apocalyptic and ecumenical *Dialogues*,[54] was effectively an order unto itself.[55] More recently, scholarly attention to Premonstratensian authors has recognized their articulation of a specifically Augustinian and canonical perspective on both their social role and their spiritual practice but failed to identify them as particularly inspired by Norbert or informed by common tendencies at Prémontré or his other early foundations; from this point of view, the Premonstratensians recede into the larger category of Augustinian canons, whatever the administrative connections among their houses and adherence to the statutes of a general chapter active from the 1130s forward. So Karl Morrison has discussed the first conversion narrative since Augustine's own, the purported Herman the Jew's *Short Account of His Own Conversion*—a work whose authenticity as the narrative of a real Jew is much disputed, but whose composition at a Premonstratensian house in Westphalia is indisputable, and whose discussion of reformed canonical life is central to its examination of spiritual transit—without mentioning the term *Premonstratensian*.[56] Still more notably, Caroline Bynum has taken the educational works of Philip of Harvengt, an eminent twelfth-century abbot of a daughter house of Prémontré, as central to her distinction of canonical

16

from monastic spirituality in the twelfth century, but she has presented Philip as Augustinian canon rather than as inheritor of Norbert or representative of recognizably Premonstratensian spirituality. While, for Bynum, Philip's injunction that canons' commitment to teaching by word and example, *docere verbo et exemplo*, defines a charism separating them from monastic contemplatives, she seeks no special grounding for this usage or the mission it frames in Norbert's preaching or in the thought or practice of Philip's confreres in the widespread communities aligned with Norbert's reform.[57]

The question framing the selection of texts translated here has been whether the legacy of Norbert of Xanten framed a coherent sense of spiritual goals and worldly mission for his followers well into the twelfth century. Scholarly perspectives referenced here as dubious about this charism's clarity, so militating against a coherent Premonstratensian identity, surely contain elements of truth. Norbert's model was complex, and his Eastern foundations differed in important regards from the Western houses more closely associated with Prémontré. His followers' apostolate was mixed like his, so more variously expressed in word and action than, for instance, the Cistercians' contemplative pursuit of charity.[58] An eventual Premonstratensian order's unity was hard won, with only difficult assertion of authority by a general chapter over German houses in particular. And the authors collected here generally failed to self-identify as Premonstratensian. Yet for them to have done so would have been anomalous. As Constance Berman has emphasized, the notion of a monastic order in the sense of a filiation bound by history and statute, with pan-European unity of liturgy, spirituality, and secular mission, can only be imagined retrospectively for the middle of the twelfth century from its later form.[59] The Latin term *ordo* meant many things to Norbert and his immediate successors, but it was most meaningful to them as characterizing adherence to the Rule of St. Augustine.[60] Norbert certainly did not set out to found an order in the sense the Fourth Lateran Council understood when it limited the proliferation of such religious associations, nor did writers such as his followers Anselm of Havelberg or Philip of Harvengt understand themselves as members of a Premonstratensian "order."[61] Nonetheless, the texts included here represent their definition and justification of their actions and attitudes as regular religious and, in Philip's and Anselm's cases, as leaders in a newly militant church, according to a reading of the Augustinian Rule shaped by Norbert's life and teaching.

The contents of this volume suggest that Norbert's followers—East and West, active and contemplative, in their writings for members of their own communities and for the wider world of Christendom—shared a discernible common vision that would, in the long run, inform the foundations begun by Norbert and those early Premonstratensian canonries' daughter houses eventually defined as an order in the canonical administrative sense, in capitular statutes, and in papal legislation. Such a view of the early Premonstratensians is supported by recent European, especially German, scholarship, notably the work of Werner Bomm.[62] A common Premonstratensian vision shaped their historical role as a large and influential regular religious movement. Attention to the white canons' self-understanding, articulated in the texts gathered here, thus adds depth and richness to moderns' understanding of the great twelfth-century reform of Western religious-life, standing in interesting counterpoint to the well-documented model of their Cistercian contemporaries and to the explosive growth of their successors among the mendicant orders a century later.

Texts assembled here are of several genres—historical, hagiographical, polemical, and educational. In their different voices they point to an eloquent silence. Ironically, Bernard of Clairvaux's description of the canon-preacher Norbert as a "stream from heaven" evokes a historical perspective of which the great Cistercian cannot have been aware: that Norbert would in the long run be known from the words of those who heard him, not his own—as it were, from the edges of his own absence. To discover him in others' perceptions requires careful comparative reading of the texts of those whom his presence inspired. The mutual juxtaposition of Norbert's followers' hagiographical and theological arguments for the reform of community life of clerics promoted by him makes important assumptions about reading medieval works, particularly about reading hagiographical works as windows on the spirituality of their primary audiences, the religious communities their subjects founded or to which they belonged. An abundant recent literature on theoretical approaches to medieval saints' lives affirms their interest as normative artifacts of spiritual life, testifying to a larger Christian community's response, sometimes resistant, to elite and clerical direction.[63] The hagiographies translated here are in that sense certainly useful, but discussion below will purport that they are useful not only in interpreting their respective immediate contexts but as representatives of a trans-historical European hagiographical Premonstratensian atelier—so as evidence of coherence of a Premonstratensian vision.[64] If any unity, however loose, is to be discerned for twelfth-century Premonstratensian life, its hagiography of the founder and his early successors is crucial to it. Given the absence of a founder's written legacy, hagiography of Norbert assumes something of a written oeuvre's place as definitive of his inheritors' distinctiveness. Here the *A* life of Norbert and the slightly later *B* version, seen in the context of virtually contemporary lives of Godfrey of Cappenberg and Oda of Rivreulle, present a textual conversation about the meaning of sanctity in the order's context—effectively a discourse on the goals and means of regular life. Analysis of these texts in such terms depends on their being read in light of the volume's other elements—historical, polemical, and educational works—in whose context their common ground is better revealed.

In sum, Herman of Tournai's *Miracles* suggest how members of established monastic communities viewed Norbert and his followers. The lives of Godfrey of Cappenberg, Norbert, and Oda explore the tension between ideals and realities in the first decades of Premonstratensian life. The apologetic and educational texts translated here, the reflections of Anselm of Havelberg and Philip of Harvengt on the status and training of clerics living in reformed community, contrast the self-understanding of these followers of Norbert with other patterns of religious life. Together, these texts frame a lively tension animating reformed Augustinian life on the Norbertine model: mixed apostolate described according to a distinctive imagery and typology; an obligation to preaching defined as teaching "by word and example"; Marian piety and spousal mysticism tangled with ambivalence about preaching to women and the embrace of women religious as souls for whom to care; and exuberant advocacy of the novelty of reformed Augustinian life as a stage in the unfolding of time toward the Apocalypse.

Further Twelfth-Century
Premonstratensian Works

Unquestionably, the texts chosen here are not the only or, in all cases, the most important works in which these themes may be discerned. Three additional works, not chosen for inclusion among the texts translated below but from authors in Norbert of Xanten's immediate following, beg mention both for their likely interest to readers of this volume and in explanation of their absence here. Among these, Herman-Judah's *Short Account of His Own Conversion* is perhaps the most intriguing and significant for understanding the spirituality of the order.[65] This autobiographical text purports to have been authored by a young Jewish banker in the retinue of the early twelfth-century bishop of Münster. This Judah ben David, who eventually took the name Herman, visited the Premonstratensian community of Cappenberg and was drawn to the holiness of the inmates even as he was intrigued by the lively theological and exegetical discussion at the court and table of Bishop Egbert. Anguished and unable completely to sever himself from his family of origin to become a Christian, the Jew eventually seized his young half-brother and fled their family. He left their father's home in Mainz with the boy, eventually entering the religious community of Cappenberg founded by Norbert and Godfrey.

The story of this Jew's conversion is a central anecdote in the hagiography of Godfrey of Cappenberg, which may well have been an earlier written account of the same conversion;[66] Herman's *Short Account* and the life of Godfrey are thus salient examples of the interrelationship of twelfth-century Premonstratensian texts and their barely perceptible connection to a larger oral discourse about the history and biography of Norbert and his followers. The appearance of the conversion story in two Premonstratensian works from within a few decades of its ostensible occurrence argues for the historicity of the incident, however richly elaborated or fictionalized in the aftermath.

Morrison has taken the story of the Jew-turned-Premonstratensian as one of three principal textual elements in his interpretation of the meaning of conversion in Western Christianity, arguing that from this interpretive posture it matters little whether the text was in fact written by the individual who experienced this religious conversion or whether the "little work" was biographical embroidery or even invention.[67] Indeed, some scholars have maintained that the *Short Account* text, which survives in manuscripts from a few abbeys near Cappenberg, contains features—most notably its impeccable Latin—arguing against its authorship by a Jewish convert trained in the language only in adulthood. Jean-Claude Schmitt, noting the proximity of the accounts of the Jew's conversion in the *Short Account* and the hagiography of Godfrey, has recently suggested that the "little work" is more broadly about conversion in the sense of transformation of life, so binding members of reformed religious communities such as the Premonstratensians and new Christians brought in from other religions. In Schmitt's view, the *Short Account* text represents the centrality of the notion of conversion in the imagination of twelfth-century reformed religious. Schmitt finds here no distinctively Premonstratensian emphasis, but he stresses the radicalism underlying representation of a Jew's conversion as an image for conversion to regular religious life.[68]

Herman the Jew's story is thus of major importance for understanding the spirituality of the twelfth-century Premonstratensians. Even if it is a pious forgery, a tale imagined by a contemporary proclaiming how a Jew and his co-religionists should convert, it was certainly composed for a reformed canonical audience.[69] It thus bespeaks its author's and his anticipated audience's vivid sense of the radicalism of the religious community to which he belonged. Its currency among the Premonstratensians and their close associates in Westphalia and the Rhineland suggests the attractiveness of its idiom to a circle that remembered the preaching and the example of Norbert of Xanten. Yet because of its compelling interest to recent scholarship on conversion and critical interpretation, the purported Herman's *Short Account* has met with two recent translations, one by Morrison himself and the other by Michael Goodich, who includes it in a volume of medieval texts regarding social and religious marginals.[70] Since so little of the work of twelfth-century Premonstratensians is available in English, it has seemed best here to include only previously untranslated works. Similarly, the great dialogues of Anselm of Havelberg are excerpted in Bernard McGinn's collection of twelfth-century apocalyptic texts.[71] It has recently been expounded, with lengthy quotations in translation, by Jay Lees in the first monographic study of this important medieval ecumenist, follower of Norbert, and founder of reformed canonical communities on Europe's Slavic frontier.[72] Necessarily, however, Anselm's apocalyptic imagination, especially his conviction of the importance of contemporary religious reform as revealing stages in the completion of time, will be of interest for discussion of his apologetic letter against the monks, translated below. Uniquely among twelfth-century historical and apocalyptic thinkers, Anselm not only accepted but advocated novelty among forms of religious life as evidence of, in his image, the higher and higher flight of the church toward the light of eternal truth.[73] Stung by the criticism of contemporaries that the reform of the regular canons and, evidently, his own discipleship of Norbert of Xanten were historically unjustifiable innovations amid a twelfth-century renewal of the church generally characterizing itself as a return to apostolic models, Anselm unabashedly advocated novelty. In so doing he and Premonstratensian authors who resumed his imagery effectively claimed priority—or at least elevation—in the great contemporary search for pathways to beatitude guided by a monastic or canonical rule.[74] But Anselm's theology of history is included here only to the extent that he implies it in his powerful rejoinder to contemporary monks' criticism of the dignity and novelty of the reform of regular canons in which he, like his master Norbert, was a powerful agent.

Finally, Philip of Harvengt's commentary on the Song of Songs has recently been demonstrated by Rachel Fulton to have been the most adventuresomely Marian and arguably the most provocative with respect to its treatment of gender and its explicit eroticism of the many twelfth-century commentaries on this Old Testament book.[75] Because Fulton's widely available volume again translates substantial passages and spotlights the distinctiveness of Philip's perspective in the wider context of medieval empathy for Christ and Mary, it has seemed better here to include lesser-known elements of his massive oeuvre, filling an entire volume of the Patrologia Latina and so overwhelming the rest of Norbert's followers' published writings in sheer volume. Once more, Philip's understanding of the Song of Songs, his Marian thought, and his sense of the gendering of mystical experience eventually expounded in his Song commentary will be seen in discussion here of his earlier life of Oda of Rivreulle to have had important influence on his literary representation of a real woman, the *magistra* of the community of sisters for whom as abbot of Bonne Espérance he had spiritual and administrative responsibility. Yet Philip's Song commentary, the lengthiest and most complex of such twelfth-century texts on the love poem understood by medievals as Solomon's, is not excerpted here. Preference in this context for complete works—texts that, albeit relatively short, show their authors' framing of complete narratives or arguments—has further militated against inclusion of portions of Philip's grand commentary.

Documenting the Premonstratensian Charism

Together, this suite of texts from twelfth-century authors answers questions about their pattern of religious life as basic for modern readers as for their medieval contemporaries. How did established local monasticism and episcopal authority respond to Norbert's charismatic preaching and community building? Why would a layperson, especially from an elite family, abandon his or her prior status and join his following rather than some other regular religious group? What meaning lay in Norbert's personal model? How did he represent himself in his worldly mission, and how were the stages in his mixed career interpreted by those who joined his religious foundations or those who followed him in prelacy on Christendom's eastern frontier? What was the role of women among Premonstratensian religious houses, given their founder's extraordinary appeal to the women of northern France, the Low Countries, and the Rhineland? What did Premonstratensian authors take to be the meta-historical meaning, the interpretive significance for the larger shape of church history, of their vocation's apparent novelty? Finally, what was the place of scriptural, theological, and rhetorical learning in the canons of Norbert's and his immediate successors' foundations?

In their response, twelfth-century Premonstratensian texts recur to two principal themes—first, community life grounded in prayer and poverty, and second, the obligation to teaching in the wider church. Herman of Tournai's understanding of Norbert as reformer and founder centers in his success as a preacher, as do both twelfth-century hagiographies of Norbert. The life of Godfrey of Cappenberg again portrays Norbert as a charismatic preacher, then emphasizes the rigor and poverty of his earliest German foundation and the struggle of Godfrey, Norbert's disciple and Cappenberg's noble donor, to participate fully in the liturgy and literacy mandated in the Rule of St. Augustine. Philip of Harvengt's life of Oda interprets the example of an ascetic woman for both the active ministry and the contemplative life of males in the Premonstratensian community overseeing her and her sisters' religious house. And Anselm of Havelberg's and, again, Philip's more explicitly apologetic works hammer the themes of mixed apostolate and teaching through preaching and exemplarity of life.

The Victorines, Rolduc, Arrouaise—other reformed canons shared with Norbert's followers a commitment to strict interpretation of the Rule of St. Augustine, and they too chose their way of life for its emphasis on "teaching by word and example." Yet it was the Premonstratensians, not these other networks of Augustinians, who quickly became astoundingly prolific. As these collected works of Norbert's followers suggest, their dynamism—compelling as it was to many Europeans of the twelfth century—was grounded in the impact of Norbert of Xanten's career as a lived gloss on that ancient rule. At least until mid-century Norbert's commitment to the people of the secular world continued to animate the communities he founded. The Premonstratensians' success sprang from the tension he embodied and Anselm of Havelberg identified as the core of canonical charism—a refusal to choose the role of either Mary or of Martha, but instead to imitate the Christ who unified and perfected both active and contemplative callings.[76]

Individual introductions to the primary texts translated here point out each work's particular themes and its historical or biographical contexts. The present general introduction, like this volume in sum, aims to facilitate intensive study of the early Premonstratensians rather than to predict such study's conclusions;

although the primary audience of this series is readers in translation, students of medieval spirituality to whom the original Latin is accessible may nonetheless find these texts' juxtaposition, comparison, and bibliographical apparatus useful. Meanwhile, some further suggestions about the distinctiveness of the medieval Premonstratensian charism proceed immediately from these works' representation of women in their authors' theological imagination and historical reality. The earliest texts represented below, Herman of Tournai's and Anselm of Havelberg's, emphasize women in Norbert's following and women as hearers of his great model, Christ. The latest work included in this volume describes a historical individual, Oda of Rivreulle, as an exemplar of Premonstratensian spirituality. Women's participation in the canonical reform of Norbert of Xanten—ironically in that they could not be clerics living in community because they could not be ordained—was evidently essential to it.

Recent scholarship on medieval women's piety has noted the success of Norbert, like others among the twelfth century's wandering preachers, in eliciting the interest of both sexes. It has likewise examined the process by which, through an accumulation of capitular and eventually papal legislation, the Premonstratensians' at first almost universally double communities—men and women celibates housed, praying, and working in close proximity—were split, their women reestablished at a distance from men's houses and finally banned from the order. Shelley Wolbrink's 2003 article on thirteenth-century Premonstratensian women demonstrates that, despite hierarchical negativity about the presence of sisters among the white canons, women's communities endured well beyond their ostensible final prohibition at the end of the twelfth century. Prior historians had taken papal prohibition of women in 1198[77] as stimulus to the development of the beguine communities prominent in the Low Countries and the Rhineland. The same geographical region saw concentrations of the white canons, and indeed the Premonstratensians were closely involved with the beguines, but the order's connection with these extra-regular women now seems grounded in the canons' commitment to supporting women's piety rather than the elimination of their own women's communities.[78]

The complexity of Premonstratensian sisters' social and institutional history aside, both lay and religious women were of patent importance to the early white canons—to the founder Norbert in his preaching, to the theologian Anselm in his grounding of canonical charism in scriptural figuration, to the teacher Philip in his choice of his sister Oda as a spiritual hero for his own times. Their importance lay not only in their inclusion among Norbert's hearers and followers but also for their indication of his wider goals. More than any contemporary except perhaps Robert of Arbrissel, Norbert of Xanten seems in his preaching to have both addressed and attracted women. This summoning of women testified to the radical ambition of his reform program. Preaching, rigor in canonical life, archiepiscopate on the pagan fringe of Europe—Norbert's various enterprises understandably left some, like Idung, skeptical, yet these widespread points of engagement mapped the plane of contemporary Christianity, and so the extent of Norbert's purpose.

As the texts translated here demonstrate, Norbert of Xanten set out to reform the world, not just the clergy. His purified, galvanized Augustinians would, as the Apocalyse loomed, add their voices to his, converting souls from France to the Slavic frontier, as well on Europe's internal frontier of gender. Philip of Harvengt was able unembarrassedly to slip from his confrere Anselm's apology for his way of life as embracing the roles of both Mary and Martha into erotic interpretation of the Song of Songs in terms of the other Mary, Christ's mother, because his master, Norbert, had left behind the great Marian mystic Bernard's squeamishness about historical women's place in apostolic life.[79] The frank inclusion of women in Norbert's universal program to reform the church in the face of the end of time brought his followers much criticism. Bit by bit they gave it up, but nowhere in the evidence for their charism does the founder's urgent inclusiveness—willingness to do all things and approach all persons—emerge as clearly as in this theological and social daring. The Premonstratensian enterprise was to that extent doomed; the realities of twelfth-century society would soon erode and diminish its ambition as the looked-for Apocalypse approached only tardily. Yet the early texts of Norbert's admirers and disciples memorialize the adventuresome charism they sought to realize. Their texts stand as a reminder to their order and to the wider

Christian spiritual tradition of the radicalism of Norbert's vision of a renewed church for all Christians led by a clergy perfected in its imitation of Christ.

Conventions in Translation

The translations collected here reflect as transparently as possible for speakers of modern American English both the content and the style of the Latin originals. Readers will immediately note the relative clarity and simplicity of the anonymous hagiographical texts and of Herman of Tournai's work. Anselm of Havelberg and Philip of Harvengt were both accomplished exegetes, and their texts bristle with scriptural and classical allusions; the pleonasm understood as elegant in their period is reduced rather than eliminated here in the interest of sensitive communication of their respectively magisterial tones. Pronouns have frequently been replaced with their referents for clarity's sake, but few other departures from the Latin have generally been necessary. Theodore Antry's translations of Herman of Tournai's work and of the two lives of Norbert offer contextually appropriate fresh translations of scriptural quotations; Carol Neel's translations of the remaining texts privilege the Douay version of scriptural references as close to the medieval Vulgate but are occasionally adjusted to support context. All scriptural references noted in texts and apparatus follow Douay numbering. All nonscriptural translations in commentary are our own unless otherwise noted.

Although the translators have in some instances examined the relevant manuscripts from the perspective of their texts' histories, all translations and textual divisions follow the principal editions cited below; readers who wish to compare translations with Latin texts will find these divisions useful, even when they have weak grounding in the various manuscripts. Bibliography on each text appears in the notes to the respective introductions, and notes to the translations stress historical details and occasional thematic emphases or interesting usages; references to sources and criticism are to English translations, where possible. Bibliographical references on the twelfth-century context and general Premonstratensian history have

27

been included above, and this volume's final bibliography adds sources and commentary either directly useful in its preparation or potentially helpful to readers interested in further investigation of these works, their authors, or Premonstratensian spirituality. Texts are presented in chronological order, as best determined by current scholarship, so reminding readers that Norbert's hagiography, though central to his later followers' self-understanding, is not the earliest articulation of their charism.

Anselm of Havelberg, *Apologetic Letter*— Introduction

Anselm of Havelberg's *Apologetic Letter*, written in 1138,[1] is the earliest text from a Premonstratensian hand represented in this volume—moreover, the first important work of one whom Norbert's principal biographer, Wilfried Grauwen, called Norbert's "very image."[2] Anselm's career took shape in Norbert's shadow during the latter part of the Premonstratensian founder's life. He first appears in imperial and ecclesiastical charters in 1129.[3] At that time, Norbert, as archbishop of Magdeburg, had newly appointed Anselm titular bishop of a see in fact abandoned in the tenth-century resurgence of the pagan Wends;[4] Anselm would finally establish residence and real leadership in the Havelland only a decade later, after a stint as papal representative in the Byzantine court and alternating periods of exclusion and enfranchisement in the royal court.[5] In the meantime Norbert's brilliant protégé seems to have been loath to serve on the Slavic frontier, but after his effective exile from the highest circles of imperial power early in the reign of the Hohenstaufen Conrad III in the late 1130s,[6] Anselm fulfilled important regional roles in the foundation of the Premonstratensian house of nearby Jerichow[7] and eventual reestablishment of episcopal authority in Havelberg itself during the crusade against the Wends.[8] In general, after Norbert's death in 1134, Anselm continued with varying levels of success to follow his patron's example as prelate, advocate of canonical reform, founder of religious establishments, and apocalyptic theologian.[9] More than any other early Premonstratensian, the bishop of Havelberg thus lived according to the personal model of his master, Norbert. Anselm's apologetic letter on behalf of the regular canons thus holds not only chronological priority among the texts gathered here but also unique significance as a reflection of Norbert's own sense of the character and importance of the canonical reform of which he was instigator.

Anselm wrote the letter translated here and conventionally known as his apologetic letter—although he seems unlikely so to have titled it himself—only four years after Norbert's death, in a period of active engagement in the court of the Saxon emperor Lothair. Jay Lees's recent biography, the first full monographic treatment of Anselm's career and written works, persuasively argues that the bishop's sense of his earthly mission had been shaped by his education at the cathedral school of Liège.[10] Drawing on C. Steven Jaeger's description of the twelfth-century "courtier bishop" as an ideal type actively engaged in the reform of the secular world,[11] Lees portrays Anselm as accepting Norbert as the proximate instantiation of this ideal. For Lees, then, Anselm was a Norbertine or Premonstratensian to the extent that Norbert himself represented that identity in his later career as archbishop—at a physical and, effectively, spiritual remove from his early foundations such as Prémontré itself, which he had organized as an essentially contemplative community.[12] Yet Anselm was Norbert's righthand agent by 1129 and, educated as he was in the urban environment of the Low Countries where Norbert first established his reputation as preacher and reformer, he may well have accompanied him to Magdeburg rather than have met him in the German-speaking east.[13] So Anselm was likely to have been at least familiar with Norbert in his earlier career as preacher and founder.

The chronology of Anselm's career after his elevation as bishop of Havelberg is meticulously detailed in Lees's study; as well, Lees synoptically interprets both the *Apologetic Letter* and the *Antikeimenon*, Anselm's dialogue in three books about the state of the church and the Catholic West's relationship to the Orthodox East composed around 1150 after nearly fifteen years' reflection on his mission to Constantinople in 1134–36.[14] Lees's monograph persuasively presents the bishop of Havelberg in his episcopal role, as in these texts, as a forceful and tendentious ecclesio-political actor on the model established in centers of courtly training such as Liège. In the present context, however, Anselm's biography is less at issue than the relationship between his literary production and texts from contemporaries in Norbert's following. Attention to the *Apologetic Letter* in this Premonstratensian context suggests a different reading, not necessarily at odds with Lees's interpretation of Anselm as courtier bishop conscientiously imitating Norbert, but from the alternative perspective of his letter's relationship to other expressions of Norbert's followers' charism. Such a reading of the *Apologetic Letter* alongside other texts translated here qualifies Lees's representation of Anselm as advocate of the *vita activa*, that is, secular engagement by regular clergy such as the Premonstratensians.[15] At the same time, seen in relation to other apologetic texts or, more exactly, normative works from the early Premonstratensians, Anselm's interpretation of the role of regular canons and his laudation here of a mixed life of action and contemplation locate his description of his and his confreres' charism solidly within the tight framework suggested by, for instance, the lives of Norbert and the works of Philip of Harvengt. Anselm would conclude his career in relative glory, far from frontier Havelberg, as archbishop of Ravenna and high councilor of Barbarossa,[16] but the text at hand offers important insight into what a canon shaped by Norbert might think and be a few years after the Premonstratensian founder's death. Here, Anselm appears the advocate of the pattern of regular religious life Norbert instituted, not the court bishop, imperial councilor, or papally appointed ecumenist of the royal charters and the *Antikeimenon.*

The immediate provocation for Anselm's *Apologetic Letter* elicits the bishop's expression of his broad spiritual ideals and sense of his and his confreres' position in the complex topography of twelfth-century religious reform. The circumstances were these: a regular canon and provost of Hamersleben near Magdeburg—an Augustinian but not a member of one of Norbert's own foundations—abandoned his life as a regular canon and sought refuge at a Benedictine monastery in Huysburg, in the Diocese of Halberstadt. The canons of Hamersleben evidently sought the return of this apostate, Peter, who was defended in his retreat to monastic life by the abbot of Huysburg, Egbert. Two short works written by Egbert in support of Peter survive, although in fragmentary form.[17] A third is entirely lost. This third letter on behalf of the former provost of Hamersleben met with Anselm of Havelberg's acerbic epistolary response in 1138.[18] Much of Egbert's argument can be reconstructed in Anselm's virtually line-by-line refutation, although it is difficult to imagine that a serious participant in the great contemporary discussion of the distinctions among and relative status of the orders should have been as logically inept and hermeneutically unskilled as Anselm claims.

Anselm's apologetic letter is thus a comment on a specific situation involving an actual historical *transitus*, the transfer of a regular religious from one house and rule to another—a situation for Anselm very like the situation later encountered by another follower of Norbert, Philip of Harvengt, when one of his own canons left the Premonstratensian community of Bonne Espérance during Philip's priorate; movement between religious communities and rules was evidently a not infrequently encountered problem in the mid-twelfth century.[19] At the same time, the bishop of Havelberg clearly intended his letter's audience to extend beyond its Benedictine recipient and his monks at Huysburg, and indeed it seems to define regular canons' charism as much for them as for others. Anselm seems in this text to have entered the general fray over the identity and hierarchy of religious communities as a champion of the Augustinians rather than simply to have taken the side of the canons of Hamersleben in recalling their provost, Peter.

For many years before Anselm wrote against Egbert's view, controversy had been building in letters, pamphlets, and public disputations about the appropriate role and rank of the canons. Although the new Augustinians vaunted their historical legitimacy and even the priority of their way of life, which they assumed had been articulated by Augustine in the last years of the fourth century, over the sixth-century Benedictine model, regular canonical life as a historical reality was indeed a novelty.[20] Established monastic communities were dismayed and critical of the canonical reform. In the early 1120s Rupert of Deutz, the great black monk, argued against the canons in his *Altercatio monachi et clerici*. Even if Norbert of Gennep was not Rupert's interlocutor in the historical debates this text purports to record, as some scholars have argued, his presence and activity as canonical founder in Rupert's own diocese of Liège—where Anselm would later be educated—at the very period in which the Benedictine apologist and theologian wrote this defense of monastic life identify Norbert and his followers as among the problems Rupert set forth in this debate and text to solve.[21] Here Rupert responded to the canons' assertion that monks should stay inside their walls by attaching the prerogative to preach to ordination. This argument made preaching an obligation for a monk as it was for a canon. Rupert then ridiculed canonical status as empty novelty, monasticism *manqué*.[22] For Rupert, monks' right to preach—and here his argument and his defensiveness regarding the Benedictines' secular role were most clearly competitive with the Premonstratensians' and the other Augustinian canons'—was the crux of the matter. The canons were upstarts, usurpers of the monks' regular status.

Egbert of Huysburg cited Rupert's authority in defending the canon Peter's *transitus* to Benedictinism as access to a higher form of Christian life, so licit. The later abbot's arguments seem to have included little new.[23] Thus, when Anselm responded, his blistering tone reflected fifteen years' resentment among Norbert's followers over Rupert's self-proclaimed victory over the advocates of canonical life. As Lees has pointed out, Anselm begins and ends his letter with an invocation of charity, whose law he declares his opponent has abrogated.[24] Whether or not the violation of Christian charity was a fair accusation against Egbert, Anselm himself was certainly culpable in effect if not intent. The militancy and sarcasm of his tone are perhaps best explained by the realistic length of the period in which this controversy had been brewing—far longer than the few months in which the status of Peter of Hamersleben had been debated. Many passages of Anselm's work reveal real bitterness at not only Egbert's but a succession of Benedictines' vaunting of monastic superiority. Later, similar tracts from other parties in the controversy, such as the *Libellus de diversis ordinibos* and Idung's *Dialogus* between a Cistercian and a Cluniac, would ring of less bitterness but also less spontaneity.[25] Anselm's text bespeaks his own absolute conviction of both the legitimacy and the necessity to the wider church of the canonical life. Here, more than in any other text in this volume, a regular canon in the immediate following of Norbert of Xanten argues for his and his confreres' importance to the universal historical church. Urgency therefore trumps charity or, in Anselm's representation, his truth is his harsh charity's gift. Unless Egbert and his kind are receptive to Anselm's news about the true imitation of Christ, they are condemned to a lesser Christianity, as are the European laity for whom they are bound to pray.[26]

In the *Apologetic Letter*'s first phrases Anselm immediately seizes the moral high ground from his Benedictine addressee and adversary. The bishop identifies himself as *pauper Christi*, poor man of Christ. This label, later adopted in self-reference by Francis of Assisi, was widely used in the twelfth century to refer to religious figures of Norbert's general ilk. Such wandering holy men as Gilbert of Sempringham and Robert of Arbrissel, like the Premonstratensian founder, began religious orders but never entirely abandoned the popular preaching in which, dressed as ragged penitents, they had established their reputation. *Pauper Christi* was a favorite self-description of Norbert himself, as was *nudus nudum Christum sequens*, a naked follower of the naked Christ.[27] Lees has noted that Anselm of Havelberg never identified himself as a Premonstratensian,[28] and indeed it would have been anomalous for him to do so, given the loose sense of all early twelfth-century religious of the term *ordo* and their tendency to self-identify generally as monks or canons rather than, for instance, as Cistercians or Victorines. Yet, as even Lees acknowledges, Anselm himself used the phrase *pauperes Christi* to refer specifically to the Augustinian canons in the filiation of Norbert's Magdeburg, whom he installed in his own diocese in the convent of Jerichow.[29] Anselm's repeated, highly affective reference to himself as Christ's poor servant strongly suggests his discipleship of Norbert.

Overall, Anselm's response to Egbert presents a survey of important scriptural texts illuminating the respective roles and relative merits of action and contemplation in both Jewish and Christian pasts. Throughout, as Lees again persuasively argues, Anselm shows primary interest in the historical level of interpretation rather than in the several figurative exegetical levels among which contemporary authors typically distributed their interest.[30] So, for instance, Anselm opens his rebuttal of Egbert's arguments by stressing the fallacy of the Benedictine's insistence that Jesus' early followers were types of later monks. Anselm's central point that the apostles were not monks—hence his mordant note that the New Testament book is the Acts of the Apostles, not the Acts of the Monks[31]—provides this short work's central theme. Everywhere in holy writ Egbert imagines contemplative models; Anselm finds instead a model of mixed life of action and contemplation. For him, then, the primary mode of Christian leadership is apostolic rather than monastic, and the regular canons of the twelfth century are closer types of the apostles than are Egbert and his confreres.

Of gospel images opened to Anselm's apologetic exegesis, most important in this letter is the story of Mary and Martha, presented with important differences in detail in Luke 10:38–42 and John 12:1–8. Giles Constable's study of the importance of this image in twelfth-century thought has clarified the importance of this New Testament pericope for contemporary monks' and canons' articulation and valuation of their respective spiritualities.[32] Anselm of Havelberg's reading is extraordinary, in this rich context, in the radicalism of his advocacy of a mixed life. Anselm retells the story of Mary and Martha, basing his relation primarily on the text of Luke. He reviews the central narrative, explaining that when Martha chides her sister, Mary, for not helping her with the tasks of serving dinner to Jesus and other friends, the guest of honor takes Mary's side. Jesus says that Mary, who has instead pensively sat by his knee, has the *melior pars* (the better part).[33] Overwhelmingly, twelfth-century interpretations of this passage assert either the superiority of the contemplative life figured by Mary or, despite Jesus' apparent preference for Mary's contemplation, the indispensability of the active life figured by Martha—the former expressed in the medieval world by monastic communities and the latter by the secular clergy and, in the twelfth century, by the regular canons.[34] But Anselm adopts a uniquely assertive and rhetorically forceful approach: that the principal exemplar of the story of Mary and Martha is neither woman but Christ himself. Therefore, neither the active nor the contemplative life holds primacy but rather the mixture of the two embodied in Jesus.[35] Anselm makes no attempt to cloak this fresh reading of a much-interpreted gospel text in patristic authority; he presents his new reading as grounded in the text's historical truth, supported by both long historical record and the lessons of recent events. Imagine, he asks his reader, a church without clerics; there could be none. Imagine a church without monks; indeed it could survive, although—and here he is truly if grudgingly charitable—it would be less lovely.[36]

By way of explanation of the meaning of contemplative experience in this exploration of *vita permixta* as the highest form of apostolic imitation—now seen as direct *imitatio Christi*[37]—Anselm extends his discussion of New Testament models of the canonical calling to the visionary experience of John, the beloved disciple. Here he broaches the most elusive aspect of twelfth-century canonical spirituality and characterizes it in terms, once more, of Norbert's characteristic imagery. When Norbert exhorted his followers, as the *Vita B* records, he called them his eaglets, urging them to flight by his example.[38] Of course imagery of the eagle for contemplative life is frequent and ubiquitous in the Christian literary tradition, but for Norbert, as for Anselm, it had particular emotional force. Anselm would later, in the first book of his *Antikeimenon*, use the image of the eagle's youth in Psalm 102's usage to figure the renewal of the church represented by the reformed religious orders of his own times.[39] Here, however, Anselm recurs to the association of the eagle with the apostle John, proximate to Christ in his earthly physicality and sensible again, as documented in Revelation, to divine presence even in his earthly life, in his apocalyptic vision.

Anselm's tone is aggressive to the point of bitterness. So evidently was Egbert's in his lost letter. But Anselm surely wins the day against his now-silenced opponent, in accumulation of authority as well as in originality of argument. He depends not only on scripturally documented history but on the subsequent record of many patristic and canon law citations. Again and again, Anselm affirms, doctors of the church, ecclesiastical councils, and popes have affirmed the integrity of clerical status, seeming to set it above monastic contemplation.[40] Anselm finally suggests that, like the John of the Apocalypse, those who imitate Christ in his teaching and preaching lead the Christians of the twelfth century even as Caleb and Joshua led the Hebrews in their search for the promised land. Such imitators of Christ look past time into a new age. Here as firmly as in the *Antikeimenon* but more figuratively, Anselm implies that the regular canons constitute a superior developmental stage in the unfolding of Christian time. Living on the edge of the new age, they effectively see into timelessness.[41] With Paul, they suggest to all Catholics the awesome beauty of the beatific vision—

not because they stand separate from the world as pure contemplatives, but because they reach toward God in contemplation and
return again to serve God's people, tumbling and climbing between
heaven and earth like the beasts of Ezekiel's vision, among them the
eagle later to become the symbol of John.[42] Anselm's harshness is
then the straightforward expression of a radically new exegesis ren-
dering the standard monastic interpretation of scriptural models
absurd, rather than the product of competition between the orders.
Anselm believes the mixed life to have been Christ's own. It was also
the way of the beloved disciple, and it is now the life the author of
the *Apologetic Letter* lives with his confreres among the regular
canons instituted by Norbert of Xanten. Contemplation is best
achieved by action; Mary and Martha are one in Christ—and in
Augustine and Norbert, in Anselm and the Premonstratensians, and
in all authentic imitators of Jesus.

Anselm's simple collapse of contemplation into action sought
to elide much medieval discussion of the priority of one or the
other. It might function similarly to defuse modern scholars' char-
acterization of the early Premonstratensians as a divided community, contemplative in their Western foundations and active in the
East. Anselm, arguably the most prominently active of the regular
canons in Norbert's following, shows himself in the *Apologetic Letter*
to hunger after both contemplative peace and mystical experience.
In the Christ whom we will soon see, he argues, this boundary dis-
solves. The canons' imperative to preach, to realize the church on
earth among ordinary Christians, expunges any pretense of distinction; to preach is by definition active, and all preaching points
toward the contemplative. Behind Anselm's apology for the regular
canons stands the model of Norbert, but here the Norbert who
preached the Apocalypse in Liège and Prémontré more than the
prince-bishop of the East.

ANSELM OF HAVELBERG, *APOLOGETIC LETTER*

Anselm, poor man of Christ,[1] called bishop of Havelberg, sends greeting to Egbert, venerable abbot of the monastery of Huysburg—for we are both called Christians, and indeed we are Christians.

He who administers acts of charity is to be embraced according to its law, but he who acts outside that law should be admonished. Otherwise—deceived by an appearance of right, considering light to be darkness and darkness light, sweetness bitter and bitterness sweet, and calling good evil and evil good—he may fall from goodness into evil. He may grasp darkness, abandoning the light, or choose bitter food unsuited to the healthy palate while spitting out sweetness. Recently, as I sat alone reading, as I often do, as it happened perusing the letters of the blessed Jerome, a certain brother came up and brought me something else to read. I took it up quickly, eager for something recent, but I found what it contained was more burdensome than boring, and I was amazed that anyone should have made the effort to undertake such a piece of writing, then continued and finished it. I noticed the heading of this text, which named you as its author, and I reread it carefully, taking notice of all it said. I found in it certain things that were superstitious and useless to say, to which you nonetheless saw fit to give credence for some negligible reason or authority you had in mind. Everyone accustomed to interpreting sacred readings should know how great an evil it is to entrust sacred scripture to one's own understanding rather than to entrust one's understanding to sacred scripture, but you argue on the basis of sacred scripture something that contradicts it. Framing this assertion in your own words, you insist that all the faithful of the Old and New Testaments alike were in fact monks. You do not hesitate to say

This translation is based on the Patrologia edition (PL 188, cols. 1091–1118).

38

openly that the passage where the evangelist Luke writes, they *had but one heart and one soul* (Acts 4:32), and so forth, pertains to the company of monks, not to the apostles and those who were with them—people at whose time even the term *monk* was unknown, whence it is that the book is called Acts of the Apostles instead of Acts of the Monks. And you adduce certain words of the blessed Augustine commenting on Psalm 132, "Lo to live as one is a good and happy thing,"[2] in which he clearly commends the apostolic and common life, but which you nevertheless ignorantly attempt to twist to mean monastic profession.

Tell me, brother, if the five hundred who saw the Lord after his resurrection, as the apostle Paul recounts,[3] were monks? Or were those one hundred twenty who were together after the Lord's resurrection and ascension into heaven, when he came upon them gathered together, were those too monks?[4] The Holy Spirit was sent to them from heaven on that day of Pentecost, sent as promised.[5] And was it then the case that all those were monks who then lived together as one happily, as brothers? You add something from the writings of John Chrysostom, which you do not quite understand because your charity seems to extend only to monks, not to all Catholics.[6] Finally, you adduce the teaching of some Rupert or other whose authority, because it is unknown in the church, is cast aside as easily as accepted.[7] But perhaps you consider him great not because he wrote great things but because he was an abbot of monks. Out of curiosity I read something that he wrote, I confess, so that I know and have seen his work, but I found the Greek proverb true of him: "A fat belly need not give birth to great understanding."[8]

But I ask, dearest brother, why do you toil so? Why do you flail at the air? Why do you dispute with such energy on behalf of the order of monks, which no thinking man would assault? You do too much, so that you please the monks but make yourself obnoxious to others. As the saying goes, do not sell bladders for lanterns[9]—unless you do so for simple boys, or the uneducated, or even for idiots who are amazed at everything new. Why do you crack such vessels[10] in your writing as will then leak? With what rashness do you presume to offer muddy water[11] to the sons of God? Those who receive the flesh and blood of Christ not—as you do— eating it entirely raw, but rather as roasted lamb,[12] are accustomed daily to drink the fountain of living water in divine speech. I fear for you and for God's sake I am fearful of you, lest while you laboriously defend the venerable cloak of Christ—that untorn cloak[13] which no Christian would attack unless he had lost his mind—you destroy it, ripping the very garment of charity. But I wonder whether you would do these things if you were not a monk. I am not a monk, but I am prepared to defend the order of monks with you. We read that many saints—many of the blessed, of the elect, of the perfect, of those full of the Holy Spirit—served according to the monastic rule of life. Clearly only someone insane or diabolical would presume to detract from that praiseworthy and desirable order. For the monastic life, preserved in its uninterrupted pattern, is altogether irreproachable, worthy of support, venerable, desirable, to be embraced, confirmed, buttressed, conserved, and generally held up, raised to heaven as the ladder of sinners and penitents.

On the other hand, the perfection of the monks should in no way diminish the perfection and sanctity of the clergy—nor do I in any way agree with the words you marshal, dearest brother, to demonstrate that the life of monks is more honorable than the excellence of the clergy. But before I respond to your opinion in this regard, I wish first to offer a few words to shed light on my own judgment. I do not say a monk is good because he is a monk; I say he is good because he is good. I do not say a cleric is good because he is a cleric, but because he is good and I love a good man. And I do not judge a layman to be either good or bad because he is a layman, but because he is good or bad, or at least I do not know him to be bad. *God is not a respecter of persons, but in every nation he that feareth him and worketh justice is acceptable to him* (Acts 10:34–35), and as the apostle says, he *will have all men to be saved* (1 Tim 2:4). Is it the role of a thinking man to roil with his writing the hearts of so many monks so long kept peaceful from the whirlwind of the secular world, or to summon them into a debate—as you say—to battle for the dignity of the monastic order, when they so gather themselves in vain, against no opponent? I think that if you could you would not fear to awaken from their sleep all the monks of Egypt and Mesopotamia, the Pauls, the Antonies, the Hilaries, the Macarii, and that very father who is no less blessed *(benedictus)* in his name than in his sanctity, Benedict—all for a useless war. But you ought indeed to fear greatly, for these very men would refute you as reprehensible. Not only would they not support you, but they would judge you harshly for your ignorance, since they are themselves the worthier of heavenly life to the degree to which they were too humble to enter the order of clerics who rule God's church.

I wonder at the effrontery and rashness with which you say they are your masters and you glory to be their disciple, since you seem neither to pertain to them nor they to you except through the common bond of Christianity by which we are all one in Christ. They were poor, so that they scarcely touched meat and suffered cold, yet they were happy, but you do something else again. Hungry, they found their food with their own hands, and they leaned on ropes and mattocks, but you do not do this. They were needy, but you are wealthy. They were afflicted, and you have consolation. They suffered, and you lead a peaceful life. They wandered in solitude,[14] and so forth, and you are secure in the midst of your people in your lofty seat—all of which things I say briefly lest in my truthful comparison I tear down the charity I intend to build and worsen the wound I propose to cure. I would prefer, while I keep silence, that you examine yourself in comparison with them. If I were speaking and pointing with my unwelcome finger, cutting to the quick with my tongue, you would be disturbed and angry—you whom I wish to see never disturbed, and whom I wish to hear and embrace as always gentle, always joyful, always benevolent, always peaceful, never troubled. Indeed, I wish to detract neither from your merit nor that of any of the monks of our times, especially since—sinner that I am, my head confounded with fear—I wish to be saved with the help of all and to be found in name and in merit among the poor men of Christ.[15]

You say that the dignity of the monastic order has been insulted because Peter, the provost of the canons of Hamersleben, who live in community following the profession established by the apostles, has become a monk but is being sought out and recalled to his original order. Clearly he deserted the canons for no good reason and ought not to have. O Christian unworthy of any dignity, now the source of controversy concerning these orders' relative rank! But perhaps you meant dignity in heaven. For heavenly rank is one thing and earthly another. If you argue concerning heavenly rank, you are of this earth, and certainly you show that you are unworthy of that higher rank but instead deserve the indignation of good men. If, however, you mean rank in heaven, why do you lament that it is insulted, for any rank or dignity is safe there, altogether free from any insult? So no earthly rank should be sought by a Christian person, nor should heavenly dignity be believed or stated by any Christian to be insulted in any way.

Further you complain about the term *regular canon*. You say that it is a novelty and therefore contemptible, as if novelty need be contemptible. Anyone who understands syllogisms knows that this is itself a contemptible argument, for everything old was new at some time, and therefore is neither more nor less contemptible because it is new or was new. Nor is something more or less acceptable because it is or will be old, but rather it should be acceptable to all good men because it is good and useful whether it is old or new. For there are ancient goods and new goods, ancient evils and new evils—and surely if the antiquity or novelty of evils does not deprive them of force, neither should the antiquity or novelty of good things bring them dignity. You seem here not straightforwardly but obliquely, as if by implication, by praising the term *cleric*, taken by itself, both to draw those to whom it applies to your own side of the controversy and to praise them for their antiquity. But what I fear you have actually done is not so much to praise clerics as to derogate regular canons while appearing to keep the peace.[16] I confess that I do not know how to answer you about this term, because "regular canon" seems to signify the same thing as if one were to say "regular regular," or "canonical canon," as though modern usage iterates the same word in Latin as in Greek as if affirming the antiquity and, now, revival of this form of religious life, or perhaps to distinguish the regular canons from those who do not live according to a rule.

But imagine that this priest Peter, having long ago professed the apostolic life and taken on the dress of poverty, might now—descending through human frivolity rather than ascending through divine election—either wish to become a monk or even carry out this wish. Should he not be rightly recalled to his first profession, especially since the authority of the holy fathers prevents such a change from happening and—if by chance it does happen—advises and powerfully commands that it be reversed? If someone superstitious thinks those fathers' authority should not be obeyed, he damns himself irre-mediably, for as the blessed Ambrose says, "Whoever does not agree with the Roman Church clearly is a heretic."[17] So Urban, pope and martyr, says, "We ordain and so ordaining universally forbid that any-one professed as a regular canon be made a monk unless—may this not happen!—he has publicly fallen into sin. And if someone should presume to violate our decree, we command that he return to the canonical order and from then on wear a monk's hood as a reminder of his presumption. And may he be last in the choir."[18]

Likewise, Bishop Gelasius says, "There came to us certain brothers who had professed the canonical life, and who said that their abbot, having cast aside both his paternal care and the canon-ical habit he had professed, had entered a monastery of monks although all his brothers were unwilling that he do so. We were dis-turbed at the presumption in this unheard-of act, and we affirmed what Urban, pope and martyr of blessed memory, had established previously, that this abbot go back without complaint to the cloister whence he had unlawfully withdrawn. Further, on account of his great presumption he must wear a monk's hood there until his death. When we saw that this was pleasing to all the brothers there, we commanded that this law be kept perpetually in the canonical order of our God omnipotent and of the apostles Peter and Paul, and that it be maintained by our authority."[19] Likewise, Urban II: "We ordain lest anyone of the canonical profession, after God's vicar's hands have been laid upon him, whether for some frivolous impulse or desiring stricter religious practice, dare to leave his clois-ter without permission of his provost and all his congregation. If he leaves, we forbid by our and God's authority that any abbot, monk, or bishop take him in without warranty of their assent."[20] Likewise, elsewhere: "We find it is a reprehensible practice among certain canons, one worthy of ecclesiastical censure and contrary to eccle-siastical tradition, to wear a cowl. Only monks ought to use that, and canons ought not to usurp the monks' habit. This practice is approved by no authority, but rather is rightly reproved by those who know what is healthy. It is repudiated and should be, and henceforward it is prohibited."[21] And again: "It is clear from evident authority that the institution of canons ranks above other such insti-tutions, and therefore it is necessary that those who are called by the name of this profession take care that they honor it in themselves, in their life and customs, rather than dishonor it. Since they hold their power from an institution of such great authority and they ought to show themselves worthy of imitation, they should be afraid—may this not happen!—to step outside of their role and so be unworthy of the kingdom of heaven."[22] And likewise, from the Council of Autun, "No monk or abbot may presume to take in a regular canon or to foster a monk if he can find a cloister of his own order where he can be cared for."[23]

Therefore, beloved brother—for we are both servants of God—I wish you to teach me by what reason or authority you may wish that a good cleric become a monk, since he who is a cleric of good life speaks, declares boldly and securely, with the prince of the apostles and with all that original holy company: Lord, *behold we have left all things and have followed thee. What therefore shall we have* (Matt 19:27)? Why, if he has sold all and given it to the poor, and now follows Christ naked?[24] Why, if he is weighed down by his cross and, prepared for all persecution, imitates Christ and his apostles? Why, if he has said nothing and done nothing of his own in this world except perhaps sin? Why, if he has renounced all things that he possessed and, hearing the words of life and learning the discipline of justice, makes himself a true and perfect disciple of Christ? If, I say, the good cleric—for I speak about the good cleric—does these and all the other things enjoined by the gospels, why does he not sit with the twelve who judge the twelve tribes of Israel?[25] For Christ, the savior and doctor of perfect salvation, causes such a man both to recline among the disciples and, crossing over to another role, to serve them.[26] Does he not? Christ says: *Where I am, there also shall my minister be* (John 12:26). Say therefore, if you can, whether a faithful God would promise something to a monk and deny it to a cleric? I recall having read this neither in the promises of the gospels nor anywhere in all of the great expanse of divine scripture, nor do I remember hearing this from anyone who has read it. For this reason I beg you to allow that everyone remain in the vocation to which he is called, and do not under the pretense of religion presume to disturb the ecclesiastical order built on the model of divine institution on the mount. Rather, humbly seek peace with all those in the Lord's house and with the company of Christians, lest, taking you as an occasion, the one way of religious life judge the other, or in the words of the gospel, *house upon house shall fall*,[27] and there be pernicious scandal in the church of God.

But perhaps you say that you have often seen and more often heard and even more often read that certain clerics crossed to the monastic life and habit, and on the other hand that certain monks were assumed into the clerical order. I confess, dearly beloved, that I too have seen these things and heard them and read that they were done—but we must diligently consider not only what has been done but how it has been done or is being done daily in the church of God. For if a man was a cleric before he crossed into a monastery, this was done or even tolerated only as a special case, not by law or rule of ecclesiastical institution. He might have been someone's relation, or a useless character, or arrogantly contemptuous of ecclesiastical discipline or canonical obedience, or a slippery follower of secular life and a flat-out liar, or perhaps even a damnation to himself or others in the church, of the sort forbidden to become monks in the fifth council of Toledo, canon 49.[28]

Many examples of the saints teach us how, according to the strict and ancient practice of the church, it might be necessary that a cleric become a monk. When clerics are infamous or criminal they are degraded from sacred orders by ecclesiastical censure, and when they are so stripped they are then put into a monastery to lament their sins. Thus it is clear—and no one of sane mind would doubt—that the order of canons is higher in the church than that of the monks, since criminals are cast out as guilty from the former and into the latter as condemned so that, grieving and weeping, they unwillingly receive punishment and penitence. But who is so mad that he would say that he had seen that criminal and infamous monks—for sons of darkness can also arise among the monks—are cast from the order of monks and received into the order of canons as a lower, abject status? When this befalls a cleric bound to canonical profession and tied by the assent of his own mouth to the cross of obedience, what does this have to do with clerics wandering without oversight?[29] For *the wicked walk round about* (Ps 11:9). If, I say, as I have often said, a good cleric led by some accident of frivolity flees the narrow path that leads to his fatherland,[30] seeks a monastery, and demands that he be made a monk—I say it plainly,

I say it openly, and if there is anyone who does not know this, I judge him to be nothing—that cleric is not to be taken in. Rather, he is to be sent back at once to his own fold whence he has wandered, breaking the bond of obedience. But if he is taken in through ignorance, because knowledge is limited or, worse, in presumption and usurpation, and is made a monk, I say with the holy Roman popes in the church and with the church generally, and I declare faithfully, that the cleric must be called back. According to the written intention of the holy fathers who forbade this to happen, he must be restored to his prior order, which he deserted in stupid and superstitious devotion.

On the other hand, if a monk holds to his religious vow inviolably, if he serves obediently under the Rule of St. Benedict, and if he is trained in frequent readings in the sense of divine scripture to be useful to the church of God, according to the example of the blessed Gregory, the great theologian and cleric, he may usefully be moved forward at the church's calling to the priesthood, even to the pontificate. From that point on he may usefully open his mouth, heretofore humbly closed in the midst of the church: *A good man out of a good treasure bringeth forth good things* (Matt 12:35). Nevertheless, whenever this happens it ought to happen according to the ordination of the fathers who have gone before. It should be thus: that he not cast aside his monastic habit but wear it hidden. Since he is shaped by canonical training he should always wear his stole on the outside. He should set aside the gradual anthem that he had sung before, bewailing his tribulation to God. From the eighth tone of *Blessed are the undefiled* (Ps 118:1) he should cross over into the true octave, learning and performing the divine office with clerics.[31] In all things, in his dress as in his worship, let him show frequently and openly that he has become a cleric, wearing underneath the black garment of human grief, infirmity, and mortality, but always showing on the outside the white linen of the newness of life and the brightness of the resurrection.[32] And he ought to preach these things ardently to the people of God.[33] Thus it is clear that the cleric has deserved for his good works to be set above the others, the monks.

Now then, let our and your Jerome come into this discussion—our Jerome because he was a priest and yours because he was a monk *not minding high things but consenting to the humble*

46

(Rom 12:16), not one who used a third tongue[34] hissing against many in our time, but one so learned as to wield three languages. Let him come, I say, into our discussion and say what he thought about clerics or about monks. Let him offer it to all, opening the book for me and you and everyone everywhere to read without embarrassment. Jerome wrote thus to Heliodorus: "Far be it from me to speak against those who, following in the footsteps of the apostles, prepare the body of Christ with sacred speech—those through whom we are Christians. They hold the keys of the kingdom of heaven, as it were, until judgment day, and they keep the bride of Christ in sober chastity. There is one role for the monk, as I have argued, and another for the cleric. Clerics feed the sheep and I am so fed. They live for the altar, and the axe is put to my root as to a tree failing to bear fruit[35] if I do not bear my gift there. I cannot claim poverty as my excuse, for in the gospel Christ praised the old widow offering the two mites that alone remained to her.[36] It is not permitted me to sit ahead of a priest, for if I have sinned he may hand me over to Satan in bodily death, so that my spirit may be saved in the day of the Lord Jesus Christ." And below, "If the pious encouragements of the brothers summon you for the same order, I rejoice for your ascent and fear for your lapse."[37] And the blessed Augustine, "A perfect monk in no way makes a good cleric."[38]

See to it, brother, that those things that were humbly written by such great men be humbly read by you. But perhaps despite such great authorities your mind prefers still to be uncertain of what you believe in this regard. Yet it is indeed certain that nothing is lacking for you to believe, even if you do so slowly and with difficulty. Where authority precedes, there the firm truth of unshaken reason follows. Therefore let what you say be true. Listen a little. You assert that the monastic profession has greater dignity than all others. And you adduce the example of the blessed Gregory, rightly saying that many other monks properly crossed over to the clerical order. Or rather, you only seem to speak rightly, but actually you are tied up in your own words. For either it is true that the monastic order is more worthy than all others and from it one cannot cross into the clerical order or, if it is permissible to cross over, then the order so left behind is not the more honorable. No one would judge that one should cross from a higher to a lower order unless because of a public lapse. Choose therefore what you wish—live either entirely without ecclesiastical orders and content with monastic life alone, or, if you think that it is permitted to rise from monastic life to ecclesiastical orders and ranks, confess with me and the whole church that you remain humbly below, lower in rank, and that clerics are truly higher. Otherwise you are caught up in this opinion you speak and teach, that a monk who wishes to be a cleric is lowering himself. But monks as well as clerics judge this absurd and reprehensible, for they preach that they are the closer to sacred orders the better their lives are found to be.

So then keep silent on your opinion, which you seem to have dreamed rather than proved through any argument or authority. As for what you glory over in your writing about the miracles of St. Benedict, they should not be adduced as an example. I wonder that you are not amazed at the apostles and that infinite crowd of those who imitate them and follow their footsteps, through whom God has done and still does so many great miracles that no talent ever suffices to enumerate them. As for what you have copied over from the dialogue of the blessed Gregory, that the venerable Benedict himself banned a priest troubled by a devil before he took orders from serving the altar—surely he did this not by authority of judgment but by way of counsel, foreknowing what evil would befall one who set aside the healthful counsel of one so great as he. As for what you then copy out from the same dialogue, that Benedict excommunicated some nuns, and your conclusion that he had the authority of ecclesiastical censure—you have not interpreted this correctly. He excommunicated them by accusing them rather than punishing them, and he afterward absolved the sisters after they were dead by true priestly authority rather than by ecclesiastical law, in the oblation he made on their behalf. He recognized that they were absolved by God, and he acknowledged that to others.[39]

When I was in the church at Rome, I saw and heard a certain abbot of Clairvaux in a rough garment, with a gaunt face—a worthy man of God, not false but a true disciple of blessed Benedict—sitting among clerics expounding divine scripture at the command of the Roman pope, Innocent II, himself an incomparably great man.[40] But the abbot did this from obedience to the pope rather than out of priestly duty. And though I am a sinner, unknowing how to loose the seal of divine scripture and so obligated to express my opinion only humbly, I will mention my own relevant experience. The same pope of the holy Roman church, while he was celebrating the collects and the solemnities of the Mass of the Virgin on the feast of the Nativity of Christ, called upon me when I chanced to be there. When the archdeacon finished reading the gospel, the pope ordered me to climb to the lectern so that, with him there and all around eager to hear, I might offer my teaching and exhortation. I did so for a little while according to the grace given me by God, not so much by my own authority—though I am a bishop—as by his, whom it is right for me humbly to obey in all things. Therefore let us not adduce as examples those things that happen by useful dispensation or special permission against those things that are confirmed in immovable law and invincible authority. Let this not happen!

I have heard that you do not fear to say—that you do not blush to say from time to time to some people—that regular canons should not hold parishes or direct the care of souls among the people. If you indeed say so, I am most vehemently amazed at your judgment. Whoever might try to assert this, which I consider that no wise man believes, does it more with spite against the canonical order than love of truth. If he understands aright, he should invite all priests to live under a rule rather than separate those living according to a rule from keeping God's sheep.[41] As for them, the malice of others should displease them to the degree to which they have set aside their own ill will, and they should credit another's correction to the extent that he applies himself to correcting himself. Undeserved insult therefore does no harm to a fruitful tree. The common usage of the whole church is clear, that no monk be taken up into an archdiaconate or archpriesthood or into any parish. Similarly, no regular canon is removed by ecclesiastical judgment or synodal trial from the care of souls or from any other ecclesiastical office or dignity; rather, he is sought out, elected, raised up by the simple people, and like a light shining in the darkness is loved and honored, teaching by word and example.[42] Therefore, whoever wishing to satisfy his own ill will tries to detract from the canonical order in this way—in what he says, why he says it, against whom he says it—is completely ignorant or, bereft of any scriptural understanding, only seethes maliciously with envy of the good.

Since I have the opportunity, I will here respond further to these envious folk. From the beginning I have had as my purpose that *their teeth in their mouth* be worn down (cf. Ps 57:7). May they come to their senses and be corrected, setting aside the fog of envy and ignorance. And now I will proceed further and respond both to your words and to those of certain other monks who boast that they are only contemplative, so—as if divine scripture spoke on their behalf—setting themselves superciliously ahead of clerics who sometimes sweat in the active life and then lift themselves up to the contemplative life. Such clerics, with the Lord himself standing at their head, either are too active to tread upon contemplatives or they are both so contemplative and active that they would spurn neither the one group nor the other, but rather love those who are good and active when they have time for sacred contemplation and again in their time of good action love the holy contemplatives. But it seems to me that you should fear, dearest brother, as greatly as I do lest—while we dispute in writing these issues discussed within established boundaries by the holy fathers for those studying lofty theology—we give offense to the contemplative life and the active life, and lest in provoking each other we destroy the charity we both ought to build. But I trust in God, because *charity*, which is *poured forth in our hearts* by the spirit dwelling there, *is patient, kind, envieth not, is not puffed up, dealeth not perversely, thinketh no evil, rejoiceth with the truth, beareth all things* (cf. 1 Cor 13:4–7). If you, who are a monk, offer a sacrifice of turtledoves, it ought not to seem to you vile or contemptible if I, who am a cleric and a poor man of Christ,[43] humbly offer the sacrifice of the poor, that is, the chicks of doves, at the temple of the Lord.

Let us see now if those of us following the active life in a praiseworthy manner, as heralds of the Old or New Testaments, are bereft of what is called contemplative life, so that they are called active because they cannot be called contemplative. Surely Abel, the first just shepherd of sheep and type of the souls of shepherds, experienced contemplation of the Divine, because his good gifts were accepted by a good God.[44] As for the just Noah, pilot of the ark of the church, was he without divine contemplation, when God effected through him the salvation of those he did not wish to perish in the flood?[45] Abraham, in faith as in flesh *the father of many nations* (Gen 17:5), is read to have contemplated God at one point in Ur of the Chaldees, at another in the land of Canaan or in certain other places, and he was made blessed in God's familiar address.[46] Jacob, father of the twelve patriarchs, who cherished Leah and Rachel, figures of both active and contemplative lives, is read to have seen God *face to face* (cf. Gen 32:30), in a heavenly way, with the Lord resting on the ladder to heaven and angels going up and down it.[47] Moses was tending the sheep of *his father-in-law Jethro, the priest of Madian, and drove the flock to the interior parts of the desert, came to the mountain of God, Horeb. And the Lord appeared to him in a flame out of the midst of a bush and he saw that the bush was on fire but was not burnt.* Therefore he said, *I will go forth and see this great sight* (Exod 3:1–3). O great vision! O magnificent contemplative experience! How was he not a contemplative when he foresaw at such a distance our beginning in the bush that *was on fire and was not burnt,* just as the blessed Virgin Mary was later pregnant without carnal concupiscence?

Likewise Moses, after he became the leader of God's people, was called onto the mountain in a cloud, away from the people's contentiousness, and was instructed concerning the Law and the ruling of the people, the ordination of the priesthood, and the arrangement of the tabernacle. As a servant to the Lord's whole house he was divinely taught, made ready through heavenly contemplation for terrestrial action. So we read that God spoke to him as friend to friend: *Make it according to the pattern that was shown thee in the mount* (Gen 25:40). Joshua and Caleb, the leaders of the same people, while they wandered to explore and contemplate the promised land, were also types of contemplatives in that they revealed the secrets of the heavenly fatherland. When they returned to the people, carrying back the bunch of grapes on a pole, they inspired them to seize that fertile land. Good teachers of virtue in God's church, they set an example by going before the people.[48] David, king and prophet, did not neglect his well-ruled kingdom for the sake of prophecy, nor did he set aside the prophecy, with which in his humility he was enriched, for a kingdom well administered. So we see that in a long succession of grace he was at one point a perfect contemplative and at another point perfect in active life, as is shown in the divine testimony: The Lord says *I have found David, the son of Jesse, a man according to my own heart* (Acts 13:22). Who would believe that Daniel, the man whom God loved in the midst of Babylon, was untouched by divine contemplation?[49] Who thinks that the three boys in the fiery furnace were not sent as contemplatives, when the Son of God was with them in the furnace?[50] And Ezekiel spoke thus about the holy animals: they *ran and returned* (Ezek 1:14). They went away intent on their contemplation, and they came back serving through their action. The Lord said to that prophet: *Go forth into the plane* and *shut thyself up in the midst of thy house* (cf. Ezek 3:22–24). What is it to go away into the field except to preach among the people? And what might it be to be shut up inside the house but then to separate the mind from that same preaching and to conserve the joy of life spiritually, within oneself, in contemplation?

Thus you see that the fathers long ago unambiguously considered a life sometimes contemplative but sometimes active to have been entirely perfect. Some of them were called seers on account of the frequent visions of the secret things of God that they saw and because they announced to the people things that had already happened or would happen. They went before the people bearing the precious bunch of grapes behind them on the rod of the Old Testament. There were still many things that they could not see, but they knew those things figuratively and in faith.

But what do you think of those who followed, who in the course of the New Testament—almost at the end of time—instead bore the same sweet bunch of grapes before them? They looked upon it directly with their blessed eyes. What a great thing they knew, what great joy they had, with what great desire for contemplation they burned—those for whom this bunch of grapes was full of the sweetness of all divinity! As we read, the Son of God himself once said when he was oppressed at the prospect of suffering on the cross, *Blessed are your eyes which see what you see, for many kings and prophets* wished *to see the things that you see, and they have not seen them, and to hear the things what you hear, and they have not heard them* (Matt 13:16–17), clearly teaching that those things that the ancients knew figuratively might now be seen unveiled. As for the Son of God and man Jesus Christ, the head of the Catholic Church, the chief of the contemplatives, the strict judge of all the proud, the lover and preserver of all the humble, he who wills spiritual grace and is its benevolent and spontaneous giver, he who is both generous to give grace and a munificent, sufficient, and bountiful donor, who *hath wrought salvation in the midst of the earth* (Ps 73:12), does it seem to you that he was one or the other, active or contemplative? Or does it seem rather that he was both contemplative and active?

If you may so direct your charity, consider our Lord Jesus Christ himself carefully and humbly according to the truth of the gospel and according to the moral interpretation fully known and conventional in the church. He was a guest at the house of the sisters Martha and Mary, of whom the one, namely Martha, rushed about doing service, so appropriately signifying the active life. But Mary, meanwhile, seated at the feet of the Lord, listened most attentively to his word, thus signifying contemplative life. Concerning her, when the Lord says, *Mary hath chosen the better part, which shall not be taken from her* (Luke 10:42), did he wish the loftier role to be understood as in comparison of Mary to both himself and Martha?[51] Did he mean rather not to himself but to Martha alone? Surely the latter. Jesus Christ sat teaching, so figuring the teaching of teachers. Mary sat silently and devoutly hearing his work. Martha rushed about serving solicitously. Direct your charity to this: Christ teaching, Mary listening, Martha serving. Three persons—which of the three to you seems worthiest? Three roles—which of the three seems to you the most worthy? As for me, I know and am confident in saying to you without any doubt that Jesus is the worthiest. And because it is clear that the person of Jesus is worthier than they, surely no one would doubt that his role was also the worthiest. Therefore, if you can, show how Mary, who was there, chose the better part in comparison with Jesus, who, when he was present, chose her. But I think that this word from the mouth of the Word came forth to Martha about Mary with respect to Martha, for I would not easily be persuaded that Mary listening and not Jesus teaching had chosen the better part. Yet it would necessarily be true according to the testimony of the word that Mary chose the better part if indeed this passage refers to those who are in the church of God only in the order of hearers, *auditores,* and not teachers, *doctores.* Thus it is also fitting that the evangelist says Jesus "chose." Those who are lower can laudably choose silence and quiet and a place to

LORETTE WILMOT LIBRARY
NAZARETH COLLEGE

listen, but they ought not themselves choose the role of teaching. They must be selected for this by others if they are indeed worthy.

What is laudable for some is reprehensible for many, so I fear for you, *since the thoughts of men are vain* (Ps 93:11), lest you be deceived and by chance think that Christ was neither contemplative nor active, especially since he seems to have had the role neither of Mary listening nor Martha ministering, but instead the role of the master teaching. But if you consider carefully what Jesus began to say and do, it will appear clearly that *a great prophet is risen up among us*, through whom and in whom *God hath visited his people* (Luke 7:16). Because of us he was perfect in action, and for us he was a contemplative higher than the heavens. The gospel says: *Jesus, being full of the holy spirit, returned from the Jordan and was led in the spirit into the desert for forty days* (Luke 4:1–2). Likewise, Jesus ascended *a mountain alone to pray* (Matt 14:23). And again, *lifting up his eyes to heaven*, he said, *I confess to you, Father*, and so forth (cf. John 17:1). Again, *Jesus, going out, went according to his custom to the Mount of Olives*. Breaking away from his disciples by *a stone's cast and kneeling down, he prayed, "Father, if thou wilt, remove this chalice from me, but yet not my will but thine be done." And there appeared to him an angel from heaven, strengthening him. And being in agony he prayed the longer* (cf. Luke 22:39–43). Again, *Jesus taketh unto him Peter and James, and John his brother, and bringeth them up into a high mountain apart, and he was transfigured before them* (Matt 17:1–2), and so forth. O divine contemplation! O great revelation of God's secrets! O open confirmation of the blessed resurrection in Moses and Elijah, who appeared in the same place! O rare and admirable representation, more delectable than can be said, of future unimaginable glory! If you, who already so many times have gloried in the contemplative life, had been there—if you were able to contemplate the son of God in such glory—you would no more be able to keep silent about such an excellent vision than were the rest of the apostles who were so found worthy. But you would glory more in yourself and about yourself for having seen this than in him who did it, especially since you do not seem to scorn many who are monks along with you for seeing lesser things—monks whose vision and contemplation are altogether unknown to you. Yet the gospel text says of Jesus that he taught crowds in the temple or on the mountain or in a little boat, that he gave sight to the blind, cleansed lepers, cured the sick, cast out a demon,[52] healed paralytics,[53] responded to the scribes and Pharisees, and argued that others were fathered by the devil but he had divine zeal.[54]

The Son of God is the model of highest contemplation and the form of perfect action. He is the paradigm of either life in one person. He showed himself to all Christians and especially to his apostles as the norm of right living in both his deeds and words. After Christ I need not describe the apostolic life for you, because they clung fervently to his commandments and footprints. So we must believe that they have instituted his life according to the doctrine of their Master, just as those blessed in the purity of their hearts see the God of gods as in a mirror in Zion, those who are blessed with compassion wish to follow his mercy in preaching the care of their neighbors, and in healing and curing and preaching. So the apostle Paul, doctor of the Gentiles in faith and truth—who said boldly, *be ye followers of me* (1 Cor 4:16)—from time to time forgets those things that are in the past and goes forth into those things of the future, reaching toward contemplation of God. At other moments, sober in that holy and inebriating cup of divine contemplation, neither losing his heavenly friend whom his embrace had just held in burning love nor neglecting his neighbor, for whom he now wished to be present and to provide an account of the same love, he cared for those entrusted to him. As is written, there is a time for embracing and a time to abstain from embracing.[55] Likewise Paul, as he actively labored to spread the gospel of Jesus Christ from Jerusalem to Illyricum, said, *our conversation is in heaven* (Phil 3:20).

John the apostle and evangelist, flying like an eagle in the heights and gazing directly upon the rays of the true sun, drank deeply from the fountain of the Lord's breast. Full of the spirit of wisdom and intellect, endowed with the special privilege of divine love, he penetrated the secrets of divinity and the hidden places of the heavens. Crossing into the active life he then taught in Ephesus and several other places, founded churches, ordained bishops, and established priests.[56] See how the living creatures of God burn and gleam like lightning![57] They wander into contemplation and return into action undiminished, rather expanded in their merit and in their reward. But you, going once into the holy of holies—if indeed

55

you have yet gone—although the highest priests go in and come out, you alone, I say, seem never to come out. How grand! How great! How sublime! How incomparable a merit! You enter once into the holy of holies—if ever you have entered—and from that moment on you have not come out, as you see it. Oh, what a great and singular privilege of contemplation in the flesh, given neither to Aaron nor any of the highest priests nor any of the apostles who saw the Lord in the flesh! O man of ineffable blessedness, alone worthy of a home in heaven! You have chosen the best part, because you have experienced full joy without ceasing, and you are now filled with rejoicing before the face of God. You know delight on his right hand, now and forever.[58] I wonder what else you may await, because if it is thus, you are well, you are blessed, and the relics of your *thought shall keep holiday* for the Lord (cf. Ps 75:11). But do not be deceived. Often Satan is accustomed to transform himself into an angel of light. While you or any devout person intends to contemplate *who inhabits light inaccessible* (1 Tim 6:16), Satan jealously runs to that person intent on the heights, seeking the truth, and obtrudes himself deceitfully. And because often he wishes to be like the highest God, he vainly imagines himself as highest. In a similitude of truth he wickedly deceives both the earthly hearts of simple folk still here in their misty abode and spirits seeking the highest of all goods, those who ardently investigate where life and truth may be. Indeed Satan's nourishment is choice, and he gains trust because the Jordan flows in his mouth. Therefore take care that you not be deceived. You have found honey; eat only what is enough, for *he that is a searcher of majesty shall be overwhelmed by glory* (Prov 24:27).

Perhaps you are angry at me for having dared to write such words, especially since you have been rapt into the third heaven and carried into paradise, and alone after Paul are accustomed to hear the hidden words *it is not granted man to utter* (2 Cor 12:4). But it seems to me that God's light has shone around you from heaven and you have prostrated yourself on the earth in his illumination, so that trembling and wordless you see little or nothing with open eyes. You must then be taken in hand and cared for by those close to you, because you have need of an Ananias to visit you and place upon you the hand of correction at the Lord's command, so that the dirty clouds of fog shutting you away from the clear light may vanish.

Then you will be filled with the Holy Spirit, strengthened by the food of scripture, so that you may defend that which as an emulator of monastic traditions you seem not justly but rashly to attack. But indeed might we find an Ananias whom you will accept? For Ananias means the grace of God. May the hand of that grace's good effect touch you and rouse you as you lie stricken. May it open for you the eyes of serene contemplation, educate you to rational compliance in your profession, and guard you from useless and empty imagination of the truth.

I think—indeed I confidently believe—that the opinion you express is not that of all monks but only yours. For what thinking man, even if he was a monk, would doubt that monks are not then contemplatives, whom I would scarcely call active even when they go about in public places outside of their communities, when they contend about their properties, when they do business in the secular world, when they extort money from their peasants, when—their silence broken—they tell empty stories and when they pass judgment on all religious life? Then again, I would scarcely doubt that some other monks are contemplatives when they kindly take in Jesus among the least of his people,[59] as they are accustomed to do, devoutly assuming Martha's part, or when others take action in writing, reading, singing, and maintaining the rhythm of the good work and usefulness of the monastery. Among them, unless I am deceived, some are so simpleminded that, as they work outside and keep watch usefully and laudably for the common needs of the monastery, they think that this is the contemplative life—namely, to sit lazily in the cloister with folded hands and in embroidered sleeves, to have a leisurely meal, to keep useless clothes, to sleep soundly, to walk aimlessly from corner to corner with slow steps, to explore the coming and going of the abbot and his absence or presence with astute questioning, to investigate outside goings-on from travelers with vague curiosity, to confound all things with a complicated array of signs, keeping a silent tongue but usurping its duty with an unquiet hand, in short abounding in all things, beyond what is necessary, living in abundance. And if anything ever seems to stand in their way, they complain constantly or mutter covertly or obstinately object openly, or feigning patience, conceal proud taciturnity under the appearance of religious devotion, and from time to time fruitlessly impose fasts upon themselves. But this fasting comes of depraved indignation rather than true piety. While they stew within in the misery and guilt of temptation, not opening themselves up to confession and penance, they drink the cup of their own bitterness as punishment. Yet among them there are still some who, climbing the tower of fortitude and humility, tasting the sweetness and community of the contemplative life richly and eagerly, from time to time are drunk with the wine of compunction and from time to time delight in being spiritually filled with fat and richness.[60]

My intent in this part of my letter has not been to discuss the order, life, and habit of canons or to describe how that life used to be, but rather to discuss the order, life, and habit of monks. Provoked by your letter, I have wished to demonstrate that the contemplative life was not only or always—or it could ever wholly be— the life of all monks to the extent that they claim. Monks are therefore usurpers when they claim for themselves before others the title of contemplation, for the true profession of the canons does not preclude that from time to time they be lifted up devoutly, by some grace, to the highest citadel of contemplation—and this can happen the better when they take on the care of others. As we already see clearly and is perfectly apparent to any monk or canon with any sense, the two orders present different purposes for their members' lives.[61] Each is good. As for whether the one or the other is more useful or necessary in the church of God, let us assume that the entire category of monks was stripped of ecclesiastical orders, as indeed it was in antiquity—and no literate person doubts that—and let us take away the category of clerics. Tell me, brother, how the church will stand, since it cannot be called or be the church without archbishops, bishops, priests, deacons, and the lower orders of clerics? Again, take away all the category of monks, and let us have in the church of God according to the ordination of Christ other apostles, indeed other evangelists, other pastors and teachers, and other orders of clerics. These suffice, do they not, *for the perfecting of the saints, for the work of the ministry, for the edifying of the body of Christ* (Eph 4:12)? Yet even if the church might be able to stand unornamented by monks, it is in fact built the more appropriately and decorated the more beautifully, wrapped as it is in the diverse orders of the elect. In this church any cleric who is minimally fit must be loved and imitated, as must any good and perfect monk, so then any cleric who lives well according to a rule is without doubt to be preferred to the best monk. I would certainly think that it is just and good for all clerics to live according to a rule and for none of them to become a monk, but those who do not wish to live according to a rule should be corrected or improved in their own order, else they should be made to be good monks.

Now I will choose persons of the two orders as examples. So that the truth of what I have said be still clearer, I will compare their desires, roles, and merits. For the sake of the word the first, named Paul, is called the apostle of the eternal King. He is styled leader of the word of God and vessel of choice for carrying the word of God before the kings and leaders. He disputed and persuaded about the kingdom of God, gathering many of the Jews, many more of the Greeks, and some of the Romans to the orthodox faith either by his preaching or his epistles, powerfully serving God rather than himself, building and planting the church of God as on a new foundation. A mighty warrior, he subjected many of the Gentiles to the laws of Christ, ascribing the name and title of his triumph not to himself but to the King of time, the immortal, invisible and only God. Thrice cut by lashes, stoned once, three times shipwrecked in fighting the good fight,[62] in staying his course, keeping the faith, waiting faithfully, knowing that the crown of justice would be aside for him, and trusting in him in whom he believed, this Paul finally achieved glorious martyrdom at Rome. He led many with him into glory and today teaches his people in the church through his admirable epistles, still bearing fruit, drawing many of the faithful after him.

But as for that other Paul,[63] he slept in the Lord as a simple monk—humble, devout, solitary, quiet, God-fearing, given to strict fasts and chary of food, ragged in his attire, sedulous in prayer, worn down by vigils and toils, seeking nothing but Christ, sufficient to himself in Christ, repenting in tears for prior sins, assiduously fearful of his own future, stable in his purpose, useful to himself alone, persevering in labor, winning no other by his teaching or his writing, unless perhaps someone by the example of his eremitical conversation. Which of these two Pauls of Christ seems of higher rank in the church of God? Which was more worthy, when his labors were done, of God's great inheritance? You would not think, would you, that it would be better for our Paul, his apostolate abandoned and his ministry—which he assumed from the Lord and fulfilled with honor among the Gentiles—neglected, to descend to the desert or to the monastery where, fearing idle speech, he might be made empty by idle silence? How much better and more useful it would be for your Paul, leaving behind his solitude, if indeed he were suited to preaching,[64] to cultivate the vine of God which our Paul had planted,[65] working alongside that Christ for whom and through whom all things are, and so begotten and nourished many sons of the church of God.[66]

Now, indeed, compare the work of these two examples and weigh their fruit or their reward. You will certainly judge that Paul the apostle is greatly to be preferred, or you will stand alone in your judgment, separate from the communion of the whole church— which is an abomination. *Every man shall receive his own reward, according to his own labor* (1 Cor 3:8). And if perhaps you say to me that neither I nor any of those who are now of the canonical order are like our first apostle, I say that is true, that you speak truth. But also I believe that neither you nor any of the modern monks whom I know is like your first monk. In saying so in no way do I mean to stop up that fountain of divine grace that now and always is generous to the faithful. Rather I do and always will rejoice that it is so open and abundant to all.

But now, because of the rudeness of those who account themselves above all others even if they are not, or at least are not alone in that lofty station, this letter is longer than I would have hoped. But that charity which compelled me to write you will likewise grant you the opportunity to read it and will alleviate the tedium of my prolixity. But it remains for the holy humility of the blessed monks to grow peaceful. Because God brings all sin to an end and takes pity on all men, so that *there is no one that can hide himself from his heat* (Ps 18:7), we deplore our imperfection. Because *man knoweth not whether he is worthy of love or hatred* (Eccl 9:1), let us be humbled *under the mighty hand of God* (1 Pet 5:6), and *whilst we have time* (Gal 6:10), *let us come before his presence in confession* (cf. Ps 94:2), fearing urgently lest we contend about order in a disorderly way such that we fall from the order of the blessed and lest, lapsing into self-exaltation, captivated by Satan in our competition with our brothers, we be Christians in vain. For we know that just as in heaven there are different orders of blessed spirits, so in this church that is still on earth there are diverse orders of the faithful. Just as here they do not fall down unless they are puffed up and hateful, so there they will not ascend to those high places without charity.

You, therefore, most beloved brother in Christ, go into your cave with your penance, grieving your sins and those of all the people, hiding in fear of the Lord and of the glory of his majesty when he arose to smite the earth. In your fasts, prayers, vigils, tears, constant meditation, and cleansing of your spirit, call faithfully upon the Lord Jesus who consoles all those who groan in prayer, and meanwhile grasp and hold the feet of his humanity until he who pities all, who hates nothing of them but *overlookest the sins of men for the sake of repentance* (Wis 11:25), takes pity too on you. But as for me, I will—with my brothers the poor men of Christ,[67] the least of the servants of God, as a little vessel in the temple of God, as the most recent of those who serve the tabernacle of the covenant—carry forward the ark of the testament with all my strength along with the other priests of God. I will serve faithfully with his other ministers, humbly rousing the Christian people as they travel to the promised land to defeat their carnal concupiscence and to conquer the throngs of spiritual evil with the trumpets of divine scripture—until, when the enemy is crushed, the walls of Jericho fall, until the Hethbite and the Amorrhite, the Chanaanite and the Pherezite, the Hevite, the Gergesite, and the Jebusite fall before the divine sword,[68] until Madian and Sisara, Jabin, Oreb, Zeb and Zebee, and Salmana are smitten by God,[69] when the Philistines and all our other adversaries are conquered and we all ascend to the heavenly Jerusalem, joyfully confessing God's name arranged in tribes, and we stand in the temple of the peaceful Solomon on a day made festive with assemblies. There the vessel of election[70] and every vessel made for honor rather than rebellion have their place. When all images have been set aside and the veil over truth removed, we will enter with the high priest into the holy of holies once and forever, when the book of extraordinary things is opened so that we know as we are known, when we will always see the king in his beauty *face to face* (cf. 1 Cor 13:12) and in always seeing will desire to see. Then there will be knowledge without error, memory without forgetting.

61

Meanwhile, however, as long as we are pilgrims away from God,[71] whatever we do, let us act in the name of the Lord.[72] Let us not make judgments against each other but fear heartily, praying lest we be tempted by that Satan whom we must resist in faith[73] and not in contention. For *God resisteth the proud but giveth grace to the humble* (Jas 4:6). In all things, therefore, spoken in my humility or your brotherhood, may charity always preside firm, whole, unshaken, untouched, thoughtful, healthy, solid. Amen.

HERMAN OF TOURNAI, *MIRACLES OF ST. MARY OF LAON*—INTRODUCTION

In addition to the twelfth-century hagiographies of Norbert known as the *A* and *B* texts, two other important sources describe the Premonstratensian founder's life. The first, *The Restoration of the Monastery of St. Martin of Tournai*,[1] the work of a Benedictine monk named Herman, includes a brief but informative passage— sixteen lines in the MGH edition—about Norbert and his followers.[2] This passage attributes Norbert's conversion to his dismay at Henry V's mistreatment of Pope Paschal II in 1110–11; Henry took Paschal prisoner in order to secure his rights in the investiture of bishops as Norbert was present in the entourage of his archbishop, Frederick I of Cologne.[3] The *A* and *B* lives of Norbert instead describe the founder's conversion as triggered by a thunderstorm in which Norbert was caught four years later on the way to Freden.

The second contemporary source shedding light on Norbert of Xanten's career beyond the representation of the two hagiographies devoted to him is entitled *The Miracles of St. Mary of Laon*.[4] This work in three books is also authored by an individual named Herman. Since early modern times the author of *The Restoration of the Monastery of St. Martin of Tournai* has usually been designated as Herman of Tournai and the author of *The Miracles of St. Mary of Laon* as Herman of Laon, but as early as the seventeenth century scholars were divided as to whether the two works were from the same hand. In the nineteenth century Roger Wilmans, who edited the newly discovered *A* text of the life of Norbert in 1856, believed that one author was responsible for both the text about Tournai and that about Laon.[5] His view was followed by Max Manitius in 1931. On the other hand, Charles Dereine, writing in 1947, followed the opinion of D. A. Stracke, who thought different hands were involved. Doubt concerning the works' authorship focused on the question of the relationship of Herman, an abbot in Tournai, to the diocese of Laon.[6]

Gerlinde Niemeyer ended the dispute over authorship of these two works in 1971 by demonstrating that the author of *The Restoration of the Monastery of St. Martin of Tournai* and the author of *The Miracles of St. Mary of Laon* were in fact the same. Niemeyer traced the whereabouts of Abbot Herman after his retirement, confirming his connections to the diocese of Laon.[7] As the principal modern textual critic of three of the most important primary sources for the early Premonstratensians—Herman of Tournai's work, translated here; the *Life of Godfrey*, likewise included in this volume; and the closely related conversion narrative of Herman of Cologne—her evaluation is definitive.

Herman of Tournai, then, the author of these two works, refers to himself as "the scum of monks,"[8] but this self-depreciation is a topos. Herman had been born into a knightly family of Tournai about 1090. His devout parents entered religious life, so Herman was raised by an uncle until such time as he could be given as an oblate to the abbey of St. Martin of Tournai in 1095.[9] In 1127 he was elected abbot there. Herman resigned his office in 1136, according to his own account due to illness described as paralysis; according to another account he was forced into retirement because of his poor leadership.[10] For the first few years after his resignation the sources are silent concerning Herman's activity. Around 1142, however, he was asked by the canons of Tournai to go to Rome in order to petition for the reestablishment of the Diocese of (Flemish-speaking) Tournai, which had been eliminated about 626 or 627 and joined to the Francophone Diocese of Noyon, although it retained its own cathedral chapter. Although Herman was successful in this endeavor and obtained permission for Tournai to elect its own bishop, nevertheless the diocese was in fact never reestablished.[11] While in Rome, however, Herman was befriended by Abbot Anselm of St. Vincent in Laon, who offered him a place to stay. The following year, after Herman had returned to Tournai, he sent Anselm a book as a token of thanks: *Passio quorundam martyrum*.[12] Sometime later Herman was once again asked by the canons of Tournai to take their case to Rome. During his second visit to Rome, while awaiting a decision, sometime between early April and late May 1143, he began to write the history of the restoration of his abbey. The case of the Diocese of Tournai dragged on until finally Pope Eugenius III named as its bishop Anselm of St. Vincent in Laon. Eugenius consecrated Anselm in March 1146.[13] Herman of Tournai, whether his paralysis as abbot was literal or metaphorical, had clearly been an effective agent in the papal Curia.

Between Herman's resignation as abbot in 1136 and his journey to Rome in 1142, the Benedictine may have traveled to Spain. In the letter to Abbot Anselm accompanying the *Passio quorundam martyrum*, Herman speaks of his journey there in order to obtain the relics of St. Vincent for Bishop Bartholomew of Laon. Apparently Herman had by this time recovered from his paralysis, if this was in fact the real reason for his resignation as abbot. Herman is last mentioned in contemporary sources around 1147 when he decided to join the Second Crusade.[14]

Herman's *Miracles of St. Mary of Laon* is written in three books gathered, respectively, around major events in the history of the cathedral and community rather than chronologically arranged. In 1112 the church burned down. In order to raise money to rebuild it, representatives of Laon took the relics of the church around France and England. The first book describes the first tour of the relics through France (June–September 1112) and the miracles that took place meanwhile. The second book describes miracles on the second fundraising journey when the Laonais took the relics through France and England (March–September 1113).[15]

The third book, excerpted here, describes the dedication of the reconstructed cathedral in 1114. It tells of the credit due to Bishop Bartholomew for the reconstruction of the cathedral and the renewal of religious life in his diocese, as well as the collaboration of Bartholomew in the foundation of Prémontré. In this book the author goes beyond his original intent to describe miracles during the efforts to raise money, turning instead to praise of Bishop Bartholomew. Of twenty-eight chapters in the third book the first nine are about Norbert and the first Premonstratensian foundation in the Diocese of Laon. They end with Norbert's death as archbishop in Magdeburg. The tenth chapter has to do with Hugh of Fosses and the changes he made at Prémontré. These first ten chapters are translated below.

According to Niemeyer, *The Miracles of St. Mary of Laon* was first drafted sometime between 1136, the date of Herman's resignation as abbot, and 1142, when he made his first trip to Rome. After his second trip to Rome, in 1143, Herman made some additions to his composition. He made still more after the consecration of Abbot Anselm as bishop of Tournai in 1146 and before he began his pilgrimage to Jerusalem during the second crusade in 1147.[16] The third book of *The Miracles of St. Mary of Laon* was thus written in three stages: between 1140 and autumn 1142, from autumn 1143 to 1144, and between summer 1146 and spring 1147.[17] Herman's sources included biographies and documents, when available, but especially oral reports and his own personal experience. He did not, however, use written historical sources.[18]

Herman's account of Norbert's activity in the Diocese of Laon and the foundation of Prémontré lies in the sections of this work composed earliest, but the information he gives about the early Premonstratensians in Book 3, chapters 6–10, belongs to the final draft.[19] The seven-year interval between the first and final redactions was the very period in which the individual foundations of Norbert began to be organized by general chapters. Chapters 2–5 on the beginnings of Prémontré thus seem to reflect the view of the bishop of Laon and his background about these developments. Chapters 6–10, on the contrary, representing the opinions of Hugh of Fosses, come from the years 1146 to 1147.[20] This is especially noticeable in chapter 8, where information is added about the period immediately following Norbert's conversion, when Hugh first met him.[21]

This text by a Benedictine is thus the earliest of the major sources for Norbert's career as preacher and founder and the earliest Premonstratensians. Herman says "not yet thirty years have passed since the bishop brought Norbert to Prémontré."[22] The great German historian of medieval religious movements Herbert Grundmann calls Herman "the most important and dependable witness for Norbert's efforts in founding Prémontré."[23] Herman is less reliable, however, for the years 1126–34. As Grauwen writes, the author of the *Miracles* here shows a lack of understanding regarding the political circumstances within the German Empire. His depiction of Norbert's election as archbishop is clearly marked by an effort to cover up the influence of the laity on the election process. Herman's description of the period of Norbert's archbishopric[24] must be compared with sources coming from Germany, since he seems to be less acquainted with events outside his own geographical area.[25]

Herman's description of Bartholomew's efforts to find a place for the preacher Norbert to settle his many followers in a religious community is more detailed than in the two hagiographies of the former cleric of Xanten. This is to be expected since Bartholomew was one of Herman's oral sources and the work praises the bishop. Not only does Herman refer to the various places where Bartholomew took Norbert but adds fuller description of the founder's vision on his initial visit to Prémontré. According to Herman's account, Bartholomew left Norbert at the spot overnight at the latter's request. In the morning he told Bartholomew that he had had a vision in the night: "a very great multitude of white robed men carrying silver crosses and candelabra and thuribles and they encircled this place singing as they went."[26]

Herman also includes important information about gender among the early Premonstratensians. Although neither hagiography mentions the presence of women in his early foundations, Herman stresses that Norbert encouraged women's participation. In the seventh chapter of the *Miracles*, among his commendations of Norbert, Herman mentions that in contrast to Cîteaux, where only men were received, it was Norbert's decision that women be welcomed as well. Herman goes on to praise the life of the women as much more strict than that of the men.[27]

Herman of Tournai thus represents a view of Norbert and his work from outside his Premonstratensian following. The two hagiographies of Norbert originated in strongholds of the white canons—Prémontré and Magdeburg—and were written by followers of Norbert to represent their and their confreres' perspective. Herman, on the other hand, was a Benedictine, and his primary goal was to praise the accomplishments of Bishop Bartholomew. Nevertheless; Herman affirms Norbert's distinctiveness and impact as a religious reformer and founder. On the one hand, his *Miracles* verifies events and opinions recorded by the Premonstratensian hagiographers. On the other hand, his *Miracles* reveals aspects of Norbert's model that would otherwise be lost: how Norbert met Bartholomew,[28] and Norbert's vision on his first night at Prémontré—this latter account quaint but symbolic. His text also reveals that Bartholomew took Norbert to other places before he chose Prémontré.[29] Herman's praise of Norbert is extreme: "Many testify that, after the Apostles, no one's life has borne such fruit in the holy church in so short a time." Herman's affirmation of Norbert's importance is most persuasive where he lauds Norbert in preference to the great Cistercian Bernard, despite his and the white monk's common Benedictine heritage.[30]

HERMAN OF TOURNAI, *MIRACLES OF ST. MARY OF LAON* (EXCERPTS)

BOOK 3
Chapter 1—The throng of people at the dedication of the church of Laon

With the help of divine mercy, from the offerings of the faithful collected throughout France and England, the work on our church was so successful that in the following year it was dedicated after the completion of the restoration. In the year of the Lord's incarnation 1112, on Thursday of Easter Week,[1] the aforementioned church had burned down. That same day Gualdric, the bishop of Laon, was cruelly slain in his residence along with some of his men. Hugh succeeded him as bishop. Hugh scarcely survived eight months, and after his death Bartholomew[2] was elected to the bishopric, as mentioned above.[3] After being consecrated bishop, Bartholomew made every effort to speed up the work on the church of Our Lady so that in two half-years[4] after the fire the solemn dedication could once again take place, that is, in the year of the Lord's incarnation 1114. The bishop and the canons decided that it be dedicated on the same day on which its solemn dedication took place each year, on the eighth day before the Ides of September,[5] namely, on the third day before the Nativity of Blessed Mary. For the dedication Lord Bartholomew gathered together with him Ralph, the archbishop of Reims, William, the bishop of Châlons-sur-Marne, Lisiard of Soissons, Godfrey of Amiens, and Hubert of Senlis.

This translation is based on Roger Wilmans's edition in MGH 14, 653–62.

Such a great throng gathered for the dedication that two hundred thousand people, men and women, old and young, were said to have been present.[6] Great was the joy in the hearts of all because after such desolation of the church—indeed of the whole city of Laon—in so short a space of time, that is within two half-years after such a profound abyss of darkness and calamity, they saw brightness shining through the mercy of God's mother. It seemed that the words of the prophet Haggai could rightly be applied to our church also. After the Babylonian captivity Haggai had prophesied concerning the restoration of the Temple in Jerusalem that *the glory of this second house will be great, even greater than that of the first* (Hag 2:10). If the careful reader wishes to look more attentively, indeed he will very easily see that after the grief of desolation an even greater glory and exaltation followed in the church of Laon than existed before. Who will be able to give a worthy report about how much the splendor of religion and this new brightness glowed afterward in the Diocese of Laon, and from there throughout almost the whole world?

After a few years Norbert, that discoverer and originator of new light and new conversion, not only of interior but also of exterior brightness, came to France[7] from Lorraine and, with the help of divine grace, planted his first vine in the Diocese of Laon. This vine, *taking root and founded in charity* (Eph 3:17), now filled the world, *extending its branches to the sea and its shoots to the river* (Ps 79:12). With the wine of its strength that *gives joy to the heart of man* (Ps 103:15), it now abundantly inebriates *many princes and judges of the earth, young men and virgins, old men and youth* (Ps 148:11–12), so that the drunken seek nothing else but to praise the name of the Lord and *to sing him a new canticle* (Ps 32:3). By putting off the old man with his acts and *putting on the new man created according to God* (Eph 4:24), they completely cast aside carnal allurements, and, as if changed from water into wine by the Lord at the wedding,[8] *they forgot what was behind them and stretched forth to those things that were ahead of them* (Phil 3:13). Thus, although they were living physically on earth, nevertheless *they tasted what was above, not what was on earth* (Col 3:1). They said with the apostle that *our conversation is in heaven where Christ sits at the right hand of God* (Phil 3:20). Joined in their minds with the heavenly seraphim, Norbert's followers continually burn with the love of Christ alone, *to whom they exhibit their bodies as a living, holy sacrifice pleasing to God* (Rom 12:1), a resplendence of virtues by which they shine from within, even preferring this in their exterior garb.[9] From the following it will easily be recognized that the aforementioned Bishop Bartholomew was a partner and participant of this sublime and glorious institute.

Chapter 2—How Bishop Bartholomew found Norbert

Pope Paschal died in Rome.[10] Then Cardinal John, who succeeded him as Gelasius and who wished to come to France, passed away at Cluny.[11] The cardinals who had come with him realized that they could not return to Rome for an election, and so, forced by necessity, they immediately elected Guy, the archbishop of nearby Vienne, to the apostolic see.[12] This Guy was a noble and industrious man, an uncle of the queen of France,[13] the wife of King Louis.[14] He was consecrated pope in the same province and was named Callixtus. Before he went to Rome, this pope wanted to hold a general council in France. He ordered all the bishops and archbishops of almost the entire West, along with the abbots and other ecclesiastical persons to gather at Reims.[15] The above-mentioned King Louis of France was also present at this council.

Bishop Bartholomew, traveling to Reims in order to attend this council with his clerics and entourage, had just passed the monastery of St. Theoderic. He saw Norbert with two clerics sitting not far from the road. Now Norbert just shortly before this had heard two voices, as he was afterward accustomed to mention. The first voice had cried out from one side: "This is Norbert and his companions." The other added from the other side: "This is Norbert and his companion." What this meant will be explained later. After hearing these two voices from the heavens, Norbert was stunned and left the road.[16] Thus sitting on the ground with his two companions and in a state of shock, Norbert looked around. Shortly thereafter the bishop approached. Unlike the priest and Levite who, turning from the road, passed by the man they had seen wounded by robbers, the bishop greeted them graciously and asked who they were. Norbert answered that he was from Lorraine and, after leaving his family and the emptiness of the world, proposed to pursue religious life. He said that the ideal of this religious life must be according to the plan and authority of the apostolic see. He continued to explain that he had stayed at Reims for three days but, because of the multitude of the rich who were continually gathering, no audience with the pope was available to him. He had left the city sad and despairing, not knowing where to turn.[17]

Then, moved by great compassion, the bishop urged Norbert and his companions to return with him to Reims, promising that he would introduce them to the pope. However, because the three were traveling on foot, the bishop ordered his men to dismount and told Norbert and his companions to mount and ride with him. On the way he questioned them diligently. He heard that Norbert was of noble origin and that he had possessed great wealth in the church at Cologne but by choosing poverty had left everything completely.

When the bishop reached Reims he approached the pope. Modestly he suggested to the pope that it was not good that, as the father of the universal church, he should speak only with the rich and turn the poor away from conversation with him. Immediately, with the assent of the pope, Norbert and his companions were brought in by the bishop and refreshed by apostolic conversation, but because Callixtus was so busy he could not entirely fulfill their desire for discussion. He promised the bishop that when the council was ended he would go straightaway to Laon and for several days rest there, speaking with these poor men further. The pope asked that the bishop send them ahead and suggested that they wait for him at Laon. Afterward, as long as they were in Reims, the bishop always kept Norbert and his followers in his company. When he returned to Laon he never permitted them to be separated from his company. Later Bishop Bartholomew received the pope in a most dutiful manner, as was fitting, when he came as he had promised. The pope then deeply pleased Norbert and his companions with his conversation.

Chapter 3—The little church of St. Martin of Laon, how Bishop Bartholomew took Norbert to many places

At that time outside the walls of the city of Laon was a little church built in honor of St. Martin, in which this same bishop many times had placed religious clerics to serve God. But since none was successful there, the church reverted to the bishop. When he saw that Norbert wished to follow a poor religious life, the bishop therefore began to persuade him to stay in this little church of St. Martin. Bartholomew also asked the pope to advise him about this.[18] But Norbert, understanding his efforts, said: "I did not leave great wealth at Cologne in order to seek lesser wealth at Laon. I do not wish to stay in cities but rather in deserted and uncultivated places." The bishop answered: "I will show you many deserted and unculti-vated places in this diocese suited to religious life, and once I have shown them to you I will give you them."[19]

Bartholomew said this and, after the departure of the pope, took Norbert and showed him not *all the kingdoms of the world and their glory* (Matt 4:8), but that very great forest of his diocese called Thierache. He took him to a place called Foigny,[20] pointing out the availability of water, pasturage, forest, and lands suitable for reli-gious life. Then Norbert, after praying, said, "Indeed this place is suitable for religious life but it is not destined for me by God." Then the bishop took him to another part of this forest called Thenaille.[21] After it was shown to him and he had prayed as before, Norbert said it too was suitable for religious life but neither was this place destined for him by God.

Then, returning to Laon, the bishop took him to the forest of the Vosges and showed him a place there called *pratum monstratum*[22] or *praemonstratus*. Whoever reads this account should see the devo-tion of the bishop who, leaving behind his episcopal business, went to great trouble to take an unknown man around so many forested and trackless places that even today seem fearsome, although they are now inhabited by many people. In those days they were still rougher and more fearful because they were remote from all human habitation, surrounded only by wolves and wild boars.

Chapter 4—How the church at Prémontré was begun

Coming to the aforementioned place of Prémontré,[23] Norbert and Bartholomew entered a little church built there in honor of St. John the Baptist in order to pray. This rightly belonged to the monastery of St. Vincent[24] at Laon. A monk from that monastery was sometimes sent there to conduct the divine office. But because after Mass was finished there was no bread to be found there unless it was brought from somewhere else, the place, along with the little church, now remained almost deserted. After the bishop finished praying, he went outside. He advised Norbert, the man of God, to rise from his prayer because night was falling and there was no place to stay, but the servant of God, Norbert, came outside and asked Bartholomew to depart with his men, letting him keep vigil there throughout the night. The bishop then quickly mounted his horse, as night was falling. He rode swiftly to Anizy but did not forget about Norbert. By means of a messenger he sent him bread and other necessities.

In the morning the bishop returned to Norbert and asked what he wanted to do. The latter was overjoyed. "I will remain here, Father, because I know that God has destined this place for me. This will be a place of rest for me, and here many will be saved by the grace of God. But this little church will not be the principal site. On another part of this mountain the many who come here will build their place of rest. Last night in a vision I saw a very great multitude of white-robed men carrying silver crosses and candelabra and thuribles. They encircled this place, singing as they went."

The bishop rejoiced greatly. Not wishing to cause any loss to the monastery of St. Vincent, to which the place belonged, he summoned the abbot of St. Vincent and gave him a more useful property in exchange. In a charter he then granted this place with the church to Norbert in freehold. The servant of God, Norbert, remained there. The bishop returned to Laon but did not cease to have a care for Norbert and his companions.

A few days later the man of God came to Laon and entered the school of Master Ralph, who had succeeded his dead brother, Master Anselm.[25] Norbert gave an exhortatory talk to Ralph's students and immediately converted seven of the richest of them who had recently arrived from Lorraine. He brought them with their great wealth to his church. But the ancient enemy, who is always accustomed to envy the advances of the servants of God, strove to harass even Norbert at the very beginning. Just as he seduced Eve in paradise and caused the apostle Judas to be depraved, so also he corrupted one of the two companions who had come with Norbert.[26] In the middle of the night this follower stole the money the students had brought, handed over to them by their teacher. Fleeing from the church, the thief sneaked away, leaving the students in great poverty and need. Then for the first time the man of God recalled the voices that, as we mentioned above, he had heard near Reims. He understood and revealed to the bishop, who consoled him in this regard, that the second voice that had shouted "This is Norbert and his companion!" meant this: that of the two companions who had come with him only one would remain. The other would leave as had Judas. Norbert understood the incident in that fashion.

But Leonius, the abbot of St. Bertinus, a very religious man and very knowledgeable in secular and divine literature, recently read this book. He immediately interpreted the voice in another way and ordered me to insert his opinion here.[27] He said that, given the time and the person approaching, it might be understood that the voice was testifying that Bishop Bartholomew was the companion of Norbert. He said: "After staying three days in Reims unable to speak with the pope, Norbert left the city sad and despairing, knowing neither what to do nor where to turn. He seemed to have no consolation besides God other than his two companions, whom he trusted would cling to him inseparably wherever he went. Then he heard the voice from above: 'This is Norbert and his companion,' as if it said to him more clearly: 'Don't despair or trust only in your two companions, because a bishop is near whom God has given you for a companion. He will take you back with him and let you speak with the pope. He will be a great consolation in your tribulations and will give you a place with a church for you to rest and bear fruit.'" Leonius, the abbot of St. Bertinus, ordered me to write these things. I obeyed him willingly, believing that he understood faithfully and well.[28]

Chapter 5—How Walter was made abbot of the little monastery of Laon

Later, when the bishop saw that a large number of men had come together and were living a religious life at Prémontré, he asked Norbert to assign some of them to the little church of St. Martin, where he was unwilling to remain although he was asked to build it up and expand it to the honor of God. Acquiescing to the bishop's request, Norbert assigned a few of his confreres there and placed Walter, a religious man, in charge of them as abbot. Through the prayer of Blessed Martin, we believe, God conferred on Walter such immediate grace that what the angel said about the girl Sarah to her father Raguel seems to be able to be said about him also: *For this reason no one was able to have her because your daughter was destined for this God-fearing man as wife* (Tob 7:12). Although many had at the request of the bishop taken on the task of governing the little church of St. Martin, no one had been successful there. But by the grace of God such good fortune accompanied Abbot Walter that within twelve years a convent of five hundred confreres was found there serving God. Hence I may with justification say it was reserved for him by God.

First the church sustained such poverty there that, besides the one donkey called Burdinus, the confreres had almost nothing else. In the morning they would take the donkey to the nearby forest of Vosges, load it with cut wood, and bring it back to Laon to buy bread for themselves from the sale of the wood. Frequently they fasted for a long time until the bread that was bought was brought to them after the hour of none. Nevertheless, with the consolation of Abbot Walter, the confreres did not faint in such need. Gradually advancing by working with their hands they grew, by the gift of God, to such abundance that from their vines they frequently have three thousand measures of wine and in their possession of land and mills, as well as cattle, they surpass almost all the monasteries in the Diocese of Laon. Such abundance of charity and hospitality is found there that, because of the continuous reception of guests and because of the daily relief of the poor, God seems in a wonderful way to multiply and expand everything to such a degree that it is numbered among the special and superior monasteries of France.

Chapter 6—How Hugh was placed in charge of the abbey of Prémontré

Afterward, Norbert was unwilling to be abbot even in the monastery at Prémontré. However, he appointed Hugh,[29] the one companion who remained with him, abbot of that place. Norbert tried to convert not only groups of men but also of women. As a result, today in various places of that same diocese we see more than a thousand religious sisters serving God in such strictness and silence that in the strictest houses of monks one can hardly find a like religious group. Nor was Norbert content to confine the throngs of his confreres within the boundaries of the Diocese of Laon. Just as bees leave the cells where they produce honey to fly elsewhere to make it, so he began to seek various deserted places to build new monasteries to which he sent confreres. Norbert determined, however, that all the abbots from every monastery following the norm or intention of his institute and rule, whether during his lifetime or after his death, should gather at the church of Prémontré each year on the feast of St. Denis.[30] This was their first mother, from whom they had gone forth. They were to gather here in order to drink as from a fountain. Once gathered together they should hold a general chapter and correct anything needing correction, whether in all houses or in each house.

Although not yet thirty years have passed since the bishop brought Norbert to Prémontré, nevertheless, by the grace of God, Norbert's followers have already produced so many monasteries that almost a hundred abbots gather there on the set feast not only from France and Burgundy but also from Germany, Saxony, and Gascony. Apart from the others, the church of St. Martin alone, still presided over by its first abbot, Walter,[31] has produced twelve other monasteries. Not only does such a great light illumine the neighboring provinces, but also a ray of this new sun has crossed the sea and has illumined the city of Jerusalem.[32]

I do not know what others think, but I believe in my heart and faithfully proclaim with my mouth that Bishop Bartholomew is a partner, participant, and cooperator in all the good things happening and still to happen in these many monasteries. For Truth says in the gospel that *whoever receives a prophet in the name of a prophet will receive a prophet's reward* (Matt 10:41). This bishop not only received the servant of God, Norbert, but also—as written above—interrupted his episcopal duties to make the effort to accompany him through so many trackless and dreadful forest places and finally to establish him firmly in the wilderness of Prémontré, and once established continued to tend to him. Clearly he will receive the sweet reward of that fruit.

The blessed Gregory, in a homily on the gospel *Anno quinto decimo* (Luke 3:1), explains the scripture cited above more simply. "It should be noted," he says, "that the Lord does not say 'he will receive his reward from a prophet' but 'the reward of a prophet,' because he knows that the one who helps the prophet by receiving him will receive the same reward that the prophet receives because of his good work."[33] To demonstrate more clearly the certitude of this, Gregory adds the testimony of the prophet Isaiah, who among the cedar, olive, fir, and other more precious trees mentions the elm, which, although it does not itself bear fruit, nevertheless is accounted by the Lord among fruit-bearing trees because it supports a vine with grapes.[34]

If anyone wishes to check this view of the blessed Gregory more carefully, I do not think that he will ridicule me for having written this but will agree with me. Bishop Bartholomew, although he appeared to be busy with ecclesiastical duties and involved in secular affairs, nevertheless—because he always took such great pains to help the servants of God who were fleeing worldly life—by the grace of God shared their pious life in his desire. Hence in the future he will not lack his reward. Since this is the case, I think that the above-mentioned Leonius, the abbot of St. Bertinus, rightly ought to be praised for that opinion in which he expressed that the heavenly voice declared the bishop to be a companion of Norbert.

Chapter 7—Multiple commendations of Norbert

To conclude briefly about Norbert, many testify that no one's life after the apostles has borne such fruit in the holy church so quickly. Although some say that Bernard, the abbot of Clairvaux, bore no less fruit in the same time, nevertheless—if anyone ponders this carefully—I think he will not deny that Norbert surpasses Bernard. The latter was not the founder of his order, for it was already flourishing at the monastery of Cîteaux in which, when he was a cleric, he took the monastic habit under Abbot Stephen after he had heard of the reputation of that way of life. From that monastery Clairvaux was founded. There Bernard was appointed the first abbot because of his sanctity. Although Bernard converted many by his preaching and by the grace of God begot many monasteries from Clairvaux, he was a great fosterer and propagator of this order but was not the first founder. Norbert, however, was first founder and by God's gift the initiator because, although his followers say they hold to the Rule of the blessed Augustine, nevertheless may we say with the blessed Augustine's permission that we view the institute of Norbert to be much more strict and much more severe than that of Augustine.

Moreover, only men are received in the monastery of Cîteaux. Norbert's decision was that women be received for conversion in addition to men. As a result we see that the life of women in his monasteries is more confined and stricter than that of men. The men, after their conversion, leave the monastery for necessary works and for other business. Frequently they are involved in ecclesiastical or even secular legal proceedings or delegations. And many times those whom we knew in their former life to have been farmers or poor folk we now see proudly riding in a religious habit. For the women, however, as soon as they have changed their lives, the rules henceforth remain permanent. They remain enclosed within the confines of the house. They never go out again. They may speak to no man, not even a brother or relative, except at the window in the church and then only with two lay brothers with the man on the outside and two women who reside with them on the inside. These attendants hear everything that is said.

As soon as women are received, at the very beginning of their conversion, their hair is cut to ear length in order to reduce all pride and carnal lust. Thus to please Christ, their heavenly spouse, they are completely disfigured in their fragile and seductive flesh out of love for him. Henceforth none is permitted to have a precious garment, only one made of wool or sheepskin. None is permitted to wear silk veils over her head as do certain nuns, but only very cheap black cloth. Although these sisters are known to be enclosed with such strictness and abasement, including silence, nevertheless the power of Christ is working in an extraordinary way. Daily we see women—not only rustic and poor, but even the noble and rich, both young widows and even little girls—who through the grace of conversion spurn the pleasures of the world and hasten to the monasteries of that institution. They hurry there as if to mortify their tender flesh. We believe today there are more than ten thousand women dwelling in these monasteries.[35]

If therefore Norbert had done nothing else, apart from the conversion of the men, but attract so many women to God's service by his exhortation, would he not have been worthy of the greatest praise? But now, since so many thousands of men and women are in the service of Christ because of his teaching, since so many monasteries of his institute shine brightly throughout the world, I do not know what others think but what so many claim seems true to me. There has been no one since the time of the apostles who in such a brief space of time has acquired for Christ so many imitators of the perfect life through his institute. And indeed if he had remained longer in the monastery at Prémontré perhaps he would have accomplished many other things. However, it pleased Divine Providence that he pursue, in the religious habit, the honor he declined in flight during his secular life. He who did not want to become a bishop before his conversion thereafter became an archbishop.

Chapter 8—Norbert refused the Diocese of Cambrai

Recently, Hugh, the abbot of Prémontré, told me that at the beginning of Norbert's conversion, when he had left the church of Cologne and his relatives, he came to Valenciennes barefoot and there found Burchard, the bishop of Cambrai.[36] In the morning, when he had heard that the bishop was going to say Mass, he came to the church and asked Hugh, who at that time was the bishop's chaplain, to allow him to speak with the bishop. Hugh, not knowing who he was, went inside and told the bishop that a foreign cleric was outside and wished to speak with him.

Once Norbert was admitted, the bishop recognized him because he had been with him frequently at the court of the emperor and knew him to be a very wealthy man. Overwhelmed with admiration the bishop's eyes brimmed with tears. "Oh, Norbert," he said, "Lord Norbert, who could have believed that you left such wealth and came on your own to such poverty? Lord God, what is it that I see about Lord Norbert whom I used to see so proudly dressed and accustomed to go about with showy arrogance?"

When Hugh, the chaplain of the bishop, saw Burchard weeping so strangely and scarcely able to speak because of excessive tears, the former asked him who this Norbert was for whom he wept so much. The bishop answered: "If you knew who he was, you would wonder that he is now like this. When the emperor gave me the Diocese of Cambrai he offered it first to this Norbert, but he was unwilling to accept or hold it. Among the canons of Cologne he was honorable and very rich. But now, as you see, he left everything for God and attempts to seek God barefoot."

When the bishop explained this, his chaplain Hugh immediately burned with love of Norbert because he himself had already thought about renouncing the world. In his heart he began to thank God, who had destined such a companion for him.[37] Therefore, just as long ago Andrew, hearing the Lord praised by his master John the Baptist, left John and followed the Lord,[38] so too Hugh, hearing Norbert so greatly praised by his lord, Bishop Burchard, whose chaplain he had been for a long time, left the bishop and clung to Norbert. After disposing of his property on Norbert's advice, Hugh became his inseparable companion in travel and preaching. He traveled barefoot everywhere with Norbert until coming to the council of Pope Callixtus at Reims, where he met Bishop Bartholomew of Laon, as we reported above.

Chapter 9—How Norbert became archbishop of Magdeburg

Because how Norbert could have been bishop of Cambrai but was unwilling has been set forth, how he became archbishop should now be explained. Many men and women leaving the emptiness of the secular world had now turned to the service of God, and Norbert's renown had extended everywhere because he had built many monasteries far and wide. Then Theobald,[39] the noteworthy count of Champagne and son of the sister of the English king, Henry,[40] sent Norbert to a certain very excellent prince of Lorraine,[41] whose daughter this count took for his wife.

Meanwhile, after the death of the archbishop of Magdeburg, clerics of that city gathered to elect another prelate. That same year Norbert was speaking privately with his friend Geoffrey, the bishop of Chartres. Norbert told Geoffrey that he knew through a vision that he would be a bishop that year, but he did not know of which city or province.[42] The clerics of Magdeburg had chosen several candidates but could unanimously agree on the election of none. They were told that two legates of the apostolic see, religious men, had come to Mainz from Rome. One of these was called Peter,[43] the other was Gerard.[44] The latter was afterward elected pope, succeeding Celestine and preceding Eugenius. The aforementioned clerics took counsel and approached the legates of the apostolic see, fearing that discord in the election might be detrimental and sedition might arise among them. They put the election in the hands of the legates, promising that they would accept whomever the legates chose. When the legates saw the great devotion of the clerics, they decided to accept no bribes offered to them through intermediaries, lest perchance the apostolic see and especially they themselves be defamed.

While they were seeking the Lord's mercy to bring this great matter to an end decently and laudably, without any shame of simony, and while they were in the church carefully dealing with wise men, behold—unhoped for and unexpected—Norbert entered the same church to pray. He was on his way from France and altogether ignorant of the ongoing election.[45] When the legates saw him they were astounded. Rejoicing that their prayers had been answered, they called together the clerics of Magdeburg and asked them if they still agreed to accept their choice. When the clerics unanimously answered that they would accept whomever the legates named without any contradiction, the latter immediately responded: "In the name of the Father and of the Son and of the Holy Spirit we choose and elect for you Lord Norbert, a man of proven religious worth who has, we believe, been given both to us and to you by the Lord God for the conclusion of this business at hand."

Shocked by this amazing, swift turn of events, Norbert was struck senseless. Not knowing whether he was awake or asleep, where he was or whence he came, he marveled to himself while he hesitated. Immediately he was seized by the clerics and dragged to the altar—not led but carried by force. The church resounded as the "Te Deum Laudamus" was sung and then, forced by the bonds of obedience, Norbert was consecrated bishop. Thus, although he fled the Diocese of Cambrai, by the will of God he received the Archdiocese of Magdeburg where, living religiously for several years and dying peacefully, he finally rested from his labors.

Chapter 10—Improvement of the church at Prémontré

Hugh, the previously mentioned companion of Norbert, whom the latter chose as abbot and who was confirmed by Bishop Bartholomew, zealously strove by his exhortation and work to water the vineyard that Norbert had planted together with him. Throughout God had mercifully granted it increase. However, Hugh saw that the little church was no longer sufficient for the great number of brothers who had gathered and who were daily multiplied by the grace of God. He knew also that Norbert, as mentioned above, had foreseen in the spirit that a larger church would have to be built on the other side of the mountain. Taking counsel with his brothers, Hugh asked Bishop Bartholomew to come—seeing that the latter was the founder and father of the place—in order to place the first stone in the foundation of the church when all the buildings had been laid out.

When the bishop arrived the entire army of God joyfully met him with a great procession, praising God exultantly. Immediately the bishop recalled the vision Norbert had told him on that first night of his arrival—how he had seen a multitude of white-robed men carrying silver crosses with candelabra and thuribles, and how they encircled the place and sang as they went. The bishop rejoiced and gave thanks to God, because what Norbert had seen in a vision, he now saw as reality.

The church, dormitory, refectory, and other buildings of this sort now there, and a kind of wall around the monastery that has been built by the aforementioned Hugh, will clearly say to everyone who comes to look that in the richest and most ancient monasteries of France there can hardly be found a like work. Truly, everyone coming and looking at it will immediately say that this was not done by or through the work of man. *It is wonderful in our eyes* (Matt 21:42; Mark 12:11). Good Jesus! With what joy Bishop Bartholomew is filled each time he comes there for a visit to see so splendid a monastery constructed in his day and by his advice and plan. It seems to me that he too could say with the apostle Paul: I have done much more than the bishops of Laon who were my predecessors; *not I, however, but the grace of God was with me* (1 Cor 15:10).

LIFE OF GODFREY OF CAPPENBERG—INTRODUCTION

In several regards, the life of Godfrey of Cappenberg translated here is unique. Among evidence for the life and thought of the early Premonstratensians it is extraordinary in its richness as a source for historical phenomena far more general than development of community life among Norbert's following. Family relations among the imperial nobility, the turmoil of church and state following from the Investitures Controversy, spiritual ferment in towns and countryside—broad issues in twelfth-century history enliven the life of Godfrey, the story of the most prominent and controversial Premonstratensian convert, the young count who abandoned his place in the highest ranks of empire to join Norbert of Xanten as a poor man of Christ. Further, the *Life of Godfrey* is important for the biography and prosopography of the medieval empire in that its subject, before his conversion a notorious player in the violence preceding the Concordat of Worms (1122), was brother of that Otto of Cappenberg to whom Frederick Barbarossa eventually gave one of the most famous of medieval objects, the so-called *Cappenberger Kopf* or portrait head of Barbarossa. Addenda to the *Life of Godfrey* clarify the meaning and circumstances of this widely known image. Otto of Cappenberg was godfather to the great Hohenstaufen, and the three-dimensional portrait seems both to have served as a memorial of his relationship with the emperor and as a reliquary for hair of John the Evangelist, an important figure in both the spirituality of the Premonstratensians and the family history of the great Swabian house from which Barbarossa sprung; the emperor's own father, another Frederick, had worn the same apostolic relic around his neck in a silver cross and he aggrandized their holdings in the decades prior to the Swabian dukes' ascent to imperial status. Ironically, then, this saint's life, central to the early Premonstratensian charism, is also the principal written source about an object of major interest for the history of imperial Germany. Hence, historians' attention to the *Life of Godfrey* has been intense and frequent, although for the most part unconcerned with its meaning for the spirituality of Norbert's early communities.[1]

Among the most important treatments of the *Life of Godfrey* in its imperial context, Herbert Grundmann's 1959 study of the portrait head persuasively determined the dating and identification of the *Cappenberger Kopf*, likewise making important contribution to the study of the hagiography in which it figures. Subsequently, Gerlinde Niemeyer addressed a lengthy essay in *Deutsches Archiv* to the *Life of Godfrey;* her work is fundamental for the new edition begun by her and recently completed by Ingrid Ehlers-Kisseler, for Scriptores Rerum Germanicarum;[2] the present translation is from the older Monumentist edition, entirely adequate for this purpose. Recent studies of Godfrey and his *vita* affirm Grundmann's and Niemeyer's work. Most important, Jean-Claude Schmitt's extended essay on the closely related *Opusculum de conversione sua* of the so-called Herman the Jew for the first time emphasizes the usefulness of considering the two texts from Cappenberg, Herman's and the *Life of Godfrey*, as thematically linked; for Schmitt, these texts are useful as documents on the twelfth-century understanding of conversion more than for their biographical information. Yet Schmitt remains unconcerned with either text as shaped or shaping a Premonstratensian spiritual idiom.[3] Here, interest lies rather in the two works' meaning for Norbert's followers, particularly in the *Life of Godfrey's* presentation of the relationship between the laity and religious reform in one of Norbert's earliest foundations and in the text's relationship to other Premonstratensian saints' lives.

Surprisingly, in the broad context of hagiography emerging from religious orders, this *Life of Godfrey* seems likely to be the oldest among such Premonstratensian texts. Its author is unknown, although he was clearly a canon of Cappenberg who did not himself directly know Godfrey but knew many who did.[4] Although Norbert was far more important a figure in the religion and politics of twelfth-century Europe than his disciple Godfrey, hagiography of the preacher, founder, and archbishop seems to have followed the composition of the *Life of Godfrey* translated here. Niemeyer has established that this version of Godfrey's *vita*, the earliest of three hagiographies of Cappenberg's noble founder eventually produced by the confreres of the reformed canonical communities he endowed, was written shortly after the return of his relics to Cappenberg in 1149 and reburial there in 1150;[5] the concluding passages of the main text, considered separately from its addenda, frame the hagiography as an element in this commemorative celebration. Internal textual evidence thus restricts the time of the *Life*'s composition to a short period, even though the one extant medieval copy is from the beginning of the subsequent century.[6] Meanwhile, the earlier of the two twelfth-century lives of Norbert of Xanten is dated only to before 1161, although it is certainly later than 1145.[7] Godfrey died in 1129, five years before Norbert. Although no hard evidence of manuscript transmission confirms that the *Life of Godfrey* is the earlier text, its author plainly states that no hagiography of Norbert himself is on hand as he composes this life.[8] Cappenberg lies between Magdeburg, where the older of the two twelfth-century Norbert lives (the *A* life) seems to have been written, and Prémontré, where it was likely emended and expanded shortly afterward as the *B* life.[9] The canonical community Norbert founded at Prémontré was thus quick to receive a copy of his first hagiography soon after its production—and to respond to it. Cappenberg seems unlikely to have continued for long in ignorance of the existence of any hagiography of the preacher and archbishop, especially since its community was—as the *Life of Godfrey* makes clear—concerned to develop a hagiography of its founders. Therefore, given the absence of evidence to the contrary, the *Life of Godfrey*'s testimony to its own priority is credible. Indeed, the circumstances of Godfrey's conversion to religious life to an extent explain why the contemporary saint whose stature in the order's context was local rather than European, despite his lofty origins, should have been first so memorialized.

Godfrey of Cappenberg and his brother, Otto, as scions of the loftiest echelon of the imperial nobility and collateral relations of the Salian and later Hohenstaufen emperors, held immense territories and were important figures in imperial diets of the early twelfth century. As partisans of royal pretensions in the Investitures

Controversy, they were implicated in the burning of the cathedral church of Münster in early 1121; at the time Godfrey was in his late twenties.[10] His hagiography tactfully omits the arson incident, but it was evidently the precipitating circumstance in his conversion to religious life; Henry V's foundation charter for Cappenberg mentions royal guilt in the affair, by implication Godfrey's as well.[11] Godfrey first encountered Norbert of Xanten, at the time making his first extended preaching tour in German-speaking lands after his foundation of a house of reformed canons at Prémontré, not long after this notable act of arson, later in the same year, when he was in a contrite and suggestible frame of mind. In May 1122, Godfrey decided not only to follow Norbert but also to convert his family's most important seat, the castle of Cappenberg, into a religious community under Norbert's authority. At first Godfrey's younger brother, Otto, took a dim view of his elder's religious fervor, but eventually Otto too was won over and himself converted to regular religious life,[12] becoming his brother's companion in community life and eventual pilgrimage to Prémontré and Magdeburg. In 1156, long after the deaths of both Godfrey and Norbert, Otto became provost of Cappenberg, and thus the effective trustee of his brother's relics and patron of the hagiographical text memorializing him.[13]

Others among the family of the counts of Cappenberg were less willing to sanction or participate in Godfrey's sudden abandonment of knightly violence and imperial courtiership in favor of repentance, poverty, and celibacy. The young count's wife wanted none of it, and her father, Frederick of Arnsberg, took up arms as his daughter's advocate, opposing her unwilling dedication by her husband to the women's community associated with Cappenberg.[14] The *Life of Godfrey* characterizes Frederick as diabolical.[15] Whether driven by satanic impulses or fatherly concern, Frederick's opposition to Godfrey's change in status was unremitting until Frederick's death in 1124. Godfrey, meanwhile, was unable to enter fully into religious life, compelled as he was to defend his territories and his donations both militarily and before royal justice.[16] At last, after Frederick's death, Godfrey was free to set out with his brother, Otto, to experience the liturgy and community of Prémontré, where he was first ordained to lower orders—and, possibly, began

to learn to read.[17] Much scholarly discussion of disunity of administration and practice among Norbert's foundations tends to ignore
the human connection recorded here as affirming Norbert's first
foundation as the touchstone and center of Premonstratensian life.

After a sojourn at Prémontré between 1125 and 1126, Godfrey
followed his master, Norbert, to the latter's new archiepiscopal see
at Magdeburg. Still traveling with his brother, Otto, the former
count soon turned homeward, however, from the Slavic frontier.
Some commentators have suggested that he was disillusioned by
Norbert's transformation from pilgrim-preacher to prince-bishop,
which must indeed have been jarring. But the text of the *Life of
Godfrey* is equivocal as to whether Norbert dismissed Godfrey,
Godfrey abandoned him in disillusionment, or Godfrey simply
wished to go home to Cappenberg.[18] In any case the former count
never reached his destination. Ill, Godfrey stopped with Otto at
Ilbenstadt, the second of the three major sites (Varlar was the third)
he had offered up for religious foundations according to Norbert's
reform. There the elder brother died. After his burial Otto continued on to Cappenberg. More than twenty years later he returned to
Ilbenstadt to negotiate the division of Godfrey's relics and the
return of some of his bodily remains to his and his brother's preferred first foundation, where Otto would become provost some
seven years later.[19]

The later hagiographies of Godfrey are of weak interest for the
self-representation and spirituality of the early Premonstratensians
because of their distance from the events they relate.[20] This first *Life
of Godfrey*, however, in its pride of place as the probable earliest in
the order's several early hagiographical models, is of great interest
for its representation of Norbert himself, for its interpretation of
Norbert's effect on Godfrey and other noble converts, for its discussion of Norbert's choice of the Rule of St. Augustine as the normative document for Cappenberg as for Prémontré, and for its
preservation—in elements in the story of the famous Herman the
Jew—of a Premonstratensian discourse on conversion. In general, it
characterizes Norbert, his canonical reform, and the meaning of
conversion in religious houses in his filiation with reference to the
personal model of the appealing, penitent arsonist of Münster,
Godfrey. Finally, the allusion in its addenda to the *Cappenberger Kopf*

opens that token of imperial might for discussion as yet another object of conversion—its literal conversion into the reliquary of a saint especially paradigmatic of Premonstratensian spiritual life, the evangelist John.[21]

The *Life of Godfrey*, if indeed it was begun in 1150 or shortly thereafter in continuation of the celebration of the return of Godfrey's relics to his home, thus became the first Premonstratensian saint's life—at least the first to survive to a modern readership—for circumstantial reasons. Like many medieval hagiographies, it was composed in honor of the translation of its subject's relics, an obvious occasion for gathering memory about a religious house's patron among those who still remembered him. But corollary reasons for remembering Godfrey of Cappenberg as a spiritual hero of the canonical community were abundant. Godfrey began his life far higher in the imperial nobility than his master, Norbert, although the latter was likewise an imperial courtier. His material gifts to Norbert's movement were huge. And he was beloved of those Westphalian communities that had previously been his possessions, where the great advocate of his memorialization was his brother and co-donor, the eventual prelate of the most important of Norbert's early German foundations. Further, the content of Godfrey's life is in some respects more paradigmatic of Norbert's followers—more useful to them in interpreting and dignifying their experience—than Norbert's own; they, like Godfrey, had heard Norbert's charismatic preaching, and his conversion was mirrored in their own. Nor was Godfrey's entry into religious life problematic, in that his transformation from noble to lay brother in his and Norbert's co-foundation at Cappenberg was simple and singular; he did not, like Norbert, blend the roles of preacher, founder, and bishop. As a layman who responded, in his anguish over his own great error in firing Münster, to Norbert's call to apostolic life, he was a characteristic new member of the reformed canonical community. Only in the loftiness of his standing and the abundance of his wealth did he differ from the many, many others who joined the many communities founded by Norbert or their daughter houses in the first twenty-five years. His abandonment of such worldly glory and the knightly prowess by which he defended his decision must have lent his life great interest for its medieval readership. When shortly after, another German

hand undertook to set forth the life of his master, Norbert, that subsequent hagiographer, who knew Godfrey's story well, faced a
thornier hagiographical problem—how to characterize the multifaceted Norbert of Xanten, whose own conversion impelled him into
multiple roles and whose interpretation demanded corresponding
complexity.

LIFE OF GODFREY
OF CAPPENBERG

Preface

One of the holy prophets, contemplating how the vastness of God's blessings overflows the human heart, wrote, *I will remember the tender mercies of the Lord, the praise of the Lord for all the things that the Lord hath bestowed upon us* (Isa 63:7). Another prophet, finding himself unworthy of such grace, said, *What shall I render to the Lord, for all the things that he hath rendered to me?* (Ps 115:12). As for me, I do not wish to be ungrateful to the author of all things for the great good with which he endows us. I therefore take up this discourse to commend God's great actions revealed especially to us, that is, to the children of our religious profession, and more generally to the benefit of all believers.[1] I speak without loftiness of style but with the help of the Holy Spirit, in a humble and simple manner, for we are forbidden by the Law to plant a grove in the house of the Lord.[2] I intend a memorial to what God has done, making no claims against another, more skillful author who may later write of these matters. In this way I avoid the sneers of the envious. As one of the saints says, *Just as charity, beautiful and modest, gratefully catches the eye of the dove, so cautious humility avoids the tooth of the dog and firm truth blunts it.*[3]

Therefore I repudiate from the start that empty laziness, lazy emptiness, by which our community has failed thus far to praise the blessed Count Godfrey, founder of the convent of Cappenberg, this very place. Yet we are enriched today with all good things by the virtues and energy of this great man, to say the least. When I contemplate the signs of his holy conversion—first the voluntary

---

This translation is based on Jaffé's edition, MGH 12, 513–30.

poverty of so great an individual, then his humble simplicity, simple humility, finally his happy end—I cannot fully express what my heart wishes to say. Godfrey, this true count, is thrice blessed because he was the retainer of the true King, he was his imitator, and his memory lives on with us, blessed throughout time. Godfrey's memory lingers always, as is written, like the fragrance of the perfumer's craft, or like honey and music in the drinking of wine.[4] I will try, then, to speak of this saint in an appropriate way and to set forth to the ears of the pious and the God-fearing what things were witnessed by our brothers.

Chapter 1

In the time of the glorious Henry, the fifth of that name to hold the Roman Empire, there was in Westphalia a certain Count Godfrey, chosen and beloved of God, born to noble parents of royal ancestry. As count, he acted in the fear of the Lord. His father was also called Godfrey and his mother Beatrix. The elder Godfrey, worthy to be numbered among the friends of God, himself had as his grandfather a count named Herman. The latter, as I have found out in many accounts of our elders, was outstandingly charitable. He was given to works of mercy and stood peacefully apart from knightly conflict. As a result he effected a miracle in his own lifetime. A certain blind man had come under this Herman's charitable care. This unfortunate used to say that divine revelation had shown him that he would regain his sight if water that had washed the count's hands touched his eyes. The blind man sought this water, put it to his eyes, and immediately he was able to see. At Herman's tomb even today his powers cause amazing things. I myself have seen offerings left by those who were healed and returned home whole.

The grandson, then, of this great Herman, our own Godfrey, was devoutly religious from his early youth. Because he was inflamed with divine inspiration, he desired to renounce his secular rank and all his worldly possibilities. He was a gentle man, respected for his mildness, praiseworthy in his benevolence, blessed with extraordinarily bright eyes, easy of speech, prudent in counsel. At the same time he was powerful in knightly skill, but ardent to fight for the highest King and, himself naked, to bear the naked cross of Christ. In the meantime, however, when from time to time he had to dress as a knight, bearing arms, he refrained from assault on others. But when he witnessed fellow knights despoiling or usurping others, as often happens, he raised his hands to heaven and wept. As one of his retainers[5] who afterward became our brother attests, Godfrey prayed in these words to the all-powerful Savior: "Lord Jesus Christ, I beseech your goodness that you free me from the midst of this iniquity and that you lead me unblemished to Judgment Day. For I know, most just of judges, that any wrong done by my men is held against me, and that any laxity or untruth on my part will bring your rightful punishment." The true, miraculous story of what followed will reveal how Godfrey's prayer was fulfilled, for God grants good things to those who walk in innocence.[6]

Chapter 2

Godfrey lived in the castle of Cappenberg, a beautiful place in a healthful, lovely setting. There the Lord repeatedly showed in truthful revelations that the count was to enter divine service. A priest named Wichman dreamed that a golden column rose up in Cappenberg and penetrated the heights of heaven. From this vision he understood that the glory of God's praise would ring forth there, and so Wichman foretold it to others long before it actually took place. Then again, a man named Egbert, a friend of the good count, saw the town of Cappenberg shining brighter than snow one night as he was traveling to see Godfrey. Cappenberg seemed to Egbert to reach as high as the clouds, pushing against the height of heaven.

Here I will mention a daughter of one of Godfrey's relations, Abbess Gerberga of Münster. This lady, famous for her holiness, loved the blessed Godfrey. She prayed constantly for him as for her own nuns. Once when she was just waking, she saw a young man standing next to her, his face shining more brightly than the stars. He spoke these words into her ear: "Cappenberg would be so suitable as the home for the convent of a spiritual congregation!" Gerberga was happy to hear this, for she had wanted this very thing for a long time. When she told her vision to the blessed Godfrey, he wisely and humbly responded in this way: "Beloved aunt, the Lord God has the power to ordain things according to his will, but by myself I cannot accomplish it." Divine Providence, as it turned out, effected the matter according to his word, fulfilling the pious desire of the holy man's heart.

At about that time Norbert, a great light of the church and famous messenger of God, came to Westphalia.[7] He was a man of admirable grace, honeyed eloquence, and great continence. Norbert was the shaper and propagator of canonical religious life, a gatherer of the servants of Christ, the founder of many convents, a powerful preacher of true penance as much in his dress as in his words, and in all these roles executor of the prophetic command *Prepare ye the way of the Lord, make straight in the wilderness the paths of our God* (Isa 40:3). Indeed, the sanctity of Norbert's life, the importance of his role as archbishop, and the holy felicity of his death are so great as to fill an entire book, should anyone wish to recount them fully.[8] When the news of the great preacher spread, our own blessed Godfrey came thirstily to this herald of salvation, bringing along his brother, the worthy lord Otto. Godfrey devoutly heard Norbert's words of exhortation. Otto, too, was beginning on his own, step by step, to spurn the worldly path through God's mercy and take up the way of holiness long since shining forth in his blessed brother. Why should I linger on more detail? Shortly afterward the two of them, having changed their secular dress, took the tonsure of religious life and the clothing of sacred profession.[9] Each vowed to serve the Lord under the Rule of St. Augustine and the obedience of the famous Brother Norbert. In the integrity of his piety, Godfrey—worthy as he was of God—encouraged his wife, Count Frederick's daughter, to take the holy veil. Godfrey as elder brother—although in this his junior concurred fully—offered their castle of Cappenberg with all their other possessions faithfully to God on the feast of the blessed virgin Petronilla.[10] Giving them for the use of Christ's poor, he made these lands into three monasteries: Cappenberg, Varlar, and Ilbenstadt. Endowing each richly with his goods, he placed them under the governance of the famous Father Norbert.

Chapter 3

It then pleased the Holy Spirit dwelling in Norbert, the messenger of truth, to raise a miraculous harvest from the Lord's fields, namely, that the brothers in the aforesaid communities should profess the Rule of the blessed Augustine.[11] They observed the Rule more strictly than had been the general practice, abstaining from fatty meat and showing the rigor of their penance in rough attire, for the Bridegroom's friend John ate of natural and woodsy food, not of delicacies, and was praised for the roughness of his garments by the Savior himself before the crowds who flocked to him in the desert. So our own way of life,[12] divine mercy accompanying it, now stretches far and wide, and we may believe that it will extend much further in the future. So we know that it was both begun in the word of the Holy Spirit and made famous by God's ordination. For did not the Lord, the leader on the journey, carry the vine from Egypt in his arm, held high? And did he not cast out the robbers and criminals who lived in this place, planting the roots of the vine that now stretches its shoots to the sea and beyond, with the support of his heavenly hand?[13] Still we fear what follows in the psalm, that a particular wild beast, our ancient enemy, root out the vine planted by God's own hand.[14] What would enable this destroyer so to do more than the cutting apart and isolation of certain of our communities?[15] We must beseech him who planted us and keeps us pure to tend his young shoots, protecting them from fire and from his own rebuke, so that he bring the tender shoot and new vine to fulfillment in the abundance of his blessing.[16]

Father Norbert himself loved the monastery of Cappenberg greatly, more than the others. I will include here what he said about it when he stayed there in the convent of the brothers: "Beloved brothers," he said, "once when I was not far from here I saw the Holy Spirit descending over this place. As I contemplated it, a great light rose up and spread around it. Glorify our God accordingly, beloved, because this truly is the mountain of his sanctification, a mountain won by him with his right hand."[17] I myself, seated in the same convent of brothers, heard these words, lest anyone befuddled by lies presume to impugn their truth. And I heard the same voice of orthodoxy go on to the chapter: "I know a brother of our profession who was studiously examining our Rule when the blessed Augustine himself appeared, not because of the brother's own merits but because of the prayers of his confreres. With his right hand Augustine held out a golden rule extending from his side. He revealed himself to the brother in glowing speech, saying, 'I whom you see am Augustine, bishop of Hippo. Behold, you have before you the rule which I wrote. If your confreres, my sons, serve faithfully under it, they will stand safely by Christ in the terror of the last judgment.'"[18] Norbert told these things humbly, as if about another man, but I believe that this revelation was to him.

I would be remiss in omitting two further great events in this place. Norbert foretold that famine would come to Westphalia and that the brothers of Cappenberg would for a time be chastened in spirit. Soon a severe famine befell, as the man of God foreknew, so that the dire calamity of starvation killed many people.[19] One day, when the brothers were about to go to their supper, they asked that some be reserved from their portion to feed their guests and the poor, since there was no bread at all for alms. Still there was none to be found, but just as the man of God had often quoted, *The Lord will not afflict the soul of the just with famine* (Prov 10:3). Behold, the Lord sent so much bread through his faithful that the brothers both filled themselves and quickly offered more to those who came to them for help. From that day on, the brothers always had enough.

Another time the holy Norbert wished to send out one of the brothers on the business of the monastery but found him laid low by a powerful fever. Norbert then commanded the brother under obedience, resting his directive in Christ's strength alone, "Go forth and return, and be fevered no more."[20] At once the brother recovered and did as the holy father directed. So the speech of the man of God both achieved his purpose and instantly banished lengthy illness.

In the same place a certain brother of praiseworthy life prayed regularly for a loyal friend who had died. The friend appeared to him one night and spoke just as he used to: "My brother, I thank you because thus far—even if my other friends and relations have forgotten me—you have never done so. Now I urge you to hold fast in your resolution, never letting your mind waver from our way of life to find another more powerful. I can show you nothing more healthful or more proper to your soul than this. I have come to declare this to your community—that the prayers of your confreres are daily recited before a golden altar in the Lord's own sight. And so I urge you never to flee the command of obedience. No other virtue will bring you merit before God in a loftier or more fruitful way."

The prophet says, may the tongue of your dogs be dipped in the blood of your enemies.[21] Many of the enemy Jews have converted and today many more convert, so that they bark at the Lord's enemies before his house. If you were to ask, "Whence so great a good?" the response would be, "From him," that is, from his grace not from themselves. I say from grace because God wrought that a Hebrew brother of our own time, who had circled around and around in error deprived of God's gift, began to investigate Christian faith with burning desire. This Jew used to dispute with Christians over the Law and the Prophets. When they spoke to him in the words of the apostle, he realized that a veil lay over his heart, and that this could best be lifted by the sign of the cross.[22] He began to cross himself, doing so secretly because of his fear of the other Jews. Because Jews seek portents, he devoted himself to fasting and prayer, asking for an indication from God that he was worthy to receive grace. When he did this with all his strength, lo! he envisioned himself standing beside Christ enthroned. A golden cross gleamed over the Lord's shoulder. Seeing some of the other Jews standing by as well, our Hebrew said, "Don't you see that this is the one of whom Isaiah said, *And the government is upon his shoulder?*" (Isa 9:6).

Fully converted by so clear a sign, he attempted to free some others of his people from the Judaic lie. He came to Mainz, to the home of his relations. There he tried stealthily to take his own brother, still a little boy, outside the city, leading him by the hand from among the Jews. But because of a malign spirit our Hebrew got lost with the boy, wandering through the streets unable to find the gate. He grew distraught in his confusion. Finally realizing that this wandering was caused by an evil spirit, he armed his forehead with the emblem of the cross. He quickly found the gate, his eyes opened, and he fled happy. The boy was freed with him and shortly afterward received the grace of baptism along with the elder brother. By the gift of heaven the younger Jew was then joined to the company of our soldiery along with his rescuer not long afterward.

Chapter 4

But enough of these matters. Now let us return to the blessed count and come to how the ancient serpent, seeing and envying Godfrey's virtues, tried with his retainers to block the saint's path. When the holy man's sanctity first emerged,[23] Godfrey's father-in-law Frederick—more an anti-Christian than a Christian—was consumed with greed. He flew into a rage and accused Godfrey of malfeasance, saying that his daughter had been seized wrongfully, that the part of his patrimony owed to her had been stolen in her fraudulent seduction. Claiming thus, Frederick beset the saint with injuries and insults, although Godfrey explained immediately, as he ought, and firmly opposed this outrage. Surrounded by several of his supporters, though, Frederick threatened his son-in-law bitterly, as if he were filled more with aloe than with honey.[24] Many who witnessed the assault were unable to contain their tears because of their reverence for so great a man as Godfrey. Meanwhile the man of God, as if strengthened by a wall of conscience upon which raging madness may not breathe, responded with a laugh, secure against all the force of that fury. Finally, Godfrey called one of his household and said: "Perhaps this unhappy man seeks to imprison me. If he does, tell Father Norbert that, even if I am thrown into a dungeon, he ought not to work for my release. I wish not only to be imprisoned for the law of God, but also to be found worthy to die in chains. For I beg God to let me suffer in prison, so that I meet his mercy and kindness the more swiftly. I wish my body, worn out in the service of Christ, to be consumed by the fire of tribulation like a worn broom thrown into the fire." So great was the steadfastness of the blessed Godfrey! He meant to suffer all things for Christ, but the good Lord kept him here for our betterment.

Frederick, however, was still spurred on by insatiable greed. Why is it not hunger for sacred riches that drives mortal hearts?[25] He besieged the castle of Cappenberg, threatening to hang Father Norbert himself before the walls. What fear or shame stands in the way of a hasty, greedy man?[26] Piling ills upon ills, he hoards his own anger until the Most High, whose recompense is patient, strikes him down with deserved reproach. Before Frederick's death was made known, one of the brothers saw in a vision that his throat was torn out by a bristly lion. Still, the diabolical serpent did not rest from his venomous envy, even when one of his many heads was cut off. Rather, he raised up more grief and tribulation for the holy Godfrey, so unwillingly offering him a greater occasion for virtue. Such is the inscrutable abyss of the judgments of God, driving the devil and all his company to serve the preferment of the elect. The blessed apostle contemplated its depth when he said, *We know that to them that love God, all things work together unto good, to such as, according to his purpose, are to be called saints.*[27] To divine power alone even evil things are good as long as they are used well, lest anything in his kingdom be left to chance.

The following story makes this point clear. A reprobate named Franco, spurred by the devil, ravished a lady who had taken the sacred veil. This fellow, armed and strutting, happened upon the blessed Godfrey, who was trying to right the matter, although he was himself unarmed. Franco said, "Who are you to try to stop me?" To this, the holy man responded in faith, as is written, *In the fear of the Lord is confidence of strength, and the just, bold as a lion, shall be without dread* (Prov 14:26; 28:1). "It is not that I keep watch against you, rather that I greatly desire you to be brought down by the teeth of our ancient enemy, whose servant you are." Franco then flew into a rage, grabbing his sword. As I might say, so that the great order of all time might know him,[28] the man of God offered the brigand his neck like a lamb led to the sacrifice. Frightened of God's will, Franco could not bring himself to strike. Why, then, would I not call this man of Christ a martyr, who not only in his spirit but also with his bared neck presented himself so freely for martyrdom? What would separate this champion from the love of Christ—tribulation, hardship, persecution, hunger, nakedness, danger, the sword? Finally Franco restored the lady, abducted and then sought with torturous effort, to her cell. The ravisher himself died not long after, pierced with the lance—a terrible death proper to sinners.

What then should I say of those several unfeeling retainers and even servile folk who assailed Godfrey with taunts that he had gone mad, that he was the follower of a charlatan and an impostor, Norbert, and that he was deserting his high place in this world stupidly, leaving himself and those in his care desolate, leaderless? Throughout, our champion suffered such attacks with a patience steady even before all these clouds of spears, and he responded from his worthy breast,[29] "If you love me, rejoice that I travel toward God, that I want to pass beyond the shipwreck of this world and go to my Creator." On the Assumption of the Blessed Virgin, a feast of great importance for us, our bishop consecrated the walls of our community, recalling how the waves of temptation and floods of persuasion pressed upon Godfrey. Some people drew him in one direction, and others pulled him the opposite way, wickedly suggesting he remain the lord of his noble, beautiful castle. The bishop himself, knowing the flesh and dragging his heart on the ground, offered Godfrey another lodging in exchange. But the knight of Christ, unconquered and standing firm upon Christ among torrent and flood, resisted the wind-driven flames steadfastly, neither worn down by fear nor broken by whirlwind. *For love is strong as death. Many waters cannot quench charity* (Cant 8:6–7). The servant of God was not delighted by the sight of his many possessions because the brightness of that precious pearl, divine charity, alone shone in his mind. So Godfrey gave away 105 retainers, along with the property to support them, and many other glorious gifts to the church at Münster—in addition to what he gave the church at Cologne and other communities—so that it might pray for him.

Chapter 5

Finally, therefore, when both material circumstance and religious practice had, after a hard struggle, been well established at Cappenberg, he was able to breathe, to foster peace in the cloister, and to release his cares in that leisure[30] that shines forth when habits are so pure that human speech cannot reveal them, as God is witness. Godfrey sought first the abnegation of his own self, willing always to face vile and lowly service and turning away the respect humbly offered him by his brothers. For he held deep in his heart what he had learned from the master of humility, who said, *Learn of me because I am meek and humble of heart, and you shall find rest to your souls* (Matt 11:29). When he heard the word of God or prayed to him, Godfrey wept many tears, testifying the burning devotion of his inner purity. One of our elders attested this, saying: "I was frequently struck with wonder about this holy man when he sat down to dine with us. Not only was he able to abstain from food to an amazing degree, but also the abundance and frequency of his tears astonished me. I asked myself, 'Good God, what is going on in this holy man? What is the reason for these groans, the cause of these tears? Is it his abundance of spiritual joy giving thanks, dwelling lovingly on the divine worship that he has established in this community forever, and which he sees in the heat of his faith? Or is it that he is so blessed in these magnificent things that he is unable to hold back such tears? Or is it rather that he is seized with desire for eternal goods so great, so unbearable, and so inconsolable that their contemplation and his fatigue of earthly things leaves him only tears?' It is healthy and praiseworthy reverence in any case, and a holy sublimity worthy of such a servant of God, whatever the compunction behind it." These things were then said by our elder, who observed Godfrey's weeping many times with his own eyes and recounted it to me in truthful and faithful testimony.

Beyond this Godfrey received the seed of the divine word in his heart. He encouraged others so much with his own lips that the father Norbert said of him with praise: "After I fall down exhausted from my preaching, I will rouse my son Godfrey in my stead, as stags do. When they are tired beyond their strength by the pursuit of hunters, they urge the other stags to run away in their stead."[31] And it is good to recall to the pious heart another of Godfrey's sayings that I learned from our brothers. He urged them to ignore unjust lips and lies of detractors, because *false honor supports—or lying infamy frightens—only the ignorant*.[32] "A lie," he said, "cannot survive for long, but sturdy truth perseveres. A lie sits upon a bolting horse, but truth upon an ass."[33] The meaning of this image is clear—the Lord who said *I am the truth* (John 14:6) deigned to sit upon an ass.

So Godfrey chastened his body according to the apostles' example, fasting continually, aware that *the greatest quiet is to wish nothing further than necessity demands—simple nourishment and one garment to cover sick limbs, easing them a little*.[34] He was content with simple things, mostly drinking water only and eating almost nothing but bread. When a few lukewarm brothers proposed to him that the rigor of the community's life should be relaxed, the holy man, his spirit full of God, responded with this image: "Those who would cross a great river in a boat begin far upstream from the intended landing, and they are forced along willy nilly with the waters. So may we, brothers, who attempt with our naked limbs to cross this great sea with its countless serpents, confirm our common intent. The sluggishness of human neglect always pulls us downward. I fear greatly lest our way of life stumble in the future, even slide down into the laxness of prior times."

Chapter 6

Once, when our count was still in secular dress, the citizens of Münster were rousing strife and waging war against him. One of Godfrey's retainers was riding out with his henchmen in that region and had collected much booty. Puffed up with his own triumph, this fellow led the many animals he had seized up to the gate of Cappenberg as the count himself stood there. But Godfrey was a friend of justice. He asked his retainer what this display might be. When he heard what had happened, he was righteously indignant. He said to his retinue: "Go tell this wicked brigand that he should stay out of my sight until he makes amends to those he has harmed and restored all that he has taken. If the people of Münster oppose me already, perhaps I deserve it because this presumptuous man despoils villagers, innocents, under the shadow of my name." The guilty man was frightened at this. No sooner did he hear Godfrey's words than he left Cappenberg as quickly as possible to return all his spoils with great care.

When we are amazed at the many wonders in Godfrey's life, we ought to marvel all the more at the good things he did when he was still a secular nobleman. This man of God showed, among other gifts of heavenly grace, extraordinary compassion even before he shed his secular possessions. He refused to disdain lepers or the sick of the lowest rank. To the surprise of his retainers, he sat down piously and humbly next to a feeble pauper as the man's attentive visitor. He drank from the wretch's filthy flask, sharing everything with the invalid, supporting him even as he would himself wish to be supported in such a state, as the apostle teaches.[35]

103

I would be remiss if I omitted what happened when our generous servant of God, still wearing the sword of a knight, was on his way to the monastery of Varlar when a beggar crossed his path. Godfrey was traveling with his servant Giselbert, whom I knew later after his conversion to monastic life. Tenderhearted, Godfrey would not allow the poor man to go away unsatisfied, so he said to Giselbert, "Is something left in our purse?" His companion answered, "Yes, lord." "Give it to the poor man," Godfrey replied. Afterward he asked again if something were left. Again it was given to the pauper. But the goodness of the holy man was not satisfied until, the third time, all that remained was given to the beggar. So the true believer and worshiper of the divine Trinity remedied poverty with a threefold gift. He said to his servant, "Let us give to the poor whatever we value, so that God's goodness see fit to strengthen the new plantation of our brothers in Cappenberg and Varlar."

Nor should I omit that Godfrey's brother, Otto, by God's grace, spread the divine service in the region of Ilbenstadt, when he was there. A powerful noble named Manegold, who had castles at Hagen and Wirberg, was slain by his enemies, along with his son. A single daughter, Aurelia, survived as heir to all Manegold's lands. Many sought her in marriage, for she was also beautiful. Otto came and persuaded her to vow perpetual chastity, stealing her away at night in danger of her life. Finally, working with papal and royal support, he distributed all of Aurelia's inheritance to God's servants. Otto himself destroyed the castle of Hagen by fire, but a religious community of brothers and sisters thrives today at Wirberg.

Chapter 7

Godfrey left all earthly things behind with great purity and simplicity of devotion, as was evident in the response with which he satisfied one Eucruvinus. At the time Godfrey was struggling to rescue the lady ravished by Franco, the story was circulating everywhere—for the rumor of falsehood and evil holds as firm as the messenger of truth[36]—that Count Godfrey had lapsed and taken back his own wife and further that he had driven all the brothers from the castle, where they were already established as a religious community, with physical violence. When these falsehoods were spread all the way to the River Meuse, Eucruvinus, the brother of our confrere Henry, arrived from his own lands hoping to take Henry away with him. When Eucruvinus greeted the count, who received him warmly and asked why he had come, he answered: "I have come, lord, to recall my beloved brother, who converted here with you. It has been widely known for some time now that you have begun to drive away all the brothers whom you received." The man of God responded swiftly: "What? Do you think that all you see here with your own eyes is false, my friend? I am amazed at tales of such impudence. How rash would I be to take back such things as no longer belong to me, and whose service is owed to God alone. The Lord knows that, even if I had taken some women's children to nurture, I would rather beg for us from door to door, carrying the little ones on my back, than dare in any way to violate what belongs to God or his servants." Those who heard Godfrey were amazed to weeping at the sincerity of so great a man and at the depth of his poverty.

I should not conceal that at that time, when Count Frederick persecuted the man of God hotly, even Frederick's cruelty— tyrannical as it was—was somewhat shaken from its fury. Around then Emperor Henry summoned and presided over a council of counts, marquesses, and other nobles at Maastricht. Frederick too was there. After the empire's business had been done, the emperor was sitting in his chancery and the great nobles outside. As is the custom, *they passed over many things as their conversation wandered.*[37] A certain prince of the Swabians, a good Christian, pretended that he did not recognize Frederick and began to reprove him facetiously in the hearing of the great conclave, referring to the conversion of our Godfrey and his brother. The prince said: "Pay close attention, heroes and fellow-knights. It is known far and wide that a true miracle of God has happened in our parts—that the two counts of Cappenberg have been divinely inspired to give all their property to the Lord God, so that their inheritance is ceded forever to poor men of Christ who serve God continually. Happy and greatly blessed are they whose nobility of spirit is so gathered up by the Lord! How happily is the will guiding their lofty plan fulfilled! In our own times these men offer a magnificent example of holiness and voluntary poverty for all Christ's faithful, as they humbly, unhesitatingly gather a following of God's poor servants. What an outrage that some son of the devil in that neighborhood, one Frederick of Arnsberg, is trying to block their sanctity, as rumor has it! Blinded by a cloud of greed such as misleads no true Christian, this Frederick launches machines of war against God himself. If such a brigand, the worst of men, were to prevail over our God, I would be loath to declare myself still the servant of a Lord who declined to avenge such insult to his name. Yet I do not despair, for the victory in that conflict will surely be God's own."

Hearing this princely ridicule, Frederick was distraught and humiliated. He cast his eyes about here and there, able neither to bear the gaze of the speaker nor, in so august a gathering and with so dark a conscience, even to murmur a response. But I found out for certain that, when he had gone home after the council, he began to behave somewhat more gently. Sending a messenger to Godfrey, he besought the man of God with great mildness to consent to come to Arnsberg to speak with him. Godfrey hoped to converse with Frederick about the remedy of his soul, so he gathered a few men loyal to him and trustingly came to Arnsberg on the feast of the Assumption of the Blessed Virgin Mary.[38] There, however, he found several captives shackled and thrown in a dungeon—for Frederick always had been cruel, putting broken men in chains. Godfrey was overwhelmed with pity in the visceral way in which he was accustomed. He approached the count immediately to plead for the prisoners. Yet at Godfrey's gentle words of supplication, Frederick stood immobile, a cliff against the sea. He would respond neither to the grace of the feast day nor the dignity of so great a man nor finally to the lamentable wretchedness of the captives. Why is it any surprise if this barbarous man gave no relief then, remaining unwilling to release even one of his captives, when even at the very hour of his death he wished no one's prayers or counsel? The impious man perished, as they say, of his flesh rotting, and the lady who cared for him died a little after. Frederick's captives rejoiced that the tyrant had fallen because they were at last released, but their freedom was in vain because some of them gave up the ghost soon after, sickened by the filth of his dungeon.

Because Godfrey was grieving over the captives, Frederick never revealed to him the reason for which he had summoned him, instead taking him around and showing him the walls he was building and the great variety of his material goods. The holy man laughed at all of this. He leaned over and whispered to one of his companions, who told me about it himself: "This man thinks I am delighted by vanities of this sort, but I humor him only because I must. I would not give the price of rotten straw for all the riches he vaunts." Then, after exhorting Frederick briefly, Godfrey hurried home, impatient of any delay. He always bore the tumult of the secular world ill, considering the silence of the cloister to be paradise and the quiet of his beloved solitude better than all Croesus's wealth. Afterward, however, when he learned of the death of his persecutor, he was mindful of mercy and filled with compassion. Forgetting Frederick's malice, he wept for him, knowing through the Spirit dwelling in him to what great punishments such a soul was subjected by God's judgment.

At about that time some of Godfrey's retainers came to him, saying, "Lord, what a great inheritance would have come to you if you had not wished to cast away the glory of this world, which you might have possessed." Responding with indignation, Godfrey said: "What is this of which you boast as great? Will I have left everything behind when I die, as this man did? Frederick is dead and now he has none of his things, nor does his earthly glory go with him to his grave. You know, Lord, that even if I had foreseen the future, I would not have put off my conversion unless perhaps to spread the service of your praise more widely. How have I done something great in leaving behind what could not by nature remain with me? It is true, isn't it, that *all things driven by time, carried away by death, are lowly in their brevity?*[39] Answer me this, I ask you. If you compared a husk of grain to a rich city, would you choose to take away the husk from such wealth because you valued it more than the great city?" They answered, "that would be stupid." Godfrey rejoined: "The healthy man, the sound man, is he who disdains to exchange the kingdom of heaven for anything in this world, however magnificent. Who will boast, who will demand to be rewarded, if he only restores to his maker what he receives of him? Nonetheless, the good Lord ordains the opportunity for our salvation only because he so deigns in his bottomless goodness."

Chapter 8

One of the brothers, a man of great dignity and holiness, said to me in a conversation about Godfrey's virtues: "Ah, who is still alive today who can really judge how saintly he was? I myself witnessed a miracle in his sacred presence that I consider greater than if I were blind and he restored my sight, if I were lame and he made me walk, or if I were deaf and he restored my hearing. Godfrey drove away the demons who attacked me with only a look from his holy face." I confess that I was amazed, and I answered, "I implore you in the name of him who is true charity that you not mislead me about something so holy and fruitful." He rejoined: "In the year when I first put off my secular dress and sought out the monastery, our ancient Enemy constantly attacked me with many irritations and arrows of temptation, so that I felt a very demon sitting on my chest, constantly vexing me, pulling my attention away from the divine office. I prostrated myself before the holy altar, struggling with all my might against this demon while he pursued me the harder. When I called upon God's help, the Lord showed the demon to me in visible form—misshapen and loathsome. But every time I was so afflicted, I ran to seek the presence of the holy Godfrey, and in his sight it was as if I were washed with dew. I felt the demon flee, and I was refreshed in body and spirit. If I could not actually see Godfrey but only hear his voice, I was still relieved quickly by a similar consolation, so that I never doubted that the power of the Holy Spirit did these things through him. Informed by the Spirit, Godfrey knew my heart without my telling and, as if taking on all my distress himself, spoke fitting words of comfort, 'My brother, take comfort, act forcefully, and whenever you are so beset as to be unable to pray one prayer to God, await his pity. Breathe in the hope of God's future consolation, for as the prophet says, *For if he hath cast off, he will also have mercy, according to the multitude of his mercies*' (Lam 3:32). So Godfrey spoke to me with gentle words, restoring the sweet things of God with his own sweet tongue, yet I suffered thus for almost a whole year. On whatever days I did not happen to see or hear the man of God, as I said before, I was battered by a terrible attack from the demon."

I have not allowed these words and deeds of our holy brother Godfrey to be hidden in silence, so that every pious soul may recognize how great his spiritual grace was. At another time, when the servant of God still carried a sword, he was constrained for the good of his brothers to come to a diet before Emperor Henry, his kinsman. Godfrey's chaplain was one Ebbo, who afterward was converted by the example of the great man, but who did not accede to the first stages of his lord's conversion. The saint took this Ebbo and a few of his servants along with him when he set forth, and Ebbo presumed to say: "How, lord, will your emperor greet your coming? How do you think he will respond to you as a poor man in pauper's dress and unkempt hair, coming to him without the usual knightly retinue?" The man of God answered Ebbo serenely: "All of this, brother, I give over to God, in whose hand the king's heart lies. Wherever he wishes, there it will incline." When Godfrey arrived at the palace, the emperor—although he was busy with many affairs—ran from afar to embrace him when he saw him, setting aside everything and calling out: "Oh, dear kinsman, I give great thanks to God that I have been able to see you. I did not imagine that today I would see so extraordinary a man as you." Henry kept Godfrey beside him in wonderful affection and great honor, holding him closer than anyone, to the shame of the chaplain Ebbo. At last the emperor parted from Godfrey regretfully and in peace.

Chapter 9

Later, the bishop of Münster, incited by many others, tried to seize the castle of Cappenberg rather than yield it into the possession of the servants of Christ. On the suggestion of many others, he offered the blessed Godfrey several other sites in the same region in exchange, but the latter resisted steadfastly, founded upon a rock.[40] Godfrey answered the bishop: "Our undertaking is inspired by God's gift, Father. All those who try to move it from this place by threat or blandishment labor in vain. For no reason will I allow that this place in my charge be given over to worldly vanity. Rather, this must happen—here, where before now knights have rampaged ungoverned, there must instead be constant divine worship. The wastefulness of the past consumes the will of those fools who walk about, as is written, *in riotousness and lusts* (1 Pet 4:3). Believe me, even if you offered four times as many possessions in recompense, I would never allow this castle to be returned to the business of the secular world."

The blessed Godfrey's great determination and forcefulness resisted the bishop so powerfully that neither he nor others pressed the matter any further. The tyrant Frederick, of whom I have spoken often, also felt the thunder of Godfrey's fearsome words, as the saint became one of those of whom we read, *If any man will hurt them, fire shall come out of their mouths, and shall devour their enemies* (Apoc 11:5). Although he was mindful of his noble birthright, Godfrey raised a leviathan against himself in his disregard of the world.[41] Then the princes of Edom were troubled, and trembling seized on the stout men of Moab. All the inhabitants of Chanaan raged.[42] Frederick especially burned with the flame of avarice, for the breath of the devil makes frost burn, and he panted over Count Godfrey's possessions on his daughter's account. He bullied Godfrey, leading an army against him. Again and again he threatened legal action, setting impiety in place of duty. Then, on the appointed day, when a great crowd had gathered and many speeches were made on both sides, the man of God hurled the flaming darts of the Holy Spirit at Frederick. Shining nobly in the purity of innocence, Godfrey said: "Ah, you wretch, why do you seethe so over these small, transient things? Why do you pant over little scraps of land, ignoring their boundaries? Will you live alone in the center of the earth? Or will you devour the entire world? So be it. But what does it profit you if you gain the whole world but harm your soul? You raise the matter of your daughter, but we all know the truth, that you are sickened by insatiable covetousness—you who, as the whole world knows, spared not even the daughter of your dead brother. Poisoned with greed, you threw her in prison." Godfrey was confident in these words, stunning many people by striking Frederick as with a blow to the chin. He went on: "Even now your face grows mottled and your flesh dark. Whether you wish it or not, the time is at hand when you will be decayed to dust and your neck returned to mud. Among the great men of the world your name is now first on people's lips, but I think you should fear that in the world to come you will deserve to be accounted not among the great but among the least, the vilest." Then Frederick answered, sneering with fear, "And you, lord, you are not so filled with God, with God's Spirit, but that I can be saved as surely as you and your lowly seducer Norbert."

As I have said, fire descending from spiritual heaven consumed the enemy of truth, torturing him without enlightening him. Not long afterward the wretch died, and this world breathed easier to be liberated from such a plague. Frederick had pounded upon our brothers now with threats, now by attacking their lands with military force. He oppressed them with such dread that, having made mutual confession with one heart along with Godfrey and their Father Norbert, they all offered their necks for slaughter, like sheep. They prepared for martyrdom. Leaving their gates open, they were confident of a swift death. But the Lord, who tests his servants through the vessels of iniquity,[43] frees them from injustice, saving the wicked to be tortured on Judgment Day. Mocking Frederick's madness and arrogance, the Lord put a ring in his nose and a rein on his lips and forced him to return on the road by which he had come, frustrated in all his efforts but unchanged in his will. That man every day sought evil for the poor men of Christ, as Saul did for David, but the Lord did not give them over into his hands. He tested them through tribulation and condemned Frederick's malice, while allowing it, in a wondrous way.

Chapter 10

Among his brothers, Godfrey shone with angelic life. All the brothers honored him appropriately, sometimes calling him count as in his former secular rank. But Godfrey, by whose humble example each was led to despise his own life, shunned this term of honor as if he feared it. He said to his brothers: "Dearly beloved, I beg you by Christ's love never to sadden me, who am servant of you all. When I was called count, I erred in many ways, as I confess. With sorrow and lamentation, I acknowledge that in those times other men under the authority of my name did many further wrongs." I must say that to confound our pride Godfrey showed his humility by making himself our house's privy cleaner, degrading himself to the lowest servitude. He had such great love of charity and of brotherhood that he himself built the guest house that one sees today and, as minister and guardian of our Lord's practice, he frequently washed the feet of the poor people there. Godfrey took on the responsibility of charity in distributing coins to individuals, showing fatherly feeling among them in all this, so that he said with true feeling like the blessed Job, *I was the father of the poor and I comforted the heart of the widow* (Job 29:16, 13), and again, I have not *eaten my morsel alone, and the fatherless hath not eaten thereof, for from my infancy mercy grew up with me and it came out with me from my mother's womb* (Job 31:17–18). So Godfrey gave away everything and offered it to the poor, so that his justice might remain for all time and his horn might be exalted in glory. An eager follower of the gospel precept, he loved his enemies in the purity of his innocence and he steadfastly suffered all the insults of his detractors with patience, possessed as he was of great-souled equanimity.

I recall here the apt description I gladly heard from someone close to us who knew the holy Godfrey well. This man said: "My brother, what more might I say to you? The man about whom you are writing was founded upon a firm rock."[44] What rank among the faithful might seek out greater miracles than his virtues? These are the wonderful marks of sanctity, the portents of divine action present only in the righteous. The prophet speaks of such virtues when he gives thanks, saying, *Thou art God that dost wonders* (Ps 76:15). Yet apart from these and other spiritual graces past human description, the holy man burned with an amazingly deep desire to cross over to Christ, panting with sighs beyond telling. So the Lord made haste to lead him from the midst of iniquity. Often, when his companions on the journey flagged, stopping to sit for a while, he would lie down and fold his hands and arms as we do with the limbs of the dead for their funerals. He would then say with a deep inner cry, moaning greatly: "Oh, may that hour of my crossing come! Oh, if you would deem it right and fit to prepare me for that hour, my lord God!"

Finally, so that Godfrey might obey his patriarch, Father Norbert said to him, *Go forth out of thy country, and from thy kindred, and out of thy father's house, and come into the land which I shall shew thee* (Gen 12:1). Godfrey obeyed Norbert's will fully, without delay.[45] As he was about to leave with his brother, the worthy lord Otto, he said: "My brother, if there is anything left which we have not tread under our feet in perfect renunciation, now let us abandon it from the bottom of our hearts in the name of Christ. Keeping nothing but what is useful for the path of obedience, let us hurry on." Godfrey thus came to Prémontré, the place the Lord chose and ordained, as its name reveals—*praemonstratum*, shown forth. There our way of life had its beginning, and there Godfrey and his brother were ordained acolytes, strengthening many by the example of their conversion. After a year Father Norbert again summoned Godfrey to accompany him to his archbishopric at Magdeburg, but the well-being of the holy Godfrey bore the splendor and noise of the secular world ill, and he began to suffer from a wasting illness. The Lord now saw fit to grant the wish of his chosen one. With Father Norbert's blessing, Godfrey set out for home by way of the monastery of Ilbenstadt, where after a short time he departed this world. As his weakness daily increased, his brother Otto and a few confreres stayed beside him in constant solicitude. When Godfrey expressed his desire to cross over now, one of his attendants said: "Stay, lord. Do not leave us desolate, for we still need you very much." The blessed man responded as if offended: "What are you saying, brother? Why do we take up the habit of penance, in which we strive every day to be mortified for Christ, if we do not wish to cross over to Christ the more quickly through those labors? I must wish a short life so that I may the more quickly see Christ's longed-for face."

At these words, when his brother Otto dissolved in grief, the blessed Godfrey said to console him: "My brother, we have given away all things for God's sake for this reason, because we always knew that, in the inevitable hour of our death, we would be prepared for the storm of God's judgment. So let us embrace this pilgrimage away from the body, making virtue of necessity, rejoicing and giving thanks that we are crossing over from toil to rest, from misery to blessedness. We cannot reach the desired reward of our labors except through the taste of death." Because calm of spirit is the beginning of death's reward, you should see in it nothing to avoid, nothing to fear. You should rather rejoice to see in holy Godfrey a faithful servant who, recognizing death's approach, grew joyful at the glory of his reward. For the Lord found him keeping watch, girded with the belt of chastity, and bearing lamps, symbols of light, in his hands.[46]

Finally, when Godfrey had been anointed with sacred oil, he gave the kiss of peace to all his confreres, saying: "Brothers, I sometimes have spoken with harshness for the sake of the grace of our way of life and in my zeal for God's esteem. If I have offended any of you, I beg you to forgive me." When he had spoken and when, grieving, they answered him in tears rather than words, he said to Otto: "My brother, I hear a voice saying, *Go ye forth to meet him*."[47] And then, after another short time, when Otto, who was constantly by his side, asked him what hope he had, the holy man responded in Latin rather than in German: "I have great hope. I would not wish for all the world to prolong this exile." After this he was silent a little while, then he said with a clear head, in sudden exaltation, "The heralds of the Lord, my maker, are come." After this he returned his spirit to his Creator. On the Ides of January,[48] when the holy church memorializes the baptism of Christ, his blessed spirit was released from the flesh and put on the bright robe of eternal life. In the year of the Lord's incarnation 1126,[49] when he was about thirty years old, he crossed over to Christ, to whom be honor and glory forever and ever. Amen.

Chapter 11

Abbess Gerberga, whom I mentioned before, dearly loved the holy Godfrey. She often made him promise when he left her that he would come back soon, whether he was living or dead. Therefore he appeared to her exactly as he went to heaven, girded with wondrous beauty and crowned with a golden diadem. Not having heard of his death, she asked him, "Why is it, beloved, that you wear a crown?" He responded: "Know that I have passed over to the palace of this highest King without delay, with no harsh trial. Therefore I am crowned with blessed immortality as the King's own son. And so that you have no doubt of this, read what is inscribed on my diadem." She looked closely and saw written, *The Lord hath clothed me with garments of salvation and with the robe of joy. He hath covered me, as a bride decked with a crown* (Isa 61:10). *Thou hast set on his head a crown of precious stones* (Ps 20:4), as holy prophecy faithfully states. And so at once, even though we here still did not know of Godfrey's death, Gerberga had Masses celebrated for him. When his brother, Otto, came home to Cappenberg after about ten days,⁵⁰ he announced to all that Godfrey's happy crossing-over had occurred at the very hour when he had appeared to their aunt.

After the departure of the holy Godfrey, the Lord did many works of healing through him. We, to whom *the light breeze of rumor scarcely reaches,*⁵¹ have not heard about all of them, nor could they be recounted easily by anyone. I nonetheless consider it worthwhile to tell about two. A great number of nuns live in a place called Elten. One of these nuns had a terrible toothache. Her distress grew worse and worse day after day, but she could find no remedy. She frantically sought help, and the Lord sent into her mind the memory of the blessed Godfrey, whom she had known in his lifetime and of whose famous virtues she had heard much about after his death. She began to beseech Godfrey with all her heart that he come to her aid, in her great pain, with his prayers before God. As soon as the trusting woman finished her petition, all her pain was gone. Furthermore, one of our brothers, who had been close to the saint while he lived, was greatly troubled and sickened by the same pain. He was advised to ask for a bloodletting in his arm, but when he did so he did not get better. At last, when he heard about the nun's cure, he too began to call upon our patron Godfrey. He was soon cured when he did so. Godfrey, servant of God, is thus with us in spirit, rejoicing with the apostle to see our way of life and the firm foundation of our faith, which is in Christ. For when one of our brothers had gotten up too swiftly to process into the hymns for matins, he sat back down on the bed and went quickly back to sleep. The procession left, but at once the man of God appeared, shining, beside the sleeper. Calling him by name Godfrey said: "My brother, get up as quickly as you can. The community is already entering the choir." At Godfrey's word the sleepy man awoke at once and quickly followed the brothers in procession.

Chapter 12

In the year of the Lord's incarnation 1148, at the eleventh indiction,[52] when Pope Eugenius presided over the apostolic see and God's faithful worshiper King Conrad returned from his pilgrimage to the Holy Sepulcher, the worthy lord Otto set out to Ilbenstadt to satisfy the desire of the brothers of Cappenberg. When he had called the brothers of Ilbenstadt together, he told them he must now remove the bones of his memorable brother, Godfrey, to Cappenberg. Otto said: "Godfrey begged this of me with great feeling as he breathed his last. Although sloth has led me to neglect his wish until now, it is right that I fulfill it at last joyfully and without further delay." But there at Ilbenstadt all were sad, deeply shaken. All shared the same powerful wish, that they never be bereft of the presence and patronage of so great a lord and founder. The brothers responded: "You lay waste to this place when you try to take its patron away. If you attempt further to do so, we will all—from the eldest to the youngest—refuse to continue such discussion about this monastery. Godfrey was offered to us, not you, and granted us through the ordination of divine grace. If God has given this, how may man presume to take it away?" To this the worthy Otto replied with his companions: "We would have been able, my brothers, to force you to accede in this matter against your will by a letter from the apostolic see. We would have acted freely and boldly toward you if we had not greatly preferred to conclude this with the peaceful agreement of your community. But we now declare that Godfrey asked for this in his lifetime because he loved the monastery of Cappenberg before all others. As for me, I cannot say otherwise. I must effect Godfrey's wish swiftly because I promised my brothers, and I too am about to die." In response, the brothers of Ilbenstadt again protested that they would break off discussion and that nothing could frighten them into yielding up Godfrey's relics because they had so strong a belief that his loss would be such a disadvantage to their establishment. When a disturbance then arose, the worthy Otto was greatly distraught. Turning his swift mind now one way, now the other, *he cast his mind about and reviewed it all.* Then, as the passage continues, *he came to this decision.*[53] Otto agreed on the urging of the brothers of Ilbenstadt to a new plan, that

Godfrey's relics be divided so that the stability of both houses be secure and peace maintained. Yet even this was begrudged him by the brothers of Ilbenstadt.

On the very day on which Godfrey's memorable relics were translated, accompanied by a great crowd,[54] from the lesser to the greater church, something else occurred. The brothers of the aforesaid monastery faithfully attested to me that it happened by divine power, and I relate it for the glory of Christ. The mother of a large family, whose name was Matthia, was burning with fever and could not be cured by anyone. She was suddenly made well before the relics of Godfrey by the omnipotence of that Physician who, when he was a man, freed the mother-in-law of Simon from her fever.[55] This Matthia at once stood up from her bed at Godfrey's sacred tomb, as others witnessed, and in gratitude addressed the holy relics with gifts of ceaseless prayers.

After these things, on the day before the Ides of February,[56] those of the relics that had come to us were received by our brothers with great devotion, so that on the following day the community was filled with joyful thanksgiving. A jubilee, that is, a year-long celebration, began for us. As we read, *Jubilee is at hand. The old hero's former fields are marked off again for him, lost liberty returns for those enslaved, the creditor forgives bad debts, and the exile seeks his father's threshold.*[57] So, as our patron returned and the grief of old subjugation was cast away, our community was granted the grace of new freedom and exultation, knowing that still richer blessing of divine favor would follow through him. Then, in the following year, on the sixteenth day before the Kalends of October,[58] his holy bones were laid to rest in worthy fashion in the new sanctuary by Werner, venerable bishop of Münster. From that time we have known from much experience that inside our house we are graced with heavenly generosity and outside we have acquired more and more, so that we remember the story that *the Lord blessed the use of his soldiers' leader and multiplied all his substance, both at home and in the fields, for Joseph's sake.*[59] Since Godfrey is the captain of our army, let us agree in our constant prayers to be governed by him, our Joseph, entrusting all things to him, because we know that all we do will be blessed and promoted forever under the shield of his merits.

Later additions[60]

The ancient lords of the castle of Cappenberg were descended from Charlemagne and the line of King Widukind through Imeza, who is buried in Xanten. They say that Charles himself gave his sister's daughter, Imeza, to Widukind in marriage, as a hostage for peace. From their descendants, whose broad generosity is still famous today, we received the manor of Wesel.[61] We are certain that Count Herman and his devoted wife, Gerberga of Huneburg, an outstanding worshiper of God, were also descended from them. We should not pass over in silence, for the sake of Christ's grace, the noble lineage extending even to us.

Almighty God, whose will is revealed in what he ordains, showed evidence of his goodness in Herman's sons, his inheritors. God saw fit to preserve one of them, even though they were all nefariously betrayed. That one was kept safe from murder for the good of those to come. A certain powerful nobleman named Ecker turned against them, plotting secretly to ambush and kill them. He did so even though he had sworn faithful allegiance to Herman and his sons and was obligated to them by benefices. This Ecker nonetheless laid a trap, then summoned Herman's sons to support him in a legal action at Lünen—ostensibly humbly but in fact treacherously. By God's will the third son, the youngest, had been wounded in the foot the day before, so that he could not go. What more might I say? The two elder brothers came upon the trap. Many knights rode out against them from the woods in that place, which still bears the name Grevenlo[62] from their murder. Both were killed, with two faithful retainers. Not long after this murder, the traitor Ecker was hung for his crime upside down from his feet, with his hands cut off. Godfrey alone, for this was the name of the one who survived, stayed home, as I have said, and so escaped. From him our saint Godfrey, the light of Westphalia, descended and took his name.

And so it happened that Godfrey and Otto, the counts of Cappenberg, left all their goods behind and submitted themselves to the yoke of Christ. They had two castles near Swabia, Krähenegg and Hildrizhausen,[63] as well as many retainers and about two thousand manors. They hastened to divest themselves of these and all

118

their other possessions as quickly as possible. Meanwhile Frederick, duke of the Swabians, came to the counts, seizing the opportunity to try to force them by reason of kinship—for their aunts were sisters—not to give their possessions away except into his control. Although he could not offer a fair price for their lands, he still wished to offer some small restitution at their discretion. The famous Godfrey and Otto set an amount for him as their kinsman with great good will, and he gave them only five hundred marks. Frederick argued forcefully that, instead of one hundred of the five, he preferred to give them relics of the apostle John—a treasury of grace commensurate with that amount of money. The worthy Otto, who had a special devotion to John, brought these memorable relics joyfully into our church and deposited them in a gilded head. With great feeling he ordained the continual burning of candles around this reliquary. He spent nearly half a mark of silver in rebuilding the fishery of the brothers, but another half for a cartload of wine to celebrate the assumption of the same apostle[64] on the bank of the Rhine—also on his feast day[65] at the Latin gate. It is right to record these things about our patron, so that there be no doubt about the truth behind this endowment, and so that all may be aroused to greater faith and more fervent devotion in the praise of the blessed apostle.

The father of the counts Godfrey and Otto was also called Godfrey, and their mother Beatrix. Their father was of Westphalian ancestry, and their mother was from Swabia. When their father, Godfrey, died, Beatrix took as her husband Henry, count of Ryetbeke, that is, the brother of Frederick, the former count of Arnsberg. This count Henry begot a daughter, Eileke, of the Countess Beatrix. Count Engelmar of Aldenburg married this Eileke and begot of her their sons, Counts Henry and Christian, and their brother Otto, as well as the Eileke who was the mother of Count Simon of Teklenburg.

THE HAGIOGRAPHY OF
NORBERT, THE A AND B *LIVES*—
INTRODUCTION

The principal sources for the life of Norbert of Xanten are two twelfth-century texts conventionally known as the *A* and *B* lives.[1] Until the mid-nineteenth century only the longer of these two works, *B*, was known to scholars; it was published in the Acta Sanctorum.[2] In 1853, however, Roger Wilmans discovered a hitherto unknown life of Norbert in a fourteenth-century codex in the Royal Library in Berlin.[3] The provenance of this codex, a miscellany in several hands, is the former Premonstratensian chapter of St. Peter in Brandenburg. Both the preceding and subsequent texts are in the same hand as the life of Norbert, but neither these three works nor the volume's other contents were necessarily copied by a Premonstratensian or anyone specifically interested in Norbert;[4] they may have come to St. Peter after production elsewhere. In 1856 Wilmans published the text of this Berlin version of a medieval life of Norbert in the Monumenta Germaniae Historica.[5] Wilmans believed that the newly discovered text predated the hagiographical work previously known and published by the Bollandists, the editors of the Acta Sanctorum. He therefore labeled his discovery *Vita A* and called the biography of Norbert already published in the Acta Sanctorum *Vita B*.

Until 1972, when a fragment of a manuscript in Hamburg was identified by Tilo Brandis as a partial copy of the *A* life,[6] Wilmans's discovery was the only known copy of *A*. The Monumentist transcription and annotation remains the only scholarly edition of this hagiography. The identification of the Hamburg fragment, however, demonstrates that there was at least one other copy of the *A* life in existence in the Middle Ages. This fragment, like the Berlin copy from which Wilmans prepared his edition, dates from the fourteenth century. It is damaged by use in bookbinding and comprises only thirty-two lines on each side of the parchment.[7] The relationship of this leaf to the Berlin manuscript remains unclear, but the hand indicates German origin.[8]

Since the discovery of the *A* life in 1853, moreover, the relationship of its text to the version of Norbert's life known as *B* has been repeatedly disputed. Although scholars generally agree that there is a close relationship between the two hagiographies, their relative dating and derivation have not been definitively established because there is as yet no comprehensive study or critical edition of the extant manuscripts of *B*.[9] Only one complete and one partial copy of *A* are extant, but the *B* life survives in more than twenty medieval and early modern copies, not all identical in content. The dates of these manuscripts range from the twelfth century to the eighteenth century.[10] Meanwhile, only four *Vita B* manuscripts contain the passage on Norbert's conversion on the way to Freden found in the *A* life, but *A* differs substantially from *B*. At least eight passages in *A* are absent in *B*. Many further minor differences are outlined in Grauwen's critical studies of the two lives and their manuscript evidence, on whose preliminary work on the *B* tradition any eventual edition will depend.[11]

Richard Rosenmund concluded in 1874 that both *A* and *B* were based on an earlier *vita*, now lost, so labeled α.[12] Grauwen, since there is no direct evidence for an α hagiography, continues to support the chronological and textual priority of the extant *A* life, arguing centrally that medieval authors added scriptural citations and miracle stories rather than removed them; for Grauwen, although the *B* life is a much longer text because of its multiplication of scriptural quotations and moralizations, its greater length presents virtually no additional historical and biographical information. From internal evidence he concludes that the *A* life was written first, probably between 1145 and 1161/64. Its *terminus post quem* is the text's mention of the pontificate of Lucius II as in the past.[13] The *B* life, on the other hand, was likely written between 1152 and 1161/64. Here the *terminus post quem* is its reference to Albero, the *primicerius*[14] of Metz, who was later archbishop of Trier.[15] No external evidence helps to date the two hagiographies of Norbert, but their closest possible respective dating suggests at most a fifteen-year gap between the two medieval lives of Norbert. Both hagiographies were thus written during the lifetime of Hugh of Fosses, who probably retired as abbot in 1161 and died in 1164.[16]

Although authorship of neither life is clear, the *A* hagiographer was likely a German who had taken part in the Rome expedition of 1132–33 and therefore knew Norbert personally. He writes about the construction of the church at Prémontré in chapter 12 as a competition between the German *(Teutonici)* and French *(Gallici)* workmen. The author of *B*, on the other hand, refers to German *(Teutonici)* workmen and "our men" *(nostrates)*.[17] In chapter 21 *A*'s detailed description of the approach to Rome and the sites of the encampments appears to be that of an eyewitness.[18] In the one complete manuscript of the *A* life, chapter 18 begins with a large historiated "A," so some scholars have argued that to this point the *A* text was composed by a Frenchman from Prémontré, and that chapters 18–23 were added by a German from Magdeburg. Perhaps the fourteenth-century scribe rightly sensed that at this point there was an important break in the narrative, but comparison of the style and vocabulary used in prior and subsequent parts nonetheless points clearly to singular authorship.[19]

The shorter, earlier *A* life, then, whose manuscript title is "The Life of Lord Norbert, Archbishop of Magdeburg,"[20] was apparently intended as a hagiography emphasizing its protagonist's virtues. The *B* life, on the other hand, is cast as a history of the order beginning with the life of the founder. Its second part, perhaps imagined as continuing with a description of the Premonstratensians' subsequent growth, was either never written or was lost. *B*'s title as found in the earliest manuscripts is "The Origins and Spread of the Premonstratensians."[21]

The *A* life is a concise text with a relatively high density of historical facts, despite a few chronological errors identifiable from other contemporary sources. *A* (and the *B* life repeats this error) dates Norbert's preaching against Tanchelm in 1125/26 after his journey to Rome, although local charters date this event to 1124.[22] Another error in *A*, again uncorrected in *B*, dates the revolt against Norbert in Magdeburg after the Council of Reims in 1131, while it actually took place in 1129.[23] The *B* life, more than twice as long as *A*, adds a prologue in which the author states the purpose of his work. Many have written, he says, about the life and deeds of Norbert, but none has done it well. Therefore, in order to put together a correct and orderly account of Norbert's life, the *B* author met with those who had been with the preacher-founder from the beginning and wrote down the events as they collectively remembered them.[24] The *B* hagiographer's mention of written sources may be rhetorical, intended to enhance his text's authority or perhaps further narratives of Norbert's life have indeed been lost. In any case, the only extant contemporary records of Norbert are the *A* life, Herman of Tournai's story of Norbert in his *Miracles*, and passages in the anonymous *Life of Godfrey of Cappenberg* appended to the *B* life. *B*'s prologue is found in twenty manuscripts and is stylistically compatible with the remainder of the *B* text.[25] Characteristic of *B*'s hagiographical posture is a lengthy, learned fifth chapter on why saints suffer.[26] Here, after Norbert's rejection at Xanten, the *B* author appears intent on portraying his protagonist as a martyr. The *B* text in fact uses the word "martyr" in describing the Magdeburgers' uprising against Norbert and subsequent events.[27] It likewise compares Norbert with Christ. When an attempt is made on Norbert's life on Holy Thursday, the intended victim tells those present not to be surprised because this was the very day on which Satan worked to betray Christ.[28] After another failed attempt on his life, Norbert remarks, "My hour has not yet come."[29] While the *A* life ends with the burial of Norbert, *B* adds a further chapter on confreres' three visions of Norbert after his death.[30] These visions later come to be represented in some iconography of Norbert[31] and seem to show that Norbert is in heaven. Such emphasis on Norbert's sanctity and Christlike traits is compatible with the *B* life's likely use as refectory reading; occasionally the author refers to the "listener."[32]

Attached to the end of the *B* hagiography are the "Additions of the Confreres of Cappenberg." These ten short chapters represent events from Norbert's life or remembrances of him. Some of their material is taken directly from the *Life of Godfrey of Cappenberg* also translated in this volume;[33] these passages' appearance in the *B* life of Norbert confirm the chronological priority of the hagiography of Godfrey. Finally, eight of the *B* manuscripts, including two from the twelfth century, add twenty-four lines of hexameter verse entitled "Blessed is Norbert."[34] The contents of the poem indicate that it was composed during the lifetime of Hugh of Fosses, therefore before 1164. Hugh is addressed in the second verse, and the present tense describes his promotion of the merits of Norbert, suggesting that the founder's successor as leader of the community at Prémontré was still alive at the poem's composition. The verses were thus likely written shortly after the B life but by an author other than that of A, B, or the Cappenberg addenda. The poem is addressed to Abbot Hugh and in praise of Norbert. Grauwen considers this poem to be a short summary of B.[35]

While the A hagiography thus remains of primary importance to historians as the oldest complete life of Norbert, the number of extant copies of B suggests its greater popularity among the medieval Premonstratensians. Some scholars have argued that the abbacy of Hugh of Fosses saw a strong movement toward centralization around Norbert's first foundation, and that the relatively wide availability of the B, probably originating from Prémontré, may have been supported by its status as the hagiography of the Norbert authorized by the first abbot there.[36]

The entire A life is translated here from the MGH edition. The following partial translation of B, based on the Acta Sanctorum edition, includes only those parts differing greatly from the A text: B's prologue, chapter 5 on the suffering of the saints, chapter 14 on Norbert's encouragement of Hugh, chapters 38 and 39 on wolves, chapter 54 on visions of Norbert after his death, the Cappenberg additions, and the poem "Blessed is Norbert."

VERSION A:
LIFE OF NORBERT,
ARCHBISHOP OF MAGDEBURG

Chapter 1

In the year of the Lord's incarnation 1115, when Pope Paschal[1] held the reins of the Catholic Church and Henry the Younger[2] was emperor, Norbert, of Frankish and Salic German stock, was a man well known in the town of Xanten. He was a cleric, a subdeacon, and was already middle aged. He was gifted by nature, handsome and well proportioned. He was eloquent, well educated, refined, and pleasant to all who knew him. His father was Herbert from the castle of Gennep near the forest of Ketela.[3] His mother was named Hedwig. His parents had decided that he would be a cleric since, because of a revelation received in a dream, they expected great things of him. While Norbert was at the imperial court and at the church in Cologne, he was held in great esteem. He enjoyed the affluence and the conveniences of temporal life to his heart's desire, living with no fear of God.

Now when Norbert had possessed all these things in abundance for a long time, it happened one day that he was hastening secretly to a place called Freden. He was dressed in silk, accompanied by a single servant. While he was on his way a dark cloud overtook him, lightning flashed, thunder roared, and—what was more inconvenient—there was no house for shelter nearby. As both he and his companion were unnerved, suddenly the terrifying sound and sight of a thunderbolt struck the ground, opening it to the depth of a man's height. From here steamed forth a putrid stench,

---

This translation is based on Wilmans's edition in MGH SS 12, 663–706.

fouling Norbert and his garments. Struck from his horse, he thought he heard a voice denouncing him. Returning to his senses and now repentant, he reflected on the words of the Psalmist: *Turn from evil and do good* (Ps 33:15; 36:27). Thus motivated, he returned home. There, caught up in the spirit of salvation through fear of the Lord, he put on a hair shirt beneath his outer garments intending to do good deeds and penance for his past life. He went to the monastery of Siegburg[4] and in that place enjoyed the holy company of Abbot Conon, under whose teaching and good guidance he advanced in fear and love of the Lord.

Chapter 2

When the Ember Days approached—days set aside by church custom for ordination to sacred orders—Norbert, still a subdeacon, presented himself to Frederick, the archbishop of Cologne. He requested that he be ordained a deacon and priest on the same day. Since this was forbidden by canon law, the archbishop asked him the reason for this sudden and unexpected desire. Norbert, after being pressed for an answer, fell at the archbishop's feet and with tearful groans expressed sorrow for his sins. Asking pardon, he protested to the archbishop his firm and unbending decision to change his life. The archbishop, after much deliberation and considering the outcome, although it was altogether contrary to reason and custom to ordain someone to diaconate and priesthood at the same time without knowing the reasons, nevertheless granted the dispensation and assented to his request.[5] When the time for the ordination was at hand and he was about to put on the sacred vestments, Norbert changed his secular garb and dressed himself in clothes that seemed more suited to religious life. Then, putting on the sacred vestments over these garments, he was ordained first a deacon and then a priest on the same day.

His desire fulfilled, Norbert returned to the abbey of Siegburg and there spent forty days in the service of God and the exercise of his priestly duties. He then returned to the church at Xanten. Taking his turn celebrating the sacred mysteries of the Mass, he preached a word of exhortation to the people who were present.[6] The following day in the chapter hall, without holding back, he admonished his fellow canons regarding salvation. Patiently and wisely he denounced, entreated, and reproached them. Because of his persistence, however, he became bothersome to some. He endured their derision and many insults, among them that a man of low station even spat in his face. After this insult Norbert restrained himself and kept quiet. He wiped his face and, remembering his sins, preferred to give in to his tears before God rather than retaliate.

At a later date, worn out with fasting and vigils, Norbert celebrated Mass in the crypt. After the Lord's body and blood had been consecrated, a large spider fell into the chalice. When the priest saw it he was shocked. Life and death hovered before his eyes. But lest the sacrifice suffer any loss he chose rather to undergo the danger and consumed whatever was in the chalice. When the service was finished, believing he was going to die, he remained before the altar and commended his awaited end to the Lord in prayer. Then he was disturbed by an itching in his nose. He scratched it, and soon the spider was expelled by a sudden fit of sneezing. Through this event both his faith in God and God's goodness to him became evident.

Chapter 3

Norbert made daily progress toward perfection. At one time he would visit the monastery of Siegburg, at another time Rolduc,[7] a church of regular clerics. But often he went to a hermit named Ludolph. This was a man of great holiness and temperance living the life of a cleric. This man was a lover of poverty and a fearless advocate of the truth. He was well known at that time, enduring untold threats and violence against himself and his brothers. Such harm was directed against them by perverse priests and clerics whom he used to admonish for their wickedness. Further, Norbert carefully inquired into the life and customs of anyone living under a rule—monks, hermits, and recluses—and by their example he made even greater spiritual progress.

Norbert then returned home and remained for two years in a suburb of Xanten at a church that was part of his property located on a mountain called Fürstenberg. He lived here as a solitary, spending his time in prayer, reading, and meditation. Through fasting and vigils he chastised his body and daily *offered a rich sacrifice* (Ps 65:15) on the sacred altar. He spent many nights without sleep. He said that the practice of night vigils was fruitful although it left the body tired and open to temptation. Thus while he kept watch one night he prayed for direction from God to help him in planning the future. Growing weak and drowsy, he supported his chin with his hand. Suddenly he heard the old enemy shouting insults: "Ha, ha! How do you expect to accomplish the many things you propose if you cannot persevere in the intention of one night?" To this the priest responded: "Who believes your threats since, from the beginning, on the testimony of Truth itself, you are a liar and the father of lies?" At this the evil spirit fled, confounded.

Chapter 4

While Norbert, amid these events and other such, was subject to the derision of many, he attended a council that Conon, legate of the apostolic see, was holding in the church at Fritzlar[8] with the archbishops, bishops, abbots, and many of the clergy and Christian people. Here, accusations were made against him by some envious people. They wanted to know why had he usurped the office of preacher and why was he wearing a religious habit although he was still living on his own and had not entered religious life, why was he wearing sheep or goat skins while still in the world. He responded: "If I am attacked concerning my preaching, it is written: *If someone turns a sinner from the error of his way, he will save his soul from death and cover a multitude of sins* (Jas 5:20). However, the power to preach is given to us at the reception of the priesthood when it is said: 'Receive the power to proclaim the Word of God.' If I am questioned about religious life, religion, pure and undefiled before God and the Father is this: *to visit widows and orphans in their tribulation and to keep oneself pure from this world* (Jas 1:27). Finally, if it is a question of clothing, the first shepherd of the church teaches us that acceptability before God is not found in precious garments. Hence we read that John the Baptist was dressed in camel hair[9] and St. Cecilia wore a hair shirt next to her skin. At the beginning of the world the creator made and gave to Adam not a purple garment but a tunic of skin."[10]

Having said this in his own defense, Norbert departed and, after the third year of his ordination, seeing that he did not benefit the men of that region either in word or in deed, decided to set out for another country. He gave and confirmed the above-mentioned church at Fürstenberg to the monastery of Siegburg, establishing that there would always be monks there serving God. He then resigned whatever benefices and income he held from the hands of Archbishop Frederick of Cologne. Moreover, he sold his houses and all else he possessed—either through inheritance from his father or in some other way by hereditary right—along with their furnishings, and gave the money to the poor. He kept for himself only his priestly vestments and a small amount of silver, about ten marks in value. Then with two companions he set out on his pilgrimage in the name of the Lord.

Chapter 5

When he had arrived at the Castle Huy located along the River Meuse, he distributed the above-mentioned silver to the poor. Leaving behind all his temporal possessions and clad only in a woolen tunic and mantle, barefoot and with his two companions, Norbert set out for St. Gilles[11] through the bitter winter. There he found Pope Gelasius,[12] successor to Pope Paschal. He asked and received pardon for the canonical offense committed when he received the two sacred orders at the same time. When the pope saw that Norbert was a prudent man and filled with zeal for God, he tried to keep him in his entourage, but Norbert humbly explained his plans to the pope and received permission to leave. He also received permission to preach anywhere, confirmed by the pope in writing.[13]

After receiving the apostolic mandate to preach and leaving St. Gilles, he came to Orléans, treading barefoot through the cold ice with deep snow up to his knees. Here he added to his company a subdeacon. Now with three companions he came to Valenciennes on Saturday before Palm Sunday. The next day he preached to the people, who received him favorably. But when asked to stay there and rest, Norbert was detained against his will because his companions were suddenly seized by illness and he had to take care of them. Soon, however, within the octave of Easter, they fell asleep in the Lord in that same city. The two laymen were buried in a suburb of Valenciennes in the church of St. Peter near the market on the left toward the west; the subdeacon who had become a monk was buried in the church of the blessed Mary located in the same town.

Chapter 6

On the Wednesday before Holy Thursday[14] Burchard,[15] the bishop of Cambrai and an honorable man, was passing through Valenciennes. Norbert, who had known him previously, went to see him. When he arrived at the gate of the house where the bishop was staying, a cleric admitted him to a room and after some conversation the bishop recognized Norbert. The bishop, absolutely amazed and dumbfounded, looking at Norbert standing there with bare, frozen feet and dressed in rough clothing, fell upon his neck with a gasp, and cried out, "Oh, Norbert, who would ever have believed or even thought this of you?" The cleric who had admitted Norbert wondered about the bishop's affection for him and asked the reason. The bishop answered: "This man whom you see was brought up with me in the court of the king. He was a man noble and abounding in delights to such a degree that he refused my bishopric when it was offered to him." Hearing this the cleric filled up with tears both because he saw his master weeping, but also because he longed for a similar way of life. Secretly he investigated where Norbert would be continuing his journey.

Norbert was suddenly seized by a serious illness while still in the city. The bishop kindly tended his illness, daily arranging visits to the sick man by the members of his court. The aforementioned cleric was among those visitors, and when Norbert grew stronger he approached him and promised to accompany him in his profession and journey. Norbert thanked God, thinking that the man was going to set out with him. But when the cleric stated that he first wanted to set his affairs in order, Norbert was troubled at his words and said only: "Ah, brother, if this is of God, it will not be undone."[16] The cleric left, promising to return and, disposing of his possessions, a little later did return to follow the man of God thereafter. The name of that cleric was Hugh.[17]

With Hugh's company, Norbert went with him about the castles, villages, and towns preaching and reconciling those at odds with one another and reducing old hatreds and wars to peace. He sought nothing from anyone, but if anything was offered he distributed it to the poor and lepers. He trusted in the grace of God that he would have the necessities of life. Because he considered himself a stranger and guest on the earth,[18] no trace of ambition could touch him; his entire hope was on heaven. He could not understand that someone could despise everything for Christ and yet use his ability to work for contemptible and abject rewards.

Norbert inspired such love and admiration by his presence that wherever he went, accompanied by his one companion, as he was drawing near the villages and towns, shepherds would leave their flocks and go running before him to announce his arrival to the people. People came to him in droves and during Mass heard words of exhortation from him about doing penance or about the hope of eternal salvation promised to everyone who calls on the Lord's name. They took pleasure in his very presence and considered themselves fortunate if they could receive him into their homes. People were amazed at this new style of life, namely, to live on earth and seek nothing from the earth. According to the gospel mandate Norbert carried with him neither purse nor sandals nor two tunics,[19] and was content with only a few books and vestments for Mass. His customary drink was water except when he was the guest of religious persons. Then he followed their practice for a time.

Frequently, when Norbert was asked to give a word of exhortation, among those who were eager to learn were others who would test him and mock him in order to impede his sermon. But in his simplicity, ignoring their abuse, he never ceased to perform the work of God eagerly. He practiced fasting and vigils, was diligent in work, pleasing in word, pleasant to see, kind toward simple people, stern against the enemies of the church—so much so that he gained the favor of all the people.

132

Chapter 7

One day when Norbert was passing through the village of Fosses, many clergy and laity gathered who admired his unusual way of life, especially since they knew his companion. Understanding that he was a minister of peace and concord, they eagerly requested that he remain with them a while, explaining that there was a feud of mortal hatred in their region that could be settled neither by nobleman nor churchman. Because of this nearly sixty men had been killed. Now, by the grace of God, even while these people were making their request, a man came along whose brother had been killed that very week due to this hatred. When they saw him, they said, "Look, here's one of those about whom we've been speaking." Calling the man over, Norbert embraced him saying: "My dear man, I am a stranger just passing through but I ask a favor of you. Grant pardon to those who killed your brother and receive your reward from God." Immediately tears came to the man's eyes. Not only did he grant pardon but submitted himself to the man of God, giving him the opportunity to reconcile other enemies and bring about peace completely.

On the following Saturday, when folks on both sides of the dispute assembled at the town of Moustier, many other people came, partly to see the man of God and partly to be present for the hoped-for reconciliation. Norbert remained praying in his room with the door closed until almost the third hour. When Norbert's companion politely informed him that the people were becoming restless, he responded that God must be served not according to the will of men but according to the will of God. But shortly after he came out after first devoutly celebrating the Mass of the blessed Virgin Mary and then a Mass for those who had died due to the feud. Afterward he preached to those who had at first drifted away but had regathered. He began: "Brothers, when our Lord Jesus Christ sent his disciples out to preach, among other things he gave them the command that whatever house they entered they should first say: *Peace be to this house* (Luke 10:5). And if a son of peace were there, their peace would rest on him.[20] Now we, who have become imitators of Christ's disciples not by our own merits but through the superabundant grace of God, announce that same peace to you.

133

Do not let your unbelieving minds disregard this peace, because it touches on everlasting peace. You are not unaware of why we have gathered. To achieve such peace is not mine nor of my doing, since I am a stranger and traveler,[21] but it is of the will and power of God. It is for you, however, to comply with his will with complete and total affection." To this the people responded with one voice: "Let the Lord, through you, command whatever is pleasing to him. We should not contradict whatever the Lord wants us to do." What more is to be said? Both sides of the dispute went out into the courtyard and, with relics placed in the space between them, they abjured their discord and made peace, confirming it by oath.

Chapter 8

Very early the next day Norbert left this place and set out for another village called Gembloux, not far distant, to deliver a sermon to the people there. He was very well received because the people heard that he was a bearer of the word of God and a bringer of desired peace. In this region also two princes had almost reduced everything to a wasteland with their incessant fighting, plundering, and burning. When the man of God heard this, moved by the cry of the people and taking pity on their destitution, he went to these leaders, first to the one, then to the other. He addressed the first man in these words: "You are great and powerful and you should be aware that your power has been granted you by God.[22] Thus you should listen to me his servant not out of respect for me but out of respect for him. I have been sent to you for your benefit and that of many. Therefore, listen to a poor traveler; receive the commands the Lord your God has passed on to you so that he may receive you. Forgive the one who has offended you so that you may be forgiven and thus the consolation of the poor and needy might bring about the remission of your sins." After hearing this, the prince, taking into consideration the man's poor clothing, his modest expression, and the quality of his speech, became submissive and said: "As you wish. It doesn't make sense to contradict this request of yours."

Accomplishing what he desired with this man, he went to the other, whose heart was hardened. From the grimness of his face and the harshness of his words Norbert knew that this was not a son of peace.[23] Refraining from his planned speech, he said to the brother who was with him: "The man is insane, but he will soon fall and be captured and trampled down by his enemies." Norbert said this and departed. His prediction was fulfilled within the week, for the prince was captured and put in prison.

Next Norbert came to the nearby village of Couroy and, because his reputation had spread in all directions, people from that vicinity came out to him. After the celebration of Mass he spoke about peace and concord, as was his custom. He began in humble exhortation to recall some who were at odds with one another due to their old quarrels. In spite of the request, one of them got up, unwilling to make peace, and ran outside. He jumped on his horse, attempting to flee, but the horse would not move, although he spurred it hard. At this the crowd gathered, some out of curiosity, some to mock, some weeping. The man himself, shaken, returned to the church and, prostrate, asked pardon. He agreed to the condition of peace to which he had been previously urged and received absolution for having offended the man of God.

In that same year the blessed Pope Gelasius, from whom Norbert had received permission to preach, departed this world. He was succeeded by Callixtus,[24] bishop of Vienne, a man of pious and holy life and worthy of memory. He was unanimously elected at Cluny and was elevated to the highest honor, dignity, and power in the see of the universal church. The aforementioned Gelasius, along with the more well-advised cardinals, had traveled in order to visit Holy Mother Church in her members. He had heard much about the church while presiding as its head—he had been chancellor for many years during the reign of Pope Paschal and others—and whatever went on in the world could not be concealed from him. Therefore Callixtus, the successor of Gelasius, held a council at Reims[25] where he both confirmed his own election and strengthened the state of the church. He approved what was right and corrected what was wrong and authorized these corrections by the power of Rome.

Chapter 9

When Norbert heard that the dignity of the apostolic see had been passed on to another, he came to this council barefoot in the fall of the year. He was joyfully received by the bishops and abbots who had gathered there. These asked him to relax somewhat the harshness of the penance he had undertaken, but he refused to give in. While meeting with the pope regarding his status, he requested that the letter of apostolic authority he had received from his predecessor Gelasius, as mentioned above, be renewed. This was granted. The pope then asked Bishop Bartholomew of Laon to look after him. There were in that diocese and even in that city some close relatives on Norbert's mother's side who were concerned about him. Due to their influence, the bishop was advised to extend a gentle hand to him for a time even though it was unwanted.

When the council was finished, the man of God, Norbert, decided to spend the winter at Laon, for he was alone and left without the comfort of companions. Until now Hugh had been his companion around his home territory, that is, around Fosses. Hugh had not yet changed his secular garb for religious dress but traveled with Norbert through places he knew to put his affairs in order. After the council Hugh left his companion and master, Norbert, going back to Cambrai with his bishop, Burchard; he did not return for two years.

At that time there flourished at Laon the school of Master Anselm and his brother Ralph. The man of God decided to attend their lectures on the psalm *Beati immaculati* (Ps 118). Drogo, a religious man and at the time prior of the church of blessed Nicasius at Reims,[26] heard about this. Norbert and he had been acquaintances and companions in school.[27] Drogo angrily wrote to him: "What is this I hear about you? You were brought up and educated in the school of the Holy Spirit, who is not slow in teaching; do you now leave that school and attend a secular school? Divine wisdom espoused you; now worldly philosophy has loved and allured you. Perhaps you say: 'Through the one to the other; I intend to reach wisdom through knowledge.' To which I say: 'The structure of your building was not begun in such a way that Rachel would follow Leah.[28] For the Holy Spirit, who made a harpist and, without the help of a grammar teacher, suddenly made a psalmist out of a sheepherder,[29] has taken you from the emptiness of the world and suddenly made you an evangelist.' Therefore, my dear friend, hear me as your prophet and know that if you wish to hold to both, without a doubt you will lose both. It is not so bad or even human for a man to sin, but to act against the Holy Spirit is serious."[30] What more? A word to the wise is sufficient. Norbert immediately withdrew, coming to his senses and turning to him about whom the Lord promises *He will teach you all truth* (John 16:13).

Not long after this the pope came to Laon. The bishop, taking counsel with the pope on how to keep Norbert there, urged the canons of the church of St. Martin in the outskirts of Laon to elect Norbert as their abbot. The canons petitioned both the bishop and the pope for Norbert. When asked and forced to respond Norbert answered the pope humbly: "Reverend father, do you not recall the duty and the labor of preaching the word of God to which I have been appointed twice now, both by your predecessor of happy memory and also by you? But lest I give the impression that I refuse to submit to authority, I assent to your wish, except, of course, for my central intention. I am in no way able to alter this calling without grave detriment to my soul. It is this: not to seek what belongs to another; in no way to demand back through secular justice or legal process what has been stolen; not to entangle anyone in the bonds of anathema for any injuries or loss suffered. To sum up briefly, I have chosen to live simply the evangelical and apostolic life rightly understood. Nevertheless, if the canons living in this church are not afraid to hold to this form of life, I do not refuse the burden."

When this evangelical institution was explained to the canons of St. Martin, that is, how they were to be imitators of Christ,[31] how they would have to despise the world and be voluntarily poor, how they would have to bear up under reproach and insult and derision and suffer hunger, thirst, nakedness, and other things of this sort, how they would have to be obedient to the precepts and rules of the holy fathers, they were immediately terrified by his words and appearance and said: "We do not want this man over us[32] because neither our custom nor that of our predecessors has known such a master. What is ours would be taken away and not returned, we would plead our case and not benefit, we would pass sentence but not be feared. Let us live as we are. God wants to chastise, not kill."[33] Thus Norbert obeyed and, since he was released from his obedience, did not disobey.

Meanwhile the bishop was trying to nourish his enfeebled guest, thin from cold and fasting, but the host was daily nourished by his visitor through the spiritual sharing of the honey-sweet word of God. For this reason Bartholomew grew very fond of Norbert and urged him with all sorts of arguments to remain in his diocese. Daily he took him around and showed him places in the hope that there might be a church he liked, or some lonely place, some wilderness, some cultivated or uncultivated spot on which to build or remain. Finally, overcome by the bishop's pleas and those of many others, both religious and noble, Norbert chose an extremely deserted and lonely place called Prémontré[34] from of old by its inhabitants. Here he pledged to remain if God would allow him to gather companions.

When winter had passed, Norbert went forth to preach. He came to Cambrai, where he attracted a young disciple by the name of Evermode,[35] a man after his own heart. Norbert's spirit so rested in him that he confided to Evermode where he wanted to be buried after he died and ordered that his new companion should never leave him without returning. After him Norbert attracted other disciples who were to be the root and foundation of a future multitude who followed this man of God.

But the snares of the old enemy were not lacking to the beginnings of this holy profession. Observing in each one his individual behavior—in one, namely, the love of contemplation, in another the desire for wisdom, in still another the intention to fast—Satan tried to impede each one. Thus it happened one night that the old adversary came to a certain man at Matins as he stood and contemplated the glorious and ineffable Trinity and said: "How happy you are, how praiseworthy in your intention. You have begun well and think you will persevere under affliction. Therefore you deserve to see the holy Trinity to which you aspire with all your heart." Saying this he appeared with three heads claiming to be the Trinity. The man was frightened, but hesitated a moment, for out of this vision came a foul odor. The man said: "O wretched, unfortunate, and most pitied of all creatures! You who were the image of God's likeness[36] and through pride lost the knowledge of this truth, how do you presume not only that you know the Trinity, but that you are the Trinity? You did not even have the strength to want to know yourself. Depart, and do not disturb me further, because I am not obedient to your deceits."

Satan departed immediately, only to return to this man later. The confrere was indeed prompt to obey, devout in prayer, assiduous in fasting, so much so that he fasted the whole year both summer and winter and no one could persuade him to take a second meal during the day except on Sundays, and even then food that was raw and uncooked. But while everyone was amazed at him, and his great abstinence and mortification in praise of God was spoken of everywhere, Satan was present again, secretly setting snares to destroy the new soldier. He was a youth, and Satan found it an insult that he had already resisted him. Therefore on Ash Wednesday, when the Lenten fast is imposed on all the faithful, such hunger and voracious gluttony seized the man that he said he could not fast and undoubtedly would die if he were forced to abstain from milk and cheese. When he was told, "It is not permitted anyone, even laypeople, to eat twice; not even little children are permitted milk or cheese," he answered with grim face and wolfish fury, "Does God want a man to die by withdrawing from him at the hour of his need to eat what he created for his use?" Finally, the confreres allowed him to eat Lenten food twice, and as much as he wished, if only he would abstain from milk and cheese.

When Lent was over Norbert returned to his confreres. But as he approached he shuddered and felt a strong wind surround him. He told those with him that evil was present. When he heard what had happened, with great sadness he ordered the man to be brought to him. When the man was brought in he was scarcely able to stand, he was so fat. And he was so filled with the spirit of gluttony that he could only cast a grim look at his master, whom he previously had loved with a special affection. The man of God, however, seeing that this was not a human infirmity but something diabolical that had overcome him, forbade that any food at all be given to him. After the confrere had fasted for some days, he considered it a delight when a quarter part of rough bread and a cup of water were given to him. And thus with the help of God he was restored to his former way of life.

Chapter 10

Sometime later Norbert set out to restore peace to some folk who were at odds with one another. Taking along Hugh, his first companion, who had been absent for some time, he arrived with him at Nivelles. There were some in this city who formerly had come to Norbert for the sake of conversion and later went away unable to bear the austerity of his way of life and rule. To insult him they did not come to see him or listen to his preaching. Moreover, they tried to turn the people away from him. But their malice was very quickly brought to naught. By the providence of God one of the citizens, a man whose daughter had been possessed a whole year by a devil, brought her with weeping and sighing to the man of God to be cured. Taking pity on the father's sorrow, the servant of God, vested in alb and stole, read an exorcism over the girl, who was then twelve years old. When he was reading the gospel over her head, the demon mockingly responded: "I have frequently heard tunes of this sort. Neither for you nor for all of these people will I leave this house. For whom should I depart? The pillars of the church have collapsed." But when the priest increased the exorcisms, the demon again responded: "You accomplish nothing, because you have not yet commanded me through the glittering blood of the martyrs." And soon the demon, flaunting his knowledge, recited the Canticle of Canticles from beginning to end through the mouth of the girl. Then, repeating word for word, he translated the same Canticle of Canticles into French. Once again he proclaimed the whole thing word for word in German through the mouth of the girl who, while she was well, knew nothing but the psalter.

However, at the insistence of the priest that he depart from the creature of God, the demon said, "If you cast me out, permit me to enter a monk who is here present." He named the man. But Norbert exclaimed to the people: "Listen to the evil of this demon who, in order to shame a servant of God, seeks to trouble him as though he were a sinner and worthy of this punishment. But do not be scandalized because such is his wickedness that he wishes to revile all good people and as much as possible make them disreputable." Having said this Norbert pressed on more intently with what he had begun. Then the demon said: "What are you doing? I will not leave today either for you or for any other. But if you hear me cry out, many of my forces, the forces of darkness, will come to battle. Ha ha! To battle! Ha ha! Now I will bring these arches and vaults down on you." At these words the people scattered, but the priest remained calm. Then the girl grabbed his stole in order to choke Norbert. When those present wanted to restrain her hands, he said: "No! Let her. If she has received the power from God, let her do what she can." When she heard this, she released him on her own.

Now since a good part of the day was gone, Father Norbert thought that the girl should be placed in holy water. This was done. And because she was a charming girl with blond hair, the priest, fearing that the devil would use her hair to keep her in his power, ordered her hair to be cut off. The demon, agitated by this outrage, attacked the priest with curses and said: "Pilgrim from France, pilgrim from France, what have I done to you? Why don't you allow me to rest? Every evil, every mishap, and every misfortune will come upon you because you vex me without cause." It was now evening. And Father Norbert, seeing that the demon had not left, was somewhat saddened. He ordered the girl returned to her father and brought to Mass the next day. He began to remove his alb and other Mass vestments. When the demon saw this, he shouted in insult: "Ha ha ha! Now you're doing well and you have not yet done to me the work that God has approved. You've spent the whole day in vain." But Father Norbert, returning to his lodging, decided not to eat until the girl was healed, and thus he passed that day and night without food.

When the next day dawned, the priest of God prepared to celebrate Mass. The girl was brought, and a great crowd of people gathered, coming to await the outcome. Norbert instructed two of the confreres to hold the girl close to the altar. After the Mass had begun and the gospel was being read over her head, the demon responded mockingly that he had frequently heard tunes of this sort. Soon, within the action of the Mass, the priest elevated the host; the demon exclaimed: "Look, look, behold he holds his little God in his hands." Demons confess what heretics deny. But then the priest of God shuddered and, taking on the spirit of truth in his very speech, began more intently to act against the demon. But the latter, being constrained, shouted out, "Behold I'm burning, I am burning, behold I am dying, I am dying!" And again, "I want to leave, I want to leave, let me go!" And while the confreres were firmly holding the girl, the unclean spirit fled, leaving behind the repulsive traces of very foul-smelling urine. He abandoned the vessel he had possessed. The girl, freed from her tormentor, collapsed and was carried in a faint to the home of her father. A little later, after taking food, she appeared completely sound, in control of herself, and perfectly healed. All this took place publicly, and the people witnessed it. Together they proclaimed the praise of God and acknowledged Norbert a man according to the true model of the apostles, in contrast to those who had previously criticized him.

Chapter 11[37]

Once Norbert was staying at Laon, intending to spend the winter with some of his powerful relatives whom he had met there, to take instruction in French, which he did not know. A pious woman from the town of Soissons heard of the reputation of the man of God. Wishing to speak with him, she secretly came to Laon on the pretext of visiting the shrines of the saints. After she had heard him preach the word of God, she complained to him tearfully that she and her husband had for a long time remained childless. She preferred, if it could be done, to be separated from her husband rather than be bound by legal or conjugal bond without the offspring for whom they had hoped. The priest said to her: "It shall not be so, but very soon you will have a son. You shall not keep him as an heir for the world but you will soon dedicate your child to the Lord. After him you will bear several others with whom you will later take yourself and your possessions to the cloister to serve God." The women believed Norbert and was not disappointed. She bore a son. She called him Nicholas because she had obtained her promise around the feast of St. Nicholas. *The child grew and was weaned* (Gen 21:8). Meanwhile a council was held in which a decree was promulgated that the Masses of priests who had wives should not be attended. Hence occasion for heresies arose to such a degree that many believed and claimed that married priests did not confect the body of the Lord on the altar.

One day this same lady, whose name was Helwig, accompanied by her sister, went around to the shrines of the saints to pray. The boy, now in his fifth year, was with her. The three entered a church, not to hear Mass, but just to pray. A married priest was standing at the altar celebrating holy Mass. O inestimable and ineffable grace of God's goodness! While the mother was praying with tears streaming down her face, the eyes of her child lay open to the divine mysteries. The boy was standing between his mother and aunt and looking at the priest. Although he could as yet not speak well, he cried out clearly, saying, "Mother, mother, look at the boy, more beautiful than the sun, whom the priest at the altar is holding, adoring as God." The mother rose from her prayer and, wondering what it was, asked the child, "Son, is that the boy hanging on the cross whom you see?" She thought he was looking at the wood of the cross. "Not at all," he said. "The priest was holding in his hands a boy of wondrous beauty whom he is now covering, wrapping him in a cloth." The mother and her sister looked, and they saw the priest covering with a corporal the chalice with the Lord's body. A threefold lesson is derived from this miracle: the uncertainty of the incredulous is removed; the faith of the pious is strengthened; the faithful, for whom this event took place, are edified by this divine revelation. From that day until the day of his death the boy Nicholas always suffered from weak eyesight. Nevertheless, he lived until the promise of Norbert, the man of God, was fulfilled. His father and mother, with property and offspring and a great number of relatives, entered the cloister and sent him as a deacon to the Lord.

Chapter 12

Father Norbert came then to Cologne and was welcomed with joy by the people who flocked to hear him preach and confess to him. They knew him previously as a youth, and now they saw him wondrously changed. Many, on hearing his words, followed him then and there, becoming imitators of the poverty of Christ.

At that time Norbert wanted to build a church in which he could receive those he brought together. For this reason he petitioned Archbishop Frederick and other prominent men to see if he could take some holy relics for patron saints. From ancient times the holy city of Cologne abounded in such relics. The bishop gave his consent; the clergy and people agreed, considering his request to be reasonable. Norbert imposed a fast on the confreres who were with him and commended this quest to God in the hope that he would let him find a venerable patron saint. That night there was revealed to one of these confreres in a vision a virgin, one of the eleven thousand virgins. The name of the virgin and the place of the mausoleum in which she was buried were also revealed. The next day, as pointed out in the vision, the body was sought and found complete in the place indicated. This body was then taken up with hymns of thanks and praise. Then two reliquaries were filled with the relics of the other virgins, the holy martyrs of the Theban Legion, the holy Moors, as well as the two Ewalds.

On the following day Norbert asked the provost and the canons of St. Gereon for relics. They gave him permission to look for them in their church and take them along with him. Norbert rejoiced and carefully commended this undertaking to God through the entire night, as he was accustomed to do. When morning came he ordered them to dig in the middle of the monastery, where there was no indication of a tomb. There a complete body without a head was found. The body had been buried with honor and great care. A costly gravestone was placed at the level of the ground, not deep, but covered by the thin marble of the pavement. The body was wrapped in green cloth damaged by age. A large cross of gold embroidery rested on his chest over his robe. The body was dressed like a soldier with leggings and spurs. The head was cut off from the upper lip. A sod of grass stained by blood lay between the body and the bottom of the sarcophagus.

When the canons and the vast number of people who had gathered saw this, they said: "This is our master and venerable patron, St. Gereon, who has been sought for many years both by us and our predecessors but could not be found because of our sins." Shouting out joyfully in a loud voice they gave thanks to God and extolled to God this worthy man, Norbert, through whom so great and so long desired a treasure deserved to be found. No one should doubt that it was St. Gereon. The evidence of his identity lay in the fact that the narrative of his death and martyrdom records that part and not all of his head was cut off. It was known that the head had been thrown by the pagans into a well, which was between the sanctuary and the nave of the church. Over the mouth of the well an altar was dedicated in his honor, but the canons did not know where the rest of the body was. Therefore the holy body was properly exhumed. Part was given to the man of God, but the rest was solemnly reinterred by the clergy and people.

Not long after, taking up the relics and gathering both lay and clerical confreres whom he had begotten for God through his preaching,[38] Norbert set out on his return trip. Everywhere congregations welcomed him honorably in their churches. A certain noblewoman by the name of Ermesind, the countess of Namur, hearing that Norbert was passing through, quickly hastened to meet him and eagerly requested that he accept a church in the village of Floreffe and there install members of his religious community. For some time she had desired to establish such a community in that church for the salvation of her own soul and those of her forebears. Norbert considered the loving devotion of the woman and undertook what she requested.

Leaving behind one of the two reliquaries, Norbert hurried on to Prémontré because Christmas was close at hand. He had with him about thirty novices, both clerics and laymen. Gathering these together with others whom he had earlier assembled, morning and evening he preached the saving word, encouraging them with comforting speech not to fall away from their good intention and the voluntary poverty they had undertaken. Whatever Norbert taught them he demonstrated through his own works *as an eagle calls its young to flight* (Deut 32:11). His exhortations were not about the earth, nor did they hold out anything earthly, but, as a dove after taking wing, he flew to rest—for the most part caught up in ecstasy—and made his hearers take flight after the example of the prophet saying: I shall take on *wings as a dove and I shall fly and I shall rest* (Ps 54:7).

Some of those who followed Norbert believed that what they heard from him was sufficient for salvation and therefore they needed neither a rule nor structure of life. But Norbert, who was prudent and circumspect—lest his holy institute falter[39] in the future and the foundation he intended to place on solid rock[40] totter—

advised them that without a structure of life and without a rule and without the instructions of the fathers, the apostolic and evangelical precepts could not be completely observed. The confreres, like sheep following their shepherd in simplicity, promised to obey him in all the things he proposed. Indeed, many religious men, both bishops and abbots, had advised him in various ways, one suggesting the eremitic life, another that of the anchorite, still another that he take up the way of life of the Cistercians. But Norbert, whose work and plans depended on heaven, entrusted his foundation neither to himself nor to others but rather to him who is the beginning of all things. He pondered these many things in his heart but finally, lest he seem to betray the canonical profession to which he and those who wished to live with him had been dedicated since their youth, Norbert ordered that the rule be accepted which the blessed Augustine had established for his followers. He now hoped to live the apostolic life he had undertaken by his preaching. He had heard that this way of life was ordained and renewed after the apostles by this same blessed Augustine.[41] By the profession of this rule then, on Christmas Day at Prémontré, one by one his followers voluntarily enrolled themselves into that city of blessed eternity.

Afterward, individuals gave their own explanations and interpretations of this rule, and their opinions were diverse. Because Norbert's writings and the works of other religious did not seem to agree, this led some to fear, some to doubt, others to be indifferent, since the foundation was not yet well rooted. "Why are you surprised?" said the man of God, or "Why are you hesitant, *since all the ways of the Lord are mercy and truth* (Ps 24:10)? Although diverse, are these ways contrary to one another? If the practice or the institution is changed, ought the bond of charity to be changed, which is love? Indeed the rule says: 'Let God be loved first, then neighbor.'[42] The institute alone does not bring about the reign of God, but rather truth and the observance of the commands of God. Therefore—given that this rule clearly binds in regard to love, work, abstinence from food, clothing, silence, obedience, regarding one another with respect, and honoring one's father—what is there that would be of further use for any religious in order to obtain salvation? But if there should arise any contention regarding color or thickness or thinness of clothing, let those who have the power to decide in this regard make a decision. Let them show from the rule, from the institution of the gospel and apostles, where whiteness and blackness or thinness or thickness is described and let the matter be settled. One thing is certain, however; the angels who were the witnesses of the resurrection are said to have appeared in white,[43] and by the authority and practice of the church, penitents wear wool. Likewise, in the Old Testament, it was customary to go out among the people in woolen garments but, in the sanctuary, by precept, linen garments were in use.[44] After the example of the angels it seems that white should be worn, and as a sign of penance woolen garments should be worn next to the skin. But in the sanctuary of God and during the divine services linen should be worn."

Those who had gathered around Norbert from the beginning gave scarcely any care or concern for corporal things. Rather, they focused all their effort on spiritual things, on following the Sacred Scriptures and Christ as their leader. Father Norbert encouraged and assured them that those who wished to remain with him could never go wrong if they put into practice the profession they made according to the gospels, the words of the apostles, and the Rule of St. Augustine. Hence they were not ashamed of the poverty of their clothing, nor did they offer any difficulty in obedience; they kept perpetual silence in every place and at all times. When convicted of excesses, they fell to the ground to humble themselves. They avoided harsh glances and unkind words even toward delinquents. Norbert wanted his confreres to mortify the body with fasting and to restrain the spirit in humility. As mentioned before, he wanted them to use woolen undergarments, and woolen garments for work; he wanted them always to wear linen breeches,[45] although he himself wore rough haircloth. But in the sanctuary and wherever the Blessed Sacrament was to be handled or celebrated, he wanted them to use linen for the sake of cleanliness and respect. This last he decreed to be done at all times.

Frequently he recommended the observance of three things, namely, cleanliness about the altar and the divine mysteries, correction of excesses and negligences in the chapter and elsewhere, hospitality and care of the poor. At the altar he urged faith and love of God; in the cleansing of one's conscience, care of oneself; in the reception of guests and the poor, love of neighbor. Indeed, Norbert never ceased to insist that no house could ever suffer want beyond what it could bear if it carefully tended to these three things.

One day Norbert was returning from Reims with some of his companions and two novices whom he had attracted by his preaching of the divine word. As they were walking along the road in silence reflecting on God, a voice from the clouds sounded in their ears: "This is the community of Brother Norbert." To this another voice on the side responded: "One of these novices is not of the community." Norbert, as well as the others, heard this. They considered the matter in silence, suspecting nothing evil; nevertheless, they were in doubt about what ought to be done. But Father Norbert, who was the most concerned, knew that it was not without purpose that God allowed these voices to be heard and carefully sought in prayer the cause of this event. Meanwhile, he considered the deeds and actions of those about whom the voices had been heard. When he realized that one of them was less devout in his confession, frivolous in his speech, restless in his behavior, inconstant in his practices, tepid in prayer, neglectful in obedience—he was an Englishman—Norbert said: "What is it, brother, that you bear in your heart? Reveal what lies hidden. If you seek God, no creature is hidden from him, because as the apostle says, *everything is uncovered and open to his eyes* (Heb 4:13). We seek the truth, and to the extent that it is granted to human frailty, we strive to walk in the truth. There is no agreement of truth with falsehood, nor any participation of the faithful with the unfaithful."[46] The man shook his head and answered flippantly: "Do you think, good Father, that I want to steal something from you? You are poor, but *to everyone who has, it will be given and in abundance. But from him who does not have even what he seems to have will be taken away from him* (Matt 13:12)." He said this and fulfilled his words by his action. At that time it happened that a man who had come to conversion had brought a little money along with what little he had. The money, all they had at the time, lay tucked behind the altar of the poor oratory. One night the Englishman, seeing that the hour was suitable for him, fled with the money. Thus in his dishonesty he increased the poverty of the poor of Christ, who suspected nothing evil. As a result there was not enough left for them to procure supplies for a day.

After many confreres had joined Father Norbert, a permanent place of residence had to be prepared. The location was very rough and altogether uncultivated, set among brush and swamps and other inconveniences. There was no place suitable at hand for living except the little chapel and the orchard next to it, as well as a small pond fed as it is today with water coming from the mountains when it rains and from the moisture of the swamps. While the man of God remained there with his companions in prayer, awaiting the consolation of God, one of them received a clear and unmistakable revelation. He reported this vision to the man of God, namely, that he had seen in a section of the property our Lord Jesus Christ on a cross, and above him seven rays of the sun shone with a marvelous brightness. A great multitude of pilgrims with their satchels and staffs hastened from the four corners of the earth, and after adoring their redeemer on bended knee and kissing his feet, they returned home. When he heard this the man of God gave thanks to the Lord.

Later Norbert called Bartholomew, the bishop of Laon, to come to consecrate the foundation they had dug and the stones, the first elements of the church. Among those present was Thomas, Lord of Coucy, who feared and respected Norbert for God's sake. Also present were Thomas's son Engelrand, still a boy, as well as many nobles, clergy, and laity, and a large multitude of people who wondered and spoke among themselves saying: "Who do you think this man is or of what faith that he does not use reason? Do you think this work is sound, though it is placed in such a wilderness and its foundation is not laid on rock or solid ground but in a swamp?" The marsh was such that it could scarcely be made solid even when a mass of rocks was thrown in. Nevertheless, this foundation ought not totter or be overturned because a foundation established by the heavenly Father will not be uprooted.[47]

Some of the stonemasons were German, some French. They vied with one another as they hastened on with the work, the Germans on one side of the church and the French on the other. The building grew very quickly and was completed in nine months, consecrated by Bishop Bartholomew. But because sad events are usually mixed with happy ones and the adverse with the favorable, a misfortune occurred on the very day of consecration. When the great crowd gathered for the feast day was pressing forward for the offertory into the area surrounding the altar, as was customary, the main altar moved and the stone broke. The consecration was voided, according to law, and all the work brought to nothing. Norbert was startled and saddened, fearing more the scandal of the weak than lacking trust in God's ever-purposeful work. Nevertheless, he recouped his strength in the Lord of consolation. With the bishop he secretly arranged a day for the rededication of the church, the octave day of St. Martin.[48] And so it happened. For this reason, as long as he lived, Norbert claimed that another dedication would have to be carried out at a future time.

Chapter 13

Afterward, Norbert went out to preach as he was accustomed. During his absence the ancient enemy laid many snares for the confreres who remained at Prémontré. To some of the confreres Satan presented himself in broad daylight along with his companions as an armed band, in the guise of those whom these brothers had left behind in the world as mortal enemies. But the confreres were terrified by the crash of arms and neighing of horses and fought back in whatever manner they could. Taking up clubs and rocks they fled; they also hastened to resist with their arms wrapped in their tunics or whatever was at hand. The fight was so bitter and so strange that they thought they were throwing weapons and that missiles were being thrown at them, that they struck and were struck, were wounding and were wounded, were killing and were killed. When many other confreres came running toward them, reproving them for acting like madmen, they said, "Don't you see that we are oppressed by our enemy and, almost cut to pieces, that we are dying, to our everlasting shame?" Then the confreres realized that these men had been deceived by an attack of demons. They sprinkled holy water, made the sign of the cross and, as the crowd of malignant spirits took flight, the others pursued them, running swiftly as though the enemy were conquered and put to flight. The confreres shouted after them loudly: "Hey, hey! Come back and resist, otherwise you will die a most shameful death if you ever dare to approach again." Later some of these confreres, coming to their

senses and realizing that they had been deceived, thereafter perse-
vered courageously and were victorious. Others, unable to bear the
ignominy of such derision, went away stung by the demon's tail.

The demon advanced against the same confreres with another
type of deceit. He filled certain of those individuals who had been
instruments of his will with such fraud that those who previously
could scarcely read anything in a book now were saying marvelous
things regarding books and prophesying great and wondrous things
about the future. One of them asserted that he knew the prophecy
of Daniel. He spoke with the assistance of the liar-demon about the
passage where the prophet writes about four and seven and ten
horns[49] and about kings and the Antichrist.[50] He drew the attention
of some rather simple souls and, if it could have been done, would
have even led into error that man of God, Simon, the venerable
abbot of St. Nicholas.[51] This confrere's arrogance had even grown
to the degree that he presumed to give a sermon in chapter to those
in attendance. He began with the words: "Be bold in war and fight
with the ancient serpent," but at the conclusion, "and you will
receive an eternal kingdom,"[52] he was unable to continue.

Meanwhile, another cleric, an instrument of this evil work,
was suddenly seized by an infirmity. He who before had spoken
only about visible things now presumed to lift his voice to heaven
to speak of the invisible and ineffable. The confreres ran to anoint
him and to hear what he was saying. He claimed great things about
himself but even greater things about those around him.
Concerning himself he claimed that that very evening he would
either be with the angels in heaven or would be standing healthy
with the rest of the confreres in choir. But about the others, as
though auguring or prophesying, he said: "When I was recently in
ecstasy, I saw one man called to eternity; another one was placed on
a throne of happiness; still another one's couch was set with the
same joy; this one a future bishop; another a rector and master of
many religious; this one to persevere in his good intention; that
other one, failing, will depart." After saying this he behaved as
though he were about to breathe his last. Then, after the space of
an hour, he heard the call for Vespers; he suddenly arose and, walking swiftly, entered the choir with the others. When those present
saw this they realized with shame that they had been fooled.

The evil enemy likewise stirred up another confrere. Like the cleric who spoke of the prophecy of Daniel, this one professed that he knew about John's Apocalypse and how to probe the secrets of heaven. The prior was notified where he was working and, through him, the convent. The confreres returned in order to hear what these new events were. The man, whose name was Reinald, was sitting before them flushed like one drunk. Another, whose name was Burchard, was sitting there weeping inconsolably. When he was asked the cause of such great grief, he said, "My good brothers, look, my rival here intended my death and, if you check his bed, you will find the instrument of my death." There was a search and under each man's bed were found signs of hatred, namely, a knife of some length and a large club. When these things were brought into the convent the prior said to them: "Brothers—would that you were brothers!— the disciples of our Lord Jesus Christ instructed and illumined by the Holy Spirit lacked envy and hatred. For the Holy Spirit is the spirit of concord, not discord; the spirit of peace, not of dissension. It is now clear from what source you have drawn evil and not good, bitter and not sweet. Hence in the name of the Lord we impose silence on you, for we shall not hear you until our Father Norbert returns." Thus the confreres were cautioned against this and other such things.

Chapter 14

Sometime later Satan seized upon a young man, the son of a lay brother, and began to torment him wickedly. The confreres, amazed and wondering at the assaults and their frequency, tied and locked up the possessed man until they could take counsel. In the silence of the night, when the prior wanted to go to the prisoner, although the doors were still closed, the demon within began to shout in a loud voice: "Now he will come in to me, now he will come in to me. Here he comes. Here comes the master with the patched tunic. Let him be cursed! Lock the door, lock it as quickly as possible lest he approach me." The prior did not stop but, knocking on the door, entered and asked standing before him, "What are you saying?" The possessed man answered: "Are you asking me what I am saying or who am I who speak? I will tell you neither. Surely you are not the master of this man or his protector or a teacher of the others? Go away," he said, "go away as quickly as possible, lest you depart shamefully injured by me." The prior was certain that this was an evil spirit, and that he had very frequently come to deceive, but now to destroy. He said: "I command you through Jesus Christ, the son of God, who on the cross overcame the snares and power by which you unjustly and fraudulently held man captive. Christ rightly took that power back, so that you may not presume to hide who you are." The devil responded, "Surely you do not force me thus?" The prior answered, "Not I; he forces you who at another time conquered you, as I've said." And the demon shouted out: "Woe is me! What shall I do? I am the one who was in the girl at Nivelles in the presence of your master, Norbert, the white dog. Cursed be the hour in which he was born!"[53]

At these words the prior called the confreres together. Humbly they undertook corporal discipline and gave themselves over to fasting and prayer. Next they approached the demon with holy water. Therefore he began to growl and shout out noisily, "Let them come to this battle, for we are many and we will crush them as grains are crushed by a millstone, and we will completely destroy them." The prior responded, "You will do so only if you have received the power." The devil said, with hands outstretched toward him, "Do you think you are their master?" With fingers extended toward their cross, he continued: "He is the master, not you. For you we do nothing, but he is the one by whom I am tormented." For the demons acknowledge and fear our Lord Jesus Christ crucified. The Jews and false Christians do not recognize him but rather curse and laugh at him. Finally, the man in whom the evil spirit resided was freed. But although he could scarcely be controlled by many, a young cleric of the community, humbly bold yet truly obedient, said, "Command me through obedience and I will hold him not with my own hands but with the hands and shackles of obedience." When he had been given the command and the others had departed, he alone held the possessed man and led him, trembling at the very sight of the young cleric, to the holy water. The demoniac was placed in the holy water, while the exorcisms and gospels were read. Kneeling, the confreres prayed and cried aloud, while imposing on themselves various physical disciplines. Finally, after the man's body had been excessively tormented, the demon appeared sitting on his tongue like a grain of very black lentil. With open mouth and tongue stretched out, he showed himself to everyone standing there and said: "Look at me! I will not leave today for any of you." To this the prior's response was, "You are a liar from the beginning, and no one should ever believe you."[54] Shortly thereafter the devil left, leaving an intolerably foul stench. Freed of its tormentor, the body immediately collapsed onto its sickbed. Only after a long rest did the man barely recover from his illness.

Now at that time a confrere of commendable holiness was stationed at the gate to give alms and welcome guests with a prayer. One night while he was lying on his bed, which for everyone consisted of fern, Satan came to him. The brother was unable to sleep. Satan was roaring and sometimes grunting and rolling the fern around the confrere's feet. This happened three nights in a row. When Satan came on that third night, the confrere said on the advice of the prior: "Wretched and most miserable one! *You were the light bearer. You rose in the morning* (Isa 14:12), dwelt in the delights of paradise but, when this was not sufficient and you said 'I shall place my throne in the north, I shall be like the most high',[55] you lost what you were, exchanging darkness for light, misery for happiness, choosing the stench of pigs for a place of delights. A worthy and suitable exchange! There is no place for you here. Be like the pigs, rolling yourself in the stench of the sewers, awaiting the time of the judgment of the dead in places that stink." The tempter departed in dismay and did not approach this confrere again in any visible form. The evil spirit is confounded and shamed when the delights he lost are cast up to him. He panics and trembles when the threats and terrors of the coming judgment are mentioned. Hence the custom of the holy church has developed that the concluding words of all exorcisms are: "I exorcise you through him who will come to judge the living and the dead[56] and the world by fire."

Therefore, when the malicious enemy had harassed the confreres many times over and found no place for deception among the simple, he crossed over with no difficulty to Maastricht, where Father Norbert was. Satan seized upon a man who was the steward of a prince. Just then an annual celebration was taking place in the town and the priest of God, Norbert, celebrated Mass in the principal church there for a great crowd of people. The demoniac, growling horribly, could scarcely be held in control. After the celebration of the Mass he was brought to Norbert with much encouragement from the people in attendance. Still clothed in the sacred vestments and, even more, girded with the strength of the Holy Spirit, Norbert approached to do battle with this most troublesome enemy. Some of the confreres asked him to spare his own health, because it was now evening and they said this was a chance incident, that not all cases could be helped. Norbert was disturbed by this and sternly rejected their proposal, saying: "You are not aware, brothers, that through the envy of the devil death has entered the world. Death has continued in the world and has no intention of leaving. Indeed, Satan inflicts himself on the world so frequently and in such a troublesome way that I grow angry. He makes the word of God ministered through me grow worthless in the hearts of those who hear it. Although he is clearly unable so to do, in his innate arrogance he secretly strives to take this word away from those who have received it. Have you not heard the words of the Lord, who says *the devil comes to take the seed of the word of God from their hearts*" (Luke 8:12)?

After Norbert said this the possessed man was placed before the altar, and the priest began the exorcism compelling the demon to leave. When he had placed the blessed salt on the demoniac's mouth, the man lunged forward and spat in Norbert's face, saying: "You have suggested that I be placed in water and beaten with harsh whips almost to the point of death. Your efforts are in vain. Your whips do not harm me, your threats do not frighten me, death does not torture, nor do the chains of death bind me." The suggestion had indeed been made that he be placed in holy water, although the raging man did not hear it. Then, when the clergy and people were standing around—some out of curiosity, some out of piety—the evil demon began through the mouth of the possessed man to reveal the shameful lives of many, recalling their adultery and fornication. His malicious mouth now revealed whatever had not been hidden in confession. Hearing what he said, everyone began to flee this way and that, only a few remaining with Father Norbert. However, as the day came to a close, those who were present, weary from the fasting and vigils of the preceding night, forced Norbert to go to the place where he was staying in order to refresh his exhausted body with food and sleep.

While Norbert sat at dinner with his confreres and some guests, it was announced that the sick man was sitting quietly and unbound before the altar, asking pardon for the curses he had dishonorably uttered. Norbert and his companions gave thanks to God, for truly that night and the next day the man appeared to be cured. But there was a mortal hatred among the citizens of that same town. Father Norbert spent the entire next day settling and putting this feud to rest, and by the grace of God he brought about complete peace among them. Then the devil who had been expelled from their hearts was unwilling to depart and returned to the same wretched man who had seemed to be cured. Immediately the man began to howl and rage. Therefore, when the priest of God had returned to the church, the people standing there said: "Are you not aware that this possessed man of yesterday is raging again? Unless he is cured as quickly as possible he will perish, consumed by his own fury." The man of God responded: "For the present he will not be able to be freed from his tormentor because this is happening to him because of his sins"—he bore the office of steward of an estate—"and he was given over to his tormentor deservedly. Leave him alone now! After the devil vexes him for some days he will be healed, once satisfaction has been shown." And that is what happened. For three days the demoniac was bitterly tormented. Afterward he was freed from the devil by God's mercy, and, in control of his mind, he returned home unharmed.

Chapter 15

As Norbert's reputation spread, Godfrey,[57] a very powerful count of Westphalia, was touched by the fear of God. He approached Norbert and shared with him his intent to give up all his property and embrace voluntary poverty. He was wealthy, powerful in arms, and well endowed with estates, servants, and handmaids. Renouncing all of these things he handed them over to the man of God to be disposed of with this stipulation, that Norbert turn the fortress of Cappenberg into a religious house and consecrate it to the service of God so that through divine mercy virtue might spring up where vice had reigned. Godfrey's wife[58] and younger brother,[59] his men and their household ministers, as well as Count Frederick,[60] his wife's father, all spoke against such action on his part. Frederick said that the donation Godfrey was making was for the most part from his daughter's dowry. Although the controversy over this matter was long and complex, finally by the grace of God Godfrey's wife gave her consent and his brother also decided to change his life. So it happened that from their possessions three churches were established, namely Cappenberg, Ilbenstadt, and Varlar. These houses were then peopled with confreres where religious life worthy of God thrives even to the present time.

Because the fortress of Cappenberg held control of Westphalia, Count Frederick, the father of Godfrey's wife—partly to indulge his ambition—alleged that this was his daughter's dowry and threatened the confreres with death unless they departed as quickly as possible. He came there with his retinue several times, threatening that if he should find Father Norbert he would hang him up with his donkey so that he could see on the scale which of them was the heavier. Bishops and other princes who were present spoke against such boastful speech and threatened Frederick with the wrath of God. By now all in the Rhineland held Father Norbert in high esteem, and they objected to anyone speaking ill of him. The confreres of Cappenberg, in their difficulty, sent to the man of God, asking his help and at the same time informing him of the boastful words of this proud man. When Norbert received the message, he gathered all his strength of faith and hope in him who said, *Have confidence, I have overcome the world* (John 16:33) and publicly announced that he, with his donkey, was going to enter that territory and place himself in the count's power. What more? Although the journey was long, nevertheless he did not change his mind. Crossing the Rhine unarmed and powerless, he entered the territory of Count Frederick. While Norbert stayed there divine vengeance came upon the count. While he sat at dinner, his stomach burst open[61] and brought an end to his evil life. With his death peace returned to the church.

After Father Norbert had returned to France, a very noble French prince, Count Theobald,[62] approached him to ask advice about his salvation. Norbert had heard that this count was very generous in giving alms and in building churches and monasteries; Norbert had heard too that Theobald was a father of orphans, spouse of widows, and steward of the poor and infirm. Therefore he did not presume to change this man's holy way of life, but advised that he continue his good work and beget an heir through marriage who would inherit these vast domains with the blessing of his forefathers. The man of God used much discretion in his advice. He wanted the above-mentioned prince of Westphalia, a plunderer of others' goods, to renounce his possessions. However, he persuaded the count of France who supported the needy with his goods to possess all as though having nothing.[63]

At that time the man of God arranged to set out for Rome. The retainers of Count Theobald were his companions on this journey and went with him as far as Regensburg. The brother of the bishop of that city was Engelbert, a powerful and noble margrave. Theobald's knights sought the margrave's marriageable daughter, obtaining her as a bride for their master. They then returned to him to announce the good news.

Norbert, however, having resumed his journey, arrived in Rome, where he was honorably received by Pope Honorius[64] of happy memory. Norbert obtained from the pope whatever he reasonably requested. When his business was finished, he set out on his return trip and came to the city of Würzburg. On this journey both he and some of his companions clearly heard that he would be the future bishop of Magdeburg. Then, while he was celebrating Mass in the cathedral of Würzburg on Easter Sunday[65] before a large gathering of people, a blind woman known to all approached him as he was consuming the body and blood of the Lord. He breathed on her eyes just after he consumed the Lord's blood, and soon after she regained her sight. Hence all the people who were present extolled the greatness of God in a loud voice. Some of the prominent citizens of the city were so touched by this event that they gave themselves and their possessions to God through Norbert. Through their generosity a church called Cell[66] was built near the city and is famous for its divine worship even to the present time. But the man of God, along with his companions, recalled the voice he had heard on his return from Rome. Fearing that he would be elected bishop there, since the see was vacant, he departed quickly and in secret. After he returned to Prémontré, he arranged for the establishment of the church of blessed Martin in the suburbs of Laon, and the church of Vivières, which is in the district of Soissons, placing some of his confreres there.

On the very day on which the confreres of Norbert had arrived at Vivières, the ancient enemy, black and in horrid attire, appeared to a peasant who was cultivating the fields. He said: "Why are you working? What are you doing? Be subject to me and I will make you rich." Thinking him to be a monk, the man responded: "Keep what is yours; we have Norbert. He will enrich us both in soul and in body." Hearing this, the demon breathed on him as though offended and then vanished, saying "Norbrec, Norbret!" as if he were tormented by the name. The peasant, however, dropped his hoe and ran screaming madly through the fields. His neighbors doing similar work in the same field came running. They saw that he was beside himself; they took hold of him and led him bound to the church of Vivières. In the evening Norbert arrived there with Anscolf, the archdeacon of Soissons, in whose jurisdiction the church lay, so that according to the local custom he might officially assign the place to the man of God. He did so. Meanwhile the demon was cruelly tormenting the same peasant. When asked his name, the demon said he was that Olybrius who had tormented blessed Margaret. Father Norbert, at the request of many, approached the possessed man and sprinkled him with holy water. Then, rubbing his gums with blessed salt and washing them with holy water, he ordered the peasant to take no food for nine continuous days unless it was seasoned with blessed salt and holy water. When the man had done this, he was healed and returned home. In the morning he came to church and, thankful, told the people the details of what had happened to him in the field.

Chapter 16

At that time a most destructive heresy arose at Antwerp, a very large and populous city. A certain heretic, a seducer by the name of Tanchelm,[67] who was remarkably shrewd and cunning, came there and found an opportunity for his false teaching. He was an evil man, an enemy of the Christian faith and of all religion to such a degree that he declared that obedience to bishops and priests was not necessary and denied that the reception of the most holy body and blood of our Lord Jesus Christ was a benefit to eternal salvation. He led many people of that region astray. As a result, the people believed everything the heretic said. About three thousand armed men were in his following, and neither duke nor prince would encounter or resist him. He wore gilded clothing and his curled hair glittered with gold and many ornaments. With lavish banquets and persuasive words he won the good favor of his listeners. Strange and astonishing! His followers drank his bathwater and carried it away, preserving it like a relic. They also willingly involved themselves in many other vile and detestable activities so that even after the heretic's death it was impossible to root out this destructive evil.

In this city was a community of twelve clerics who, forced by the circumstances of this error, handed over their church[68] along with some of its revenue to Father Norbert and his confreres. They did so through the agency of the bishop,[69] hoping that through the merits of Norbert and his confreres the fury of this great plague of heresy might be removed and, with the darkness of ignorance dispelled, the light of truth might be restored. Norbert accepted this church and the aforementioned clerics built another church for themselves in the same city. Both churches remain to this day dedicated to the service of God. And thus it happened that the people who were falsely led astray by that depraved seducer were brought back to the path of truth and justice through the work of the pious preacher Norbert and his confreres.

Chapter 17

One thing further. During the winter when the man of God was at Prémontré he took the opportunity at night to speak a word of exhortation to the confreres. Some were thirsty, and water was brought from the spring. When Norbert claimed that the water was not clean, those who had brought it protested that the vessel had been washed and that they had brought the purest of water. Norbert insisted, however, that no one drink the water. After lighting a lamp, the confreres looked carefully at the bottom of the vessel and found a large, repulsive worm crawling in the jar. They were astounded because it was winter, when worms of this sort were not usually found, and because the spring from which they recalled drawing the water was very clean, as was the vessel. The confreres now burst forth in praise of God because they had been rescued by Father Norbert from the snares of the enemy. In various ways that ancient foe tried frequently to deceive the confreres at Prémontré. Even when they absented themselves to take care of the needs of nature, he appeared to them in frightful images and threatened them with various fantasies. One of them, however, gathering his courage and strength of mind, said to himself, "How long shall I endure the falsehood and fantasies of this most troublesome enemy?" Rising, he rushed at the devil and sent him flying. Thus from that time on he remained immune to such illusions.

The malicious enemy appeared to yet another confrere as he was tending to his private needs and kept him there senseless, from the beginning to the end of Matins. Finally, however, the constancy of the confrere won out over the importunity of the devil for, making the sign of the cross, he leapt through the doorway where the demon seemed to be. When the brother found no one opposing him, he realized that this had been an empty demonic illusion, and thus gaining a spirit of freedom he henceforth feared nothing of this sort.

One night the devil also came to terrify Father Norbert as he was intent on prayer in the church. The devil stood there in the form of a frightful bear striking fear in him with its teeth and claws. The man of God was somewhat frightened by the unexpected appearance but soon came to himself and recognized the snares of his persecutor. After a while he regained his courage in prayer and said: "What do you want, bloody beast? Your claws are without substance, your frightful teeth are air, and your hairy pelt empty smoke and vapor passing away like the shadow that vanishes with the sun. You were formed in the image and likeness of God and, although you were light, by your pride you merited the darkness. Depart now, I command you, because there is nothing in common between Christ and Belial, *between light and darkness, between the faithful and the unfaithful* (2 Cor 6:14). Depart quickly! You know you can harm no one without permission." The liar then disappeared, unable to endure the truth.

Now the time had come when the above-mentioned Count Theobald along with his friends was, at the set time and place, to meet his bride, her father, and the gathering of her relatives. Father Norbert had also been invited. But the bride, detained by illness, did not meet him, and this gave cause for suspicion that perhaps some regret or deception intervened in this arrangement. Hence Father Norbert was asked to continue on and carefully investigate the cause of this delay. Norbert agreed to this request and set out to bring to a close the concern of this marriage he had undertaken to arrange.

As a farewell to his confreres at Prémontré, Norbert sent them a little money, which he had received, so that they might add 120 poor in his name to the number of 500 poor whom he fed at the time of famine, and that the brothers might care for these people with fraternal charity. He had no hope of returning to remain with the confreres any longer. Hence he left them this memorial of his name, following in this the example of the true master who, *when he had loved those who were his, loved them to the end* (John 13:1).

Chapter 18

In the year of the Lord's incarnation 1125, the archbishop of Magdeburg, the metropolitan of Saxony, died. After his death the election of a future bishop was difficult because three eminent persons were named as candidates. Because the electors were unwilling to withdraw from the candidates of their choice, the matter was brought to the hearing of the emperor, the most serene Lord Lothair.[70] Gerard,[71] the cardinal legate of the Roman see, who after Pope Honorius governed the Catholic Church as Pope Lucius,[72] was with the emperor at that time. On his advice, because the electors could not agree, the emperor decided to appoint Norbert as archbishop of Magdeburg, after taking counsel with Adelbert,[73] archbishop of Mainz, and Albero,[74] the *primicerius* of Metz.

Norbert at that time had been at the court to preach the word of God. Therefore, after calling together the electors and after much discussion, the emperor himself appointed Norbert archbishop. The aforementioned cardinal legate of the apostolic see, on the authority of the pope, confirmed this sincere and commendable act of the emperor, immediately sending messengers after Norbert, who was preparing to depart. Amid a great roar of acclamation he was presented to the prince while all the leaders of the church of Magdeburg cried out, "He is our choice for our father and bishop; we approve him as our shepherd." Although Norbert protested as much as he could, he was compelled by those surrounding him and finally brought to his knees before the emperor, forced to accept the crosier placed in his hands. Meanwhile the cardinal addressed Norbert in these words: "By the authority of almighty God and the blessed apostles Peter and Paul and the lord Pope Honorius, I order you not to speak against the call of God in any way. Rather, as a faithful and prudent servant dutifully administer the 'money' of the word of God that you have received for distribution so that when the Lord comes to reckon with his servants to whom he has given money for their use, you may be found worthy to hear from him: *Well done, good and faithful servant, because you were faithful over a few things, I shall place you over many. Enter into the joy of your Lord* (Matt 25:21)." Finally, yielding to numerous arguments and the apostolic authority, Norbert accepted the yoke of the Lord, not without much weeping; thus dismissed by the emperor, he set out for Saxony to the place destined for him.

At Norbert's approach to the city, the people gathered. All gave thanks that they had deserved to receive a man of holy reputation as the shepherd of their souls. Gazing at the city of Magdeburg, to which he was being led, he entered barefoot. After he was received in the church he entered the palace accompanied by many people. However, since he wore a shabby cloak, he was not recognized and was turned away by the doorkeeper. But when the porter was reprimanded by others, Father Norbert said smiling, "Do not be afraid, you know me better and see me with a clearer eye than those who force me to this palace to which I, poor and simple, ought not be raised."

After Norbert was consecrated bishop[75] he began to be a *faithful steward* (Luke 12:42) of his household. He called together the administrators of the diocesan property and *undertook a reckoning* (Matt 25:19) of the income of the diocese. This accounting was found to be so modest that it could scarcely cover the expenses for

163

four months. Although the church at Magdeburg had been established and raised up by imperial power, endowed and expanded by
much generosity, nevertheless it had been greatly reduced by the
negligences and extravagances of the archbishops. To restore it,
encouraged by the will of God, Norbert as archbishop took back
the possessions of the church appropriated by the hands of the violent. By so doing, he afforded them the opportunity to malign him.
He became hateful to everyone who had at first acclaimed him with
praise. But he did not hesitate to suffer insult for the name of the
Lord.[76] Hence by censuring, both when convenient and when
inconvenient, by rebuking, by entreating,[77] he tried to renew the
face of his church both by spiritual and physical increments. Among
the many things he promptly did, he obtained the church of the
blessed mother of God and ever-virgin Mary from the emperor and
the cathedral chapter, as well as from the canons of that church. He
placed the confreres of his order in this church as he had so long
desired. Here, by the grace of the Holy Spirit, they devoutly administer the divine services to this very day.

In response to Norbert's good work, however, the indignation
of his rivals was stirred up. On the very solemn day of the Lord's
Supper, while Norbert was receiving penitents for confession, a man
clothed in penitential garments came to the door of the house. He
asked the porter to be admitted for confession. The porter indicated
this to the man of God, who said, "Do not let him in." When the
man persisted in knocking, the others stood back and finally admitted him. The man of God looked at this man carefully from a distance and said, "Do not approach, but stand there and do not move."
Norbert called the palace servants, who were outside, and ordered
them to remove the young man's garment. When he was stripped
there appeared secured to his side a sharp knife about a foot and a
half in length. When asked why he had come so armed, the young
man fell at Norbert's feet trembling, stunned, and fearing death,[78]
and confessed that he had been sent to kill the man of God. After
hearing the names of those who had hired him to commit the crime,
all were amazed that household members and secretaries—men at
whose hands official matters were handled—were found to be at the
heart of this betrayal. The just Norbert, however, calmly responded
that it was no wonder that the ancient enemy was preparing these

snares for him, since on this same most sacred night he persuaded the Jews to proceed to the death of our Lord Jesus Christ. Norbert was happy that he was found worthy to share in the Lord's passion, especially on that day when mercy is given to those without hope, pardon to sinners, and life to the dead.

At another time a cleric of Norbert's' household attempted at night to strike him with a knife as he was leaving with his clerics for the celebration of Matins. But by mistake he struck another of the clerics, ripping his garment. And when the man shouted that he was wounded, the attacker, knowing by the sound of the voice that it was not the archbishop, said, "I did not think it was you but he whom I was planning to kill." The archbishop had gone ahead, mixed in among the others, fearing just such an event as though having prior knowledge of the future. Therefore, when others were pursuing the fleeing attacker to capture him, the man of God said: "Let him flee. You should not render evil for evil. He did what he could and what God permitted."

In the midst of all these events Father Norbert had not forgotten his first foundation in the church at Prémontré. Lest perhaps the confreres gathered there be in danger without a shepherd, he sent messengers to grant them free election. He made a recommendation, suggesting a person who was suitable and of proven religious value, and this is the one whom the confreres unanimously—a unanimity pleasing to God—agreed upon. The one who was elected was at that time staying with Father Norbert. On the day on which the confreres chose him, he learned of his election through a vision in the night. He claimed that in the vision he stood with Father Norbert before our Lord Jesus Christ, and that he was received by the right hand of the Savior from the hand of Norbert, who said, "O Lord, to your most holy majesty I present this man whom you entrusted to me." When the news regarding the unanimous choice of the confreres arrived, Norbert addressed the one elected in the presence of the confreres who were with him, saying: "Through election by the confreres you will succeed me in the house of our poverty. Go therefore in the name of the Lord, for the hand of the Lord will be with you until the end."

After receiving Norbert's blessing, the chosen one departed, taking two confreres with him, one of whom was appointed abbot in Antwerp, the other in the church at Floreffe. The shepherd-elect, however, went on to Prémontré and became a renowned abbot of that church. Soon he appointed abbots from among his confreres for the churches at Laon and Vivières, and for the one called Bonne-Espérance. He determined to come together annually with these abbots in a set place for the reparation of any decline of the order, for eradicating excesses, and for the healthy restoration of anything necessary. From then on the confreres of the order established by the venerable Father Norbert increased throughout the world even to the present day.

Chapter 19

Around this same time Pope Honorius of blessed memory passed away. Innocent[79] succeeded him by canonical election but was unable to take possession of the Roman see because of the intrusion of Pierleoni[80] and the sedition of Pierleoni's relatives. Innocent left and went to France, where he was honorably and fittingly received. There he presided at the Council of Reims,[81] where archbishops and bishops and a multitude of prelates and the faithful of Christ gathered from diverse lands. Here the interloper Pierleoni was excommunicated and the election of Innocent confirmed. Archbishop Norbert was present. Besides the many concerns of the universal church, he consulted regarding the private needs of his own church and obtained the confirmation of the apostolic see regarding many useful privileges. When his affairs were in order he returned home.

On Norbert's return,[82] however, he found an unexpected and disturbing situation. Something that happened in the cathedral seemed, according to the authority of the canons, to require its reconsecration. The elders of the city spoke against this, claiming that the consecration ought not be repeated since it had been celebrated on the authority of many kings and bishops. Norbert, on the contrary, responded that he would never celebrate the divine mysteries there unless the anathema were removed from the church. Soon he announced the outcome of the matter publicly, pointing out that he was bound to do as the custom of the holy fathers decreed in cases of this sort. Therefore, on the following night Norbert and two other bishops, along with the cathedral provost and many of his clergy clothed in sacred vestments, entered the church and performed the customary office of consecration with sincere devotion. When the office was completed, however, while the clergy were still in their sacred vestments, there was much shouting and tumult among the people outside. Indeed, the whole city was in an uproar because of a rumor that the archbishop had smashed the altars, opened the sanctuary, broken up the tombs and reliquaries and laid them aside for himself, then under the darkness of night decided to flee with all of these things as well as the treasures of the church.

Hearing the clamor of the populace, those who were with the man of God were terrified. Norbert himself was undaunted and wanted to go out to the people, but his companions kept him from doing so. They said that an uprising could not easily be settled at night. They forced Norbert to climb into a fortification, which in former times had been built by Emperor Otto for a church tower. The church itself was never finished because of Otto's death. There Norbert and those who were with him sat down, still robed in sacred vestments, and awaited death. Once settled in the tower they celebrated the solemnity of Matins in honor of the blessed Paul, whose feast was being observed.[83] They sang the praises of God while the tumult of the people besieging them increased. At this point some of the confreres resolutely awaited the outcome of the situation, while others faltered and, groaning, said, "Oh, why did we follow this man here to die with him in our sins?" The holy man consoled them as much as he was able: "Don't be frightened, my dear brothers. What we have endured is of God; what we are enduring is of God. When some good work is assailed by God's enemies, it is by his permission." Saying this he prayed more fervently for them that they might not weaken,[84] and from their lack of prayer his own devotion increased. He later claimed that he feared death less than that his confreres might give up from despair. The hostile crowd continued to gather throughout the whole night, but the priest of God and those with him redoubled their prayer.

In the morning some of the enemy made an advance on the tower while others attacked the archbishop and his clerics with

167

arrows. Then, unexpectedly, certain men who were said to have sworn to kill Norbert boldly climbed to the top of the tower. When the man of God saw them attacking with drawn swords, he stepped forward lest they kill others in their rage. He said: "You are seeking one man. I am here.[85] Spare these who have not deserved the sentence of death." When the attackers saw him still clothed in his purple pontifical vestments, they were suddenly struck by the grace of God and, falling at his feet, sought and received pardon. Once his adversaries, they now became his defenders. Others, however, quickly followed and, assuming the archbishop was beheaded, tried to kill one of his soldiers who was in their way. They drove a sword into his neck all the way to his throat and, thinking him dead, left him half alive. When the man of God saw this, leaping into the midst of the crowd, he put himself in death's way rather than have anyone die while he remained alive. But when the one who had struck down the soldier saw Norbert, he was full of fury and boldly struck at the shoulder of the archbishop with his still bloody sword. The sword glanced off but did not inflict a wound; nevertheless, the blood on the sword spattered the fringes of Norbert's episcopal miter. Thereafter the stains from the blood were always visible.

While this was taking place, some who did not seem to be participants in this uprising placed in their midst the relics of the saints, which were brought from the churches. They said that it was a disgrace that the shepherd was attacked by his flock, but in so saying they feigned kindness. They too were trying to force him, while he was in this predicament, to remove those confreres whom he had stationed there, as was stated above, from the church of the blessed Mary. But Norbert absolutely refused, claiming that as long as he lived this act—to their regret confirmed by imperial power and apostolic authority—would not be overturned by them.

While the people awaited the outcome of this crisis and the end of such tumult, the count of the city arrived. He was returning from a journey and, unaware of the uprising, came upon the rioters. Separating them one from another, he set a day on which everyone who had a just complaint against the bishop might come and receive justice. At the orders of the judge the people departed. But the priest of God entered the cathedral over which the riot had taken place to say Mass and render boundless thanks to God. When

Norbert approached the altar, he said to those gathered around, "Look, everything which had been reported broken and stolen is whole and safe." Then he celebrated Mass there but read the epistle and gospel himself because all his ministers, exhausted from weariness and fear, had left. When Mass was finished he entered the palace happy, elated, and thankful that the Lord had delivered him from such tribulation.[86]

Chapter 20

The uproar of the evildoers still did not cease. They complained that they had been deceived because the venerable priest had evaded their trap. So they made a pact among themselves that on an appointed day they should all come together drunk so that if they did anything wrong it would be attributed to drunkenness rather than to premeditation. And they agreed that if anyone went against this decision his home would be confiscated. When this plan was relayed to the princes of the territory, who seemed to care for the archbishop because they knew he was a just and holy man, they advised Norbert to leave for a while. He refused and joyfully awaited the martyr's palm. The day agreed upon arrived and, when the signal was given, the citizenry began to make a great deal of noise and shouting. When the bishop asked what this was all about, he was told that a large mob was trying to expel his confreres from the church of the blessed Mary. But he smiled and said, "It is not to be, because a foundation which the heavenly Father has planted cannot be uprooted."[87] Then, as the people began to gather, horses were prepared and he was forced to leave. He went to the abbey of Saint John the Baptist[88] in the outskirts of the city. There he spent some time putting his affairs in order. He then went to Gevekenstein Castle to rest from all this turmoil. When he found this castle closed to him—for his enemies, arriving ahead of him, had seized the fortification—he went to a nearby church of canons where he remained for several days praying that God would direct his way in accord with his will.

While Norbert remained there in a humble and saddened frame of mind, peace was restored with the help of God and the mediation of those who were loyal to him. His adversaries gathered contritely and were humbled before him. He received them kindly and demanded only one thing of them, that they immediately be reconciled to his wounded soldier. This they accepted most willingly and repaired the soldier's ruined house, giving him forty silver marks in compensation for the wound he received. After this the fortress, previously closed to Norbert, was opened to him and he was received there with honor, surrounded by a band of many nobles. All the people praised God for the constancy of such a bishop, who remained undefeated, secure in body and spirit, in spite of the evident danger of death.

These events took place in the third year of Norbert's archiepiscopacy. After this he ruled for five years and from day to day gave honor to the ministry entrusted to him by God, advancing in all religion and virtue, preserving the unity of the holy church, and resisting and protesting against those who disturbed it and against all schismatics, embracing the good, giving counsel to the desolate, supporting the poor and orphans and widows, fostering and helping to spread religious orders, while setting an example of religious life, presenting himself affably both to the lesser and the greater as the dignity of his office could bear. Mindful of the divine generosity and grace, he daily offered to the Lord his God an upright conscience with a pleasant and charming demeanor.

Chapter 21

A very serious schism raged at that time. The Catholic Pope Innocent worked here and there among faithful people, and the schismatic Pierleoni occupied the see of Rome with the help of his relatives and supporters, committing many crimes in the city against the laws and statutes of the fathers. Because of this, Emperor Lothair, after holding council with the princes of the empire, arranged an expedition to Italy in order to oust the sacrilegious Pierleoni with the material sword because he resisted the spiritual sword. Father Norbert joined this expedition, obedient to the command of Pope Innocent and at the call of the emperor. Though frail in body he was nevertheless prompt and resolute in spirit.

Afterward, on this expedition, how necessary and useful Norbert was for the church emerged clearly.

Now while the emperor halted with his army in a place the inhabitants call Valentano and Pope Innocent was staying at Viterbo, legates from Rome sent by Pierleoni approached the emperor. They tried in various ways—by entreaty and by bribes, as well as by reasoning—to persuade the emperor to support him. When these attempts failed because Father Norbert spoke against them, Pierleoni's retainers demanded a hearing and appealed to a tribunal of justice. With this device they won over to their side the minds of some of the princes as well as of the rest of the faithful to some degree. Hence Norbert, concerned for the peace and honor of the Catholic Church, hastened to Pope Innocent and explained what was happening in the camp. Norbert advised the pope insistently not to put off providing for himself and his people. Although Norbert was told that it was not fitting for the sovereign pontiff to be subject to the judgment of man or be present at tribunals, Pope Innocent, freely and honorably looking to his own interest, put himself at the disposal of Prince Lothair, saying that he would allow himself to be permanently imprisoned if he did not present himself for examination by the royal tribunal at the place and time set for him.

So the deception of Pierleoni, who sought the papacy like a roaring lion,[89] was brought to naught. Innocent gradually became more acceptable to all those with sound judgment. Next Lothair moved his army and advanced on Rome following the difficult circuit through Orte and Narni,[90] encamping first on the hill of thieves,[91] then boldly within the walls of the city on the Aventine close to Santa Sabina. Finally he placed Pope Innocent on his throne in the Lateran Palace.

Later, when the day arrived on which Lothair was to be consecrated emperor by Pope Innocent, Rome was suddenly thrown into confusion and uproar, fearing that the solemn imposition of the imperial crown by Innocent would bring the inevitable deposition of Pierleoni. And so it happened. From this time on Innocent began to grow strong and gain power, and Pierleoni's power grew weak and declined. Pope Innocent then, along with the cardinals and bishops and his entire clergy, solemnly welcomed Lothair as he entered with his forces, consecrating him emperor amid the cheers of all present.

After his coronation, however, the emperor unwisely requested that the pope grant him the right of investiture of the bishoprics, that is, that the freedom of the churches be handed over to him for the honor of the empire and the solidification of the bond he had pledged with the pope. The pope seemed inclined to grant this request. Since none of the many bishops present spoke out against this abuse, Archbishop Norbert stepped into their midst in the presence of the emperor and his military and said: "Father, what are you doing? To whom are you exposing the sheep entrusted to you? Are you leaving them open to be torn to pieces? Will you reduce to a maidservant a church free when you received it? The chair of Peter demands the deeds of Peter. I promised obedience to Peter and to you for the name of Christ, but if you do what is asked of you, I will speak against you in the face of the church." Thus Father Norbert pleaded his case. And so the emperor backed off from his improper request and the pope from his illicit accession to it.

This same Emperor Lothair was a God-fearing man, an active leader of war, distinguished in arms, prudent in counsel, frightful to the enemies of God, an ally of justice, an enemy of injustice. His courage was known in Sicily, renowned in Saxony, and as long as he lived the Roman Empire he governed remained firm with the help of God. He too loved the man of God, Norbert, and was often guided by his advice and through him was daily nourished by the word of God.

One day a soldier in the emperor's army was ill and troubled by an evil spirit. Tearfully the soldiers presented this man to the pope to be cured. Objecting to their intrusion, the pope went inside to his chambers and left the possessed man in church to the care of Father Norbert and the few who were with him. Norbert took pity on the man and said to his confreres, "Let us approach the Lord in a spirit of humility and contrition to see if perhaps he may deign to look upon the work of his hands in this poor man." He said this and immediately looked for a quiet place to pray. After Norbert gave way to tears and groans from noon until evening, he obtained the cure of the infirm man. As it grew dark, after many horrid words, the evil spirit left his victim. The man himself collapsed into the hands of those caring for him and fell asleep. After a little while he woke and got up healthy. The man of God urged him to go to confession and, both for the remission of past sins and in thanksgiving, Norbert ordered the recovered demoniac to abstain for several days from rich foods. The archbishop told him directly that, if he should stray from this rule of abstinence, the same punishment that he just escaped would happen again. Thus cleansed and reconciled to God the formerly possessed man proceeded to Pisa with the man of God. There he misused his freedom. Because he did not do what he should have, he suffered what he did not wish. While he was staying in Pisa, he was not on his guard but out of curiosity wandered around alone. He was suddenly seized and miserably tormented. Once again he was delivered by the grace of God through the ministry of the priest of God.

Chapter 22

Physical strength began to forsake the man of God after these many labors. Worn out by long and severe penitential austerity, his health declined both from the strain of the journey and from the corrupt condition of the air. Nevertheless, he returned from Italy and was brought with great difficulty to his city of Magdeburg. There he lay for four months, overcome with great weakness. Finally, after having administered his diocese wisely and faithfully for eight years, fully conscious and giving his blessing to those in attendance, he died in blessed peace. As Augustine said, one could not die badly who had lived well.[92] It was the year of the Lord's incarnation 1134, the Wednesday after Pentecost, the eighth day before the Ides of June,[93] in the fifth year of Pope Innocent, in the ninth year of the reign of Lothair.

Chapter 23

Now after the bishop died, great contention arose between the cathedral and the church of blessed Mary concerning the place of his burial. The canons of the cathedral claimed that it was worthy and just, because Norbert had been the head of the churches of that city, that his bones should bring honor to the principal church, there awaiting the coming of the sovereign judge. There Norbert held the title of the church no matter how long he lived. The confreres of the church of blessed Mary, on the contrary, said that Norbert had not only been the archbishop but also a special father to them and their provost till the end. Therefore they ought to have his body, especially since devotion to him demanded that he be buried and rest among his confreres and sons whom he had begotten for God by the seed of the word of God.

To settle this argument a delegation was sent to Emperor Lothair so that if he himself judged in this matter it would be considered settled. Meanwhile Norbert's body lay unburied and day after day was brought to those different monasteries of the city where vigils and prayers due to the faithful departed were devoutly celebrated. Although the heat was intense, Norbert's body emitted no odor of corruption over so many days. The messengers who had been sent out returned eight days[94] later, and by command of the emperor the body was taken to the church of blessed Mary and buried before the altar of the holy cross. Some years later it was moved to the choir, where it awaits the final day in the hope of a blessed resurrection desired greatly by every faith-filled soul.

VERSION B:
LIFE OF NORBERT (EXCERPTS)

Prologue[1]

Every faithful and pious soul no doubt comes closer to meriting the love and glory of almighty God the more he hears good about another. Such a soul believes much more easily, and wishes and hopes that the same good be conferred on him by that same God. He who does not believe does not imitate such virtue, and whoever does not imitate it will never attain that goal. Just as the homeland we seek in the exile of this life is true, so is the way by which we strive for it true and singular. Along this way, blocked as it is by many errors and great difficulties, the examples of holy men—among other benefits of divine dispensation—have been present to us from the beginning of the world. If we follow in their footsteps we will the more eagerly seek the joys of eternal happiness and the more surely attain them. Some of these examples are from the past and recorded by others. We can read them. Other examples, however, we ourselves have seen and continue to see. Since, for the Christian on his journey, nothing is so fitting and necessary for grasping the rewards of eternal glory as to shape his life by good practices and to occupy himself with praiseworthy endeavors, he therefore gratefully seeks with devotion to discover in the lives of such memorable men whatever commendable features he can, so that in continual meditation he may reflect on the worthy deeds of those whose virtue he strives to emulate.

The unfaithful and wicked, however, *whose God is their belly* (Phil 3:19) and whose greatest good is physical pleasure, do not fear immediately to judge as false and deceptive whatever they read or

---

This translation is based on the Patrologia edition, PL 170, cols. 1253–1350.

hear because it is foreign to their own endeavors and experiences. Because their conscience is foul and impure, they hate justice and suspect truth. They do not cease to turn the simple from the way of salvation and subvert these ordinary folk by the example of their own corrupt and wretched lives. Because of the obstinate and reprehensible shamelessness of such men, when I decided to write about the Premonstratensians,[2] who are in our own times praised for their devout and holy life and approved before God and men, I was forced to omit many things—or at most mention them only briefly—although they are known to everyone, lest corrupt people dare to deny them. On the contrary, when I considered the deeds of those about whom I am writing and I observed their growth, I realized that in a mysterious way theirs is the work not of men but of God. Recalling the gospel passage in which the good Master and Savior of all, Jesus Christ, said, *By their fruits you shall know them* (Matt 7:16) and *a bad tree cannot bear good fruit* (Matt 7:18), I investigated the tree from which so much good fruit had come. And when I inquired a little more carefully into the origin and source of the matter, I encountered Father Norbert of pious and revered memory. Concerning this man, as the course and order of this story requires, I shall briefly record a few things I have heard told about him from the legitimate and faithful testimony of others, as well as facts that I myself know.[3] So that I do not bore the reader with my wordiness, I will take care to narrate these events clearly and arrange them by chapter as carefully as I can.

I begin my story with the same father, the first of this community. I point out that, although many have written of his life and deeds,[4] I have found none who pursued the matter fully and in proper order. So that I not make the same mistake, some of those who had been constantly with him from the beginning met together and after careful examination decided that the specifics of the events should be written down in a timely sequence as they are agreed to have happened by most of those consulted.[5]

Chapter 5—Why the saints suffer evil they do not cause[6]

If, as scripture says, *Nothing happens on earth without a reason* (Job 5:6), then it is the highest and principal glory of a rational creature to understand the reasons for those things that happen. Certainly no one doubts that the saints suffer adversities in this world. I do not say why such hardships befall, but they do. These adversities are worth noting and should be recognized because the reason for them is obscure if their outcome is unknown. When the reason is understood, however, each person easily moves toward his goal freely and at will, depending on how thought dictates the usefulness or loss of what is proposed to him for imitation or avoidance.

In everything carefully considered there are two aspects, namely, the cause, by the cognition of which the interior reasoning of the soul is fed, and the effect, by the use of which the exterior sense of the body is aided. From this comes a double perception of things. The one, known through experience, pertains to the exterior sense of the body; the other, known through cognition, pertains to the interior reasoning of the soul. Since the natures of the soul and the body, that is, reason and sensory experience, are different and their movement contrary, it frequently happens that either reason, when it is exercised, weakens sensory perception and removes the ongoing ability to sense, or, on the contrary, that sensory perception, growing stronger, blocks the reason and dulls the sharpness of understanding. Consequently, reason, when the bodily sensation is subjected to it, aims toward virtue and acts strongly. But sensory experience, if reason is overpowered, tends toward pleasure and acts like an animal. From this it follows that men given over to the senses of the flesh and accustomed to the corporeal neither seek reasoning nor look for a cause. They think everything comes from accidental and unexpected causes. Those, however, in whom reasoning thrives and the natural light of reason shines carefully inquire and easily observe not only that nothing happens without a certain and rational cause, but that it cannot so happen. Therefore, if you see a man entangled in visible affairs, subject to the judgment of the senses, attending to the care of the flesh, speaking of chance events and fortune, blaspheming Mercury,[7] do not ask him why holy, just, and good men suffer in this world so many evils that they did not cause, because someone like this does not care to know what good men suffer or to imitate what they do. But for him to whom *to live is Christ and to die is gain* (Phil 1:21) and who can truthfully say with Paul *the world is crucified to me and I to the world* (Gal 6:14)—for this man salvation is a serious concern. This man without a doubt solicitously and carefully adverts to what the saints, for a time in this life at least, suffer for the debt of the human condition, and where they are led through such patience by the clemency of divine mercy.

In this distinction three things should be noted in particular: what each one suffers, why he suffers, and what is the result. This can be stated more briefly: punishment, cause, and end. Concerning punishment, the apostle says: *Because through many trials it is fitting that we enter the kingdom of God* (Acts 14:21). And again: *The sufferings of this time are not worthy to be compared to the future glory that will be revealed in us* (Rom 8:18). Concerning cause, we read: "It is not the punishment that makes the martyr but the cause."[8] In this regard we read in the gospel: *Blessed are those who suffer persecution for the sake of justice* (Matt 5:10). Finally, concerning the end, it is written: *God will wipe away every tear from the eyes of his saints* (Rev 21:4). And again, in the Book of Wisdom: *These are the ones we once held in derision* (Wis 5:3). And other references follow.[9]

Of these three, punishment is the first in cognition, then follows the end. Nevertheless, in imitation end precedes and punishment follows. End spurs us on to desire. Punishment tests if we are able. Cause in the middle distinguishes between the sons of the kingdom and the sons of Gehenna, as between the chaff and the grain, between those who suffer because of justice and those who are punished according to justice. For this reason God, by whose providence the whole world is governed and administered, in order to reveal himself as a most powerful and just creator and disposer of all created things, has not prohibited anyone from being evil. He has, however, subjected those who are evil to the laws of his sovereignty through their own evil desire. Through his omnipotence he brings it about that, just as something was made from nothing by him and through him, evil men become good by him and through him, and those who want to be good and try to be good are perfected through the agency of evil men. God neither separates nor

178

disjoins the good and evil but permits them to be mixed together at the same time.

These four concepts, good and something, nothing and evil—both in the order of consideration and in the condition of their nature—are somehow gradually disjoined from one another. For however much nothing differs from something, no doubt to the same degree evil through punishment is less, because it is nothing. And good through merit is greater, because similarly it is something. Thus God, like a king in his domain, disposes and orders everything everywhere through his all-encompassing wisdom. He allows free rein for the desire of evil men or blocks their way to whatever they desire as he sees fit. However, he prepares the will of good men by anticipating it and aids its accomplishment by his support.

So that what has been said may become clearer, both positions should be proved from sacred scripture. In Psalm 103, after commemorating certain works of God, the Holy Spirit says: *How highly exalted are your works, O Lord! You have made all things in wisdom* (Ps 103:24). And again, after enumerating a few things briefly, he adds: *that dragon which you formed to amuse him; all things wait for you to give them food in due time* (Ps 103:26–27). Undoubtedly "to give them food" is to open the way to what men desire to obtain. What we read in the gospel where the devils ask the Lord Jesus Christ to enter into the swine[10] corresponds to this. For where the prophet says "they wait," in the evangelist Matthew we read "they asked." And where the former says "you give to them," the latter says "go." The former says "they will gather"; the latter says "they went away." After this the prophet continues: *If you turn away your face they will be troubled* (Ps 103:29), that is, to block their way by restraining the perverse will and by holding it back with invisible bonds. The Book of Tobit presents something similar: *Then the Angel Raphael laid hold of the devil and tied him up in the desert of Upper Egypt* (Tob 8:3).

Concerning God's antecedent mercy Psalm 58 says: *And his mercy will come before me* (Ps 58:11). Concerning his consequent mercy Psalm 22 says: *And his mercy will follow me* (Ps 22:6). The rest of the words of either psalm from beginning to end attest to this sense. The first psalm begins with adversity and, as if God's mercy is not yet anticipated, continues by describing tribulation. The second begins with prosperity, as if his mercy is indeed already anticipated,

179

and describes divine blessings on the Psalmist. Hence the prophet first prays with a groan: *Deliver me from my enemies, my God* (Ps 58:2), and in the second he speaks with joy: *The Lord rules me and I will lack nothing* (Ps 22:1).

Good men share temporal good and bad fortune with evil men indiscriminately. Sometimes the more virtuous they are, the greater their share. Good fortune comes to good men so that they may believe it comes from God and is dispensed by him. But it comes to evil men so that those who are good or who wish to be good may not consider it important. Likewise, temporal misfortunes fall to the lot of good and evil men. They befall the good so that they may be tested, purified, and prepared; they befall the evil so that they do not think God has forgotten or neglected their crimes and iniquity. Thus the depth of God's counsel is more worthy of greater respect the more incomprehensible it is to the human intellect. We too, then, fearing the punishments of the evil and desiring the rewards of the good, should not harden our hearts to what we hear and know. Challenged by the examples of the good and the evil as by a call from God, let us strive with the help of our Lord to pursue our goals, reform our lives, correct our actions, put our conduct in order, and better our senses, wills, and intentions.[11]

Chapter 14—How Norbert encouraged his companion[12]

The holy Norbert, who had recently received Hugh as his new companion requested from God, admonished his follower to be strong. Norbert feared that Hugh would waver before his penitential severity. Lest he shrink from poverty, Norbert set before Hugh the example of St. Lawrence, who distributed the treasures of the holy Pope Sixtus.[13] Norbert wanted him gradually to put aside the dryness of worldly heat and draw from the font of heavenly refreshment and sweetness. He promised Hugh what was promised by Truth, namely, that whoever drinks from that font will not thirst forever.[14]

Norbert also taught Hugh how a sinner ought to be reconciled to and approach God—with what efforts, with what labors, and with what virtues any just person might reach the company of good spirits. He pointed out the greatness of the virtue of humility by which we come to heaven, of the simplicity by which we enter there; he pointed out too the nature of that obedience by which we reach the knowledge of the secrets of God, of that patience by which we attain strength of mind, of that chastity bringing us close to God, of that virginity in which we walk with God, of that poverty offering us the kingdom of heaven.[15] These and like thoughts the man full of God repeated many times from day to day by way of exhortation.

Chapter 38—The wolf quickly tamed[16]

At another time, when some confreres were in the forest to cut wood, they found a wolf devouring a deer. Shouting, they sent him running and took the deer that the wolf in his hunger had brought down. They took it home with them and hung it in a corner unsuspectingly. But the wolf followed them, as if complaining about the wrong done to him, and, at the door of the house they entered, sat like a house dog, seeming to demand what had been taken from him. Others coming in, not knowing what had happened, shouted at the wolf to chase him away, as is usual, but looking at them with a friendly face he did not budge. When the man of God was told about this, he called together all the confreres and inquired what this was about. He said that such a wild animal would not have assumed this mild appearance without a reason. Fearful, the confreres who knew the reason came forward and sought pardon as for a great offense. They explained what had happened, that they thought the reason for the wolf's presence was the wrong they had inflicted on him. When the man of God heard this, he said: "Give him back what is his. You have acted unjustly by taking what was not yours." Finally, the wolf, after taking his prey, departed in peace, harming no one.

Chapter 39—Another wolf letting go of a sheep at a boy's command[17]

A shepherd boy asked what he should do, since he did not have dogs, if a wolf should steal a sheep from him. Jokingly he was told that on behalf of his master Norbert he should command that it dare not take or harm the sheep. Not long after, this same lad was watching the sheep in the pasture as usual. A wolf came and took one of them and quickly ran off with it. The confrere saw this from a distance and, remembering his orders, began to shout loudly: "Where are you fleeing faster than usual, evil thief? Put the sheep down. Put it down, I say. I command you on behalf of my master. Do not harm it, and do not presume to carry it farther." The wolf immediately put the sheep down unharmed and, hoisting it on his shoulders, the lad hastily carried it back to the others.

Whether the following pertains to the same young man or another is unknown. Nevertheless, it is known that another day, when a confrere who was a cleric had been sent to guard the animals in the field, a wolf stood by the sheep the whole day, even while their shepherd was present. As if offering support to the sheep's keeper, the wolf showed no sign of wildness. When evening drew on and it was time to drive the flock in, just as on one side the confrere was forcing the flock to enter, so on the other side the wolf was doing the same. Once the flock was inside and the confrere had closed the gate, leaving the wolf outside, the wolf struck the gate with his paw, as best he could, as if complaining about a wrong done to him and asking that due reward be given to him. He continued to strike the gate, showing that he wanted to enter and receive a portion of food.

When the man of God, Norbert, heard this he asked, "Why do you not open to a guest who is knocking?" When the answer was given that it was not a guest but a wolf imposing himself inconsiderately, and that none of them could get him to leave, Norbert called the confreres together. He inquired about the occasion for the wolf's presence. When the confreres were all silent, he summoned the cleric whom he had sent in the morning to guard the flock. He asked who had helped him to guard the flock, and though the brother was afraid to indicate what had happened, he did not dare to conceal the matter about which he was asked. He said: "It is the wild animal who is knocking at the door. It was with me today and helped me guard the flock entrusted to me as if it had been entrusted to him until the sheep were shut behind the gate."

When the man of God heard this, he said: "Give the wolf some food; he is seeking a reward for the service he gave. *The hireling is deserving of his food*" (1 Tim 5:18). When at the command of the man of God some meat was tossed to the wolf, he seized it as if in reward and left. Not long after, the wolf came and took bread from the hand of a young man who was guarding the calves.

What does this mean, confreres?[18] Wild animals who lack reason may nonetheless grow mild and obey men, yet man, who is rational, closes his ears and does not obey, as if *he who fashioned the eye would not see* (Ps 93:9). Unfortunate man does not hear that *when his ways please God, all his enemies will be at peace* (Prov 16:7). And elsewhere: *The world will fight against the unwise* (Wis 5:21). The man of God preached this to everyone. He taught this to his men, and in this way flying before them,[19] he demonstrated everything by his actions.

Chapter 54—Three visions of Norbert after his death[20]

Proof of Norbert's salvation and the hope he represents should not seem incredible in the judgment of any of the faithful, especially when he appeared in his own likeness after his death to some who surely should be believed. To those who asked about his condition, he gave such response with God's permission that no one carefully attending to it should doubt its truth and certainty.

On the same day and hour on which Norbert's soul was separated from his body, a confrere saw him in a white garment, just as he looked in life, holding an olive branch in his hand. When the confrere asked him somewhat fearfully whence he came and where he was hastening, Norbert answered: "I was sent from paradise, whence I have brought this green olive branch, and I go quickly to transplant it to the place of my poverty, that is, to Prémontré." The confrere, excited about so unaccustomed a vision, began to think about what this might mean. He reported his vision to some at the abbey, for he was at one of its granges. His confreres committed the day and hour of the vision to memory and waited to see what it might mean, what might follow so clear an apparition. After they heard about the death of their master, they realized the vision took place on the same day on which his soul was released from his body.

Norbert also appeared in his own likeness to another confrere, a priest, as if standing before him. But immediately the image of the man Norbert was changed into a flower of wonderful brightness like a lily, and angels then took the flower and carried it off to heaven. Waking up very early, the confrere ran to his prior to receive permission to celebrate Mass in order to commend to God the soul of his pious father, Norbert. When the prior asked for the meaning of so sudden a request, he explained what had happened. The prior ordered him to remember the day. That day was found to be the burial day of the man of God.

Another of those whom God had given Norbert at the beginning of his conversion[21] clung to him faithfully and affectionately and grieved in his heart about the departure of his master, the more because he had no certitude about Norbert's salvation. He humbly begged God persistently in prayer that he might receive some answer about the mercy that the Lord might in his grace confer on his soldier Norbert, a truly repentant sinner. One night Norbert appeared to this confrere in a very beautiful house handsomely illumined by the brightness of the sun. The brother recognized his master, the sight of whom he fervently desired in some way to enjoy. He quickly fell at Norbert's feet and humbly begged him to reveal something about his condition and the mercy he had received from God. Norbert lifted the brother from the ground, threw his arms around his neck, and said to him: "My son, you are asking something difficult. Yet, because to him who keeps knocking the door is opened,[22] come, let us sit down." A very beautiful chair had been arranged there. When the two had sat down Norbert said to the confrere: "It was said to me, 'Come, my sister,[23] rest.' I am in peace and at rest. But I have not yet lost the tremendous fear of judgment at which even the angels stand in fear." Satisfied with this pleasing and hoped-for response, the confrere, fearing that Norbert might leave because his follower's request had been granted, said, "Most beloved father, I ask you to tell me if you were offended that I did not come to you when, still alive, you commanded me to come." Norbert answered, "You will come." And after this he vanished. It was true. That confrere was going to go to him but some business impeded him, and he did not go.

May Almighty God grant that, as this promise portends, the confrere might come to Norbert[24] so that the man of God may transform him whom he left behind as his companion and successor—heretofore a participant in the wretched and painful tribulation of this world—into a sharer in the joys of eternal felicity, the blessings received from God. May Norbert do so through him who lives forever, maintains his mercy, and gives it to all who obey him in doing good and who walk in the way of salvation, justice, and truth.

What more is to be said? Should any of the faithful despair about the salvation of such a man who both lived as already described and with God's permission, after his death, showed these signs of his salvation? Perhaps someone will say, "I hear what is written, but I doubt whether what is written is true because it is unproven to me." Believe if you wish. The writer here brings the truth of the matter to bear in the truth of Christ, because he either witnessed these events he wrote about in Norbert's life or he heard about them from truthful witnesses who had seen them[25] and were still alive when he committed the above work to memory through this writing. The only incidents that might not be eyewitness accounts are certain events the author learned from Norbert himself about what he did before he left his country and his relatives[26] and put aside the burden of secular property.

May those who come after us live and strive to commit to memory whatever has been done and told by Norbert and by the confreres of this order who have gone before us. Even if some do not accept this narrative completely, or everyone is not completely pleased with it, it cannot cause harm to the well disposed, even if it should happen that it does not benefit the ill disposed and detractors.[27]

Additions made by the brothers of Cappenberg[28]

Chapter 1—What sort of person Norbert was, how great he was

We, Norbert's sons at Cappenberg,[29] desire to add what has been discovered by us concerning our father lest in the pursuit of your paternal blessing we appear to your holiness,[30] Hugh, to be ungrateful. We have a book that contains the life of our founder, a man worthy of God. In it is written, at about that time Norbert, a great light of the church and famous messenger of God, came to Westphalia. He was a man of admirable grace, honeyed eloquence, and great temperance. Norbert was the shaper and propagator of canonical religious life, a gatherer of the servants of Christ, the founder of many convents, a powerful preacher of true penance, and in all the roles the executor of the prophetic command *Prepare ye the way of the lord, make straight in the wilderness the paths of our God* (Isa 40:3).[31]

Chapter 2—Norbert predicted a famine would come to Westphalia

I would be remiss in omitting two further great events in this place. Norbert foretold that famine would come to Westphalia and that the brothers of Cappenberg would for a time be chastened in spirit. Soon a severe famine befell, as the man of God foreknew, so that the dire calamity of starvation killed many people. One day, when the brothers were about to go to their supper, they asked that some be reserved from their portion to feed their guests and the poor, since there was no bread at all for alms. Still there was none to be found, but just as the man of God had often quoted, *The Lord will not afflict the soul of the just with famine* (Prov 10:3). Behold, the Lord sent so much bread through his faithful that the brothers both filled themselves and quickly offered more to those who came to them for help. From that day on, the brothers always had enough.[32]

Chapter 3—Norbert dispelled a fever by his word

Another time the holy Norbert wished to send out one of the brothers on the business of the monastery but found him laid low by a powerful fever. Norbert then commanded the brother under obedience, resting his directive in Christ's strength alone, "Go forth and return, and be fevered no more."[33] At once the brother recovered and did as the holy father directed. So the speech of the man of God both achieved his purpose and instantly banished lengthy illness.[34] What follows was also written at Cappenberg.[35]

Chapter 4—The confreres' life according to a rule

It then pleased the Holy Spirit dwelling in Norbert, the messenger of truth, to raise a miraculous harvest from the Lord's fields, namely, that the brothers in the aforesaid communities should profess the Rule of the blessed Augustine. They observed the Rule more strictly than had been the general practice, abstaining from fatty meat and showing the rigor of their penance in rough attire, for the bridegroom's friend John ate of natural and woodsy food, not of delicacies, and was praised for the roughness of his garments by the Savior himself before the crowds who flocked to him in the desert. So our own way of life, divine mercy accompanying it, now stretches far and wide, and we may believe that it will extend much further in the future. So we know that it was both begun in the word of the Holy Spirit and made famous by God's ordination. For did not the Lord, the leader on the journey, carry the vine from Egypt in his arm, held high? And did he not cast out the robbers and criminals who lived in this place, planting the roots of the vine that now stretches its shoots to the sea and beyond, with the support of his heavenly hand?[36] What follows was also added there.[37]

Chapter 5—The Rule of blessed Augustine

I heard the same voice of orthodoxy go on to the chapter: "I know a brother of our profession who was studiously examining our rule when the blessed Augustine himself appeared, not because of the brother's own merits but because of the prayers of his confreres. With his right hand Augustine held out a golden rule extending from his side. He revealed himself to the brother in glowing speech, saying, 'I whom you see am Augustine, bishop of Hippo. Behold, you have before you the rule, which I wrote. If your confreres, my sons, serve faithfully under it, they will stand safely by Christ in the terror of the last judgment.'" Norbert told these things humbly, as if about another man, but I believe that this revelation was to him.

Up until this point what has been written here comes from the book of our founder.[38] Now, if you will, let us treat briefly and lovingly those things that are noted neither in your book nor in ours,[39] according to what we find true.

Chapter 6—The Lord's blood appearing on the paten of Father Norbert's chalice

The following event took place at Floreffe. When our memorable father was there celebrating Mass, during which he was certainly accustomed to proceed very devoutly, suddenly just before communion he saw a large red drop of the Lord's blood in the middle of the paten. He called Brother Rudolph, our sacristan, who was then his deacon. "Do you see, brother, what I see?" He said: "I see, my Lord." And Norbert began to weep profusely because of this great event. It is due to this miracle becoming known, we believe, that we have been instructed to wash the paten.[40] The observance of this custom among us began at this time, since until then it was unknown to us.

Chapter 7—The veil of St. Servatius

We read in the life of blessed Servatius[41] that, after the death of that very holy bishop, while the people watched with wonder, a silk cloth brought by angelic hands was placed over his venerable body. For this reason this silk cloth is honored with the highest reverence in the church at Maastricht and is also preserved and stored with special care.

When the man of God came to Maastricht, he asked to see this silk cloth. But those in charge of it all began to make an excuse, especially since no one dared to look into the case in which it was kept. What can we say? The man of God eventually was granted his request, but when in his presence they opened the sacred repository, suddenly the silk cloth—I am going to say something strange—by some marvelous and divine power moved and flew away. It drifted around the basilica for some time until, unfolded, it hovered high up in the church near the ceiling as if borne up by wings. When the people saw this, some gasped in amazement while others were almost fearful with grief that it was being taken from them. The man of God considered the matter in silence and then began Mass. While he was saying Mass, the silk cloth refolded itself and softly settled above the priest's extended arms. He took it respectfully and restored it to its place. From this event I do not doubt that God has declared both the glorious merit of Bishop Servatius as well as the faith and power of prayer of his servant Norbert.

Chapter 8—The death of a robber

In the place that is called Bolanden, where a monastery of our confreres flourishes, there dwelled a powerful plunderer of others' possessions. This man, among his other violent crimes, had some time before seized the income of wine properly belonging to the church of Magdeburg and in particular intended for the celebration of Mass. When Archbishop Norbert came there, as a confrere of that place recounted to me, he was not silent on behalf of the church entrusted to him. Norbert summoned the robber and, although he was fearful, openly said, "Sir, why do you presume to inflict this injustice on blessed Maurice,[42] rashly seizing the annual income set aside for Mass and putting it to your own use?" When the man pompously responded that this was not invasion of property but a legitimate part of his inheritance, the man of God answered with prophetic spirit, "Know, brother, that this coming year you will be driven back from this plundering by the judgment of God." As he predicted, so it happened. That same year the unfortunate man was killed by his enemies.

Chapter 9—Warfare foretold by Norbert

At another time, when Norbert was taking part in an expedition of King Lothair, he arrived with the king at Augsburg, where he predicted the famous conflict between the people of that city and the king.[43] Before entering any church to pray, this thrice-blessed man was accustomed to say on bended knees at the threshold of the basilica, "Peace be to this house and to all who dwell there."[44] When, therefore, Norbert entered the church of the aforementioned city and had completed his prayer, he summoned his deacon from whom we know this, revealing to him what he knew through the spirit. He said: "Brother, I asked peace for this place. I asked for peace, but nevertheless I have found here the rejection of peace.[45] Therefore, I carefully commend to your safekeeping our pallium and whatever else is in your custody, because confusion and great conflict hang over this place." Thus it happened. The next day, after many lay prostrate and wounded by the king, the citizens were punished for their rashness. Finally, they were received into the king's favor only with difficulty, even after much tribute money was paid.

Chapter 10—Norbert's healing of a demoniac

On another occasion when a demoniac was brought to him—to be brief—Norbert blessed water mixed with salt, and when he approached and began to sprinkle the water, the evil spirit departed before he came to the man. These are a few of the many things we have discovered, about which we do not think it right to be silent because in both the law[46] and the gospel[47] we are warned not to neglect the honor of our father. He who has left us such great examples of perfection will not cease to intercede for us with Christ—as we securely trust—so that even here we may walk in the footsteps of so

great a predecessor and, at the end of our suffering, deserve to be
welcomed with him into eternal glory. Amen.

Blessed is Norbert[48]

Blessed is Norbert, first father of this order.
 I rejoice that you, Father Hugh,[49] foster his merits.
 Surely blessed, he spurned worldly heights
 and, subject to the yoke of Christ, dutifully sowed the seed
 that all around has borne a marvelous fruit,
 fruit through which the cloister rule saves many,
 fruit joyfully filling the heavenly storehouses.
 An astounding spirit, a divine fire,
 marked him out and made him known for learning.
 He burned with heavenly light. He was a peer of the great
  doctors.
 Crowned with merit, he bears an imperishable name.
 He constantly loved true poverty.
 With courageous faith he put Satan to flight.
 Vessel of the Eternal Word, minister of peace,
 he secured peace, reconciling discord.
 Advanced to episcopal office
 he was outstanding, a cross for the wicked, an example for
  the good.
 In all affairs of the church he was a shining star.
 Blessed is he who could stand secure before swords.
 Conscious of no wrong in himself, he does not grow pale
  with guilt[50]
 or hesitate to die, but is bound to the love of Christ.
 Blessed is he who, when the Lord comes, will have troops
 whom the good judge will choose from our order.
 May grace protect us at this time of trial. Amen.
 Here ends the life of our glorious father, Norbert.

Philip of Harvengt, "On the Knowledge of Clerics"— Introduction

Of the authors whose works are gathered in this volume, only Philip of Harvengt, prior and later abbot of one of the earliest of Premonstratensian foundations, Bonne Espérance in Brabant, is known to have lived into the final quarter of the twelfth century, dying in 1183 in the community where he had spent most of his long life.[1] A direct convert of Norbert in the early 1120s, Philip was drawn away from the schools of Laon[2] to spend a long career as canon, prelate, and prolific author. His works fill an entire volume in the Patrologia Latina.[3] Philip had been among the earliest members of Norbert's young community at Prémontré. In 1126 or 1127 he and a few others were sent by the founder to plant a daughter foundation at Bonne Espérance in Hainault. Soon after, Philip became prior at the new establishment under the same Abbot Odo who figures prominently in his text about the woman saint, coincidentally called Oda, on whom he later wrote a hagiography.

As prior of Bonne Espérance, Philip met with extreme difficulties. Already beset, by his own account, with malicious rumors about his ethics and leadership, Philip was in the late 1140s embroiled in a controversy similar to that about which, nine years earlier, Anselm of Havelberg had written his *Apologetic Letter.* As in the earlier instance, a canon sought to leave his community and join a monastic house. Now, however, the controversy was closer to home, and as it turned out far more damaging for Philip than his controversy with Egbert of Huysburg had been for Anselm of Havelberg. The errant canon of the 1140s was a member of Philip's own house, Bonne Espérance; although the monastery to which he fled was a Cistercian neighbor, its case was advocated by Bernard of Clairvaux himself. The matter was appealed to the papacy. Perhaps because the pope at the time was the Cistercian Eugenius III, the Premonstratensians lost.[4]

The personal consequences for Philip were disastrous. In the aftermath the canons' general chapter removed him from his priorate and sent him and a few other disgraced confreres into exile from Bonne Espérance. When the community continued to be in turmoil during their absence, the general chapter recognized that Bonne Espérance's problems extended beyond its leadership and restored Philip to his priorate in the early 1150s. Apparently fully rehabilitated, he was elected abbot some five years later. In the more than two decades of his subsequent abbacy he seems to have administered the community successfully.[5] At least he was involved in no more such heavily documented controversies. Nor, however, did he produce major scriptural commentaries or theological works, such as his exile may have encouraged.

Philip of Harvengt's long career as prior and then abbot of Bonne Espérance was thus shaped by tumult, and his small work "On the Knowledge of Clerics"—despite its educational content—is evidence of the wide disputes in which he and his Premonstratensian confreres found themselves in the middle years of the twelfth century. In this text comparison between canonical and monastic charisms with respect to the importance of scriptural learning, teaching, and preaching sharpens and focuses the authors' advocacy of rigorous intellectual training; Philip's conflict with Bernard over whether a white canon might leave his house to join the white monks is here in the background. On a still larger scale a former student in the cathedral schools but here an advocate of a distinctively canonical pattern of religious education, Philip enters forcefully into contemporary discussion of the relationship between action and contemplation among religious orders and the relationship of education within the cloister to the mixed apostolate he saw as ideal for the contemporary priesthood.

Philip's work "On the Knowledge of Clerics" is one of a series of educational works, tracts on the formation and secular role of the regular canons. His writings on the training and status of clerics are often cited as the respective parts of a synoptic work, *On the Education of Clerics*. So titled, the six related texts occupy some 541 of the 1398 columns in the Patrologia Latina volume devoted solely to Philip's works. Recent scholarship on the abbot from Harvengt and the spirituality of regular canons continues to cite *On the Education of Clerics* as a grouping of treatises made up of parts entitled "On the Status of Clerics," "On the Knowledge of Clerics," "On the Silence of Clerics," "On the Justice of Clerics," "On the Continence of Clerics," and "On the Obedience of Clerics."⁶ In fact, however, the overarching title was invented by a seventeenth-century editor, Philip's later confrere and successor as abbot of Bonne Espérance, Nicholas Chamart, whose 1621 edition of Philip's works depended heavily on a single manuscript codex.⁷ This codex represents all of the short texts that Chamart then grouped as *On the Education of Clerics*, but it nowhere indicates that the author intended them as comprehensive or integrated. In the PL, Migne repeated Chamart's editorial grouping without comment. As a result—in respect to twentieth-century reception of Philip's work on the identity and formation of regular canons, as in many instances in twentieth-century medieval studies—a miscue in the PL has led to misleading scholarly interpretations. Indeed, a rough parallelism links Philip of Harvengt's various works on the canonical life surviving in the Brussels copy, but primary evidence of his intent to frame them as an encyclopedia of clerical education is completely lacking. This essential point about the shape of Philip's work was made in 1977 by Norbert Weyns but has been largely overlooked by professional academics, like much of the exacting scholarship on the history of the Order of Prémontré published in its *Analecta*.⁸ Philip's "On Knowledge" in fact bears a complex relationship to the other essays conventionally grouped as *On Education*, as well as to his Song of Songs commentary and other elements in his literary production, but here it will be considered as a small, freestanding work rather than as an arm of a comprehensive treatise on Augustinian canons and their education.

In itself, then, "On the Knowledge of Clerics" is interestingly tendentious. Philip argues here for literacy, scriptural learning, and prioritization of intellectual and contemplative over material and pastoral concerns for all clerics, especially for clerics in community. His discussion of these topics models what he understands to be optimal process for learning, interpreting, and communicating the message of the Vulgate Bible, which he represents as the fountain of all appropriate knowledge. Here Philip shows himself a skilled exegete, as Henri de Lubac's many references to his specific readings and his general discussion of hermeneutics—not only in "On the Knowledge of Clerics" and the related treatises, but also in his correspondence—affirm;[9] Philip was characteristic of his generation in embracing four levels of interpretation of a given passage, and in this small work he is again characteristic of mid-twelfth century authors in moving from direct textual commentary toward the *sententiae*, that is, the grouping of biblical texts on a given topic in support of a wide-ranging theological discussion that would soon become central to theological education.[10]

In "On the Knowledge of Clerics" Philip's argument that learning is essential to members of canonical communities is grounded in typological readings of the scriptural texts about Old Testament priestly figures and of the evangelists, Paul, John in the Apocalypse, and Christ himself as exemplars of priestly comportment with respect to *doctrina*, understood as both their own education and their responsibility to inform others. This short work, although it compactly presents this follower of Norbert's central educational thought and is therefore important to clarification of the twelfth-century Premonstratensian charism, may seem unwelcoming to a modern readership unaccustomed to reading scriptural exegesis as medievals' self-articulation. Here, however, Philip is concerned to teach "by word and example" how the well-trained, hard-working cleric invests himself in continuing study; here his word becomes his example, which he holds up for his reader as the manner of reading and interpretation to which he should himself aspire.

Philip begins abruptly, plunging directly into the reading—figurative interpretation of scripture—that he identifies as the grounding of canonical spirituality as well as intellectual life. Following the canonical books in order, he identifies and expounds models of priestly scriptural reading and interpretation from Exodus through the Apocalypse, everywhere militating against an implied argument that either good works or contemplative disengagement from secular affairs can substitute for knowledge of the literal content and multiple levels of figuration in both Old and New Testament texts. Having pointed out to his reader that priestly leadership was effective for the ancient Hebrews because it was grounded in knowledge of law, he sets aside potential clerical claims of inadequacy for preaching by expounding the model of Jeremiah. As he points out, the prophet at first protested God's directive to preach with claims of humility, as having only childish understanding. In Philip's view, however, Jeremiah is a type of the cleric of his own times who is bound to overcome his own reticence and speak the divine will.[11] This discussion is an important transition in Philip's text; he urges not only that the members of his clerical audience maintain high intellectual standards, but that their central secular obligation is to engage with an illiterate laity in their preaching.

Philip's forcefulness in the matter of clerical preaching begs the question of his audience. At his writing, he was prior—albeit in exile from his own community—of canons living according to the Rule of St. Augustine, but his own Premonstratensian affiliation has frequently been understood even in his own generation, the immediate succession of the founder Norbert, to have largely abandoned active apostolate for a life on the contemplative Cistercian model. Scholars have understood this turning away from secular involvement especially to have characterized the Western circaries of the order, such as Brabant, which embraced his own house of Bonne Espérance.[12] Yet here Philip patently advocates preaching grounded in scriptural learning such as that which formed the core consistency in his master Norbert's varied and far-flung career. The discordance between Philip's urging of his clerical and Augustinian audience toward preaching to the laity and scholarly assumptions of the twelfth-century Premonstratensians' contemplative isolation has led Caroline Bynum, for instance, to doubt that "On Knowledge" was written for his own confreres. Instead, she views this and others of his educational and apologetic texts for canons conventionally grouped as *On the Education of Clerics* as directed toward a broader audience of Augustinians or, still more generally, priests, presumably to be read by his own brothers as exemplars of a higher form of clerical life, and by others who might so appreciate them.[13]

Yet later passages in Philip's "On the Knowledge of Clerics," from its exegesis of Jeremiah's reluctant acceptance of his prophetic imperative, argue against such interpretation. The abbot's text rings, like so many works of his contemporary Bernard, of abbatial collation in the chapter house. He pauses occasionally to gather his audience's attention—*fratres carissimi*, beloved brothers.[14] Most provocatively, having discussed Christ himself as exegete and Paul's injunctions to Timothy to set learning ahead of works, Philip narrows his discussion to clerics living in community. Here the specificity of his description of canonical life, although it does not specifically refer to the model of Norbert of Xanten or list by name his foundations or their filiation, seems to reflect the specific characteristics of the Premonstratensian network of religious houses. As Rachel Fulton's analysis of Philip's Song of Songs commentary persuasively argues, the abbot from Harvengt adventuresomely wished to refound the intellectual life of the canonical community in a Marian imagery of the relationship of learning to faith; Martianus Capella's old story of the liberal arts in the marriage of Mercury and Philology would be replaced by the new romance of the soul and her lover, Christ.[15] Although scriptural learning would thus be brought to support mystical encounter, it would retain its active end—the preaching that remained a consistent theme of Norbert's and the Premonstratensians' worldly engagement and apologetic from the founder's conversion through Philip's educational writings. Thus, Philip's "On the Knowledge of Clerics" seems to have been composed for a Premonstratensian audience, most narrowly the canons of Bonne Espérance, and generalized for a wider readership, rather than intended for Augustinian canons in general.

Comparison of Philip's readings of the many biblical passages he gathers here with their long respective exegetical traditions is outside the scope of this discussion, but some of his remarks are especially noteworthy. For instance, as Lubac notes, his assertion that tears open up difficult passages in scripture is distinctive.[16] In the rhetorically powerful finale to this generally reserved treatise, Philip's urging of his reader to cling to his determination to unlock the secrets of difficult passages even to the point of tears and his linkage of his reader to the speaker of the Apocalypse, for whom this act of ablution yields interpretive clarity, inspire and encourage the reluctant student of scripture, at once validating and pointing past his feelings of frustration.[17]

In terms of its relationship to the other texts in this volume and their development of recognizable Premonstratensian idiom, Philip's dynamic, highly affective focus on the apostle John as scriptural reader is especially persuasive that this text is normative of a Premonstratensian charism with respect to scriptural learning and preaching. Because authors in Norbert's immediate circle consistently look past Norbert and Augustine, respectively the reformer and inaugurator of regular communities of clerics, to John of the gospel and the Apocalypse as their paradigm, Philip's exegesis of the opening of the seals has emphatic meaning for his *fratres carissimi*; the same John had been, with Christ himself, Anselm of Havelberg's exemplar of the canons' mixed life of action and contemplation.[18] When the abbot urges tears of frustration as a means to dissolve the hiddenness of difficult scriptural passages, he figures in human bodily substance the mixed life of action and contemplation his confreres carried across Europe. For Philip, contemplation brought the amendment of heart that would open the most obscure of texts and—so released—its reader was bound to communicate its meaning to the Christian community at large. Reading, among the regular canons, even more among the Premonstratensians, might be improved by the contrition cultivated throughout the monastic centuries, but the cleric living in community—the canon of Bonne Espérance and his confreres in more than a hundred foundations in their coalescing "order" across the continent—answered the still higher calling of sharing his knowledge, as had Ooliab, Jeremiah, and John.

Meanwhile, for Philip, other distractions should be shorn away. Indeed, parish work and ecclesiastical offices were to be shunned, not because preaching or modeling of scripturally informed life was inappropriate for the cloistered cleric, but because they distracted from his continual transit of the pathway between disciplined contemplative reading and active preaching. Here, the abbot's discussion of the efficacy of tears recalls the fervor of his Marian commentary on the Song of Songs and his discussion of the life of the exemplary woman, Oda of Rivreulle. Philip had read and interpreted Oda's experience as scripturally modeled. Here, in "On the Knowledge of Clerics," he invites his brothers literally to predicate their lives in time on biblical learning. *Docere verbo et exemplo* (teaching by word and example) is indeed the core of Augustinian experience, and the Premonstratensian pattern of cultivating that art is distinctive, efficacious, and transformative of both the cleric and his worldly hearers.

PHILIP OF HARVENGT, "ON THE KNOWLEDGE OF CLERICS"

Here I speak simply, setting things forth one at a time. If we truly wish to know whether clerics must surely have knowledge of holy scriptures, we may easily find that out in the same writings. In Exodus, when the holy text mentions the building of the tabernacle, it speaks of Beseleel's building it with Ooliab: *The Lord has filled them with the spirit of wisdom and understanding and knowledge in all manner of work* (Exod 31:3). Here, the tabernacle built in the desert signifies the church of our times. Beseleel and Ooliab signify the clerics to whom responsibility for building the church is commended. Men glory wrongly in the name of cleric if they attain the position of teachers even if they are themselves unlearned, so true clerics must be filled with the spirit of wisdom, understanding, and knowledge—with all learning. Otherwise clerical status may be their downfall rather than a lofty achievement. When such men had been set in office to frame the church, what would they have done if they had not known to wield the tool of learning? Beseleel and Ooliab are rightly said to signify clerics because the meaning of their names fits this interpretation. Beseleel means "in God's shadow," and Ooliab, "my Father, my protection." Such men—those who are divinely ordained to the dignity and office of the clergy for the building of the church—indeed linger in the shadow and the protection of the Lord. Lest they be cut off at the root for the aridity of sterile ignorance, they bear fruit in the shade and refreshing shade of salutary knowledge.

In Deuteronomy, when Moses carefully tells the people whom God commanded him to instruct what must be done, he clearly explains how necessary such great knowledge is to clerics: *If thou perceive that there be among you a hard and doubtful matter in judgment*

This translation is based on the Patrologia edition, PL 203, cols. 1387–92.

between blood and blood, cause and cause, leprosy and leprosy, and thou see that the word of the judges within thy gates do vary, arise, and go up to the place which the Lord thy God shall choose. And thou shalt come to the priests of the Levitical race, and to the judge that shall be at that time, and thou shalt ask of them, and they shall show thee the truth of the judgment. And thou shalt do whatsoever they shall say and they shall teach thee according to his law (cf. Deut 17:8–11). We realize that for us judgment between blood and blood, cause and cause, leprosy and not leprosy is hard. Obtuse as we are, we cannot distinguish between sin and justice, sin and injustice. Blood here signifies exactly that, and sin means sin, as Hosea says: *Blood hath touched blood* (Hos 4:2). And I think that cause signifies cause and justice signifies justice, for David says, *Judge me, O God, and distinguish my cause from the nation that is not holy* (Ps 42:1), that is, my justice from an unjust people. Leprosy and not leprosy mean sin and freedom from sin, as in Leviticus: *If the stroke of leprosy be in a man, he shall be brought to the priest* (Lev 13:9).

Too often we perceive a greater sin as lesser, and conversely, we take a greater justice to be the lesser, or what is leprosy as not, or vice versa. Therefore when we consider matters in our own minds, we often change our views, thinking now this, now that to be the more correct, as if we see the pronouncements of judges change within ourselves. So the text says: *The words of the judges within thy gates do vary* (Deut 17:8). Here I believe that the gates signify our five senses, through which either life or death may enter our soul. As Jeremiah says: *So death has entered and come up through our windows* (cf. Jer 9:21). And David speaks to the just soul: *Because he has strengthened the bolts of thy gates* (Ps 147:13). The judges are our thoughts, which either accuse or excuse us in their judgment, as the apostle speaks of *thoughts accusing or defending* (Rom 2:15). So the words of judges vary within our gates when uncertain thoughts turn within our heart. The ignorant man often yields to them, when it seems that the one rightly resists the other. So that he not struggle in doubt any longer, the text says: *Arise, and go up to the place which the Lord thy God shall choose. And thou shalt come to the priests of the Levitical race and thou shalt ask of them* (cf. Deut 17:8–9). The place the Lord has chosen is the church. Jacob says of it: *Truly, that place is holy* (cf. Gen 28:16). And Moses says: *Beware lest you offer your holocausts in every place that thou shalt see, but in the place which the Lord shall choose* (Deut 12:13–14). So the Lord said to Solomon: *I have heard thy prayer, and have chosen this place to myself for a house of sacrifice* (2 Para. 7:12). And a little after: *I have chosen, and have sanctified this place, that my name may be there forever* (2 Para. 7:16). The place of the Lord's choosing, dearest brothers,[1] is the congregation of holy clerics, the convent of religious life to which Moses, that is, divine law, warned those whom he saw dying of the disease of ignorance to enter in humility. The members of that gathering are Levites, priests, that is, clerics of the tribe of Levi—not their descendants in the flesh but the inheritors of their office, not in transient but in perpetual succession. Concerning them the Lord says in Exodus: *They shall be priests to me by a perpetual ordinance* (Exod 29:9). So the text says: *Thou shalt ask of them, and they shall show thee the truth of the judgment* (Deut 17:9). Indeed, those judges show the truth to those who ask, for devoting themselves to scriptural study and holding mentally to its commandments, they try diligently to fulfill what they learn—to educate others to fulfill those commandments as much by word as by example.[2] So the text says: *You shall do whatsoever they shall say and what they shall teach thee, according to his law* (Deut 17:10–11). We ought to listen with complete obedience to those whom we see are themselves obedient. Those whom study improves are thereby helped to live well, and they who have learned the law can teach others according to it. As one of the pagan poets says, "No one can say what he does not know."[3]

And how, I ask you, can a cleric know the law unless by applying himself diligently to divine reading? So it is that the text then says: *He shall copy out to himself the Deuteronomy of this law in a volume, and he shall read it all the days of his life so that he may learn to fear the Lord his God, and keep his words and ceremonies that are commanded in the law* (Deut 17:18–19). Clerics must devote themselves to reading if they wish to fulfill the divine command, so that they may learn in their reading how to serve God and keep his words and ceremonies as set forth in his law. Lest we doubt that clerics of this sort are pleasing to God, he promises through Jeremiah that he will give them to his people as shepherds, as a great gift: *I will give you pastors according to my own heart, and they shall feed you with knowledge and doctrine* (Jer 3:15). Because the Lord confirms that those who offer up knowledge and doctrine please his heart, we understand that those who do not nourish with knowledge and doctrine perhaps displease him. So again God says through Hosea: *Because thou hast rejected knowledge, I will reject thee, that thou shalt not do the office of priesthood to me* (Hos 4:6). And below: *There shall be like people like priest* (Hos 4:9).

The prophet Ezekiel says when he was sent to teach the children of Israel: *I looked, and behold, a hand was sent to me, wherein was a book rolled up, and he spread it before me, and he said to me, Son of man, eat this book, and go speak to the children of Israel. And I opened my mouth, and he caused me to eat that book* (Ezek 2:9—3:2). The literary figure here is metonymy, in which the vessel signifies what it contains or the contents signify the vessel. This figure of speech frequently appears in both divine scriptures and in secular writings. There is no doubt that book or volume here by metonymy figures scripture, literally contained in a roll. So, in a beautiful image, the prophet and priest who is sent to the children of Israel is first fed with the volume. Because the office of the cleric is to enrich others with the page of knowledge, he should himself not suffer hunger, and he who is ordered to regurgitate healthful learning ought not to fast from the same knowledge. How could he offer the vital nourishment of doctrine if, weighed down by aversion to study, he did not wish to erase deadly ignorance with it? Ignorance is inexcusable, and so negligent a will is blameworthy.

When Jeremiah was called to the office of preaching, he seems not have been dedicated to seeking knowledge, and he humbly resisted undertaking such work because of his ignorance. He accounted for his ignorance gracefully, saying: *Lord God, behold, I cannot speak, for I am a child* (Jer 1:6). He spoke as if to say, do not place upon me the office of a teacher because I am untaught—not because I do not wish to speak, but because I have not yet been able. I am not marred by the stain of negligence but hindered by immaturity. The Lord, knowing that Jeremiah had responded in modesty, did not condemn him for deceit but cut away his anxious fear in pity, with a generous promise. The Lord said: *Say not, I am a child, for thou shalt go to all that I shall send thee, and whatsoever I shall command thee, thou shalt speak* (Jer 1:7). This is to say that we should not refuse what we are commanded on account of our immaturity, for no age of life may refuse God's commands. Humility's true commandment is what obedience dictates. When Jeremiah then asked, how may I fulfill your commandments, since he who has not learned to speak should keep silent? the Lord said, *Behold, I have given my words in thy mouth* (Jer 1:9), as if to say, the powerful grace of my generous hand grants you what your age and maturity deny. I will give you such words that will be understood to be learned, and you need no longer complain that, though untaught, you are forced to teach others.

Finally, in the gospel the Lord accused the Sadducees of not knowing scriptures, so that they did not believe that their souls would return to their bodies in the resurrection. When they asked him whose wife the woman who had married seven brothers would be at the resurrection, he responded to them: *You err, not knowing the scriptures nor the power of God* (Matt 22:29). When the Lord said *not knowing the scriptures*, it was important that he added *nor the power of God*. You see with what great force he spoke against ignorance of scriptures, such that when someone did not know them, he was certain that person did not know God's power. For if the Sadducees had known scriptures, they could not have been ignorant of God's power. If they read with understanding, they could not doubt the power of the resurrection those scriptures preach. According to John, when Christ was tormented by the people, unrecognized by the unruly crowd, certain lost souls proffered testimony from the scriptures. Knowing neither what they were saying nor what they supported, they pressed their error on others who would therefore perish too. Some said, *This is the Christ*, but others answered, *Doth the Christ come out of Galilee? Doth not the scripture say that Christ cometh of the seed of David, and from Bethlehem the town where David was? So there arose a dissension among the people* (cf. John 7:41–43). As you see, this great dissension among the crowd was because the people did not understand scripture and so could not recognize Christ, even though they looked upon him in the flesh. A little later the priests and the Pharisees said to the ministers whom they sent to Jesus to arrest him: *Why have you not brought him? Are you also seduced? Hath any one of the rulers or of the Pharisees believed in him? But this multitude that knoweth not the law is accursed* (cf. John 7:45–49). Perhaps the Pharisees spoke truly, because indeed the crowd ignorant of the law was accursed, but those same Pharisees who thought that they knew the law and did not were also accursed. Nicodemus, who was one, said to them: *Doth our law judge any man, unless it first hear him, and know what he doth? They answered and said to him, Art thou also a Galilean? Search the scriptures and see that out of Galilee a prophet riseth not* (John 7:50–52). You see that everywhere here they returned to the scriptures and tried to convince one another by the scriptures' testimony, but the wretches were defeated by their own reasoning even as they believed they had won.

Nicodemus rightly warned them to investigate scriptures, for if they examined them as carefully as he, they would defer to their truthful testimony rather than set it aside. So the Lord himself warned them in John: *Search the scriptures, for you think in them to have life everlasting, and the same are they that give testimony of me* (John 5:39). Who doubts that he incurs God's just wrath if he has not diligently searched scriptures, when they hear that the Lord commanded this in the gospel? In a beautiful passage he said not that you have life everlasting in these things, but *you think in them to have life everlasting.* The Pharisees did not understand scriptures but falsely believed that they did, so they did not in fact have eternal life in them. Therefore the Lord said, *Search the scriptures.* Why? *The same are they that give testimony of me.* And he says thus, if you wish truly to have eternal life, which is nothing other than me, study scriptures, which offer testimony about me so that in searching them you may find me, and when you have found me, you will have eternal life. And so he says, if you truly wish to have eternal life, which is not except through me, search the scriptures offering testimony about me so that you may find me in searching them, and when you have found me you may have eternal life. He says to them: *You will not come to me that you may have eternal life* (cf. John 5:40). So those who do not wish to search scriptures seem not to wish to come to Christ, nor do they seem able to have life even if they can falsely believe so.

Finally, the Lord himself, when he chose apostles who were uneducated and illiterate to confound the learned, nevertheless allowed them to remain uneducated but took care to move them toward the deep secrets of knowledge as time went on. For that reason, when he climbed the mount and opened his mouth, he taught them, saying: *Blessed are the poor in spirit* and so forth (Matt 5:3). And below, when he had ended his many parables for the same apostles, he offered this closing: *Have ye understood all these things? They say to him, yes. He said unto them, therefore every learned scribe is like to a man that is a householder, who bringeth forth out of his treasure new things and old* (Matt 13:51–52). He offers a testimony worthy of those who understand it, whom he says are like the father of a family because they understand what is said, offering new and old from their treasury. The father of a family is Christ himself. His treasure is holy scripture, new and old. Its rewards are for the just, and its punishments for the unjust. Because the grace of the gospel is revealed to the just, they receive the reward of eternal life as a new gift, but the unjust receive punishment as they always have from ancient times. In this passage the father is concerned to offer new and old things, as when Christ promises punishment for the unjust and enjoyment of life for the just. The learned scribe is like Christ himself when he carefully understands those things that are in scriptures, when he writes them out in his heart as on tablets, with the pen of memory, and when he does not doubt that they bring salvation for all who understand them.

The Lord invited the apostles and those who take their places to study, coaxing them. A little afterward, when Peter said to him *Expound to us the parable* (Matt 13:36), he responded reprovingly, *Are you also yet without understanding?* (Matt 15:16). For he excited them to study not only with gentle persuasion but also with harsh reproof, lest they provoke him to anger by remaining sluggish and lazy. According to Luke, he chastised the two disciples going to the town of Emmaus, saying: *Oh, how foolish and slow of heart you are to believe in all things that the prophets have spoken* (Luke 24:25). He interpreted the things about him in all the scriptures beginning with Moses and all the prophets. Then a little later, when the disciples had recognized him and he had disappeared from their eyes, they said to each other: *Was not our heart burning within us, while he spoke in the way, and he opened to us the scriptures?* (Luke 24:32). The evangelist John says that the disciple who ran with Peter to the tomb had believed what the woman had said, that the Lord had been taken away. As for why he believed so rashly the explanation is added: *He saw and believed, for as yet they knew not the scripture* (John 20:8–9). This is as if to say, if he were aware of the scripture he would not have so rashly believed what was false. According to Luke the incredulity of those going to Emmaus is reproved, and according to John the credulity of those

others is reproved, but their errors in both cases come from ignorance of the scriptures. Therefore the Lord, after his resurrection
when he was about to ascend into heaven and leave his disciples
behind for a while on earth, wished that they be ignorant of scriptures
no longer, lest in that ignorance they wander from the straight path
of living or of teaching. Thus far, even though he had taught them
many things in such time as there was, he had still left behind many
things that must be taught, perhaps so that they might take them in
more ardently and hold them more tenaciously once they possessed
them. When the Lord was about to leave them, he said: *Go ye unto the
whole world, and preach the gospel to every creature* (Mark 16:15). And
lest the preachers of the truth limp in their knowledge and the
unlearned stagger in their faith, he said: *All things must needs be fulfilled that are written in the law of Moses, and in the prophets, and in the
psalms, concerning me* (Luke 24:44). And the evangelist added: *Then he
opened their understanding, that they might understand the scriptures*
(Luke 24:45). What scriptures? The law of Moses, the prophets, and
the psalms, in which three things the whole of the Old Testament is
indicated—this he made clear to the apostles, as Luke testifies.

But lest anyone think that understanding of scriptures is
appropriate for the apostles alone and not for the clerics who hold
their place in the church, and that therefore he who is impatient of
study and toil may choose instead to yield to his distaste for them,
let him hear how Paul worked to educate his disciples, whom he had
ordained as clerics, and to commend them when they were educated
worthily and laudably. He says to Timothy: *Attend unto reading, to
exhortation, and to doctrine* (1 Tim 4:13). This is to say, do not think
you are a cleric in order to wander about unoccupied or perhaps to
involve yourself in secular business, but so that you may truly
progress, embrace reading. So that your progress may be evident to
all, embrace doctrine and exhortation as well. And lest anyone
believe that only a little time might suffice to accomplish these
things and that he need not devote himself to studies of this sort
with appropriate concentration, the apostle adds: *Meditate upon these
things, be wholly in these things, that thy profiting may be manifest to all*
(1 Tim 4:15). Doing these things you bring about the salvation of
both yourself and those who hear you. You see how useful it is for
the cleric to linger in reading and exhortation, so that not only does

he merit salvation himself but he glories greatly in the salvation of his hearers. In another letter the apostle commends the same Timothy: *But thou hast fully known my doctrine, manner of life, purpose, faith, long-suffering, love, patience* (2 Tim 3:10). When he is about to add the further virtues, Paul sets doctrine first so that he may mark it as a school and a kind of melting furnace, from which by polishing and study the list of virtues comes. And a little later he admonishes the same reader: *But continue thou in those things which thou hast learned, and which have been committed to thee* (2 Tim 4:14). This is as if to say, you believe that such great power comes from me that I may reach sanctity by doing what you direct, so he adds, *because from thy infancy thou hast known the holy scriptures, which can instruct thee to salvation by the faith which is in Christ Jesus* (2 Tim 3:15). All scripture is divinely inspired, and so is useful. When the apostle instructs Titus, he says: *In all things show thyself an example of good works, in doctrine, in integrity* (Tit 2:7). Here, when he is about to say *in integrity, in gravity*, he first says *in doctrine*, because a cleric is only a false example of good works if he is unwilling to embrace doctrine, the mother of virtues. Thus the apostle forcefully commends these things to the Corinthians: *In all things you are made rich in him, in all utterance and in all knowledge* (1 Cor 1:5). And in another letter he writes to them: *You abound in word and knowledge* (cf. 2 Cor 8:7). Lest the Corinthians wrongly consider the apostle contemptible for his own lack of knowledge, he glories humbly about it in the same letter: *I suppose that I have done nothing less than the great apostles, for although I be rude in speech, yet not in knowledge* (2 Cor 11:5–6). He means by speech that volubility and fluency preferred and sought assiduously by some who would speak rather than live well, wishing to seem rather than to be and to be placed ahead of others rather than to progress. One may lack such elegance of words and ornament of style without danger, but a cleric cannot lack knowledge of scriptures without blame.

When one is assigned in infancy to learn to read, without other obligations, and entirely committed to that task, what living person is so dull that he cannot obtain learning, even if he might not be very diligent? Therefore must he be reproved for neglect and laziness, if he is so distorted in his sense of order as to wish to do nothing. He has been chosen for this, to put knowledge ahead of all else. Many, when they have left behind their boyhood and reached the age of puberty, wish to exercise their liberty perversely. Impatient of study and toil, they cast aside discipline, deserting their prior nest, and they fall rather than fly. Released from the constraints of the schoolboy, they discover the vices of heedless youth, and because they realize that their elders will no longer drive them by the rod, they are glad to wander freely through fields of pleasures. Perhaps they are concerned to gather riches or wish that honors come to them, so they are the more set against study to the degree that they wish for these false excesses. They think it is enough simply to be able to read, if they see themselves raised high by riches and honors, for they judge it happier to glory in financial prosperity than to suffer tribulation and toil for the sake of learning. It seems to them that knowledge is good for nothing but to bring temporal honors and riches, and if by chance this profit comes easily for them, then they consider it superfluous to work to achieve it. They do not ponder the commandment of divine wisdom: *Receive my instruction, and not money. Choose knowledge rather than gold* (Prov 8:10). They learned this as boys, when as a blessing of their youth they were still subject to their parents and teachers, but when they should have achieved greater progress in the passage of time, laziness compels them to forget. So we see many who are heaped with riches and profits, decked with ecclesiastical offices, but who nevertheless are simple, idiots, and illiterate, so that when they come among clerics gathered for one reason or another, they scarcely dare to speak Latin among them. And if by chance they do presume to do so, their speech does not reflect scholarly training. Of this divine scripture says: *What doth it avail a fool to have riches, seeing he cannot buy wisdom?* (Prov 17:16).

But just as some are distracted from the work of learning by harmful prosperity, so many are kept from it by poverty, or so they say. Realizing that they do not have the desired financial support and unwilling to suffer from the slightest want, they prefer to remain among their own people without learning than to be in want among strangers for learning's sake. Comforting themselves in this circumstance, they fall prey to their very consolations. They refuse to invest effort in study and labor, giving themselves to the pleasures of sluggishness and leisure. The less they busy themselves with literary studies, the more they succumb to deathly pleasure, because when laziness takes away one's appetite for persisting in honest work, it compounds the reason for neglect. Thus, when these people refuse to attain knowledge because of the burden of poverty, they encounter the ruin of their habits. While in their reprehensible laxness they grow sluggish about honorable and useful pursuits, they burn the more reprehensibly for base and harmful pursuits. Once they believe that they cannot attain the joys of transitory prosperity by being upright clerics, they fall fearlessly into every sort of corruption, pulled hither and yon by their desires. They become involved in secular cares, valuing the marketplace more than the church. In acquiring temporal possessions they become imprudently, even shamefully inquisitive, losing their desire to maintain clerical honor. Now, all barrier to sin removed, they retain nothing of a clerical status but the title, and even in that they glory falsely, since the name is violated by the reality. Yet most of them presume to compound their perdition, taking sacred orders. Although they know nothing or, worse, because they know nothing, they hasten to invade the place of learning, which they ought especially to avoid because their ignorance is inappropriate to this status.

For because learning is undoubtedly appropriate for every cleric and still more for him who is raised to the rank of priesthood, Malachi criticizes an unlearned priest: *The lips of the priest shall keep knowledge* (Mal 2:7). Yet unlearned clerics, as if to balance the disadvantages of their situation with material goods, dare boldly to appropriate to themselves the rank of priest and are snared as dangerously in their downfall as they have, though unlearned, audaciously seized the place of the learned. Because in their laziness they seek to learn nothing from scriptures by great effort, they do not know how to guard their life and their rank with appropriate religious practice. Because they did not seek first to obtain knowledge, they cannot afterward show its works. The divine word speaks against this: *A man, well instructed and taught, will look to himself* (Sir 40:31). Although unlearned clerics have neither knowledge nor suitability as guardians, they nevertheless presume to teach their ignorant people, and they do not fear to usurp the magisterial role wiser men hesitate to take. Divine scripture gracefully repudiates their presumption and, in praiseworthy fashion, commends

Ecclesiastes to their disgrace: *Whereas Ecclesiastes was very wise, he taught his people* (Eccl 12:9). This is as if to say, blush, you who knowing nothing do not fear to enter the place of knowledge, who without sitting on the footstool of discipleship presumptuously leap to the master's high seat, although Ecclesiastes himself did not presume to teach the people without first attaining wisdom. Therefore, because they repudiate wisdom and can neither experience spiritual preferment or offer others salutary doctrine, but by their teaching kill those whom they should bring to life, indeed they choose not to live through wisdom but to die through ignorance. Against this divine scripture says: *May they have learning and wisdom, which grant life to their possessor* (Eccl 7:13). So clearly, although the world has many clerics, the number of the ignorant is infinite. Of those, none or perhaps only a few can truly excuse their lack of learning in seeing themselves as rich or poor. They do not hear the counsel of a certain wise man—rather of wisdom itself—admonishing them healthily: *Draw near to me, ye unlearned, and gather yourselves together into the house of discipline* (Sir 51:31). And another wise man says: *He that rejecteth wisdom and discipline is unhappy* (Wis 3:11).

Not only are those who purport such excuses distanced by their noxious torpor from the desire for learning, but so are many who renounce the secular world for the rule of the cloister. They seem commendably ardent to serve God but nevertheless grow reprehensibly sluggish about diligent reading. God has led them out from engagement in the marketplace so that they may free themselves in the cloister for the utmost attention to spiritual business. Therefore, I consider them more reprehensible than can be expressed if they are bored by meditating on divine law with appropriate assiduity. For divine law is sacred scripture. A cloistered cleric ought entirely to be involved in it, if he is concerned to oppose the secular world the more perfectly, according to what he has vowed and, unspotted by earthly things, to make his *conversation in heaven* (Phil 3:20) along with the apostle. The prophet David spoke of divine law as *the unspotted law of the Lord, converting souls* (Ps 18:8). Sacred scripture is appropriately said to be unblemished law from its effect, because with grace assisting it purifies its readers from earthly feeling, and it turns around those souls whom temporal attraction has misled in ignorant error. It converts them by recalling, informing, and enlightening them.[4] Scriptural testimony shows that the things we see pass away quickly and do not endure endlessly. What else can recall those who are small in understanding from the love of visible things and to inform them to seek invisible things? So the prophet adds: *The testimony of the Lord is faithful, giving wisdom to his little ones* (Ps 18:8). Scripture is the Lord's testimony, as he says himself in the gospel: *Search the scriptures. The same are they that give testimony of me* (John 5:39). Therefore the cleric ought to linger upon this law day and night if he is concerned to glory the more fully in the beatitude of the perfect. When he has learned the law by reading and meditating, he ought to pour it forth to those who seek it in preaching.[5] So Malachi speaks of the cleric in a mystical figure: *They shall seek the law at his mouth* (Mal 2:7). And another wise man says, *Despise not the discourse of them that are ancient* (Sir 8:9), since from them you learn understanding so that you will yourself be able to give appropriate response in time of necessity. Many who are cloistered, as I was beginning to say, refuse to attend to reading. What is worse, they either openly or subtly criticize those who do, thinking that anyone engaged in transient business is lazy or idle. They find it irritating to sit, read, and meditate, and they seek to be occupied with extraneous matters. If by chance no business is entrusted to them, they complain with sinister murmuring, suspecting their superiors. They say that not enough is assigned to them if they have no outside obligations, even though, as they say, they are prepared to fulfill their assignments and serve the needs of their brothers. If they do undertake extraneous business, they rejoice that they are now not constrained to sit and read. Flattered as they are to have such assignment, they are freed more than they should be to talk and to run about. Since they are let loose for those things on the outside that they wish to do, they return only rarely to the inner and spiritual business of reading and meditation. Even if they plan to attempt it again, they are blocked, turned back by their own distaste to the pattern they enjoy. Many of them neglect to attend to their reading for long because they do not understand it all, and although scripture is difficult, they imagine that their future reading will not be so. Therefore, shutting their books, they revert to transitory things, and if they lack a place or permission for these occupations, they still think about them. They are more eager to wander outside, free of

213

mind, than to search out the hidden meanings of scripture with diligent focus.

Scripture demands a studious reader, not someone whose mind wanders and is easily distracted. Most of it is obscure so that it may be the more meticulously investigated and, once understood, retained the more gratefully. When its meaning is hidden, the reader should not then step back but focus on it the more fully, so that his skillful investigation uncover what Christ is loath to impart to the neglectful reader. For those who wish to find Christ alone must knock, demanding his answer devoutly, for he rejoices to open up the riddles of scripture to those who ask (Matt 7:7–8; Luke 11:9–10). Mark the evangelist seems to me to express this beautifully after he has recorded that Christ told the parable of the sower to the crowd standing about: *When he was alone, the twelve that were with him asked him the parable. And he said to them, to you it is given to know the mystery of the kingdom of God* (Mark 4:10–11). When, I ask you, my brothers, do we find Christ alone, except when we push aside all the tumult of the world from our hearts so that nothing inappropriate stands in the way of our reading or blocks our meditation? Then we can focus our understanding on the sacred page in order to recognize Christ the more fully in the benefit of reading, and love him whom we know, cling to him whom we love. When we eliminate whatever stands in the way of our reading and in our reading think of nothing other than to please Christ, then surely we find him alone. And to them who find him he gives the spiritual understanding of scripture. Therefore he says to them, *To you it is given to know the mystery of the kingdom of God* (Mark 4:11)—to you, that is, who have constantly desired to know, and to you who have asked me when I was alone. So according to Matthew, when he had said, *To you it is given to know the mysteries of the kingdom of heaven*, he added, *but to them it is not given. Because it was given to the apostles it was not given to the others, and Christ sets forth the cause, saying: For he that hath, to him shall be given, and he shall abound, but he that hath not, from him shall be taken away* (Matt 13:11–12). This is to say, he who has diligence will receive understanding. He who urgently inquires and reads will find the grace to comprehend. But as for him who does not have diligence, this same understanding, which he has either from natural talent or some bit of knowledge, is taken away from him. Nothing useful comes of it. We must therefore pray to Christ when he is alone that he lift the veil of obscurity over the letter of the law and the cloud of blindness over our heart, because the book that has brought letters to our knowledge does not delight as long as it is sealed with seals we cannot break.

But if prayer alone does not suffice to open the book and unfasten its seals, we should not then cease, lest it seem that the reader or prayer has faltered and been negligent in his weariness. We must do what the apostle John says that he did: *I saw in the right hand of him that sat on the throne a book written within and without, sealed with seven seals. And no man was able, neither in heaven or upon earth nor under the earth to open the book, and I, John, wept much because no man was found worthy to open the book nor to see it* (Apoc 5:1, 5:3). But John tells then what usefulness his tears had: *And one of the ancients said to me, weep not. Behold the lion of the tribe of Judah, the root of David, hath prevailed to open the book, and to loose the seven seals thereof* (Apoc 5:5). And after he had said that: *And I saw, and behold in the midst of the throne and of the four living creatures, and in the midst of the ancients, a lamb standing as it were slain, and he came and took the book out of the right hand of him that sat on the throne, and he opened the book* (Apoc 5:6–8). When, therefore, those things which are in the scriptures are sealed with the covering of the letter, they are not opened to us as we read and wish to know them.

We must then knock for the highest master and, if words of prayer do not bend him to reveal them, we must pour forth tears as well. Usually these are effective with God, for they soften his severity. He does not still deny to one who weeps what he did not wish to grant to one who prayed. If we feel that our understanding is so clouded that the reading is empty for us and that we press against a veil covering the meaning of the text, then we must pour forth a stream of tears to wash away the covering over the scriptures. When the earnest reader weeps in his desire to understand, his exterior eye is clouded for the moment, but then his interior eye grows clear in a new way, and that which had before seemed hidden is now pellucid to him. Even if it is his face, not the scripture, that is washed with tears, still the scripture too is washed clean in a way impossible to explain. While the former is cleansed in a physical sense, the effect surely passes to the latter. Indeed, the transformation is more for spiritual than physical eyes when the sense emerges clearly. What was hidden, wrapped in seals of cloudiness, the reader sees now as freed from all obscurity—a wonderful thing. We speak of it not so much from experience as from the firm testimony of divine reading. Although we speak of it, we know it not so much from experience as from the solid proof of divine reading, because the grace of understanding is not given to all to whom the benefit of knowledge is offered. The apostle John knew it, however, from experience. When there was no one who could open the sealed book, *I wept much* (Apoc 5:4), and after those tears what had been hidden was clear to him. Here we see plainly how much effort we must bring to our reading—and ardor to our understanding—even if we cannot achieve all we desire because our eye is clouded. We ought to invoke God in our prayers and beg his grace with tears.

These and many different testimonies are more than sufficient to show that knowledge of scriptures is appropriate to clerics and should be sought by them with the greatest care, but not because their involvement in something else needful should be criticized, for that other need is indeed appropriate to the clerical order. Clerics can rightly obtain ecclesiastical roles and from time to time indulge in manual labor, if charity or necessity has forced them urgently to do so, but not because levity has lured them to it. The apostle himself bore great concern for churches because charity constrained him, and he labored with his hands when necessity pressed. Finally when he instructed Timothy, he did not forbid him from labor but rather set it in its rightful place, so that he could show that from time to time it was fitting for a cleric to do manual work if he knew what place it should hold. A cleric should set study of scriptures first and pursue it diligently. He should do manual labor with patience, not enjoyment, so that spiritual delight draws him to the former but only unwelcome temporal necessity constrains him to the latter. As the apostle says: *Exercise thyself unto godliness, for bodily exercise is profitable to little, but godliness is profitable to all things* (1 Tim 4:7–8). By godliness he means attentive study of the scriptures. Through such study, with grace assisting, the cleric ought to know God better, love him thus known more devotedly, and worship him so loved more perfectly. Progressing in these things he may thus become, in a spiritual sense, a temple of God even as he provides a holy example to others in his knowledge and life. A little afterward the apostle adds: *Attend unto reading, exhortation, and doctrine* (1 Tim 4:13), and again, *Take heed to thyself and to doctrine* (1 Tim 4:16), in so doing effecting both your own good and that of those who hear you. Therefore Paul admonishes Timothy especially: *For bodily exercise is profitable to little* (1 Tim 4:7). Because Timothy knew that Paul frequently was burdened with manual labor, for the apostle's letter to the Corinthians says that he has been in great need, Timothy wished to imitate him like a good disciple, so that in all things he might be like his master. But because necessity did not weigh Timothy as it did the apostle, nor demand that the strength of his body supply much labor, Paul advised moderation, so that he not take his fervor too far but recall it to appropriate measure. So Paul said that *bodily exercise is profitable to little* (1 Tim 4:7). He did not say useless, so that he seemed entirely to condemn labor, but of little use, wishing to show clearly the limits of its use. Work is indeed useful when it maintains the health of the body, returning it still more eager for reading. Work is useful, Paul says, when it serves reading and the other spiritual offices as their inferior, not with that order reversed and upended so that it persistently dominates. Work is useful for the cleric when he does not presume to take the first seat but, mindful of his proper rank, rejoices to choose the last. It is useful when a cleric controls the work so that it not exceed its bounds, so that desire for reading not yield to levity. Therefore, it is of little use with respect to godliness, which apostolic truth testifies is useful for all things: *Godliness is profitable to all things, having promise of life that now is and of that which is to come* (1 Tim 4:8). Through such godliness spiritual riches and glory come more richly in this life, and eternal joys are the reward of justice in the next. So David says: *Glory and wealth shall be in his house, and his justice remaineth for ever and ever* (Ps 111:3). And Solomon says: *Length of days is in her right hand, and in her left hand riches and glory* (Prov 3:16). Therefore the cleric ought to keep this resolve first and foremost, that he open himself to the desire for inquiry and knowledge of truth, and that he not engage in manual labor or the care of churches because of curious levity but in obedience to pure and sincere charity.

PHILIP OF HARVENGT,
LIFE OF ODA—INTRODUCTION

Although Philip of Harvengt's oeuvre has received little attention from modern scholars compared, for instance, to the works of
his German confrere Anselm of Havelberg, its importance has
recently been emphasized by Rachel Fulton in her massive study of
medieval spirituality from the Carolingian period to the twelfth
century. In her discussion of Philip's relationship to the great contemporary development of Marian piety and empathy with the suffering Christ, Fulton argues for the originality of the theological
contribution of this immediate follower of Norbert of Xanten,
identifying him as the most adventuresomely erotic twelfth-century
interpreter of the Song of Songs.[1] Her affirmation of the interest for
the history of spirituality in the abbot of Bonne Espérance's long-
neglected commentary invites exploration of this work's relationship to other Premonstratensian documents. Philip's life of Oda of
Rivreulle,[2] which interprets in terms of the Old Testament book's
imagery the experience of a woman whom he personally knew, is of
special importance to fuller understanding not only of his own complex exegesis of the Song of Songs but also that commentary's place
in the wider context of Premonstratensian thought and practice.

The circumstances of the composition of the *Life of Oda* support such analysis of this hagiographical text. Saints' lives are sometimes assumed to be early works of medieval authors; young
religious were often encouraged to develop their writing in hagiographical exercises.[3] This hagiography, however, offers internal evidence of composition shortly after its subject's death in 1158, when
Philip, by then in his fifties, was already abbot. In that capacity, as
his account affirms, he celebrated the funeral of his friend and subject.[4] Philip's *Life of Oda* was thus composed after his principal large-
scale works, the Song of Songs commentary and the cluster of texts

on the education of canons conventionally known as *On the Education of Clerics*, both of which were likely written before his abbacy. The *Life of Oda* speaks to Philip's leadership of Bonne Espérance and the associated women's community at Rivreulle as to gender and spiritual practice among the order's many double communities, with their strongly Marian piety.

Like Philip's Song of Songs commentary, the hagiography of Oda is in large part written in *Reimprosa*, filled with internal rhyme intended to enhance and render memorable its reading aloud. Philip of Harvengt is, as Fulton notes, "not an easy author."[5] His *Life of Oda* is, from a modern perspective, burdened with pleonasm—again a positive choice of contemporary literary aesthetic—and so laden with scriptural allusions that identifying them is superfluous except where they function as important images. Despite the heavy application of craft in its composition, however, Philip's representation of Oda presents important evidence for the social and institutional history of the new order of Prémontré. The author seems to have known his subject for two decades. In the period between the 1130s, when she was first associated with Bonne Espérance, and her death in 1158,[6] her leadership at Rivreulle and her local repute as a spiritual advisor and model of charity were well established. Philip's hagiography of Oda thus works to clarify the much disputed role of women among the early Premonstratensians.

Catherine Mooney's recent collection of essays about medieval males' hagiographical representations of the experience of contemporary women emphasizes the extent to which such narratives represent the normativity of male authors rather than the experience of female subjects; to discern the reality of saintly women's lives or the character of their spiritual experience from their portrayal by, typically, their confessors is difficult at best. Some *beatae* so memorialized seem to have had more agency than others in the production of their own hagiographies.[7] Given the absence of other information about Oda of Rivreulle, Philip's representation of her has more importance as the exemplar of a Premonstratensian woman saint than as an individualized portrait. Nonetheless, in some regards Oda's story is so idiosyncratic as to suggest a lively historical reality.

The young girl Oda showed a proclivity to holiness that her parents feared. Pious enough, they nonetheless wished their daughter, apparently an only child, to marry well. In order to forestall her entry into religion, they contracted with the family of another local youth to marry the two teenagers. Philip's account of the abortive wedding reveals some timeless features of adolescent-parent relations as well as specifically twelfth-century details of the history of marriage. The girl flatly refused to accept her young husband, to the consternation of all the adults, especially her father. While the latter chased the young man, who had ridden off in profound embarrassment, the unhappy daughter shut herself in her mother's bedchamber and mutilated her face.[8] Whether Oda understood herself here to imitate Agnes and Perpetua or whether allusions to such martyrs or virgins is Philip's device to honor Oda's self-sacrificial act,[9] the modern reader immediately recognizes distressingly familiar behavior and sympathizes with friends' and parents' grief; as Rudolph Bell has noted, young females' self-mutilation as escape from social expectations, especially sexual expectations, is chronologically ubiquitous.[10] As Caroline Bynum has further pointed out, assessment of its pathology or suitability is culturally determined.[11] In the context of twelfth-century canon law's and social custom's construction of marriage as invalid without the consent of both parties,[12] Oda was thus able to achieve her own release from her unwilling betrothal. She does what she wants. She joins the Premonstratensians.

Throughout Philip of Harvengt's exposition of the young girl's developing piety and maturing desire to enter regular religious life, the hagiographer weaves the imagery of the Song of Songs. As Ann Matter's study of historical exegesis of the Song of Songs notes, male authors typically accepted the grammatical gendering of all human souls as feminine in their allegorization of the voices of the canticle as a human soul's—the bride's—in conversation with Christ, her male lover.[13] Here, however, no such regendering is needful, because the already feminine Oda begins even as a youngster to meditate erotically on her divine lover. At her very wedding she answers the priest's question whether she will accept her young husband with the proud assertion that she already belongs to a divine spouse.[14]

Philip's reader is prepared—as the wedding guests are not—for Oda's forceful and scripturally informed refusal. Her hagiographer's description of her inner life in the period before her parents' attempt to marry her preemptively has predicted this answer. In Oda's extreme youth, already "her beloved tarried in delight between her two breasts and she spoke with him continually in her heart as in the marriage bed"; rather than suffer earthly marriage, she "chose rather to be lifted to the mountain of myrrh, that is, to the lofty discipline of regular life." Philip locates the girl's wished-for, lingering mystical encounter with Christ in "the hills of Lebanon…a community of religious women blossoming in full, pure holiness."[15] As Fulton points out, the Song of Song's *A bundle of myrrh is my beloved to me, he shall lie between my breasts* (Cant 1:12) had been the text for one of the most challenging and original passages in Philip's commentary on the Old Testament book. There he explained that the female speaker of the canticle might be understood as at once mother of Christ and the Bridegroom's lover: "Truly the breasts of the Virgin seem to figure that twofold love with which she loves to love her Bridegroom as God and man—as God inasmuch as he is the Creator and Lord of all creatures, as man inasmuch as he is her son by the grace of a wonderful and ineffable birth."[16] In Philip's life of the saint of Rivreulle, the daughter of the well-meaning, mundane parents becomes a type of the heavenly Virgin in the highly affective dissolution of the boundary between motherhood and eroticism. Perhaps the young Oda imagined such heights of feeling as a result of the Premonstratensians' preaching on the Song of Songs, even before she sought them out as her protectors and counselors, or perhaps Philip only so imagined his woman friend's internal life. In either case, his *Life of Oda* presents to its principal audience at Bonne Espérance and Rivreulle a model of passionate spirituality, a mysticism at once Marian and spousal. Philip's portrayal thus explores, in the life of a woman, the contemplative ends of his own community of Bonne Espérance—or, more properly speaking, his and Oda's communities of Rivreulle and Bonne Espérance. As the hagiographical text makes plain, Oda was in her lifetime both counselor and model for men as well as women. Philip attests to his and his canons' respect for her spiritual stature.

Yet the woman saint portrayed by Philip merits memorialization for her sisters and the associated men's community not only through her reputation as a mystic but also for her charitable acts. Her virginity and poverty are exemplary, as is her physical and psychological suffering in the period in which she is afflicted with a skin disease initially thought to be leprosy. Her gentle administration of the women of Rivreulle and her acts of charity to the sick and the poor of the secular world, however, make her famous outside the convent—as Philip says, punning on her name and the name of the first abbot, Oda and Odo, spreading the *odor* of her sanctity.[17] Oda's work at Rivreulle's hospice included her sacrifice of her own small comforts to those who were still needier. In his hagiographical representation of her, Philip—like Norbert of Xanten and Anselm of Havelberg—constructs a regular religious' exemplarity according to her identity as "poor for Christ's sake."[18]

Evidently women were respected members of early Premonstratensian double communities, and their work in the hospices such as Rivreulle's was valorized both for its contribution to society at large and as a means toward the sisters' own spiritual preferment. Oda cannot, as Philip's life describes her, have been fully cloistered, with respect either to her service to the poor or her interaction with Premonstratensian men. Her own life at Rivreulle—despite the contemplative emphasis lent it by Philip's focus on imagery from the Song of Songs—was to that extent active. Her hagiographer's representation of her experience, while it surely served to encourage contemplation among his literate confreres and their sisters, likewise supported active ends. Oda's example, Philip of Harvengt reminded his reader, was useful for the preaching he again affirms as central to his community's charism.[19]

PHILIP OF HARVENGT, *LIFE OF ODA*

Prologue

The ancient pagans, blind though they were in their error, eagerly praised their poets, even though those writers' tales were poorly written and empty of content. Still, the ancients aggrandized with glorious titles the names of those who—cloaking truth in clouds of lies—cultivated vice rather than virtue. How much more fitting it is, then, for us to carry forward with great fanfare our own philosophers, advocates of truth, lovers of justice and virtue? For they carefully wrote down whatever was worthy of being preached[1] in the thoughts of great teachers or in the deeds of illustrious men, so these examples might be read about in the future and remain widely known. Indeed, in all centuries up to our times, our authors have carefully preserved the memory not only of men but also of women who were wonderfully virtuous beyond their sex, so that the healthful breeze of their great repute might reach others who might then be inspired by their examples.

In this evening of the world, as our times decline, no such shining light should be concealed beneath a bushel but rather should be raised up to light all in God's house.[2] Anyone who keeps such knowledge to himself rather than spreading it to the ears of many—whether because he is puffed up with his own learning or corrupted by envy or simply lazy—deserves to be harshly criticized. On the other hand, he who raises up praiseworthy models in churches and preaches about them at every crossroad brings himself grace. The first of the apostles did thus when, as the scribes and the Pharisees were preventing him from speaking in the name of Jesus, he

---

This translation is based on the Patrologia edition, PL 203, cols. 139–74.

retorted: *We cannot but speak the things which we have heard and seen* (Acts 4:20). For as someone said, "If one wishes to shape the company of praise, he should be the first to proclaim the good someone else has wrought in words or deeds."³ A good man enjoys no possession unless he shares it. Therefore, though my literary talent is unpolished and I achieve neither the logic of Socrates, the argument of Demosthenes, or the rich eloquence of Tully, nonetheless—depending more on devotion than knowledge—I take up the life of this virgin in my simple speech, as if stammering. She gleamed forth in my own times, brilliant in her virtue, before my very eyes. I commend myself to her merits so that my mouth may be worthy to open in her praise, so that my weak beginning may grow in strength and I may not fear the criticism of a later reader or tremble before an accusatory judge but hide from such storm and rain under the shelter of her prayers.

The Life Begins

In the middle of the night heaven is decorated with the lovely variety of its gleaming stars, as the gift of light removes fearsome shadows from the world. So in the deep blackness of our earthly pilgrimage the company of the saints shines wonderfully in the varied brilliance of their merits. They are brighter than the beauty of all the stars as they shed their many rays of virtues throughout the world. This welcome diversity feeds the eye of the onlooker, since it presents no confusion or dissonance but always returns to itself as into the habitation of its heavenly city, where there are many mansions,⁴ different orders,⁵ varieties of brilliance. Among them abides one God, all things to all, the inextinguishable light, the undying life, the unfailing peace, the unblemished beauty. In this order of eternal thrones the various saints take their rank according to the exaltation of their titles and the degree of their blessedness—those whose bodies were broken in a winepress in witness to God as well as those who were cooked on the griddle of temptation in flesh and spirit, sweating through many fasts, vigils, and travails. Among all these sacrifices virginal chastity has a high place. Because of its lofty merit it is ranked close to the King of glory, the spotless Lamb.

Such is the high status the worthy virgin Oda desired to reach through him by whose will the author and consecrator of her virginity might guard her undefiled, inviolate until her life reached a glorious end.

Pope Innocent then had charge of the universal church, Lothair served the Roman Empire in the West, Philip's son Louis held the kingdom of the Franks, the venerable Reinald was bishop of Reims, Lithard oversaw the Diocese of Cambrai, and Baldwin of Holland was prince of Hainaut.[6] At that time the maiden Oda was born of eminent parents in that region, in the castle called Allouet. Her noble parents, her father, Gilbert, and her mother, Thescalina, were both outstanding in their piety as well as in their ancestry. This wise maiden, of lofty origin through both her parents in the flesh, wished to preserve her inborn nobility from life's corruption. Cutting off such itching of the flesh as corrupts women's gentleness from its very origin, she distanced herself from the seduction of the world and from all illicit affections, committing herself fully to the school of virtue and nobly decorating her youth with the flower of chastity and the title of modesty. She thought as did the pagan poet that she did not deserve the rank of her parents unless she earned it herself.[7] Boethius too says, "You are not splendid without your own eminence; borrowed brightness pales."[8]

Therefore Oda made up her mind already as an adolescent to dedicate her virginity to her heavenly spouse. She meditated daily, like the dove that leaves behind the swamps of earthly delight and ventures freely, as it should, to the mountain of holy life, building her little nest in a niche of humble rock. She aspired in her vows as the Song of Songs says, *I will go to the mountain of myrrh* and the hills of Hebron (cf. Sg 4:6). Oda saw many others constrained by the poisonous freedom of licentiousness. Knowing that such baseness is not corrected except according to a monastic rule, she chose rather to be lifted to the mountain of myrrh, that is, to the lofty discipline of regular life. And because the lily of chastity is often lost among the thorns of transitory vanity in the mud of the low places, she wished to be carried toward the hills of Lebanon, that is, to a community of religious women blossoming in full, pure holiness.

After Oda made this vow she remained sheltered in the care of her family up to the age of puberty. Shut away from the things of the world, she kept to herself from the time she adopted this resolve. So that hateful talk not wound her innocence, she avoided like vipers the company and the conversation of girls absorbed in luxury and laziness. She saw only maidens who spoke of honor and friendship and whose private deeds cast no shadow on their public reputation. Although her face glowed with lovely color and although she spoke sweetly, with maidenly reserve, all her beauty and dignity came from within, because her beloved tarried in delight between her two breasts[9] and she spoke with him continually in the quiet of her heart as in the marriage bed. So she feared or rather scorned the lustful speech and looks of young men, for their eyes announce shameful things and their mouths speak vanity. They come upon a vulnerable heart and are swollen with emptiness, rashly driven by carnal pleasure. But as for Oda, nothing earthly occupied her mind, and day by day she kept her vows.

Constantly, joyfully impassioned by her love, the girl called upon a certain male relation to whom she was especially close. Trembling with fear, she revealed her holy passion to him fully, beseeching him with many tears and asking that he carefully keep from her parents the secret she had entrusted him, begging that he help her achieve what she wished. Indeed, because no action seemed swift enough to her eager mind, she redoubled her entreaties, worried that he might change his mind the next day. She asked that she be taken immediately to the Lord Odo of Bonne Espérance[10] so that she might practice religious life with him and his community. But because trust is never safe and a friend easily becomes fearful when involved in secret plans, even as the maiden in her dove-like simplicity thought her plan was going forward secretly, her kinsman indeed changed his mind. Wounding her trusting heart, he went to her mother and father and told her secret, so blocking the road he should have prepared.[11] As soon as her parents found out, they were confused and agitated, distraught over the news. Taking counsel with each other, they decided to undercut Oda's plan for chastity with a marital bond.

So Oda's parents set out to find a husband for the girl—one who in family, habits, wealth, and rank was worthy of marrying her. From far and wide they gathered many friends and relations to discuss marriage alliance between their children. A young man named

Simon was eager to accept the bride offered by her father and relations, and his family was equally approving. But while the young man gloried that he would be happy in so fine a marriage, he urged that the promise be fulfilled as soon as possible—that it be confirmed without delay in a sacramental bond. When this was agreed on both sides, a day was chosen for celebrating the union.

Meanwhile the holy maiden hung between hope and fear, troubling thoughts filling her mind. She was frightened by the prospect of the marriage she so wished to avoid. At the same time she heard bruited about by everyone the secret she had entrusted to the ear of one man. She who had declared that she would not know a man's bed in delight now heard that she was to be married on the next day. As she was already preparing to leave the home of her father and to reach the holy place she desired, she thus met with a great obstacle, struck with new fear that she lose the seal of her virginity. But what is knowledge without personal witness? Indeed, it is not virtue—or does not seem to be—when a hardworking athlete does not sweat from exercise in the arena of temptation, or when the fierce south wind does not press her with all its power, or the northwestern wind does not batter her often with its free breeze, or when she does not fend off the poisoned arrows of her enemies even as they threaten to overcome her. For virtue *(virtus)* is so called because its strength *(vires)* prevails over difficulties. Virtue has in it nothing obtrusive or flashy; neither is it especially conspicuous without being tested. And when it is neither proved nor tested it is not virtue, any more than he who is never battered can bring great courage to a struggle. So it is that the Lord of virtues allows his champions to be tempted, that their temptation bring a favorable outcome. For such reasons God disposed that his handmaiden Oda battle with the enemy in a triumphant struggle, for he wished her to be well prepared for battle on the training ground. Practice makes performance easier. God allowed, even willed, that she be tested so that instead of falling in feminine weakness under the battle standard before the enemy's assault, she might be a wonderful spectacle for all—a humble, defenseless girl sent into battle alone against the gigantic, armed Goliath rightly to win the victor's palm, defeating the enemy before a great throng of men.[12]

228

Seeing various windstorms of temptations stirring against her and the enemy preparing battle against her with all his strength, the maiden retreated into herself and roused that beloved who rested in delight in the humble dwelling of her heart. To him she opened up all her complaint, announcing the enemy drawn up before her gates. She asked that the Lord send his help from his holy place, that her loins be girded with strength, for she knew that she needed to battle strength with strength. Urgently she commended to Christ the chastity she had dedicated to him while still a little girl. So that she might run with foot and heel unbruised along the path of truth she had chosen, she prayed that the bonds be broken with which Satan had prepared her ruin and scandal. Meanwhile she pounded, repeating her prayers urgently, upon the door of her heavenly lover.[13] He awoke and listened affectionately to the voice of his bride. He opened the door to her and kindly consoled the gentle spirit of his lover, pressing upon her the interior kiss of love. And lest she suffer from dread at night or be fearful of temptations, he prepared that bread of fortitude that is pure delight and sweetness, promising to defend her on her day of trial. As if she were a fertile field in which good seed had been planted, divinely consoled by its scent the maiden set aside her fears. She who just a bit before was bent by any breeze now laughed at the rage of the weather, the sounding of the sea, and the whirling of the winds. Meanwhile Oda's many-faced enemy connived with his snares against the flower of her virginity. She tried all the harder to live purely, setting forth in free flight to a refuge of solid rock. Having set her tent in impregnable crags, she fearlessly faced the multitudes besetting her. Even though she was inexperienced at warfare with forces encamped against her, still she gloried, hoping so to provoke the enemy more than she was provoked. Secure, she said with Paul: *Neither trial nor sword nor death nor any creature shall be able to separate us from the love of Christ.*[14]

The day of the wedding was at hand. It was talked about widely, and the house was decorated with pictured tapestries and various other ornaments. The family gathered, decked out and merry. All kinds of beautiful array were assembled to dress the maiden, but she did not involve herself in these wonderful preparations, remaining solemn throughout. Instead, she took on manly courage; as someone says, "A wonder is nothing to him who considers even a great thing nothing."[15] The father, knowing that his daughter abhorred his plan for her, was deeply afraid that—if he insisted that she be married unwilling—she would be overtaken by unbearable grief and incurably sickened, or perhaps driven to run away somewhere from which she could not easily be brought home.[16] As he turned over these troubles in his heart, he finally decided to put them to rest with a lie. As Oda lay down for bed the night before the wedding, he spoke to her gently but falsely: "It is wrong that the flower of your youth fall and wither in this place, that your rosy freshness be darkened by grief. You should be joyful in your growing up, enjoying many things, many riches, exchanging this dark sorrow for bright happiness. Banish all this heaviness from your mind and stop wounding your loving parents with your sad face. Do not be afraid of what is not fearsome. You think your wedding day will be tomorrow, but I will put it off to some more appropriate date, saying I am too busy with other affairs." Oda took her father's words to heart and fully embraced them, taking falsehood for truth. Not knowing what the next day would bring, she rejoiced as if she had won the first engagement of a battle.

When night had passed and the sun rose on the new day, the young man to whom Oda was betrothed arrived at the prescribed time with a great crowd of his relations—girls, their parents, many noble maidens and ladies, all bedecked with fancy and costly garments. Because the church was a long way off, the great throngs of guests gathered in the courtyard of Oda's father. The girl was summoned. Because she was accustomed to obeying her parents, she complied immediately, emerging not as a bride into her parent's doorway but as a warrior-maiden into the arena.[17] Such great love of chastity filled her breast that she showed it clearly not only in her words but also in her actions. And when the priest, as was the custom, asked the bridegroom Simon three times whether he consented of his own free will that the maiden Oda be joined to him, he responded that he had come for this, that he wished heartily to do all that conjugal law required. But when the priest turned to the maiden and asked whether she wished to accept him as spouse in the accustomed way, she blushed deeply and bowed her head, not answering anything the priest said, as though she thought whatever display he made for eyes or ears was empty and meaningless.[18] Some of those standing about attributed her silence to arrogance and some to bashfulness.

One of the ladies close by Oda's side, taking note of her maidenly modesty, addressed her thus, sweetly and softly: "Do not fear, noble girl, to give your assent. It was honorable and modest, when you were questioned, to be silent first once and then twice, but you will be thought ignorant and contemptuous if you do not know or do not wish to open your mouth when it is right to do so. There is *a time to keep silence and a time to speak* (Eccl 3:7). For a young person to speak little even in her own behalf is wise, but she ought to answer when asked yet again lest she be rebuked for taking her reticence too far. Do not insult the dignity of so many important people or seem too contemptuous to respond—a bad example to other girls your age—to the priest's third question. Open your noble lips and offer the response he wishes."

To this the maiden spoke: "You ask urgently whether I wish to have as my husband this man whom you name to me. Know then that I intend to accept neither him nor any other. I am joined in love to him to whom alone I offer my faith, to whom since I was a little girl I have wished to dedicate my virginity. I cannot in any way be separated from his embraces by the love of a man, by any gifts, by any threats or blows of my parents."

At Oda's response the entire throng was dumbstruck, but Simon blushed deeply at the insult to him. Covering his embarrassment at his rejection with arrogance, he boasted untruthfully that he did not in any case want a girl who was unable to speak. Then he went away glowering and indignant, turning his back like an enemy and riding away on a fast horse with his people. The girl's relations and those who remained with them, no less embarrassed, berated her harshly and raised dark suspicions about what she had said with a pure heart, good conscience, and true faith. An eye muddied with ill will finds it hard to see the truth, choosing rather to condemn good thoughts than to judge carefully, considering clearly what is not obvious. So when Anna prayed tearfully in the Temple of the Lord, but no one within heard her trembling voice, the priest Heli, his eyesight dimmed by age, saw her prayerful mouth and countenance, but the old man judged wrongly that she was belching up

231

drink rather than groaning. He said, *Digest a little the wine, of which thou hast taken too much* (1 Kgs 1:14). But a firm, clear intention is not easily changed, nor is a pure conscience frightened by invidious carping. As the apostle says to the Corinthians, *But to me it is a very small thing to be judged by you, or by man's day* (1 Cor 4:3). Therefore, a wise maiden takes her stand with a calm mind and serene appearance in the midst of Babylon. The strong north wind cannot penetrate the citadel of her virginity because the daughter of Jerusalem is surrounded by the valley of all sanctity and chastity, so she scorns the suitors of luxury and the eye of petulance, having nothing in common with the daughters of Ascalon. So Oda's father, fearful lest the accusations of bad faith mar his good name, took some of his retainers with him and went to bring back the young man whom she had insulted as soon as he could, to join her in the marriage he had promised whether she wished it or not. *But a net is spread in vain before the eyes of them that have wings* (Prov 1:17).

When Oda found out that her father was still plotting against her, as the crowd still stood talking about what had happened, she seized the opportunity to slip away to the house and shut herself in her mother's bedchamber. She locked the door and prayed that God come to her assistance. Seizing the sword hanging at the head of the bed, she tried to cut off her nose, but her hand trembled. Unaccustomed as she was to the weapon, her girlish stroke failed to cut through the harder part. She berated it, "Sword, are you so blunt that your edge cannot destroy the beauty of my face?" Speaking thus, she gathered herself and pressed the iron harder, mutilating her nostrils. A torrent of precious blood flowed into her lap. So she ruined her splendid appearance.[19] What a wonderful heart this maiden had! To make herself ill-matched to this secular world, she chose to live with her nose mutilated, defacing the beauty of a form that might be seduced rather than painting it in false beauty with lying colors, so attracting wanton looks. She preferred to be a handmaid of Christ with dirty skin and humble dress, to be abject in his house, and to be reputed among the servants of David—even the least of them—rather than to cover the filth of her neck with abundant ornament, deceitfully, or to perfume herself as prostitutes do in summoning adulterers in their sickness.

We read of holy women—married as well as virgins—who have plunged swords into their breasts or dove into deep waters or died throwing themselves into fire. As their own avengers, they have blocked bold assaults with death and so have bought the glorious name of martyr. As I see it, the maiden Oda was no less a martyr. Her garment of flesh was ripped away neither by her own hand nor by her persecutor's, nor did the torture wear her down. Nevertheless, she bathed herself in the blood of Agnes and guarded her white garments until she might retire from the world. How would she have died for Christ, had she needed—this woman who lived in the flesh but outside it, disfiguring herself for his love? I believe this a still greater martyrdom, surpassing all manner of torments—when someone lives in the flesh but outside it, castrating himself for the kingdom of heaven.[20] As most people believe, such martyrdom is like when a man dies willingly for the faith, setting neither home nor wife nor children nor himself before his belief. For virginity is the highest and best state, although it is prescribed in no law and decreed nowhere. It is wrongful only if one is already bound by a vow or has willfully dishonored an undertaking.

The Lord says, *He that can take, let him take it* (Matt 19:12). And the apostle says, *Now concerning virgins, I have no commandment...but I give you counsel* (1 Cor 7:25). Also, the blessed Fulgentius says in his sermon commending virginity, "Virginity cannot be commanded, but it can be wished."[21] Many magnificent men have conquered great evils with their strong resistance and overcome many obstacles set against them in concerted attack, only later to find their ardor drained of all the strength of its holiness when the desires of the flesh wore them out, so that even feminine softness then subdued them, weak and unwarlike. He who—held up by grace—prevails against this filth, against this enemy, and makes no place for corrupting influences either in his flesh or in his mind, is truly praiseworthy, for he does wonders in his own lifetime. Therefore the virgin Oda is indeed a martyr, because there is no virginity without martyrdom, and virginity tames the troublesome rebellion of the body with the strong restraint of chastity. It marks its face with the cautery of a sword when it is displeased with a beauty it finds harmful. It says this in action rather than words, as

Agnes did: "I have set a sign on my face, that I may receive no lover but Christ."²² But now I turn back to my story.

Those friends and relations who were still at the house began to worry about what the girl was doing locked away in secret. They tried to find out what was going on first by listening, then by looking. They heard Oda's voice murmuring to herself. Beating on the door, they first asked and then demanded that she unlock it. When she did not respond or open up, they were afraid she had died either by the sword or from her great grief. Throwing themselves on the door, they broke it down with an axe. Seeing that she had cruelly attacked herself and that she had lost a great deal of blood, that her face was already cold and pallid, they raised a great outcry, unspeakably horrified. Oda's mother, viewing the face of her daughter so deformed, fell on her face and struck her aged, withered breast. Dragging long sighs from deep down, she poured forth heavy waves of tears, bewailing this lamentable tragedy and proclaiming herself the most wretched of all women. The news came swiftly to the ears of Oda's absent father. Stricken with grief he hurried home on his horse. Seeing all the blood flowing from the face of his daughter and his daughter's grandparents pulling the white hair from their heads with the bitter sobs, his whole house in weeping as if over a death, he could scarcely bear it. He burst into tears, inconsolable in his grief. Even his masculine restraint could not lighten his anguish or moderate his tears. The cithara played songs of grief; the voice of joy was turned to sorrow.²³ Happy applause grew silent on sad hands, and deep sighs mingled with groans. The chorus of girls preparing to lead a festive dance put aside their sweet song and took up a dirge. The splendid preparation for the wedding was shadowed in clouds and covered with a cloak of grief. What is more amazing, Oda herself never wept, as if—secure in her vow—the sad lamentations of all those about her struck a deaf ear, and she was unafraid.

When Odo, the abbot of Bonne Espérance, was informed of these things, the virtue of the famous woman moved him. He summoned two of his brothers in religious life, bidding them to offer her support, restoring her with their consolation and asking attentively what she wished to do. The father of the maiden welcomed them generously, accepting their efforts joyfully, and Oda herself greeted them with devoted service as very messengers from heaven's throne. When they were alone with her, they inquired, and she laid out the plan she desired to follow, believing that they would help her. She asked her father not to block her chosen path of chastity with further marriage plans, begging that he gladly give her his permission that she leave the secular world now that she was unfit for marriage and, as it were, already repudiated.

At first her father still refused to assent, arguing against her, declaring it wrong for her to undergo the confinement of voluntary poverty and strict religious life when, as heir of his many possessions, she might retain her famous name and in her blossoming youth be joined to a man of her own age in lawful marriage. Then Oda said: "If you do not accede to my request, releasing me to freely follow my heavenly calling—if I am unable because of your opposition to seize the baton that I was sent into this stadium to carry in the race—I will at once spoil the flower, as you call it, of my youth. I will destroy myself and cut myself down so that not only will I be undesirable to a nobleman but even to a peasant. But I will also add to your head a grief that you will be unable ever to forget. Why do you try to marry me off unwilling, with such empty solicitude? Why do you not instead realize that one who is dead to the world cannot live in it? Know this, Father, that if there were no other hope for what I wish, if the only means to the happy progress of my life were that you serve me with your body in the mud as a bridge on which I might walk—that you lie down that I might cross you—then I would not hesitate cheerfully to tread upon your body. Scorning you, stepping on you, I would hurry to give thanks in the place I have chosen." With these or like words she struggled against her loving father heatedly until he despaired of winning. His heart was greatly troubled but finally, sorrowfully, he assented to her wishes.

Having given his permission, Oda's father summoned his guests and asked that with their leadership and protection she be able to pass quickly out of Egypt. They, supporting his petition, returned to the monastery as quickly as possible and told their story to the abbot as it had unfolded. Odo rejoiced at their news. Taking a few brothers with him, he hurried himself to meet the maiden. When she saw him she threw herself humbly at his feet and described her wishes to him in her own eloquent voice. After the two had pious conversation and came to agreement over the issue on which they were meeting, Oda bid farewell to her parents and the secular world, so leaving her home and family. Taking on the dress of religious life from the same abbot, she entered the cloister of obedience under his leadership. Manly in her courage, she undertook the discipline of monastic profession with the holy women there.

Poor as I am in my own life, as in my literary craft and talent, I cannot adequately tell with what fervent desire for sanctity she made swift progress, with what great humility and obedience and other virtues she reached perfection. So that an excellent end may follow a good beginning, a contractor first calculates the cost before he lays the foundation of his tower, lest either the funding or the building material be inadequate to the task so it is a laughingstock to passersby because of some ridiculous flaw or incomplete masonry, or lest the construction of his tower leave the foundation so poorly laid as to offer a hiding place for robbers or a place fit for burying the dead. Therefore Oda set her feet from the first toward the lofty mountain peak, avoiding the wet sands in the depths of deep humility, so that the construction of her tower might rise up straight and grow to be a temple holy in the Lord. So she made sure that she set her feet in the path of God's truth. Because she took Christ's light, sweet yoke[24] on her slim neck, she set her steps while singing in her heart even in the valley of tears. The Lord put in her mouth that new song which none might sing in a foreign land except she of whom the Apocalypse says, *she joined the hundred thousand virgins.*[25] That is the song of virgins alone, of those who follow Agnes wherever she has gone.[26] Oda subdued her flesh with such abstinence from food and drink that her dry belly had no means to resist, and so that neither softness nor bloating might push her chastely sober mind toward fleshly love. As the pagan poet says, "Without Ceres and Bacchus, Venus grows cold."[27] Whenever a throng of vices militated against her or the wind blew against her, she was never impatient but drove her little ones under a sheltering rock like a ram, with great patience. So she crushed the head of the devious serpent into the earth with her heel.[28] What follows here reveals how greatly she wished to sweat in the workshop of virtue.

Shortly after Oda had spurned the deadly glory of the world and bent her neck to the yoke of obedience, and after she had forsaken soft clothes and sweet food, willingly binding her foot with the shackles of poverty and want, her harsh regimen and meager food wore down her slim, delicate body, eroding her prior health. Her robust constitution was weakened by indigestible, coarse food, and her lovely skin was infected by dark swellings. Her sisters, noticing how quickly her maidenly freshness had turned into pallor and how her spotless skin had broken out in unsightly sores, suspected that she was stricken with leprosy. They began at first to murmur to one another that she should be separated from their company and removed from their dwellings. When this suggestion began to be made openly by everyone, some of the women who thought they understood such matters looked carefully at Oda's sores and judged her indeed a leper, so she was ordered to build a hut outside the wall. According to filthy human judgment she who was clean in mind and body was made to dwell away from the others as though she were unclean. But Oda, as a humble handmaiden of Christ, bore this shame bravely, knowing that virtue is perfected in weakness. She sustained wrongful insult to her name as if she were grateful for it. Oda thus went away willingly into the place where she had been isolated, without objecting to what false suspicion alleged about her. One of the oldest sisters was chosen as her companion, so that she might console Oda with maternal affection as if she were a young calf, providing for her generously even though her face was diseased. But this woman, irreverent and immature in spirit despite her age, refused to obey, saying that she did not have the strength. In fact, she feared contact with disease, preferring to rebel rather than to bring comfort to Oda in her infirmity. This disrespect was punished according to the rule's discipline. Then, after white-haired childishness had denied her this honor, young girls of the community finally showed Oda prompt service.

Never did Oda complain about so many misfortunes; rather, her spirit grew from the difficulty it encountered. She was raised to the highest point of sanctity through suffering, through being treated as refuse in the loss of her home. Throughout she kept before her eyes the image of him who, stricken on our behalf, had neither beauty nor comeliness and still suffered on the cross. He spoke with her. He talked with her constantly. He bent her thoughts into his, gazing at and kissing her hand when hateful disease caused it to swell. The wise virgin knew, with everyone who has professed this soldiery, that such suffering is necessary because, as one of the pagans says, "Patience is easier than to correct a wrong."[29] And as the apostle says, *Tribulation worketh patience, and patience trial, and trial hope, but hope confoundeth not* (Rom 5:3–5). And as Symmachus says, hope—always counseling patience in hardship—is in safety.[30] So Oda prayed to the Lord the more devoutly and secretly that her ship should emerge undamaged from so many dangers and that he might bring her to an easier time. She did not consider it a matter of great moment if she suffered anything harsh or heavy, for she was certain that he would reward her for her suffering with eternal life. But after her travail in this arena was widely reported, after her foot was calloused in hardship, he who does not suffer his people to be tested more than they can bear lightened his scourge. Oda's disease passed, and he recalled her healthy into the convent with the others. All those of this obedience heard of her devout practice, and it was clear that she was inferior to no one in this discipline. She embraced the keeping of the laws so fully that she considered nothing she was asked harsh or unbearable, but thought it welcome and light.

Therefore, only a short time after her conversion, Oda was chosen *magistra*, mistress of her sisters by the abbot of this monastery. And because she preceded her companions in virtue, she served as a mirror and a rule for them. When she was made prioress she was not puffed up with pride because of her responsibility; rather, the added obligation of more complete service made her still more humble and devout. Viewing herself more as a mother than a leader, she nurtured her daughters with warmth and encouraged them to the summit of religious life so that they all gave her filial love and respect, rejoicing under her leadership and example to be directed to their betterment. Oda's life was a kind of homily accessible equally to wise folk, mature in their understanding, and to the foolish. Her purity and consistency allowed no lukewarmness or dissolution to weaken her sisters' strength but drew them to her in love and bound them in affection. Thus her model shaped Christ more fully in their hearts. "To say one thing and feel another"[31] is base, but what she did always corresponded to her words, fitting them as though from the same mold. As her charges' mistress, she exercised her authority against their faults, disciplining them according to the rule in order to remove all corruption at its source, then bandaging and treating the wound with healthful medicine. Toward the sick and the poor she—herself poor and grieving for Christ's sake—offered such profound compassion that not only did she provide them with what they needed, taking charge of them with a mother's solicitude, but also, whenever she knew of anyone suffering poverty or illness, she endeavored to help him as best she could by secretly offering such few things as she had. For she used to say that theft was pious if it helped the sick, as if serving Christ in a naked beggar.[32]

In sum, such great holiness shone in Oda's countenance and honor in her customs, maturity in her counsel, usefulness in her words, integrity in her flesh and spirit, abundant charity in all her acts of love, that the greatness of her virtue exceeded human nature's corruption. Even in her mortal body she engaged in celestial conversation. We ought not to wonder, then, that she tasted drink from that full vessel as did the apostle whose conversation was in heaven.[33] The splendor of Oda's grace could not be hidden in her convent but shone far and wide. The fragrance of her name's ointment,[34] its vessel broken open in the house of obedience, spread everywhere to attract many men as well as women to follow the righteous path. But it was not the approval of the many that made her famous, but rather the proven virtues of her mind. Such virtues carry one who possesses them, even though he is set in a corner or hidden under a rock, into everlasting fame.

At last, when Oda had lived out her days and a crown was already set aside for her for the merit of her labors, the Lord, who had called to her and made her just, pleased to end her pilgrimage, its route completed, and to carry her from the shipwreck-ridden shores of this world to his peaceful halls in a glorious assumption. She was stricken by fever and fatigued by long illness. Deadly pain afflicted her chest. Long bodily penance had already weighed down her exhausted body, as if gnawing away on the little that was left around her vital spirit. An evil humor obstructed her breathing, and fits of coughing spread it through her entire belly, so that the illness extended its roots, worsening daily. The dross of her body was burned entirely away, as in a furnace, that she might be so tested and purified as to deserve a crown in the king's heaven. Even though she had very little strength, she bore her suffering courageously, thanking

God that he had stricken her, ordaining that she undergo this suffering. Day and night she emptied herself in prayer and meditated on the face of the Lord in confession. Standing before him, she tried her own case diligently before the eyes of her strict judge. Harshly, she corrected whatever displeased her about herself, and whatever was displeasing to her in herself, as did the Mary who bathed his feet with her tears.[35]

When this oppressive sickness had already lasted half a year, Oda was so weak as to be bedridden. An even worse pain deep in her chest portended that she would soon find release, that the vessel that had contained her as she was sanctified was about to meet its mortal end. Her natural hunger and ability to keep food down failed her, so that she was not hungry and vomited anything she ate. Then she was given the unction of the dying, and her soul looked toward heavenly things from a body that only half lived. Forgetful of what lay behind it, it reached out toward what was ahead. Commending herself with constant prayers and tears to Christ, whom she had tried to serve perfectly in her lifetime, Oda waited for her suffering to end in happiness. Her sorrowing daughters stood around their holy virgin mother and asked, weeping, that when she was carried to heaven she not forget them. But Oda, distressed that these words seemed boastful, responded tearfully: "Why, my daughters, do you importune me, a sinner of little moment, with things appropriate only for the apostles and others of the saints? Avoid these words, I ask, and beseech rather that grace be granted my failings and that the bosom of Abraham receive me crossing over hence. Commend my end in your prayers to him in whom the saints live and through whom all things are."

Finally, as the Easter holiday was at an end, she had almost reached the point where her long illness had purged the ferment of her body to purity. When the sacred mysteries of our redemption had been celebrated, she received the viaticum of salvation. She died on the twentieth of May, in the year of the Word's incarnation 1158, as the day slipped into evening, lying before the abbot, brothers and sisters singing the accustomed prayers and psalms for her. When the holy virgins realized she had gone to her rest, they were so moved with grief that their faces were clouded with pallor. They bewailed their loss inconsolably, with tears and sighs. Keeping watch over her body with prayers and weeping, they led her blessed soul with psalms and hymns onto the mountain of the Lord and into his holy tabernacles. As the following day dawned, Oda's body was carried to the abbey by the brothers.[36] There, when holy sacrifices had been made to God in her memory, she was buried by Gregory, venerable abbot of Elne,[37] and by Philip, abbot of this place. The aforesaid Odo, with many other brothers, stood about her as was fitting. Although her body was begotten in weakness, it will rise again in strength; begotten in mortality, it will rise again in immortality; begotten in ignobility, it will rise again in glory.

Oda's happy and blessed soul was found worthy to go out from Egypt on that day on which the true paschal Lamb returned freedom to the true Israelites—in which Christ arose from the dead no more to taste the bitter fruit of this vine. She whom the glory of new resurrection marked in the first world is happy and blessed to have crossed over into Galilee—she who then was worthy to see King Solomon in his glory, when his mother crowned him on the day of solemnity and joy, on the day of his betrothal.[38] The maiden Oda is now happy, worthy of praise according to her name, for the name Oda means praise. So the Psalmist, mindful of the blessings of God, calls him not merciful but mercy itself: *My God, my mercy.*[39] Already that holy maiden sees and tastes how sweet her Lord is,[40] *not only through a glass in a dark manner* (1 Cor 13:2), for these things are fleeting, but she walks in the light of God's countenance and rejoices all the day in his name with that chorus of the blessed who have prevailed in the struggle. She sleeps in happy sleep in the arms of the heavenly spouse, drunk in the richness of the house of God. He does not suffer that anyone rouse her or make her wake, as long as she should wish to indulge in the sleep of such blessed rest. Although our Oda may be free of worry in her blessedness, nevertheless she is always watchful in her loving attention to her brothers and sisters. She beseeches God's clemency for their peace and safety, praying that he keep them and their home free from their enemies' attacks. I hope that blessed Oda may offer this favor as well to me, who have undertaken to write of her life of love and devotion at the request of her sisters—even if I have offended in my speech or if I have overstepped my bounds in the way I have written. And I hope that she will guide me with the oar of her prayers as I struggle on the wide sea. Then may I easily reach my goal although my vessel is fragile.

So that God may find us worthy, when his victory at last devours death, to join Oda in the land of the living, let us confess his holy name and rejoice in praising him who lives and reigns through all time. Amen.

NOTES

Introduction

1. The outstanding study of medieval Premonstratensian spirituality remains François Petit's: *La spiritualité des Prémontrés aux XIIe et XIIIe siècles*, Etudes de théologie de d'histoire de la spiritualité 10 (Paris: J. Vrin, 1947). Despite profound intervening changes in the study of medieval religious life, Petit's analysis, emphasizing the works of Norbert's follower Philip of Harvengt in focusing on Marian piety and empathy for the suffering of Christ, presents striking parallelism to recent work on affective piety in the twelfth century. See Petit, *La spiritualité des Prémontrés aux XIIe et XIIIe siècles*, esp. 156–70 and 249–52; Rachel Fulton, *From Judgment to Passion: Devotion to Christ and the Virgin Mary, 800–1200* (New York: Columbia University Press, 2002), esp. 351–404.

2. Wilfried M. Grauwen's authoritative biography of Norbert treats only his years as archbishop: *Norbertus, Aartstbisschop van Maagdenburg (1126–1134)*, Verhandelingen van de Koninklijke Academie voor Wetenschappen, Letteren en Schone Kunsten van Belgie, Klasse der Letteren 40, no. 86 (Brussels: Paleis de Academiën, 1978). A revised edition is in German: *Norbert, Erzbischof von Magdeburg (1126–1134)*, 2nd ed., trans. Ludger Horstkötter (Duisburg: Prämonstratenser-Abtei S. Johann, 1986). Grauwen's various further articles, mostly in Dutch, treat additional aspects of Norbert's career; several are listed in the bibliography.

In the absence of a complete biography and in view of the relative inaccessibility of works in Dutch for most readers, however, Kaspar Elm's collection of articles on Norbert are the best single resource on his career and relevant bibliography: *Norbert von Xanten: Adliger, Ordensstifter, Kirchenfürst*, ed. Kaspar Elm (Cologne: Wienand, 1984). Especially useful contributions to this volume include Grauwen, "Die Quellen zur Geschichte Norberts von Xanten," 15–33; Alfons Alders, "Norbert von Xanten als rheinischer Adliger und Kanoniker an St. Viktor," 35–67; Franz J. Felten, "Norbert von Xanten, vom Wanderprediger zum Kirchenfürsten," 69–157; Stefan Weinfurter, "Norbert von Xanten als Reformkanoniker und Stifter des Prämonstratenserordens," 159–84; and Elm, "Norbert von Xanten: Bedeutung, Persönlichkeit, Nachleben," 267–318. This collection's particular value lies in the multiplicity of perspectives it offers, emphasizing Norbert's multiple roles as leader and reformer.

Among discussions in English, Jay T. Lees's chapter on Norbert and the early Premonstratensians in his monograph on Norbert's disciple Anselm of Havelberg is especially useful, solidly grounded in sources and recent scholarship as well as persuasive with respect to its presentation of the Premonstratensian founder as a powerfully active exemplar of the reform movement: "Anselm and Norbert of Xanten, 1129–1134," in *Anselm of Havelberg: Deeds into Words in the Twelfth Century*, Studies in the History of Christian Thought 79 (Leiden: Brill, 1998), 22–47. Despite the dates in the chapter's title, Lees discusses Norbert's career and model in general.

3. André Vauchez's lively survey, for instance, describes Norbert as paradigmatic of early twelfth-century preacher-hermits and cites Anselm of Havelberg's call to imitation of Christ, but presents the two as respective expressions of contemporary spiritual tendencies rather than builds connections between them and others who participated in Norbert's reform: *The Spirituality of the Medieval West from the Eighth to the Twelfth Century*, trans. Colette Friedlander, Cistercian Studies 145 (Kalamazoo, MI: Cistercian Publications, 1993), 98–99, 108–15. Similarly, Giles Constable's magisterial essays on twelfth-century spirituality treat Norbert, Anselm, and Philip of Harvengt, again as mutually distinct canonical voices: *Three Studies in Medieval Religious and Social Thought: The Interpretation of Mary and Martha, the Ideal of the Imitation of Christ, the Orders of Society* (Cambridge: Cambridge University Press, 1995), 49, 71–72, 182–87.

4. Among many representations of the origins and growth of the Premonstratensians in surveys of medieval religious life, R. W. Southern's is normative, stressing comparison with the Cistercians especially on the issue of women's reception: *Western Society and the Church in the Middle Ages* (London: Penguin, 1990), 312–18. Herbert Grundmann's work on twelfth-century religious movements remains fundamental, especially with respect to the Premonstratensians' place in religious reform (210): *Religious Movements in the Middle Ages: The Historical Links between Heresy, the Mendicant Orders, and the Women's Religious Movement in the Twelfth and Thirteenth Century, with the Historical Foundations of German Mysticism*, trans. Steven Rowan (Notre Dame, IN: University of Notre Dame Press, 1995).

5. Herman of Tournai, *De miraculis S. Mariae Laudunensis*, ed. Roger Wilmans, MGH SS 12, 658–59.

NOTES

6. PL 182, col. 162. Bernard's characteristically evocative epithet for Norbert was "coelesti fistula."

7. A notable recent exception is Werner Bomm's article on several of the authors whose works are gathered here: "Augustinusregel, *professio canonica* und Prämonstratenser im 12. Jahrhundert: Das Beispiel der Norbert-Viten, Philipps von Harvengt und Anselms von Havelberg," in Regula sancti Augustini: *Normative Grundlage differenter Verbände im Mittelalter*, ed. Gert Melville and Anne Müller (Paring: Augustiner-Chorherren-Verlag, 2002), 239–94. See also Carol Neel, "Philip of Harvengt and Anselm of Havelberg: The Premonstratensian Vision of Time," *Church History* 62 (1993): 483–93.

8. Among studies of the theme of apostolic life in the twelfth-century reformation, see especially Giles Constable, "Renewal and Reform in Religious Life: Concepts and Realities," in *Renaissance and Renewal in the Twelfth Century*, ed. Robert L. Benson and Giles Constable (Oxford: Clarendon Press, 1982), 37–67, esp. 53–56.

9. See, for instance, Vauchez, *The Spirituality of the Medieval West from the Eighth to the Twelfth Century*, esp. 91–95, 117–18. On the Gilbertines, see Brian Golding, *Gilbert of Sempringham and the Gilbertine Order, c.1130–c.1300* (Oxford: Clarendon Press, 1995); on Fontevrault, see *Robert of Arbrissel, a Medieval Religious Life*, trans. Bruce L. Venarde (Washington, DC: Catholic University of America Press, 2003). On Norbert as wandering preacher, Johannes von Walter's study retains importance: *Die ersten Wanderprediger Frankreichs: Studien zur Geschichte des Mönchtums* (Leipzig: A. Deichert, 1906), 199–229.

10. On Tanchelm, see Jeffrey Burton Russell, *Dissent and Reform in the Early Middle Ages* (Berkeley and Los Angeles: University of California Press, 1965), 56–68; Walter L. Wakefield and Austin P. Evans, *Heresies of the High Middle Ages* (New York: Columbia University Press, 1991), 96–101.

11. PL 182, col. 162.

12. "[S]ub qua si bene militaverint confratres tui, filii mei, securi Christo stabunt in extremi terrore iudicii" (*Vita Godefridi capenbergensis [sic]*, ed. Philip Jaffé, MGH SS 12, 577).

13. For a recent discussion of Augustine's life in community, see James J. O'Donnell, *Augustine: A New Biography* (New York: HarperCollins, 2005), 19–24, 88. For a lucid précis of the history of canons and especially the influence of Augustine and his Rule, see Adolar Zumkeller, *Augustine's Ideal of the Religious Life*, trans. Edmund Colledge (New York: Fordham University Press, 1986), 89–95.

NORBERT AND EARLY NORBERTINE SPIRITUALITY

14. M. A. Claussen, *The Reform of the Frankish Church: Chrodegang of Metz and the* Regula canonicorum *in the Eighth Century* (Cambridge: Cambridge University Press, 2004). See also William D. Carpe, "The *Vita canonica* in the *Regula canonicorum* of Chrodegang of Metz" (PhD diss., University of Chicago, 1975).

15. Alders, "Norbert von Xanten als rheinischer Adliger und Kanoniker an St. Viktor," 35–39.

16. For lucid surveys of the medieval canonical reform, see Vauchez, *The Spirituality of the Medieval West from the Eighth to the Twelfth Century*, 95–100; François Petit, *La réforme des prêtres au moyen-age: pauvreté et vie commune* (Paris: Editions du Cerf, 1968), 10–20. See also Hubert Schopf, "Augustiner-Chorherren," in *Kulturgeschichte der christlichen Orden in Einzeldarstellungen*, ed. Peter Dinzelbacher und James Lester Hogg (Stuttgart: Alfred Kröner Verlag, 1997), 38.

17. Jakob Mois, "Geist und Regel des hl. Augustinus in der Kanoniker-Reform des 11.—12. Jahrhunderts," *In Unum Congregati* 6 (1959): 52–59. On the Rule of St. Augustine in general, see George Lawless, *Augustine of Hippo and His Monastic Rule* (Oxford: Clarendon Press, 1987), with editions and translations of the various versions, 74–118.

18. *Sacrorum conciliorum nova et amplissima collectio*, ed. J. D. Mansi (Florence, 1759), vol. 19, col. 898.

19. See Stefan Weinfurter, *Salzburger Bistumsreform und Bischofspolitik im 12. Jahrhundert. Der Erzbischof Konrad I von Salzburg (1106–1147) und die Regularkanoniker* (Cologne: Böhlau, 1974).

20. Schopf, "Augustiner-Chorherren," 39. Norbert likely first learned of the Augustinian Rule at Klosterrath (Rolduc); (see Stefan Weinfurter, ed., "Introduction," in *Consuetudines canonicorum regularium Springirsbacenses-Rodenses*, CCCM 48 [Turnhout: Brepols, 1978], vi–x).

21. Luc Verheijen argues that the *Disciplina monasterii* was compiled by Alypius, although Norbert certainly believed it was Augustine's (see *Règle de Saint Augustin*, ed. Luc Verheijen, 2 vols. [Paris: Etudes augustiniennes, 1967], 2:164–69).

22. Mois, "Geist und Regel des hl. Augustinus in der Kanoniker-Reform des 11.—12. Jahrhunderts," 54.

23. Gelasius II had dispensed Springiersbach from the more difficult dietary and liturgical requirements of the *Ordo monasterii* in 1118. Honorius II mandated similar changes for Prémontré in 1126–29. See Weinfurter, "Norbert von Xanten als Reformkanoniker und Stifter des Prämonstratenserordens," 171–72; Stefan Weinfurter, "Norbert von Xanten—

246

NOTES

Ordensstifter und 'Eigenkirchenherr,'" *Archiv für Kulturgeschichte* 59 (1977): 70.

24. See Acts 2:42–47; 4:32–35.

25. Idung, *Cistercians and Cluniacs, the Case for Cîteaux: A Dialogue between Two Monks, an Argument on Four Questions,* trans. Jeremiah F. O'Sullivan et al., Cistercian Fathers 33 (Kalamazoo, MI: Cistercian Publications, 1977), 86.

26. The *A* version of Norbert's *vita* is published as *Vita Norberti archiepiscopi Magdeburgensis,* ed. Roger Wilmans, MGH SS 12, 663–706; the *B* version as *Vita Norberti* in AASS Juni 1, 807–47, and PL 170, cols. 1253–1350 (references below to the *B* version are to the PL text, which iterates the AASS edition); *A* in its entirety and *B* in part are translated below. Herman's *Restoration* is already available in English translation, but his related *Miracles of St. Mary of Laon* is excerpted among the present volume's texts. See Herman of Tournai, *Liber de restauratione monasterii Sancti Martini Tornacensis,* in MGH SS 14, 266–327; idem, *Restoration of the Monastery of St. Martin of Tournai,* trans. Lynn H. Nelson (Washington, DC: Catholic University of America Press, 1996). See also Herman of Tournai, *De miraculis S. Mariae Laudunensis* (ed. Wilmans).

The summary here of the major events of Norbert's life is based on the *A* and *B* hagiographies and Herman's two works, as affirmed and corrected in modern scholarship, with specific passages cited only for direct quotations and instances in which sources offer conflicting information. References to *B* are to both AASS and derivative PL versions because of the PL's likely wider availability to readers of this volume.

27. MGH SS 12, 671.

28. PL 170, col. 1260.

29. MGH SS 14, 315.

30. Wilfried M. Grauwen, "Norbert doet afstand van zijn goederen. De stichting van Fürstenberg, aug.-sept. 1118," *AP* 71 (1995): 5–24.

31. MGH SS 12, 675.

32. PL 170, col. 1277.

33. See MGH SS 12, 678; PL 170, col. 1283; MGH SS 12, 655; PL 156, col. 991.

34. MGH SS 12, 678; PL 170, col. 1283.

35. MGH SS 12, 679; PL 170, col. 1284.

36. MGH SS 12, 656.

37. Weinfurter, "Norbert von Xanten—Ordensstifter und 'Eigenkirchenherr,'" 74–76.

38. MGH SS 12, 697.

39. Bruno Krings, *Das Prämonstratenserstift Arnstein a. d. Lahn im Mittelalter (1139–1527)* (Wiesbaden: Historische Kommission für Nassau, 1990), 120.

40. *Regesta pontificum Romanorum*, ed. Philip Jaffé, 2nd ed. S. Löwenfeld et al., 2 vols. (Leipzig 1885–88; repr. Graz: Academische Druck- und Verlagsanstalt, 1956), no. 7244.

41. Stefan Weinfurter, "Norbert von Xanten im Urteil seiner Zeitgenossen," *Xantener Vorträge zur Geschichte des Niederrheins* 5 (1992): 14.

42. MGH SS 12, 697; cf. PL 170, col. 1330.

43. "Les premiers statuts de l'ordre de Prémontré," ed. Raphael Van Waefelghem, *Analectes de l'ordre de Prémontré* 9 (1913): 1–74. See also Eugene J. Hayes, "Rightful Autonomy of Life and Charism in the Proper Law of the Norbertine Order" (PhD diss., Catholic University of America, 1990), 261–82.

44. Pl. F. Lefevre and W. M. Grauwen, *Les statuts de Prémontré au milieu du XIIe siècle*, Bibliotheca Analectorum Praemonstratensium 12 (Averbode: Praemonstratensia, 1978). Cf. Hayes, "Rightful Autonomy of Life and Charism in the Proper Law of the Norbertine Order," 283–99.

45. *Regesta pontificum Romanorum* (ed. Jaffé-Löwenfeld), no. 8451.

46. See Krings, *Das Prämonstratenserstift Arnstein a. d. Lahn im Mittelalter (1139–1527)*, 121; Walter Froese, "The Early Norbertines on the Religious Frontiers of Northeastern Germany" (PhD diss., University of Chicago, 1978), 125–55.

47. *Regesta pontificum Romanorum* (ed. Jaffé-Löwenfeld), no. 12813; cf. Krings, *Das Prämonstratenserstift Arnstein a. d. Lahn im Mittelalter (1139–1527)*, 122, 122n62.

48. Krings, *Das Prämonstratenserstift Arnstein a. d. Lahn im Mittelalter (1139–1527)*, 122, 122n63.

49. Albert Hauck, *Kirchengeschichte Deutschlands* (Berlin: Akademie Verlag, 1958), pt. 4, 376–78. For a useful map with distinctive sigla for communities founded in different periods, see *Atlas zur Kirchengeschichte: Die christlichen Kirchen in Geschichte und Gegenwart*, ed. Hubert Jedin et al. (Freiburg: Herder, 1970), 54.

50. Krings, *Das Prämonstratenserstift Arnstein a. d. Lahn im Mittelalter (1139–1527)*, 122, 122n64.

51. Franz Winter, *Die Prämonstratenser des zwölften Jahrhunderts und ihre Bedeutung für das nordöstliche Deutschland: Ein Beitrag zur Geschichte der Christianisierung und Germanisierung des Wendenlandes* (Berlin 1865; repr. Aalen: Scientia, 1966), 228–51; Froese, "The Early Norbertines on the Religious Frontiers of Northeastern Germany," 90–124.

NOTES

52. See text-specific introductions for discussion of the authorship and dating of each work.

53. Some of Adam's sermons are available in translation: *Adam of Dryburgh, Six Christmas Sermons: Introduction and Translation*, ed. and trans. M. J. Hamilton, Analecta Carthusiana 16 (Salzburg: Institut für Englische Sprache und Literatur, 1974). On Adam, see also James Bulloch, *Adam of Dryburgh* (London: SPCK, 1958).

54. Anselm of Havelberg, *Dialogi*, PL 188, cols. 1139–1248. Only Book I of three has received a modern critical edition: *Dialogues, Livre I: revouveau dans l'église*, ed. and trans. Gaston Salet, Sources Chrétiennes 118 (Paris: Editions du Cerf, 1966).

55. See Winter, *Die Prämonstratenser des zwölften Jahrhunderts und ihre Bedeutung für das nordöstliche Deutschland*, 228–51; Froese, "The Early Norbertines on the Religious Frontiers of Northeastern Germany," 90–124.

56. Karl Morrison, *Conversion and Text: The Cases of Augustine of Hippo, Herman-Judah, and Constantine Tsatsos* (Charlottesville: University of Virginia Press, 1992), 39–75. Morrison offers a full translation of the *Short Account* text, 76–113. See also Karl Morrison, *Understanding Conversion* (Charlottesville: University of Virginia Press, 1992), esp. 53–57. Gerlinde Niemeyer carefully compares the biographical content of Herman's work and the extant corroborative texts and documents to argue that the convert was provost of the Premonstratensian double community (men and women) of Scheda, near Cologne (Herman of Cologne, *Opusculum de conversione sua*, ed. Gerlinde Niemeyer, MGH Quellen zur Geistesgeschichte des Mittelalters 4 [Weimar: Herman Böhlhaus, 1963], 8–25).

57. Caroline Walker Bynum, Docere verbo et exemplo: *An Aspect of Twelfth-Century Spirituality*, Harvard Theological Studes 31 (Missoula, MT: Scholars Press, 1979), esp. 49–55, 181–97. See also Caroline Walker Bynum, "The Spirituality of Regular Canons in the Twelfth Century," in *Jesus as Mother: Studies in the Spirituality of the High Middle Ages* (Berkeley and Los Angeles: University of California Press, 1982), esp. 36–40.

58. For a study gathering the texts and activities of a medieval order around a central theme of its charism, see Martha G. Newman, *The Boundaries of Charity: Cistercian Culture and Ecclesiastical Reform, 1098–1180* (Stanford, CA: Stanford University Press, 1996), esp. 235–43.

59. Constance Hoffman Berman, *The Cistercian Evolution: The Invention of a Religious Order in Twelfth-Century Europe* (Philadelphia: University of Pennsylvania Press, 2000), esp. 221–36.

60. See, for instance, the *A* life for Norbert's multiple usages of *ordo* for canons in general, the Cistercian paradigm, and Augustinian life (MGH SS 12, esp. 695–97).

61. Norman Tanner, ed., *Decrees of the Ecumenical Councils* (London: Sheed and Ward, 1990), 1:242. See especially Werner Bomm's conclusions linking Anselm of Havelberg and other early Premonstratensians to Norbert's personal model ("Augustinusregel, *professio canonica* und Prämonstratenser im 12. Jahrhundert: Das Beispiel der Norbert-Viten, Philipps von Harvengt und Anselms von Havelberg," 276–94).

62. See again Bomm's synthetic essay on the Premonstratensians among other Augustinian traditions ("Augustinusregel, *professio canonica* und Prämonstratenser im 12. Jahrhundert: Das Beispiel der Norbert-Viten, Philipps von Harvengt und Anselms von Havelberg," 239–94).

63. Among works whose discussions of the uses of hagiography are fundamental for this study, see Pierre Delooz, *Sociologie et canonisations*, Collection scientifique de la faculté de droit le l'Université de Liège, fasc. 30 (Liège: Faculté de droit, 1969); André Vauchez, *La sainteté en occident aux derniers siècles du moyen age: d'après les procès de canonisation et les documents hagiographiques* (Rome: École française de Rome, 1981); Peter Brown, *The Cult of the Saints: Its Rise and Function in Latin Christianity* (Chicago: University of Chicago Press, 1981); Michael Goodich, *Vita perfecta: The Ideal of Sainthood in the Thirteenth Century*, Monographien zur Geschichte des Mittelalters 25 (Stuttgart: Anton Hiersemann, 1982); Donald Weinstein and Rudolph M. Bell, *Saints and Society: The Two Worlds of Western Christendom, 1000–1700* (Chicago: University of Chicago Press, 1982); Thomas Heffernan, *Sacred Biography: Saints and Their Biographers in the Middle Ages* (Oxford: Oxford University Press, 1988); Thomas Head, *Hagiography and the Cult of Saints: The Diocese of Orléans, 800–1200* (Cambridge: Cambridge University Press, 1990); François Dolbeau, "Les hagiographes au travail: collecte et traitement des documents écrits (IXe - XIIe siècles). Avec annexe: une discussion chronologique du XIIe siècle (édition de BHL 5824e)," in *Manuscrits hagiographiques et travail des hagiographes*, ed. Martin Heinzelmann, Beihefte der *Francia* 24 (Sigmaringen: Jan Thorbecke, 1992), 49–65; Patrick Geary, *Living with the Dead in the Middle Ages* (Ithaca, NY: Cornell University Press, 1994).

64. Few such studies of orders' hagiographies exist. A notable exception is Simone Roisin's work on Cistercian hagiography in a region where Norbert had earlier preached (*L'hagiographie cistercienne dans le diocese de Liège au XIIIe siècle*, Receuil de travaux d'histoire et de philology, ser. 3, fasc. 27 [Louvain: Bibliothèque de l'université, 1947]).

NOTES

65. See note 56 above. Among more recent scholarship on the convert Herman, see Arnaldo Momigliano, "A Medieval Jewish Autobiography," in *History and Imagination: Essays in Honor of H. R. Trevor-Roper*, ed. Hugh Lloyd-Jones et al. (London: Duckworth, 1981), 30–36; Jeremy Cohen, "The Mentality of the Medieval Jewish Apostate: Peter Alfonsi, Hermann of Cologne, and Pablo Christiani," in *Jewish Apostasy in the Modern World*, ed. Todd M. Engelman (New York: Holmes and Meier, 1987), 20–47; Avrom Saltman, "Hermann's *Opusculum de conversione sua*: Truth or Fiction?" *Revue des études juives* 147 (1988), 31–56; Aviad M. Kleinberg, "Hermannus Judaeus's *Opusculum*: In Defense of Its Authenticity," *Revue des études juives* 151 (1992), 337–53; Michael Goodich, ed., *Other Middle Ages: Witnesses at the Margins of Medieval Society* (Philadelphia: University of Pennsylvania Press, 1988), with commentary (74–76) and partial translation (76–87).

66. See Saltman, "Hermann's *Opusculum de conversione sua*: Truth or Fiction?" 52.

67. Morrison, *Conversion and Text*, 40–41.

68. Jean-Claude Schmitt, *La Conversion d'Hermann le Juif: Autobiographie, Histoire et Fiction* (Paris: Editions du Seuil, 2003), esp. 235–40.

69. See, for instance, Jeremy Cohen's recent discussion of Herman's *Short Account* in *Living Letters of the Law: Ideas of the Jew in Medieval Christianity* (Berkeley and Los Angeles: University of California Press, 1999), 291.

70. See Morrison, *Conversion and Text*, 76–113; Goodich, *Other Middle Ages*, 76–87.

71. Bernard McGinn, *Visions of the End: Apocalyptic Traditions in the Middle Ages* (New York: Columbia University Press, 1979), 114–16. McGinn, in his comments on Anselm among his contemporaries, notes that Anselm's *Dialogues* offers "perhaps the most original early twelfth-century thought on the meaning of history in the Church" (109).

72. As Lees notes, Anselm called his three books of dialogues *Antikeimenon*, more properly translated as "antitheses." We retain the more conventional translation of the Latin *Dialogi* here, for reader's ease of bibliographical reference, although the author's title more accurately reflects the intent of his work (*Anselm of Havelberg*, 4, 8).

73. In McGinn's translation, "And so it happens that by the wondrous dispensation of God, as from generation to generation one always sees the growth of new forms of religious life, the youth of the Church is renewed like that of the eagle (Ps. 102:5). By this it is both able to fly

higher in contemplation and with almost unblinded eyes can behold the rays of the true sun more plainly" (115).

74. Carol Neel, "Philip of Harvengt and Anselm of Havelberg: The Premonstratensian Vision of Time," *Church History* 62 (1993): 493.

75. Fulton, *From Judgment to Passion*, esp. 357–59. On the Virgin in Song commentaries in general, see E. Ann Matter, *The Voice of My Beloved: The Song of Songs in Western Medieval Christianity* (Philadelphia: University of Pennsylvania Press, 1990), 151–77.

76. See below, introduction to Anselm's *Apologetic Letter.*

77. Innocent III, PL 214, cols. 173–74.

78. Shelley Wolbrink, "Women in the Premonstratensian Order of Northwestern Germany, 1120–1250," *Catholic Historical Review* 89 (2003): 387–408. Wolbrink's notes summarize the extensive scholarship on the order's women. See also Carol Neel, "The Origins of the Beguines," *SIGNS: A Journal of Women in Culture and Society* 14 (1989), 321–41.

79. Bernard had counseled the Premonstratensians against receiving women (PL 182, cols. 199–201).

Anselm of Havelberg, *Apologetic Letter*—Introduction

1. Jay T. Lees, *Anselm of Havelberg: Deeds into Words in the Twelfth Century,* Studies in the History of Christian Thought 79 (Leiden: Brill, 1998), 54. See also Jay T. Lees, "Charity and Enmity in the Writings of Anselm of Havelberg," *Viator* 25 (1994): esp. 54–58, where he persuasively supports Gabriella Severino's argument for 1138 rather than a later date for the *Apologetic Letter* (Gabriella Severino, "La discussione degli 'Ordines' di Anselmo di Havelberg," *Bulletino dell' Istituto storico italiano per il medio evo et Archivio Muratoriana* 78 [1967]: 78n1). Lees comprehensively surveys the bibliography on Anselm, the most important element of which is Kurt Fina's series of essays collectively entitled "Anselm von Havelberg: Untersuchungen zur Kirchen- und Geistesgeschichte des 12. Jahrhunderts," *AP* 32 (1956): 69–101, 193–227; *AP* 33 (1957): 5–39, 268–301; *AP* 34 (1958): 13–41.

2. "das getreue Abbild Norberts" (Wilfried Grauwen, *Norbert, Erzbischof von Magdeburg (1126–1134),* 2nd ed., trans. Ludger Horstkötter [Duisburg: Prämonstratenser-Abtei S. Johann, 1986], 164). In the prior Dutch edition of this volume, Grauwen described Anselm as Norbert's "trouwe evenbeeld" *(Norbertus, Aartsbisschop van Maagdenburg (1126–1134),* Verhandelingen van de Koninklijke Academie voor

NOTES

Wetenschappen, Letteren en Schone Kunsten van Belgie, Klasse der Letteren 40, no. 86 [Brussels: Paleis de Academiën, 1978], 225).

3. Lees, *Anselm of Havelberg*, 17.

4. Ibid., 28.

5. Ibid., 42–47.

6. Ibid., 48–63.

7. Ibid., 64–68.

8. Ibid., 88–97.

9. Ibid., esp. 33, 47.

10. Ibid., 14–15.

11. C. Steven Jaeger, "Cathedral Schools and Humanist Learning, 950–1150," *Deutsche Vierteljahrschrift für Literaturwissenschaft und Geistesgeschichte* 61 (1987): 569–616, esp. 571.

12. Lees, *Anselm of Havelberg*, 24–29.

13. Lees argues from negative evidence that Anselm first encountered Norbert in Saxony (ibid., 29–30).

14. *Dialogi* (PL 188, cols. 1139–1248). Book 1 appears in a more recent edition: *Dialogues, Livre I: Renouveau dans l'église.*, ed. and trans. Gaston Salet, Sources chrétiennes 118 (Paris: Cerf, 1966). The passages most interesting for Anselm's thought about religious orders and the shape of time are translated by Bernard McGinn (*Visions of the End: Apocalyptic Traditions in the Middle Ages* [New York: Columbia University Press, 1979], 114–16).

15. Lees consistently represents Anselm as solidly on the active side of the contemplative-active continuum (see *Anselm of Havelberg*, esp. 24–29, 158).

16. Ibid., 112–22.

17. Walter Zöllner, "Ekbert von Huysburg und die Ordensbewegung des 12. Jahrhunderts," *Forschungen und Fortschritte* 38 (1964): 27.

18. See Lees, *Anselm of Havelberg*, 54, 54n22, 136, 136n23, 162.

19. For a useful summary of the issue of *transitus*—primary texts and scholarship—with emphasis on the Premonstratensian perspective, see Douglas Roby, "Philip of Harvengt's Contribution to the Question of Passage from One Religious Order to Another," *AP* 49 (1973): esp. 69–71.

20. For a compact introduction to the twelfth-century controversy between monks and canons, see Giles Constable and Bernard S. Smith, "Introduction," in *Libellus de diversis ordinibus et professionibus que sunt in aecclesia*, 2nd ed., ed. Giles Constable and Bernard S. Smith (Oxford: Clarendon Press, 2003), xi–xiii, xviii–xix.

21. See John H. Van Engen, *Rupert of Deutz* (Berkeley and Los Angeles: University of California Press, 1983), 324; Caroline Walker Bynum, *Docere verbo et exemplo: An Aspect of Twelfth-Century Spirituality*, Harvard Theological Studies 31 (Missoula, MT: Scholars Press, 1979), 109n10; Rachel Fulton, *From Judgment to Passion: Devotion to Christ and the Virgin Mary, 800–1200* (New York: Columbia University Press, 2002), 298–99.

22. Van Engen, *Rupert of Deutz*, 328.

23. See Fina, "Anselm von Havelberg," 93–97.

24. As Lees succinctly notes of the *Apologetic Letter,* "this is not a work of love" (*Anselm of Havelberg*, 163; see also Lees, "Charity and Enmity in the Writings of Anselm of Havelberg," 58–61).

25. See Constable and Smith, "Introduction," xv; Jeremiah F. O'Sullivan, "Introduction," in Idung, *Cistercians and Cluniacs, the Case for Cîteaux: A Dialogue between Two Monks, an Argument on Four Questions*, trans. Jeremiah F. O'Sullivan et al., Cistercian Fathers 33 (Kalamazoo, MI: Cistercian Publications, 1977), 11.

26. PL 188, col. 1138.

27. See, for instance, PL 170, col. 1272: "considerans apud se quod nudam crucem nudus utique sequi deberet." On the term *pauper Christi*, see Ernst Werner, *Pauperes Christi: Studien zu sozial-religiösen Bewegungen im Zeitalter des Reformpapstums* (Leipzig: Koehler and Amelang, 1956), esp. 195–97. For further bibliography with specific reference to the Premonstratensians, see Lees, *Anselm of Havelberg*, 31n41.

28. Lees, *Anselm of Havelberg*, 30.

29. Johann Martin Lappenberg, ed., *Hamburgisches Urkundenbuch* 1 (Hamburg: Leopold Voss, 1907), 170 (no. 180).

30. See Lees, *Anselm of Havelberg*, esp. 26, 36–38, 151–61.

31. PL 188, col. 1119.

32. Giles Constable, "The Interpretation of Mary and Martha," in *Three Studies in Medieval Religious and Social Thought: The Interpretation of Mary and Martha, the Ideal of the Imitation of Christ, the Orders of Society* (Cambridge: Cambridge University Press, 1995), 3–141; for special reference to Anselm of Havelberg, see 49.

33. PL 188, cols. 1131–32.

34. Constable, " The Interpretation of Mary and Martha," esp. 44, 49, 49n187. Although a few later authors adopted this perspective, Anselm evidently pioneered it.

35. André Vauchez takes Anselm as exemplary of this posture, new to the twelfth century (*The Spirituality of the Medieval West from the Eighth*

to the Twelfth Century, trans. Colette Friedlander, Cistercian Studies 145 [Kalamazoo, MI: Cistercian Publications, 1993], 98–99).

36. PL 188, col. 1136.

37. As Constable has noted, Anselm's mentor, Norbert, had been prominent among early twelfth-century preachers who urged direct imitation of Christ ("The Ideal of the Imitation of Christ," in *Three Studies in Medieval Religious and Social Thought*, 182–83, 183n233).

38. PL 170, col. 1291.

39. Anselm, *Dialogues*, 104.

40. PL 188, cols. 1121–22.

41. PL 188, cols. 1130–31.

42. PL 188, col. 1134.

Anselm of Havelberg, *Apologetic Letter*

1. Anselm opens by identifying himself, with Norbert, as *pauper Christi*.

2. Augustine, *Enarrationes in psalmos*, ed. Eligius Dekkers and Jean Fraipont, 2nd ed., CC 38 (Turnhout: Brepols, 1990), Ps 132:1.

3. See 1 Cor 15:16.

4. See Acts 2:8.

5. See Acts 2:1.

6. Here, as he generally does, Anselm cites the name of his authority, but so generally that it is impossible to identify the text.

7. Anselm refers to Rupert of Deutz, whose hostility to the regular canons was notorious (see John H. Van Engen, *Rupert of Deutz* [Berkeley and Los Angeles: University of California Press, 1983], 333–35). Egbert had likely referred to Rupert's *Altercatio monachi et clerici, quod liceat monacho praedicare*, a work of the early 1120s (PL 170, cols. 537–42).

8. See Hans Walther, ed., *Carmina medii aevi posterioris latina* 2.3, *Proverbia sententiaeque latinitatis medii aevi* (Göttingen: Vandenhoeck and Ruprecht, 1965), 21505b, p. 285. Anselm here may intend an unkind reference to Rupert's physique.

9. If this was indeed a medieval Latin proverb, it is undigested in Walther.

10. Cf. 2 Chr 26:10.

11. Cf. Jer 2:18.

12. Cf. Exod 2:8, 15.

13. Cf. John 19:24.

14. Anselm idealizes the hermit preacher, likely adverting to Norbert.

15. Here Anselm returns to the theme of *pauperes Christi.*

16. Anselm's text is here difficult to follow, given that Egbert's letter, which he seems to follow and critique almost word by word, is lost. Egbert seems to have praised clerics but pilloried the notion of regular clerics.

17. Anselm here apparently cites not Ambrose of Milan, at least directly, but Gregory VII purporting to quote Ambrose (*Registrum*, PL 148, col. 568). This and many of Anselm's canon law citations are difficult to trace exactly because he writes before Gratian's and later scholastics' definitive collections.

18. Urban II would thus be cited by Gratian, *Decretum* C. 19 q. 3 c. 2, in *Corpus iuris canonici*, 2nd ed., ed. Emil Friedberg (Graz: Akademische Druck- und Verlagsanstalt, 1959), 1:840. Anselm presumably draws directly from Urban's letter.

19. Again, Anselm apparently refers directly to a letter attributed in his source to Gelasius's letter, but the text is inaccessible in modern editions.

20. Gratian, *Decretum* C. 19 q. 3 c. 3, in Friedberg, *Corpus iuris canonici*, 1:840.

21. See Chrodegang of Metz, *Regula canonicorum*, PL 89, col. 1081.

22. Symphosius Amalarius, *Forma institutionis canonicorum*, PL 105, col. 914.

23. This important council in the Gregorian reform was held in 1077 (*Decretum* C. 19 q. 3 c. 1, in Friedberg, *Corpus iuris canonici*, 1:840).

24. Norbert had also described his mission as "nudus nudum Christi sequi" (*Vita Norberti*, PL 170, col. 1272).

25. Cf. Matt 19:28.

26. Cf. Luke 12:37.

27. Luke 11:17.

28. Anselm's citation here is wrong. The fifth council of Toledo was largely about relations between the church and the Visigothic kingdom, and it promulgated no such canon. The sixth council of Toledo made related pronouncements about familial connections of the clergy, and Anselm may have intended to reference these (José Vives, ed., *Concilios Visigoticos e Hispano-Romanos*, *España Cristiana*, Textos 1 [Barcelona: Consejo Superior de Investigaciones Cientificas, 1963], 240).

29. Here again Anselm responds directly, apparently, to Egbert's allusion to clerics outside of regular communities, whom regular governance might improve.

NOTES

30. Cf. Matt 7:14.

31. Anselm uses musical imagery for the relatively joyful role of clerics (see Jay T. Lees, *Anselm of Havelberg: Deeds into Words in the Twelfth Century*, Studies in the History of Christian Thought 79 [Leiden: Brill, 1998], 146).

32. Anselm refers directly to Norbert's choice of attire for his followers.

33. Anselm again emphasizes the regular cleric's imperative to preaching.

34. Cf. Sir 28:16.

35. Cf. Matt 3:10.

36. Mark 12:42.

37. Jerome, *Epistolae*, PL 22, col. 352.

38. Cf. Augustine, *Epistolae*, PL 33, col. 228. Anselm exaggerates; Augustine claimed only that the good monk, not the perfect monk, might not be a good cleric.

39. Gregory the Great, *Dialogues*, trans. Odo John Zimmerman (New York: Fathers of the Church, 1959) 2.23, pp. 91–93.

40. Bernard preached before Innocent in September of 1136, and Anselm—as he notes below—on Christmas of the same year (see Lees, *Anselm of Havelberg*, 51).

41. Anselm argues firmly for the appropriateness of regular canons' care of souls.

42. "verbo et exemplo docens" (PL 188, col. 1129).

43. Again Anselm stresses his self-identification as *pauper Christi*.

44. See Gen 4:4.

45. See Gen 6:7–8.

46. See Gen 12ff.

47. See Gen 28.

48. See Num 13.

49. See Dan 2:19.

50. See Dan 3:92.

51. See Giles Constable, "The Interpretation of Mary and Martha," in *Three Studies in Medieval Religious and Social Thought: The Interpretation of Mary and Martha, the Ideal of the Imitation of Christ, the Orders of Society* (Cambridge: Cambridge University Press, 1995), 3–141, esp. 49.

52. See Matt 11:15.

53. See Matt 4:24.

54. See John 8:44.

55. See Eccl 3:2–8.

56. Anselm adverts to the Premonstratensians' reading of John's experience as paradigmatic of their own.

57. See Ezek 1:14.

58. See Ps 15:11.

59. See Matt 25:40.

60. Cf. Ps 59:5.

61. When Anselm here refers to purpose, *propositum*, his usage is very close to the modern charism.

62. Cf. 2 Tim 2:4.

63. Here Anselm means the early monk Paul of Thebes, known as Paul the Hermit, whose life was rewritten by Jerome from Greek sources (Jerome, *Vita sancti Pauli primi eremitae*, PL 23, cols. 17–28).

64. Anselm returns to the priority of preaching in the life of the church.

65. Cf. Luke 20:9.

66. The Latin of the text emphasizes the maternal role of the preacher in such language as "parturisset," "enutrisset" (PL 188, col. 1137). Cf. Caroline Walker Bynum, *Jesus as Mother: Studies in the Spirituality of the High Middle Ages* (Berkeley and Los Angeles: University of California Press, 1982), 122–24.

67. A final time, Anselm adduces Norbert's familiar imagery of his following.

68. Cf. Josh 11:3.

69. Cf. Judg 4:2ff.

70. Cf. Acts 9:15.

71. Cf. 2 Cor 5:6.

72. Cf. 1 Cor 10:31.

73. Cf. 1 Pet 5:9.

Herman of Tournai,
Miracles of St. Mary of Laon—Introduction

1. Herman of Tournai, *Liber de restauratione monasterii sancti Martini Tornacensis*, ed. Georg Waitz, MGH SS 14, 266–327. See also Herman of Tournai, *The Restoration of the Monastery of Saint Martin of Tournai*, trans. Lynn H. Nelson (Washington, DC: Catholic University of America Press, 1996).

2. MGH SS 14, 315; Herman of Tournai, *The Restoration of the Monastery of Saint Martin of Tournai*, 120–21.

NOTES

3. Wilfried M. Grauwen, *Norbert, Erzbischof von Magdeburg (1126–1134)*, 2nd ed., trans. Ludger Horstkötter (Duisburg: Prämonstratenser-Abtei S. Johann, 1986), 31.

4. Herman of Tournai, *De miraculis S. Mariae Laudunensis*, MGH SS 12, ed. Roger Wilmans, 653–60.

5. Grauwen, *Norbert, Erzbischof von Magdeburg (1126–1134)*, 17; R. Wilmans, "Introduction," in Herman of Tournai, *De miraculis S. Mariae Laudunensis* (ed. Wilmans), 653n1.

6. Grauwen, *Norbert, Erzbischof von Magdeburg (1126–1134)*, 17.

7. Gerlinde Niemeyer, "Die Miracula S. Mariae Laudunensis des Abtes Hermann von Tournai: Verfasser und Entstehungszeit," *Deutsches Archiv für Erforschung des Mittelalters* 27 (1971): 135–74.

8. "frater Hermannus, omnium monachorum peripsema" (PL 156, col. 964).

9. *Lexikon des Mittelalters*, ed. Robert Auty (Munich: Artemis, 1977–99), 4:2169.

10. Hugh of Marchiennes, an opponent of Herman in the monastery who later became abbot of Marchiennes (see Niemeyer, "Die Miracula S. Mariae Laudunensis des Abtes Hermann von Tournai," 147, 147n86).

11. Ibid., 147–50.

12. Ibid., 149.

13. Ibid., 152.

14. Ibid., 142.

15. Ibid., 136.

16. Ibid., 167–68.

17. Ibid., 171.

18. Ibid., 172–73.

19. Ibid., 172.

20. Ibid., 174.

21. "Domnus siquidem Hugo Praemonstratensis abbas mihi nuper narravit" (MGH SS 12, 659).

22. MGH SS 12, 658.

23. Herbert Grundmann, *Religious Movements in the Middle Ages: The Historical Links between Heresy, the Mendicant Orders, and the Women's Religious Movement in the Twelfth and Thirteenth Century, with the Historical Foundations of German Mysticism*, trans. Steven Rowan (Notre Dame, IN: University of Notre Dame Press, 1995), 21.

24. MGH SS 12, 660.

25. Grauwen, *Norbert, Erzbischof von Magdeburg (1126–1134)*, 18.

26. MGH SS 12, 656.

27. MGH SS 12, 659.
28. MGH SS 12, 655.
29. MGH SS 12, 656.
30. MGH SS 12, 658.

Herman of Tournai,
Miracles of St. Mary of Laon (excerpts)

1. April 25, 1112.
2. Bartholomew, bishop of Laon 1113–50, died June 26, 1158.
3. PL 156, col. 965.
4. See Wilfried M. Grauwen, "De eerste kerk- en kloosterbouw te Premontre, 1122," *AP* 71 (1995): 37–51, esp. 44n36. Grauwen suggests that by "two half-years" Herman means the summers of 1113 and 1114.
5. September 6, 1114.
6. Surely Herman exaggerates.
7. 1119.
8. Cf. John 2:1–11.
9. Herman here adverts to the white of the Premonstratensian habit.
10. Paschal II died January 21, 1118.
11. Gelasius II died January 29, 1119.
12. Callixtus II, elected February 2, 1119.
13. Adele.
14. Louis VI (1108–37).
15. The Council of Reims was held October 20–30, 1119.
16. Cf. MGH SS 12, 684; PL 170, col. 1295.
17. Cf. MGH SS 12, 677; PL 170, col. 1283.
18. Cf. MGH SS 12, 678; PL 170, col. 1283.
19. Cf. MGH SS 12, 679; PL 170, col. 1284. See also Wilfried M. Grauwen, "Bartholomeus van Laon en Norbert op zoek naar een vestigingsplaats, begin 1120," *AP* 70 (1994): 199–211.
20. A Cistercian abbey was later built at Foigny (PL 156, col. 1000).
21. A Premonstratensian abbey was later built at Thenaille (ibid.).
22. The meadow shown.
23. MGH SS 12, 679; AASS Juni 1, 820; PL 170, col. 1284. Prémontré is eighteen kilometers west of Laon.
24. A Benedictine abbey.
25. Both *Vita A* and *Vita B* mention only that when winter had passed Norbert went to Cambrai and there gained Evermode as a disciple

260

NOTES

(cf. MGH SS 12, 679; AASS Juni 1, 820; PL 170, col. 1284). Herman's inclusion of Norbert's sojourn in the urban schools, omitted in the hagiography, perhaps reveals his Premonstratensian subjects' ambivalence about such education.

26. Cf. MGH SS 12, 684; PL 170, cols. 1295–96.

27. Herman's acknowledgment of Leonius's contribution reveals a powerful cooperative and oral process behind the construction of this text.

28. Herman is happy to repeat and accept multiple interpretations of Norbert's roadside revelation.

29. Hugh of Fosses, abbot of Prémontré from 1128 to 1161/64.

30. October 9. It was in fact Hugh who began calling the abbots together annually for what eventually became a general chapter.

31. In 1151 Walter succeeded Bartholomew as bishop of Laon.

32. St. Samuel was founded in 1141.

33. PL 76, col. 1165.

34. Cf. Isa 41:19.

35. Herman's enthusiastic account of the Premonstratensians has both supported and, likely, misdirected scholarship concerning them. Evidently he exaggerates their numbers, and his description of their strict claustration accords poorly with other evidence—including hagiographical evidence such as the *Life of Oda*—that they were involved with the order's hospices for the laity.

36. Cf. MGH SS 12, 675; PL 170, col. 1274. Herman is concerned to affirm his personal contact with Norbert's follower Hugh, so supporting the accuracy of his account.

37. Cf. MGH SS 12, 675; PL 170, cols. 1274–75.

38. Cf. John 1:40–42.

39. Theobald (1125–52) was the son of Adele, sister of Henry I of England and daughter of William the Conqueror. His father was Stephen of Blois.

40. Henry I, 1100–1135.

41. Wilmans identifies this passage as erroneous (MGH SS 12, 660). Cf. MGH SS 12, 689; PL 170, col. 1308.

42. Cf. MGH SS 12, 690; PL 170, col. 1309.

43. Only Herman mentions him as present. Wilmans thought this was Pierleone, the later antipope, Anacletus II (MGH SS 12, 660; cf. Wilfried M. Grauwen, *Norbert, Erzbischof von Magdeburg (1126–1134)*, 2nd ed., trans. Ludger Horstkötter [Duisburg: Prämonstratenser-Abtei S. Johann, 1986], 97).

44. Lucius II, 1144–45.

261

45. Cf. MGH SS 12, 693–94; PL 170, cols. 1322–23; cf. Grauwen, *Norbert, Erzbischof von Magdeburg (1126–1134)*, 95–106.

Life of Godfrey of Cappenberg—Introduction

1. *BHL* 3575. See Herbert Grundmann, *Der Cappenberger Barbarossakopf und die Anfänge des Stiftes Cappenberg*, Münstersche Forschungen 12 (Cologne: Böhlau, 1959, especially 17–45; Gerlinde Niemeyer, "Die *Vitae Godefridi Cappenbergensis*," Deutsches Archiv für Erforschung des Mittelalters 23 [1967]: 405–67); Wilfried Grauwen, "Norbert en de stichtung van Cappenberg, 1122," *AP* 68 (1992): 43–75; Andreas Leistikow, *Die Geschichte der Grafen von Cappenberg und ihrer Stiftsgründungen: Cappenberg, Varlar und Ilbenstadt* (Hamburg: Kovac, 2000), especially 21–80.

2. We are indebted for this information to Rudolf Schieffer at MGH.

3. See, for instance, Jean-Claude Schmitt, *La Conversion d'Hermann le Juif: Autobiographie, Histoire et Fiction* (Paris: Editions du Seuil, 2003), 87–89. Schmitt is concerned to establish Herman's text in the locality and community of Cappenberg, but not in the wider Premonstratenisan context.

4. See, for instance, MGH 12, 525, c. 10, where he tells a story about Godfrey he has heard "a quodam familiarem nostrum, qui optime noverat sanctum virum."

5. MGH 12, 528. On the manuscripts and histories of the texts of the various lives of Godfrey, see Niemeyer, "Die *Vitae Godefridi Cappenbergensis*," 405–13.

6. Ibid., 412.

7. On the dating of the first life of Norbert, see Wilfried M. Grauwen, "Inleidung tot de *Vita Norberti A*," *AP* 60 (1964): 13–17.

8. "sancti quoque transitus felicitate si quis ad plenum dicere voluerit, singularis profecto libri ad hoc solum institutione magnitudine opus erit" (MGH SS 12, 516).

9. Wilfried M. Grauwen, "Inleiding tot de *Vita Norberti B*," *AP* 66 (1990): 136–40, 191–94.

10. Niemeyer, "Die *Vitae Godefridi Cappenbergensis*," 422–23.

11. Ibid., 423, 423n42.

12. MGH SS 12, 516. See Niemeyer, "Die *Vitae Godefridi Cappenbergensis*," 420.

13. Otto, the former count, rather than another Otto, then provost, had brought his brother's relics home, suggesting that he maintained charge of this familial legacy (MGH 12, 527–28).

14. The *Life of Godfrey* glosses over Jutta's resistance to Godfrey's plan for her celibacy (MGH SS 12, 516). See Niemeyer, "Die *Vitae Godefridi Cappenbergensis*," 447. Jutta finally may have escaped religious life.

15. MGH SS 12, 518–19.

16. MGH SS 12, 521–23.

17. MGH SS 12, 525. Godfrey was ordained as an acolyte, as was his brother, Otto, suggesting that like most contemporary nobles who had not been raised for entry into religion, they lacked the learning necessary for higher orders. Since Otto was eventually provost of Cappenberg, he presumably learned in adulthood.

18. "Post annum vero revocatus ad patrem Norbertum, iam archiepiscopum Magdeburgensem, cum seculi pompam vel strepitum sancti viri aegre ferret aspectus, Domino electum suum remunerare disponente, lenta coepit pulsari aegritudine, acceptaque benedictione patris Norberti, ad Elofstadense declinavit coenobium, ubi hoc ordine post non multos dies migravit" (MGH SS 12, 525). Cf., for instance, Niemeyer, who finds Godfrey here "im Gegensatz zu Norbert" ("Die *Vitae Godefridi Cappenbergensis*," 447).

19. MGH SS 12, 527.

20. Niemeyer, "Die *Vitae Godefridi Cappenbergensis*," 406–11.

21. Anselm of Havelberg took John as exemplary in his *Apologetic Letter* (PL 188, cols. 1133–34).

Life of Godfrey of Cappenberg

1. The hagiographer identifies his primary audience as his confreres, not necessarily at Cappenberg only, but imagines that others will hear of Godfrey's life, presumably through his confreres' preaching.

2. Cf. Deut 16:21.

3. Augustine, *De trinitate*, ed. W. J. Mountain, CC 50 (Turnhout: Brepols, 1968), 2 (proem.).

4. Cf. Eccl 49:1–2.

5. The hagiographer here uses the term *minister*. The retainer to whom he refers was one of Godfrey's unfree knightly subordinates, one of the *ministeriales* who occupied a stratum more privileged than the servile class but still unfree, beneath the nobility. This group was unexampled in

NORBERT AND EARLY NORBERTINE SPIRITUALITY

feudal Europe outside the empire (see Karl Bösl, "'Noble Unfreedom':
The Rise of the *Ministeriales* in Germany," in *The Medieval Nobility: Studies
on the Ruling Classes of France and Germany from the Sixth to the Twelfth
Century*, ed. and trans. Timothy Reuter, Europe in the Middle Ages:
Selected Studies 14 [Amsterdam: North Holland, 1978], 291–311).

6. Cf. Ps 83:13.

7. 1121.

8. The hagiographer here suggests that the life of Norbert is as yet
unwritten—at least that he and the community of Cappenberg have not
seen it. Since *A*, the earlier of the two twelfth-century lives of Norbert,
itself of German origin, is loosely dated to between 1145 and the mid-
1160s, this suggestion in the *Life of Godfrey* text implies a still earlier, if very
loose, dating. The author of Godfrey's life seems to believe that his is the
first hagiographical work among religious foundations connected to
Norbert.

9. 1122.

10. May 31.

11. Notably, the hagiographer identifies Cappenberg and its sister
houses as Augustinian communities, rather than identifying them with the
Order of Prémontré increasingly organized in the course of the twelfth
century.

12. "et ecce hic ordo noster" (MGH SS 12, 516). The author here
again refers to a particular interpretation of the Rule of St. Augustine and
a network of religious communities founded by Norbert rather than the
sort of formal religious order to which the term *ordo* later applies.

13. Cf. Ps 79:9–12.

14. Cf. Ps 79:14–16.

15. The author emphasizes the importance of the mutual affiliation
of Cappenberg and its sister houses.

16. Cf. Ps 79:17.

17. Cappenberg was also called *Mons Speculationis* or *Mons Syon* (see
Norbert Backmund, *Monasticon praemonstratense*, 2nd ed., vol. 1, pt. 1
[Berlin: Walter de Gruyter, 1983], 186).

18. Cf. Augustine, *Confessiones*, ed. Luc Verheijen, CC 27
(Turnhout: Brepols, 1981), 3.11.19. The *Life of Godfrey* account of this
vision imputes Norbert's apocalyptic interpretation to Augustine.

19. 1124.

20. Cf. 1 Kgs 19:15.

21. Cf. Ps 67:24. Here begins the hagiographer's excursus on the
conversion of Herman-Judah also known from the supposed convert's own
text (Herman of Cologne, *Opusculum de conversione sua*, ed. Gerlinde

NOTES

Niemeyer, MGH Quellen zur Geistesgeschichte des Mittelalters 4 [Weimar: Herman Böhlhaus, 1963], 114–16, esp. c. 17.

22. Cf. 2 Cor 3:15.

23. 1122.

24. Cf. Juvenal, *Satura* 6.181.

25. Cf. Vergil, *Aeneid* 3.56–57.

26. Here the hagiographer borrows a hexameter verse from an unidentified source.

27. Rom 8:28.

28. Cf. Vergil, *Eclogues* 4.5.

29. The hagiographer again uses an unidentified hexameter fragment.

30. Again, the author's verse source is unidentified.

31. See Florence McCulloch, *Medieval Latin and French Bestiaries*, University of North Carolina Studies in the Romance Languages and Literatures 33, rev. ed. (Chapel Hill: University of North Carolina Press, 1962), 173. Godfrey here seems to have followed a medieval tradition about the sagacity and community of stags, who were figures for Christ, but his specific suggestion about their decoying strategy is unusual.

32. Horace, *Epistulae* 1.16.39.

33. Cf. Augustine, *Ennarationes in psalmos* 32.2.2.

34. Pseudo-Columbanus, "Versus ad Hunaldum," *Opera*, ed. G. S. A. Walker, Scriptores Latini Hiberniae 2 (Dublin: Dublin Institute for Advanced Studies, 1957), 184.

35. Cf. 1 Thess 5:14.

36. Cf. Vergil, *Aeneid* 4.188.

37. Vergil, *Aeneid* 6.160.

38. August 15.

39. Prudentius, *Contra Symmachum*, in *Opera*, ed. Maurice P. Cunningham, CC 126 (Turnhout: Brepols, 1966), 2.112–13.

40. Cf. Matt 7:24–25; Luke 6:48.

41. Cf. Job 3:8.

42. Cf. Exod 15:15.

43. Cf. Gen 49:5.

44. Cf. Ps 111:9.

45. The year 1125.

46. Cf. Matt 25:1–13.

47. Matt 25:6.

48. January 13.

49. *Recte* 1127 (see MGH 12, 526n39). See also Gerlinde Niemeyer, "Die *Vitae Godefridi Cappenbergensis*," *Deutsches Archiv für Erforschung des Mittelalters* 23 (1967), 413.

50. January 22.
51. Vergil, *Aeneid* 7.646.
52. In fact in 1149.
53. Vergil, *Aeneid* 4.285–287.
54. January 13.
55. Cf. Matt 8:14–15.
56. February 12.
57. Arator, *De actibus apostolorum*, ed. Arthur Patch McKinley, CSEL 72 (Vienna: Holder-Pichler-Tempsky, 1951), 2.678.
58. September 16, 1150.
59. Cf. Gen 30:5.
60. There follow several brief addenda.
61. See Niemeyer, "Die *Vitae Godefridi Cappenbergensis*," 437.
62. The grave of the counts.
63. See Niemeyer, "Die *Vitae Godefridi Cappenbergensis*," 426.
64. June 24.
65. May 6.

The Hagiography of Norbert, the A and B *Lives*—Introduction

1. The *A* life of Norbert is *BHL* 6248; *B* is *BHL* 6249; the Cappenberg addenda are *BHL* 6250. For a comprehensive description, comparison, and overview of the two *vitae*, see Wilfried M. Grauwen, "Inleiding tot de Vita Norberti A," *AP* 60 (1984): 5–48; idem, "Inleiding tot de Vita Norberti B," *AP* 66 (1990): 123–202.
2. AASS Juni 1, 807–47; PL 170, cols. 1253–1350.
3. Berlin, Staatsbibliothek Preussischer Kulturbesitz, Ms theol. lat. 79, fols. 90r–110v.
4. Grauwen, "Inleiding tot de Vita Norberti A," 42.
5. MGH SS 12, 670–703.
6. See Wilfried M. Grauwen, "Een fragment van de Vita Norberti A te Hamburg," *AP* 60 (1984): 153–62.
7. The text corresponds to Wilmans's edition: MGH SS 12, 686, ll. 8–23. It presents the passage concerning the devil stories at Prémontré, the quarrel between Reinald and Burchard, and the beginning of the devil story of the porter.
8. Grauwen, "Een fragment van de Vita Norberti A te Hamburg," 156.

266

NOTES

9. Wilfried M. Grauwen, *Norbert, Erzbischof von Magdeburg (1126–1134)*, 2nd ed., trans. Ludger Horstkötter (Duisburg: Prämonstratenser-Abtei S. Johann, 1986), 21.

10. Wilfried M. Grauwen, "De handschriften van de Vitae Norberti," *AP* 70 (1994): 5–101.

11. Grauwen, "Inleiding tot de Vita Norberti A," 24–30.

12. Richard Rosenmund, *Die ältesten Biographieen des heiligen Norbert* (Berlin: Ernst Siegfried Mittler und Sohn, 1874), 31.

13. Lucius II (1144–45); MGH SS 12, 694.

14. The *primicerius* was a dignitary of a diocese either in charge of the liturgy or perhaps director of the cathedral school.

15. The past tense of the verb is used (AASS Juni 1, 836; PL 170, col. 1323).

16. Hugh died on February 10, 1164, but Philip is listed as abbot of Prémontré from 1161 onward.

17. MGH SS 12, 685; AASS Juni 1, 823.

18. MGH SS 12, 701–2.

19. Grauwen, "Inleiding tot de Vita Norberti A," 9–12.

20. "Incipit vita domni Norberti Magdeburgensis archiepiscopi" (Berlin, theol. lat 79, fol. 90r). Cf. Grauwen, "Inleiding tot de Vita Norberti B," 125.

21. "Prologus in librum de iniciis et incrementis premonstratensium" (Munich, Bayerische Staatsbibliothek, Clm. 17.144, fol. 3r). The provenance of this manuscript is the Premonstratensian abbey of Schäftlarn. Cf. Grauwen, "Inleiding tot de Vita Norberti B," 125–27.

22. Walter L. Wakefield and Austin P. Evans, *Heresies of the High Middle Ages* (New York: Columbia University Press, 1991), 96–101, 672–73; Jeffrey Burton Russell, *Dissent and Reform in the Early Middle Ages* (Berkeley and Los Angeles: University of California Press, 1965), 56–68, 265–69.

23. MGH SS 12, 697–98; AASS Juni 1, 840. Cf. Grauwen, *Norbert, Erzbischof von Magdeburg (1126–1134)*, 217.

24. AASS Juni 1, 807; PL 170, col. 1254.

25. Grauwen, "Inleiding tot de Vita Norberti B," 127–29.

26. This chapter is found in only four manuscripts and in only one of the five extant twelfth-century manuscripts (ibid., 175–77).

27. AASS Juni 1, 841; PL 170, col. 1334.

28. AASS Juni 1, 838; PL 170, col. 1327.

29. AASS Juni 1, 839; PL 170, col. 1328. Cf. John 2:4.

30. AASS Juni 1, 844; PL 170, cols. 1341–44.

31. Johannes Chrysostomus van der Sterre, *Vita S. Norberti canoni-corum Praemonstratensium patriarchae, Antverpiae apostoli, archiepiscopi Magdeburgensis ac totius Germaniae primatis* (Antwerp, 1622). Among this volume's thirty-four engravings by Theodore Galle, see esp. pls. 32 (death of Norbert) and 33 (Norbert lying in state).

32. AASS Juni 1, 818.

33. MGH SS 12, 516–17.

34. This poem is found in eight manuscripts, but in only two from the twelfth-century (Prague, Lobkowitz 484; Lobkowitz 513) (see Grauwen, "De handschriften van de Vitae Norberti," 73–81). Two other manuscripts include the poem in the list of chapter headings but do not represent it in their texts (see Grauwen, "Inleiding tot de Vita Norberti B," 183).

35. Grauwen, "Inleiding tot de Vita Norberti B," 184.

36. Ibid., 167–68.

Version A: *Life of Norbert*

1. Paschal II (1099–1118).

2. Henry V (1106–25).

3. Between Nijmegen, Gennep, and Cleves.

4. Benedictine monastery southeast of Cologne.

5. Augustine of Hippo, whom Norbert took as his model in the foundation of religious communities, also had had such an irregular ordination. On the circumstances of Augustine's ordination, see James J. O'Donnell, *Augustine: A New Biography* (New York: HarperCollins, 2005), 25–26, 231–33.

6. In the period, preaching was primarily an episcopal function, so Norbert's early determination to preach is extraordinary, pointing toward his later career as an itinerant preacher.

7. Church of Augustinian canons in present-day Kerkrade in the Netherlands (Prov. of Limburg), not far from Aachen.

8. The council opened in late July 1118.

9. Cf. Matt 3:4.

10. Cf. Gen 3:21.

11. St.-Gilles-du-Gard was a pilgrimage site south of Nîmes.

12. Gelasius II (1118–19).

13. This extraordinary privilege became central to Norbert's later mission.

14. Wednesday, March 26, 1119.

15. Bishop of Cambrai (1114–30).

NOTES

16. Cf. Acts 5:39.

17. Hugh of Fosses would become abbot of Prémontré (1128–61/64).

18. Cf. Heb 11:13.

19. Cf. Matt 10:10; Luke 9:3; Luke 10:4.

20. Cf. Luke 10:5–6.

21. Cf. Ps 38:13; 1 Pet 2:11.

22. Cf. Wis 6:4; Rom 13:1.

23. Cf. Luke 10:6.

24. Callixtus II (1119–24).

25. October 20–30, 1119.

26. Benedictine monastery.

27. Norbert was clearly previously well-schooled, and this passage illumines his ambivalence about the teaching of theology in the urban schools, a theme his follower Philip of Harvengt would later take up in "On the Knowledge of Clerics."

28. Cf. Gen 29:15–30.

29. David. Cf. 1 Sam 16:23.

30. Cf. Matt 12:32; Luke 12:10.

31. Cf. 1 Cor 4:16.

32. Cf. Luke 19:14.

33. Cf. 2 Cor 6:9.

34. Prémontré is eighteen kilometers west of Laon.

35. Evermode became provisor of Gottesgnaden and later provost of Our Lady's Church in Magdeburg (1138) and still later was bishop of Ratzeburg (1154–78).

36. Cf. Ezek 28:12.

37. This story is not found in the *B* life of Norbert.

38. Cf. 1 Cor 4:15.

39. Cf. Matt 15:13.

40. Cf. Luke 6:48.

41. This chapter reemphasizes the commitment to revival of apostolic life Norbert shared with the other principal twelfth-century reformers of religious life.

42. This is the opening sentence of the *Ordo monasterii*, the strict version of the Rule of St. Augustine adopted at Prémontré (*Regula*, in George Lawless, *Augustine of Hippo and His Monastic Rule* [Oxford: Clarendon Press, 1987], 74–75).

43. Cf. John 20:12.

44. Cf. Exod 28:42–43.

45. Cf. Exod 28:42.

46. Cf. 2 Cor 6:14–15.
47. Cf. Matt 15:13.
48. November 18, 1122.
49. Cf. Dan 7:19–27.
50. Cf. 1 John 2:18, 22; 2 John 7.
51. St.-Nicholas-au-Bois, a Benedictine abbey nearby.
52. The complete antiphon is found in the Office of the Apostles, the Magnificat antiphon for the Second Vespers of Barnabas (June 11) and Bartholomew (August 24) and for the First Vespers of Matthias (February 24).
53. Cf. Jer 20:14.
54. Cf. John 8:44.
55. Cf. Isa 14:13–14.
56. Cf. 2 Tim 4:1.
57. Died January 13, 1127, at Ilbenstadt.
58. Godfrey's wife was Jutta.
59. Otto of Cappenberg, died 1171.
60. Frederick of Arnsberg, died 1124.
61. Cf. Acts 1:18.
62. Theobald II of Champagne, IV of Blois, died 1152.
63. Cf. 2 Cor 6:10.
64. Honorius II (1124–30).
65. April 11, 1126.
66. The abbey of Oberzell.
67. Died 1115.
68. St. Michael's Abbey.
69. Burchard of Cambrai (1114–30).
70. Lothair was actually not crowned emperor until June 4, 1133.
71. Gerard Caccianemici, cardinal priest, later Pope Lucius II (1144–45).
72. Actually, the pontificates of Pope Innocent II (1130–43) and Pope Celestine II (1143–44) fell between those of Honorius II and Lucius II.
73. Adelbert I of Mainz (1110–37).
74. Later archbishop of Trier (1131–52).
75. Norbert was consecrated bishop by his suffragan bishop, Udo of Naumburg, on July 25, 1126.
76. Cf. Acts 5:41.
77. Cf. 2 Tim 4:2.
78. Cf. Jdt 13:30; Acts 10:25.
79. Innocent II (1130–43).
80. As antipope he took the name Anacletus II (1130–38).
81. October 18–29, 1131.

82. According to Grauwen, the uprising at Magdeburg took place in June 1129. Therefore the sequence of events is out of order as the text here presents it (see Wilfried M. Grauwen, *Norbert, Erzbischof von Magdeburg (1126–1134)*, 2nd ed., trans. Ludger Horstkötter [Duisburg: Prämonstratenser-Abtei S. Johann, 1986], 217–19).

83. June 29–30, 1129.

84. Cf. Luke 22:32.

85. Cf. John 18:7–8.

86. Cf. Ps 33:18.

87. Cf. Matt 15:13.

88. Benedictine abbey of Berge.

89. Cf. 1 Pet 5:8.

90. Orte and Narni are located north of Rome.

91. Located south of Rome.

92. Augustine, *De disciplina christiana* (PL 40, col. 676).

93. June 6, 1134.

94. Since Norbert was buried on June 11, 1134, this calculation must be wrong.

Version B: *Life of Norbert* (excerpts)

1. PL 170, col. 1253–54.

2. "cum proposuerim scribere de Praemonstratensibus viris" (PL 170, col. 1254).

3. The *B* hagiographer is concerned to note that he writes from firsthand accounts.

4. "Praeterea sciendum est, cum multi hujus vitam et gesta conscripserint, nullum omnino invenirem qui rem plenarie et ex ordine persequatur" (PL 170, col. 1254).

5. The *B* author thus claims that his text represents a consensus of Norbert's immediate companions.

6. PL 170, cols. 1263–68.

7. The god of reason.

8. Augustine, *Sermones de sanctis* (PL 38, cf. cols. 1293, 1459, 1460).

9. The *B* text here suggests that this chapter is excerpted from another written work.

10. Cf. Matt 8:31.

11. Chapter 5's extended proto-scholastic discourse on the meaning of saints' suffering has no clear principal source.

12. PL 170, cols. 1277–78.

13. Sixtus II (257–58).

14. Cf. John 4:13.

15. Cf. Matt 5:3.

16. PL 170, cols. 1315–16. This and the subsequent story of Norbert's and his followers' relationship with wolves anticipate stories of Francis of Assisi.

17. PL 170, cols. 1316–19.

18. The B hagiographer here indicates that his anticipated audience is his community and perhaps other Premonstratensian communities. The extent to which he theologizes in these wolf stories again anticipates the Franciscan fascination with the moral exemplarity of animals.

19. Cf. Deut 32:11.

20. PL 170, cols. 1341–44. These three appearances, not found in the A life, are intended to prove Norbert's blessedness.

21. The author likely means after the establishment of Prémontré. Norbert's earliest followers died at Valenciennes between March 30 and April 6, 1119.

22. Cf. Matt 7:7–8; Luke 11:9–10.

23. Sg 5:1. Norbert's feminine soul, *anima*, is here addressed as sister, *soror*.

24. Thus Hugh was still alive when the B life was written.

25. Here the B text turns back, as if in review, on the prior passages, affirming the firsthand authority of this account of Norbert's life.

26. Like Abraham (cf. Gen 12:1).

27. The B author assumes an active discussion of the truth of aspects of Norbert's story among his confreres and outside critics of their founder.

28. PL 170, cols. 1343–50.

29. The speaker of the first Cappenberg additions is concerned—unlike either the A or B hagiographer—to identify his community, perhaps because he expects his text to travel elsewhere.

30. Hugh of Fosse. Cf. Wilfried M. Grauwen, "Inleiding tot de *Vita Norberti B*," *AP* 66 (1990): 165–67.

31. This passage is taken directly from the *Life of Godfrey* (MGH SS 12, 516).

32. Chapter 2 is taken from the *Life of Godfrey* (MGH SS 12, 517).

33. Cf. 1 Kgs 19:15.

34. Chapter 3 is again taken from the *Life of Godfrey* (MGH SS 12, 517).

35. The Cappenberg additions imply the contribution of another voice.

36. Cf. Ps 79:9–12. Chapter 4 is thus far drawn directly from the *Life of Godfrey* (MGH SS 12, 516–17).

37. The compiler of the Cappenberg additions again suggests a further voice or still later addition.

38. Chapter 5, except for the concluding lines, is taken from the *Life of Godfrey* MGH SS 12, 517.

39. The compiler of the Cappenberg additions here contrasts the material of his *B* text of the life of Norbert and the *Life of Godfrey*, writing as if conversing directly with another community from which his own has received a copy of "your book."

40. Cf. H. J. Lentze, "Der Messritus des Prämonstratenser-ordens," *AP* 26 (1950): 143; W. M. Grauwen, "Norbert et les débuts de l'abbaye de Floreffe," *AP* 51 (1975): 20–23.

41. The passage cited is not in the AASS version of the life of Servatius, fourth-century bishop of Tongres, whose cult flourished in the Low Countries in the twelfth century (AASS Mai 3, 208–31).

42. Patron of the Archdiocese of Magdeburg.

43. August 28–31, 1132.

44. Cf. Luke 10:5.

45. Cf. Luke 10:6.

46. Cf. Exod 20:12; Deut 5:16; 27:16; Sir 3:6–9; 7:29; Mal 1:6.

47. Cf. Matt 15:4; 19:19; Mark 10:19; Luke 18:20; Eph 6:2.

48. PL 170, col. 1350.

49. The poet, whose relationship to the compiler of the Cappenberg additions is unclear, directly addresses Hugh of Fosses.

50. Horace, *Epistolae* 1.1.61.

Philip of Harvengt, "On the Knowledge of Clerics"—Introduction

1. Philip's principal biographer is G. P. Sijen, whose series of articles on the abbot and his works determine the principal events of his life and establish a basis for later criticism: "Philippe de Harveng, abbé de Bonne-Espérance," *AP* 14 (1938): 37–42; "Le passabilité de Christ chez Philippe de Harveng," *AP* 14 (1938): 189–208; "Les oeuvres de Philippe de Harveng, abbé de Bonne-Espérance," *AP* 15 (1939): 129–66. See also Rachel Fulton's review and emendation of Sijen's account (*From Judgment to Passion: Devotion to Christ and the Virgin Mary, 800–1200* [New York: Columbia University Press, 2002], 295–96).

2. Fulton, *From Judgment to Passion*, 295.

3. PL 203.
4. See Fulton, *From Judgment to Passion*, 295–96.
5. Ibid.
6. Cf. Caroline Walker Bynum, *Docere verbo et exemplo: An Aspect of Twelfth-Century Spirituality*, Harvard Theological Studes 31 (Missoula, MT: Scholars Press, 1979), esp. 12–13, 25n30, for a valuable summary of scholarship on Philip's educational works. See also Giles Constable, "The Ideal of the Imitation of Christ," in *Three Studies in Medieval Religious and Social Thought: The Interpretation of Mary and Martha, the Ideal of the Imitation of Christ, the Orders of Society* (Cambridge: Cambridge University Press, 1995), 185. G. P. Sijen had noted, in his basic study of Philip's works, that these were in fact separate treatises: "Les oeuvres de Philippe de Harveng, abbé de Bonne Espérance," *AP* 15 (1939): 150–54; on "On the Knowledge of Clerics" specifically, see 151–52.
7. Brussels, Bibliothèque Royale Ms. II.1158.
8. Norbertus I. Weyns, "A propos des *Instructions pour les clercs (De insitutione clericorum)* de Philippe de Harveng," *AP* 53 (1977), 71–79. See also Werner Bomm, "Augustinusregel, *professio canonica* und Prämonstratenser im 12. Jahrhundert: Das Beispiel der Norbert-Viten, Philipps von Harvengt und Anselms von Havelberg," in *Regula sancti Augustini: Normative Grundlage differenter Verbände im Mittelalter*, ed. Gert Melville and Anne Müller (Paring: Augustiner-Chorherren-Verlag, 2002), 264–65, 265n85.
9. See Henri de Lubac, *Exégése médiévale: les quatre sens de l'écriture*, 2 pts. in 4 vols. (Paris: Aubier, 1959–64), pt. 1, 2:293–95.
10. Philippe Delahaye, "L'organisation scolaire au XIIe siècle," *Traditio* 5 (1947): 211–68, esp. 238–39.
11. PL 203, cols. 695–96.
12. Jay T. Lees, for instance, refers to "the schism in the order into what might be called western Premonstratensians and eastern Norbertines" (Lees, *Anselm of Havelberg: Deeds into Words in the Twelfth Century*, Studies in the History of Christian Thought 79 [Leiden: Brill, 1998], 31).
13. Bynum, *Docere verbo et exemplo: An Aspect of Twelfth-Century Spirituality*, esp. 54.
14. PL 203, col. 295.
15. Fulton, *From Judgment to Passion*, 378–84.
16. Lubac, pt. 2, 1:209n9.
17. PL 203, col. 705.
18. Cf. Anselm of Havelberg, *Apologetic Letter* (PL 188, cols. 1133–34).

Philip of Harvengt, "On the Knowledge of Clerics"

1. Philip here directs his remarks to *fratres carissimi* (PL 203, col. 695). He might be embracing a more general audience, but the specific context in which he mentions clerics living in community suggests that he refers to his own Premonstratensian confreres.

2. "et tam verbo quam exemplo ad eadem implenda alios edocere" (PL 203, col. 695). Philip's phrase turns on the more frequent "docere verbo et exemplo," which Caroline Bynum has noted is the characteristic expression of the regular canons' mission. For Bynum's discussion of Philip's perspective, see *Docere verbo et exemplo: An Aspect of Twelfth-Century Spirituality*, Harvard Theological Studes 31 (Missoula, MT: Scholars Press, 1979), esp. 50–55.

3. Cf. Hans Walther, ed., *Carmina medii aevi posterioris latina* 2.4, *Proverbia sententiaeque latinitatis medii aevi* (Göttingen: Vandenhoeck and Ruprecht, 1965), 25884, p. 464, and 25942, p. 473.

4. "animas quas errore ignorantiae illecebra temporalis pervertit; revocando, informando, illuminando convertit" (PL 203, col. 703). Philip's Latin plays on the common root of the Latin terms for conversion and perversion, stressing the theme of conversion as lifelong turning from the secular world.

5. Here Philip emphasizes the obligation of even the cloistered cleric to preach.

Philip of Harvengt, *Life of Oda*—Introduction

1. Rachel Fulton devotes an entire chapter to Philip's Song commentary (*From Judgment to Passion: Devotion to Christ and the Virgin Mary, 800–1200* [New York: Columbia University Press, 2002], 351–404). She emphasizes that Philip's "highly erotic, albeit unambiguously Marian" exegesis (352) is unembarrassed by its implication of incest (357). See also G. P. Sijen, "Les oeuvres de Philippe de Harveng, abbé de Bonne-Espérance," *AP* 15 (1939), 143–47.

2. *BHL* 6262. On Bonne Espérance and the women's community at nearby Rivreulle, see Norbert Backmund, *Monasticon praemonstratense*, 2nd ed. (Berlin: Walter de Gruyter, 1983), 2:394. Backmund offers loose dates, 1140–82, for the establishment of a separate women's community. Philip's *Life of Oda* implies that she initially, in the late 1130s, moved directly to

Bonne Espérance, but by her death in 1158 the women's house had been removed (PL 203, cols. 1369, 1374: "corpus...ad abbatiam deportatum est").

3. For instance, Philip's earlier contemporary Rupert of Deutz wrote a life of Augustine of Hippo that he later dismissed as juvenalia (John H. Van Engen, *Rupert of Deutz* [(Berkeley and Los Angeles: University of California Press, 1983], 47). On Philip's other hagiographies, all of which are based on earlier lives, unlike the *Life of Oda*, see Sijen, "Les oeuvres de Philippe de Harveng, abbé de Bonne-Espérance," 154–65; on the *Life of Oda*, see Sijen, "Les oeuvres de Philippe de Harveng, abbé de Bonne-Espérance," 163.

4. PL 203, col. 1574.

5. Fulton, *From Judgment to Passion*, 362.

6. On Oda's dates, see Bernard Ardura, *The Order of Prémontré: History and Spirituality*, trans. Edward Hagman, ed. Roman Vanasse (De Pere: Paisa, 1995), 86–88.

7. Catherine Mooney, "Voice, Gender, and the Portrayal of Sanctity," in *Gendered Voices: Medieval Saints and Their Interpretation*, ed. Catherine Mooney (Philadelphia: University of Pennsylvania Press, 1999), 6–15.

8. PL 203, col. 1366. On women saints' self-mutilation, see Jane Tibbetts Schulenberg, *Forgetful of Their Sex: Female Sanctity and Society* (Chicago: University of Chicago Press, 1998), 139–55; on Oda, see 147–48.

9. Philip adverts directly to the "blood of Agnes" (PL 203, col. 367), and both his proem (cols. 1339–40) and his reference to Oda as champion in her parents' doorway (col. 1364) suggest Perpetua's life and martyrdom. Philip likely knew the pseudo-Ambrosian life of Agnes (PL 17, cols. 725–28). See also Jacqueline Amat, ed. and trans., *Passion de Perpétue et de Félicité suivi des Actes*, Sources Chrétiennes 417 (Paris: Editions du Cerf, 1996), esp. 136.

10. Rudolph Bell, *Holy Anorexia* (Chicago: University of Chicago Press, 1985), x-xii.

11. Caroline Walker Bynum, *Holy Feast and Holy Fast: The Religious Significance of Food to Medieval Women* (Berkeley and Los Angeles: University of California Press, 1987), esp. 297–302.

12. Michael M. Sheehan, "Choice of a Marriage Partner in the Middle Ages: Development and Mode of Application of a Theory of Marriage," *Studies in Medieval and Renaissance History* 1 (1978): 1–33, repr. in *Medieval Families: Perspectives on Marriage, Household, and Children*, ed. Carol Neel (Toronto: University of Toronto Press, 2004), esp. 157–68, 180.

13. E. Ann Matter, *The Voice of My Beloved: The Song of Songs in Western Medieval Christianity* (Philadelphia: University of Pennsylvania Press, 1990), esp. 123–42.
14. PL 203, col. 1361.
15. Ibid.
16. Philip of Harvengt, in Fulton, *From Judgment to Passion*, 359 (her translation).
17. PL 203, col. 1372.
18. "propter Christum pauper" (ibid.).
19. PL 203, cols. 1359–60.

Philip of Harvengt, *Life of Oda*

1. On the role of preaching among regular canons of the twelfth century, see Caroline Walker Bynum, *Docere verbo et exemplo: An Aspect of Twelfth-Century Spirituality*, Harvard Theological Studies 31 (Missoula, MT: Scholars Press, 1979), 14–21, 88–95. Here Philip effectively urges that his *Life of Oda* be employed as a resource for preaching. He thus envisions a primary audience of his confreres but a secondary audience of laypeople.
2. Cf. Matt 5:15.
3. Philip's reference is obscure.
4. Cf. John 14:2.
5. Philip here uses the term *ordo* in a general sense, to mean "pattern of life," but he may also suggest the variety of religious orders much discussed in his times (see Giles Constable, "The Orders of Society," in *Three Studies in Medieval Religious and Social Thought: The Interpretation of Mary and Martha, the Ideal of the Imitation of Christ, the Orders of Society* (Cambridge: Cambridge University Press, 1995), 249–341, esp. 324–41).
6. As Bernard Ardura notes, Oda was born about 1120 and lived for nearly forty years (*The Order of Prémontré: History and Spirituality*, trans. Edward Hagman, ed. Roman Vanasse [De Pere: Paisa, 1995], 83–86).
7. Ennodius, *Panegyricus Theoderico regi* (PL 63, col. 175).
8. Boethius, *Philosophiae consolationis* 3, prosa 6.22.
9. Cf. Sg 1:12.
10. Philip mentions no separate women's community at this point; the women of Bonne Espérance had not yet been removed to nearby Rivreulle.
11. Cf. Matt 11:10.

12. Cf. 1 Sam 17:4. See also Jacqueline Amat, ed. and trans., *Passion de Perpétue et de Félicité suivi des Actes*, Sources Chrétiennes 417 (Paris: Editions du Cerf, 1996), 10.4–7, pp. 136–38. The image of Goliath here recalls Perpetua's famous dream of battle against the tall Egyptian.

13. Cf. Luke 13:25.

14. Cf. Rom 8:35.

15. Philip's reference is obscure.

16. Here, remarkably, Oda's father is sensitive to his daughter's feelings. Here more than anywhere else in the text, the tenderness of Oda's family about her complex feelings rings true—even before their disastrous physical consequences are known.

17. The allusion to Perpetua's combat is again obvious (Amat, *Passion de Perpétue et de Félicité suivi des Actes*, 10.7–14, pp. 138–42).

18. The translation here accepts the PL's alternate reading of *supervacuum* for *superbum*. On women's consent as essential for valid marriage, see Michael M. Sheehan, "Choice of a Marriage Partner in the Middle Ages: Development and Mode of Application of a Theory of Marriage," *Studies in Medieval and Renaissance History* 1 (1978): 1–33, repr. in *Medieval Families: Perspectives on Marriage, Household, and Children*, ed. Carol Neel (Toronto: University of Toronto Press, 2004), esp. 178–80.

19. See Jane Tibbetts Schulenberg, *Forgetful of Their Sex: Female Sanctity and Society* (Chicago: University of Chicago Press, 1998), 147–48.

20. Cf. Matt 19:12.

21. Philip is in fact quoting Ambrose, "Imperari virginitas non potest, sed optari" (*De virginibus*, ed. Franco Gori, Bibliotheca Ambrosiana 14, pt. 1 [Milan: Bibliotheca Ambrosiana, 1989], 1.5.23–24). Fulgentius had said, "virginitas enim voluntatis res est, non necessitas" (*Libri ad Monimum* 3.12.13 [PL 65, col. 193]).

22. Philip here seems to paraphrase a letter about Agnes attributed to Ambrose (*Epistolae* [PL 17, col. 736]).

23. Cf. Job 30:31.

24. Cf. Matt 11:30.

25. Rev 14:3–4.

26. Cf. the invitatory of the Common of Virgins (*Breviarium Praemonstratense* [Mechlin: H. Dessain, 1953], Pars hiemalis, p. 118).

27. Terence, *Eunuchus* 4.5.6.

28. Cf. Gen 3:15.

29. Hans Walther, ed., *Carmina medii aevi posterioris latina* 2.2, *Proverbia sententiaeque latinitatis medii aevi* (Göttingen: Vandenhoeck and Ruprecht, 1965), 13685b, p. 719. Cf. Horace, *Odae* 24.19–20.

30. Philip's reference is obscure.

NOTES

31. Walther, *Carmina medii aevi posterioris latina*, 2.7, 34642c, p. 128.

32. Cf. Matt 25:38–40.

33. Cf. Phil 3:20.

34. Here and repeatedly, Philip puns on Oda's name's similarity to the English-Latin cognate *odor:* "fractum in domo obedientiae optimum nominis ejus unguentum tanto circumquaque diffusum est odore" (PL 203, col. 1372).

35. Cf. Luke 7:37–44.

36. At this point it is clear that Oda and her sisters lived separately from the canons, at Rivreulle.

37. See Ardura, *The Order of Prémontré*, 88. Philip was now abbot after the retirement of his predecessor, the Odo who had received Oda. Philip and Oda were evidently friends with the local Cistercians at Elne, despite his earlier difficulties with Clairvaux and Bernard.

38. Cf. Sg 3:11.

39. Cf. Ps 58:10.

40. Cf. Ps 33:9.

BIBLIOGRAPHY

Manuscripts

Berlin. Staatsbibliothek Preussischer Kulturbesitz. Lat. fol. 295.

Berlin. Staatsbibliothek Preussischer Kulturbesitz. Theol. lat. fol. 79.

Berlin. Staatsbibliothek Preussischer Kulturbesitz. Theol. fol. 80.

Brussels. Bibliothèque royale de Belgique. Ms. II, 1158.

Hamburg. Staats- und Universitätsbibliothek. Scrin. 17, frag. 21.

Munich. Bayerische Staatsbibliothek. Clm. 17.144.

Editions and Facing Translations

Adam of Dryburgh. *De ordine et habitu atque professione canonicorum ordinis Praemonstratensis.* PL 198, cols. 439–610.

———. *Ad viros religiosos: Quatorze sermons d'Adam Scot.* Edited by François Petit. Tongerloo: Librairie Saint Norbert, 1934.

———. *Adam of Dryburgh: Six Christmas Sermons, Introduction and Translation.* Translated by M. J. Hamilton. Analecta Cartusiana 16. Salzburg: Institut für Englische Sprache und Literatur, 1974.

Ambrose of Milan. *De virginibus.* Edited by Franco Gori. Bibliotheca Ambrosiana 14, pt. 1. Milan: Bibliotheca Ambrosiana, 1989.

———. *Epistolae.* PL 16, cols. 875–1280.

Anselm of Havelberg. *De ordine canonicorum regularium.* PL 188, cols. 1091–1118.

———. *Dialogi.* PL 188, cols. 1139–1248.

———. *[Dialogi].* *Dialogues, Livre I: renouveau dans l'église.* Edited and translated by Gaston Salet. Sources Chrétiennes 118. Paris: Editions du Cerf, 1966.

281

————. *Epistola apologetica.* PL 188, cols. 1091–1118.

Arator. *De actibus apostolorum.* Edited by Arthur Patch McKinley. CSEL 72. Vienna: Holder-Pilcher-Tempsley, 1951.

Arno of Reichersberg. *Scutum canonicorum.* PL 194, cols. 1489–1528.

Augustine of Hippo. *De trinitate.* Edited by W. J. Mountain. CC 50. Turnhout: Brepols, 1968.

————. *Enarrationes in psalmos.* Edited by Eligius Dekkers and Jean Fraipont. 2nd ed. CC 38. Turnhout: Brepols, 1990.

————. *Epistolae.* PL 33.

————. *Regula.* In Lawless, *Augustine of Hippo and His Monastic Rule,* 63–118.

————. *[Regula.] Règle de saint Augustin.* Edited by Luc Verheijen. 2 vols. Paris: Etudes augustiniennes, 1967.

————. *Sermones de sanctis.* PL 38, cols. 1247–1484.

Bernard of Clairvaux. *Epistolae.* PL 182, cols. 67–716.

Breviarium praemonstratense. Edited by Hubert Noots. Rev. ed. 4 vols. Mechlin: H. Dessain, 1953.

Chrodegang of Metz. *Regula canonicorum.* PL 89, cols. 1057–1120.

Concilios visigoticos e hispano-romanos. Edited by José Vivos. España Cristiana, Textos 1. Barcelona: Consejo Superior de Investigaciones Cientificas, 1963.

Consuetudines canonicorum regularium springirsbacenses-rodenses. Edited by Stephan Weinfurter. CCCM 48. Turnhout: Brepols, 1978.

Decrees of the Ecumenical Councils. Edited and translated by Norman P. Tanner. 2 vols. London: Sheed and Ward, 1990.

Ennodius. *Panegyricus Theoderici Regis.* PL 63, cols. 167–84.

Fulgentius. *Libri ad Monimum.* PL 65, cols. 151–206.

Gratian. *Decretum. Corpus iuris canonici.* Vol. 1. Edited by Emil Friedberg. 2nd ed. Graz: Akademische Druck- und Verlagsanstalt, 1959.

Gregory the Great. *Homilia in evangelia.* PL 76, cols. 1075–1312.

Gregory VII. *Registrum.* PL 148, cols. 283–644.

Hamburgisches Urkundenbuch. 4 vols. in 7. Edited by Johann Martin Lappenberg. Hamburg: Leopold Voss, 1907–67.

BIBLIOGRAPHY

Herman of Cologne. *Opusculum de conversione sua.* Edited by Gerlinde Niemeyer. MGH Quellen zur Geistesgeschichte des Mittelalters 4. Weimar: Herman Böhlaus, 1963.

Herman of Tournai. *Liber de restauratione sancti Martini Tornacensis.* Edited by Georg Waitz. MGH SS 14, 266–327.

———. *De miraculis S. Mariae Laudunensis.* PL 156, cols. 961–1018.

———. *De miraculis S. Mariae Laudunensis* (excerpt). Edited by Roger Wilmans. MGH 14, 653–62.

Idung of Prüfening. *[Dialogus.] Le moine Idung et des deux ouvrages "Argumentum super quatuor questionibus" et "Dialogus duorum monachorum."* Edited by R. B. C. Huygens. Spoleto: Centro italiano di studi sull'alto medioevo, 1980.

Innocent III. *Regesta.* PL 214.

Jacques de Vitry. *Historia occidentalis.* Edited by John Frederick Hinnebusch. Fribourg: University Press, 1972.

Jerome. *Epistolae.* PL 22, cols. 325–1191.

———. *Vitae sancti Pauli primi eremitae.* PL 23, cols. 17–28.

Philip of Harvengt. *Commentaria in cantica canticorum.* PL 203, cols. 181–490.

———. *De institutione clericorum.* PL 203, cols. 665–1206.

———. *In cantica canticorum moralitates.* PL 203, cols. 489–534.

———. *Passio s. Agnetis.* PL 203, cols. 1387–92.

———. *Vita beati Augustini.* PL 203, cols. 1206–34.

———. *Vita beatae Odae.* PL 203, cols. 1359–74.

Prudentius. *Opera.* Edited by Maurice P. Cunningham. CC 126. Turnhout: Brepols, 1966.

Pseudo-Columbanus. *Opera.* Edited by G. S. A. Walker. Scriptores Latini Hiberniae 2. Dublin: Dublin Institute for Advanced Studies, 1957.

Regesta pontifucum Romanorum. Edited by Philip Jaffé. 2nd ed. S. Löwenfeld et al. 2 vols. Leipzig 1885–88; repr. Graz: Akademische Druck- und Verlagsanstalt, 1956.

Rupert of Deutz. *Altercatio monachi et clerici quod liceat monacho praedicare.* PL 170, cols. 537–42.

———. *Annulus sive dialogus inter Christianum et Judaeum.* PL 170, cols. 559–610.

———. *De vita vere apostolica.* PL 170, cols. 609–64.

Sacrorum conciliorum nova et amplissima collectio. Edited by J. D. Mansi. 53 vols. Florence, 1759.

[Statutes.] "Premiers statuts de l'Ordre de Prémontré." Edited by Raphael van Waefelghem. *Analectes de l'Ordre de Prémontré* 9 (1913): 1–74.

[Statutes.] *Statuts de Prémontré au milieu du XIIe siècle.* Edited by Placide Fernand Lefèvre and Wilfried Marcel Grauwen. Bibliotheca Analectorum Praemonstratensium 12. Averbode: Praemontratensia, 1978.

[Statutes.] *Statuts de Prémontré réformés sur les ordres de Grégoire IX et d'Innocent IV au XIIIe siècle.* Edited by Pl. F. Lefèvre. Louvain: Bibliothèque de l'Université, 1946.

[Statutes.] Milis, Ludo, ed. "De Premonstratenzer-Wetgeving in de XIIe eeuw: Een nieuwe getuige." *AP* 44 (1968): 181–214; *AP* 45 (1969): 5–23.

Symphosius Amalarius. *Forma institutionis canonicorum.* PL 105, cols. 215–934.

Urban II. *Epistolae et privilegia.* PL 151, cols. 283–558.

Vita Godefridi comitis capenbergensis [sic]. Edited by Philip Jaffé. MGH SS 12, 513–30.

[Vita Norberti A.] Vita Norberti archiepiscopi Magdeburgensis. Edited by Roger Wilmans. MGH SS 12, 663–706.

[Vita Norberti B.] Vita Norberti. AASS Juni 1, 807–47.

[Vita Norberti B.] Vita sancti Norberti. PL 170, cols. 1253–1350.

Source Translations into English

Anselm of Havelberg. *Dialogues* [excerpt]. Translated by Bernard J. McGinn. In *Visions of the End: Apocalyptic Traditions in the Middle Ages*, 114–16. New York: Columbia University Press, 1979.

Gregory the Great. *Dialogues.* Translated by Odo John Zimmerman. New York: Fathers of the Church, 1959.

Herman of Cologne. *[Short Account].* Translated by Michael Goodich. In *Other Middle Ages: Witnesses at the Margins of Medieval Society*, edited by Michael Goodich, 76–87. Philadelphia: University of Pennsylvania Press, 1998.

———. *[Short Account.]* "A Short Account of His Own Conversion." Translated by Karl Morrison. In *Conversion and Text: The Cases of Augustine of Hippo, Herman-Judah, and Constantine Tsatsos,* edited by Karl Morrison, 76–113. Charlottesville: University of Virginia, 1992.

Herman of Tournai. *The Restoration of the Monastery of St. Martin of Tournai.* Translated by Lynn H. Nelson. Washington, DC: Catholic University of America Press, 1996.

Hugh of St. Victor. *On the Sacraments of the Christian Faith.* Translated by Roy J. Deferrari. Cambridge: Medieval Academy of America, 1951.

Idung of Prüfening. *Cistercians and Cluniacs, the Case for Cîteaux: A Dialogue between Two Monks, an Argument on Four Questions.* Translated by Jeremiah F. O'Sullivan et al. Cistercian Fathers 33. Kalamazoo, MI: Cistercian Publications, 1977.

Libellus de diversis ordinibus et professionibus qui sunt in aecclesia. Edited and translated by Giles Constable and Bernard S. Smith. Rev. ed. Oxford: Clarendon Press, 2003.

[Passio Perpetuae.] Passion de Perpétue et Félicité, suivi des Actes. Edited and translated by Jacqueline Amat. Sources Chrétiennes 417. Paris: Editions du Cerf, 1996.

Secondary Works

Alders, Alfons. "Norbert von Xanten als rheinischer Adliger und Kanoniker an St. Viktor." In *Norbert von Xanten,* 35–67.

Arduini, Maria Ludovica. *Ruperto di Deutz e la controversia tra Cristiani ed Ebrei nel secolo XII.* Studi storici 119–21. Rome: Istituto Storio, 1979.

———. "Ruperto, san Norberto e Abelardo: per l'edizione delle 'Opera minora Ruperti abbatis Tuitensis.'" In *Medioevo e latinità in memoria di Ezio Franceschini,* edited by Annamaria Ambrosioni et al. Milan: Vita e Pensiero, 1993.

Ardura, Bernard. *Abbayes, prieurés et monastères de l'ordre de Prémontré, en France, des origines à nos jours: Dictionnaire historique et bibliographique.* Nancy: Presses Universitaires, 1993.

————. *The Order of Prémontré: History and Spirituality.* Translated by Edward Hagman. Edited by Roman Vanasse. De Pere: Paisa, 1995.

————. *Prémontrés: Histoire et Spiritualité.* Centre Européen de Recherches sur les Congrégations et Ordres Religieux 7. Saint-Etienne: Publications de l'Université, 1995.

Atlas zur Kirchengeschichte: Die christlichen Kirchen in Geschichte und Gegenwart. Edited by Hubert Jedin et al. Freiburg: Herder, 1970.

Backmund, Norbert. *Geschichte des Prämonstratenserordens.* Grafenau: Morsak, 1986.

————. *Die mittelalterlichen Geschichtsschreiber des Prämonstratenserordens.* Bibliotheca Analectorum Premonstratensium 10. Averbode: Praemonstratensia, 1972.

————. *Monasticon praemonstratense: Id est historia circariarum atque canoniarum candidi et canonici ordinis praemonstratensis.* 3 vols. Straubing: Cl. Attenkofer, 1949–56; vol. 1, rev. ed. Berlin: Walter de Gruyter, 1983.

Bell, David N., ed. *The Libraries of the Cistercians, Gilbertines, and Premonstratensians.* Corpus of British Library Catalogues 3. London: British Library, 1992.

Bell, Rudolph. *Holy Anorexia.* Chicago: University of Chicago Press, 1985.

Berlière, Ursmer. "Rupert de Deutz et saint Norbert." *Revue Bénédictine* 7 (1890): 452–57.

Berlin. Preussische Staatsbibliothek. *Verzeichniss der lateinischen Handschriften der Königlichen Bibliothek zu Berlin.* Edited by Valentin Rose and Fritz Schillman. Handschriften-verzeichnisse der Königlichen Bibliothek 12. 3 vols. Berlin: A. Asher, 1893–1999.

Berman, Constance Hoffman. *The Cistercian Evolution: The Invention of a Religious Order in Twelfth-Century Europe.* Philadelphia: University of Pennsylvania Press, 2000.

Berschin, Walter. "Anselm von Havelberg und die Anfänge einer Geschichtstheologie des hohen Mittelalters." *Literaturwissenschaftliches Jahrbuch,* n.s. 29 (1988): 225–32.

BIBLIOGRAPHY

Bewerunge, Norbert. "Der Ordenseintritt des Grafen Gottfried von Cappenberg." *Archiv für mittelrheinische Kulturgeschichte* 33 (1981): 63–81.

Bischoff, Guntram, "Early Premonstratensian Eschatology: The Apocalyptic Myth." In *The Spirituality of Western Christendom*, edited by E. Rozanne Elder, 41–71. Kalamazoo, MI: Cistercian Publications, 1976.

Bockhorst, Wolfgang. "Die Grafen von Cappenberg und die Anfänge des Stifts Cappenberg." In *Studien zum Prämonstratenserorden*, 57–74.

Bomm, Werner. "Anselm von Havelberg. *Epistola apologetica*. Über den Platz der Prämonstratenser in der Kirche des 12. Jahrhunderts. Vom Selbstverständnis eines frühen Anhängers Norberts von Xanten." In *Studien zum Prämonstratenserorden*, 107–83.

———. "Augustinusregel, *professio canonica* und Prämonstratenser im 12. Jahrhundert. Das Beispiel der Norbert-Viten, Philipps von Harvengt und Anselms von Havelberg." In *Regula sancti Augustini*, 239–94.

Bondéelle-Souchier, Anne. *Bibliothèques de l'Ordre de Prémontré dans la France d'ancien régime*. Histoires des bibliothèques médiévales 9. Paris: CRNS, 2000.

Borger, Hugo, and Friedrich Wilhelm Oediger. *Beiträge zur Frühgeschichte des Xantener Viktorstiftes*. Düsseldorf: Rheinland-Verlag, 1969.

Bosl, Karl. "'Noble Unfreedom': The Rise of the *ministeriales* in Germany." In *The Medieval Nobility: Studies on the Ruling Classes of France and Germany from the Sixth to the Twelfth Century*, edited and translated by Timothy Reuter. Europe in the Middle Ages: Selected Studies 14. Amsterdam: North Holland, 1978.

———. *Regularkanoniker und Seelsorge in Kirche und Gesellschaft des europäischen zwölften Jahrhunderts*. Munich: Verlag der bayerischen Akademie der Wissenschaften, 1979.

Brandis, Tilo. *Die codices in scrinio der Statts- und Universitätsbibliothek Hamburg 1–110*. Katalog der Handschriften der Staats- und Universitätsbibliothek Hamburg 7. Hamburg: E. Hauswedell, 1972.

Braun, Johann Wilhelm. "Studien zur Überlieferung der Werke Anselms von Havelberg I: Die Überlieferung des Anticimenon." *Deutsches Archiv für Erforschung des Mittelalters* 28 (1972): 133–209.

Bredero, Adriaan H. "The Announcement of the Coming of the Antichrist and the Medieval Concept of Time." In *Prophecy and Eschatology*, edited by Michael Wilks. Oxford: Blackwell, 1994.

Brown, Peter. *The Cult of the Saints: Its Rise and Function in Latin Christianity.* Chicago: University of Chicago Press, 1981.

Brussels. Bibliothèque royale. *Catalogus codicum hagiographicum.* Ed. Society of Bollandists. Analecta Bollandiana 5–8. Brussels: Palleunis, Cauterick and De Smet, 1889.

Bulloch, James. *Adam of Dryburgh.* London: SPCK, 1958.

Bynum, Caroline Walker. *Docere verbo et exemplo: An Aspect of Twelfth-Century Spirituality.* Harvard Theological Studies 31. Missoula, MT: Scholars Press, 1979.

———. *Holy Feast and Holy Fast: The Religious Significance of Food to Medieval Women.* Berkeley and Los Angeles: University of California Press, 1987.

———. *Jesus as Mother: Studies in the Spirituality of the High Middle Ages.* Berkeley and Los Angeles: University of California Press, 1982.

Carpe, William D. "The *Vita canonica* in the *Regula canonicorum* of Chrodegang of Metz." PhD diss., University of Chicago, 1975.

Châtillon, Jean. *Le mouvement canonial au moyen age: réforme de l'église, spiriualité et culture.* Bibliotheca victorina 3. Paris: Brepols, 1992.

Chénu, Marie-Dominique. *La théologie au douzième siècle.* Paris: J. Vrin, 1957.

Claussen, M. A. *The Reform of the Frankish Church: Chrodegang of Metz and the Regula canonicorum in the Eighth Century.* Cambridge: Cambridge University Press, 2004.

Cohen, Jeremy. *Living Letters of the Law: Ideas of the Jew in Medieval Christianity.* Berkeley and Los Angeles: University of California Press, 1999.

———. "The Mentality of the Medieval Jewish Apostate: Peter Alfonsi, Hermann of Cologne, and Pablo Christiani." In

BIBLIOGRAPHY

Jewish Apostasy in the Modern World, edited by Todd M. Endelman, 20–47. New York: Holmes and Meier, 1987.

Colvin, H. M. *The White Canons in England.* Oxford: Clarendon Press, 1951.

Constable, Giles. "The Language of Preaching in the Twelfth Century." *Viator* 25 (1994): 131–52.

———. *The Reformation of the Twelfth Century.* Cambridge: Cambridge University Press, 1996.

———. "Renewal and Reform in Religious Life: Concepts and Realities." In *Renaissance and Renewal in the Twelfth Century,* 37–67.

———. *Three Studies in Medieval Religious and Social Thought: The Interpretation of Mary and Martha, the Ideal of the Imitation of Christ, the Orders of Society.* Cambridge: Cambridge University Press, 1995.

Crusius, Irene. *"...ut nulla fere provincia sit in partibus Occidentis, ubi ejusdem religionis congregationes non inveniantur....* Prämonstratenser als Forschungsaufgabe." In *Studien zum Prämonstratenserorden,* 11–32.

Cygler, Florent. *Das Generalkapitel im hohen Mittelalter: Cistercienzer, Prämonstratenser, Kartäuser und Cluniazenser.* Vita regularis, Studien 12. Münster: LIT-Verlag, 2002.

Delahaye, Philipe. "L'organisation scolaire au XIIe siècle." *Traditio* 5 (1947): 211–68.

Delooz, Pierre. *Sociologie et canonisations.* Collection scientifique de la faculté de droit de l'Université de Liège, fasc. 30. Liège: Faculté de droit, 1969.

De Smet, J. M. "De monnik Tanchelm en de Utrechtse bisschop-szetel." *Scrinium Lovanense: Mélanges historiques Etienne de Couwenberghe.* Recueil de travaux d'histoire et de philologie, ser. 4, fasc. 24, 207–34. Gembloux: J. Duculot, 1961.

Dickinson, J. C. *The Origin of the Austin Canons and Their Introduction into England.* London: SPCK, 1950.

Dolbeau, François. "Hagiographie latin et prose rimeé: deux examples rédigées au XIIe siècle." *Sacris erudiri* 32 (1991): 223.

———. "Les hagiographes au travail: collecte et traitement des documents écrits (IXe-XIIe siècles). Avec annexe: une discussion chronologique du XIIe siècle (édition de BHL 5824e)." In

Manuscrits hagiographiques et travail des hagiographes, edited by Martin Heinzelmann. Beihefte der *Francia* 24. Sigmaringen: Jan Thorbecke, 1992.

Doppelklöster und andere Formen Symbiose männlicher und weiblicher Religiosen im Mittelalter. Edited by Kaspar Elm and Michel Parisse. Berliner Historischer Studien 18. Ordensstudien 8. Berlin: Duncker and Humblot, 1992.

Dräseke, Johannes. "Bischof Anselm von Havelberg und seine Gesandtschaftsreisen nach Byzanz." *Zeitschrift für Kirchengeschichte*, n.s. 21 (1901): 160–85.

Edyvean, Walter. *Anselm of Havelberg and the Theology of History*. Rome: Catholic Books Agency, 1972.

Ehlers-Kisseler, Ingrid. *Die Anfänge der Prämonstratenser im Erzbistum Köln*. Rhenisches Archiv 137. Cologne: Böhlau, 1997.

Elm, Kaspar. "Norm und Praxis bei den Prämonstratensern im Hochmittelalter." In *Regula sancti Augustini*, 335–87.

———. "Norbert von Xanten. Bedeutung—Persönlichkeit— Nachleben." In *Norbert von Xanten*, 267–318.

Erens, A. "Les soeurs dans l'ordre de Prémontré." *AP* 5 (1929): 5–26.

Evans, Gillian R. "Unity and Diversity: Anselm of Havelberg as Ecumenist." *AP* 67 (1991): 42–52.

Felten, Franz. "Norbert von Xanten: Vom Wanderprediger zum Kirchenfürsten." In *Norbert von Xanten*, 69–157.

Fina, Kurt. "Anselm von Havelberg: Untersuchungen zur Kirchen- und Geistesgeschichte des 12. Jahrhunderts." *AP* 32 (1956): 69–101, 193–227; *AP* 33 (1957): 5–39, 268–301; *AP* 34 (1958): 13–41.

Flachenecker, Helmut. "*Consuetudines* und Seelsorge. Zum Selbstverständnis der Prämonstratenser." In *Regula sancti Augustini*, 295–33.

Froese, Walter. "The Early Norbertines on the Religious Frontiers of Northeastern Germany." PhD diss., University of Chicago, 1978.

Fulton, Rachel. *From Judgment to Passion: Devotion to Christ and the Virgin Mary, 800–1200*. New York: Columbia University Press, 2002.

BIBLIOGRAPHY

Funkenstein, Amos. *Heilsplan und natürliche Entwicklung: Forme der Gegenwartsbestimmung im Geschichtsdenken des hohen Mittelalter.* Munich: Nymphenberger, 1965.

Geary, Patrick. *Living with the Dead in the Middle Ages.* Ithaca, NY: Cornell University Press, 1994.

Genicot, Leopold, and Paul Tombeur, eds. *Index scriptorum operumque latino-belgicorum medii aevi: nouveau répertoire des oeuvres médiolatines belges.* Pt. 3. Vols. 1–2. Edited by Michael McCormick. Brussels: J. Duculot, 1977.

Goodich, Michael. *Vita perfecta: The Ideal of Sainthood in the Thirteenth Century.* Monographien zur Geschichte des Mittelalters 25. Stuttgart: Anton Hiersemann, 1982.

Goodich, Michael, ed. *Other Middle Ages: Witnesses at the Margins of Medieval Society.* Philadelphia: University of Pennsylvania Press, 1998.

Goovaerts, André Léon. *Écrivains, artistes, et savants de l'ordre de Prémontré: dictionnaire bio-bibliographique.* Brussels, 1899–1907; repr. Geneva: Slatkin, 1971.

Grauwen, Wilfried Marcel. "Bartholomeus van Laon en Norbert op zoek naar een vestigingsplaats, begin 1120." *AP* 70 (1994): 199–211.

———. "De eerste kerk- en kloosterbouw te Prémontré, 1122." *AP* 71 (1995): 37–51.

———. "De handschriften van de Vitae Norberti." *AP* 70 (1994): 5–101.

———. "Een fragment van de Vita Norberti A te Hamburg." *AP* 60 (1984): 153–62.

———. "Inleiding tot de Vita Norberti A." *AP* 60 (1984): 5–48.

———. "Inleiding tot de Vita Norberti B." *AP* 66 (1990): 123–202.

———. "De regelkeuze en de eerste professie te Prémontré, Kerstmis 1121." *AP* 72 (1996): 33–52.

———. "Norbert doet afstand van zijn goederen. De stichting van Fürstenberg, aug-sept. 1118." *AP* 71 (1995): 5–24.

———. "Norbert en de stichting van Cappenberg, 1122." *AP* 68 (1992): 43–75.

———. "Norbert et les débuts de l'abbaye de Floreffe." *AP* 51 (1975): 5–23.

————. *Norbert, Erzbischof von Magdeburg (1126–1134)*. 2nd ed. Translated by Ludger Horstkötter. Duisburg: Prämonstratenser-Abtei S. Johann, 1986.

————. *Norbertus Aartsbisschop van Maagdenburg (1126–1134)*. Verhandelingen van de Koninklijke Academie voor Wetenschappen, Letteren en Schone Kunsten van België, Klasse der Letteren, Verhandelingen 40, n. 86. Brussels: Paleis der Academiën, 1978.

————. "Die Quellen zur Geschichte Norberts von Xanten." In *Norbert von Xanten*, 15–33.

————. "De religieuze vorming van Norbert te Siegburg. Was er een ontmoeting met Rupert van Deutz, 1115–1118?" *AP* 71 (1995): 236–63.

Grundmann, Herbert. "Adelsbekehrungen im Hochmittelalter. *Conversi* und *nutriti* im Kloster." In *Adel und Kirche: Gerd Tellenbach zum 65. Geburtstag*, edited by Josef Fleckenstein and Karl Schmid, 325–45. Herder: Freiburg, 1968.

————. *Der Cappenberger Barbarossakopf und die Anfänge des Stiftes Cappenberg*. Münstersche Forschungen 12. Cologne: Böhlau, 1959.

————. "Gottfried von Cappenberg." In *Ausgewählte Aufsätze* 1. Schriften der Monumenta Germaniae Historica 25, 169–80. Stuttgart: Anton Hiersemann, 1976.

————. *Religious Movements in the Middle Ages*. Translated by Steven Rowan. Notre Dame, IN: University of Notre Dame Press, 1995.

Hauck, Albert. *Kirchengeschichte Deutschlands*. 5 vols. Berlin: Akademie Verlag, 1958.

Hayes, Eugene J. "Rightful Autonomy of Life and Charism in the Proper Law of the Norbertine Order." PhD diss., Catholic University of America, 1990.

Head, Thomas. *Hagiography and the Cult of the Saints: The Diocese of Orléans, 800–1200*. Cambridge: Cambridge University Press, 1990.

Heffernan, Thomas. *Sacred Biography: Saints and Their Biographers in the Middle Ages*. Oxford: Oxford University Press, 1988.

Heresies of the High Middle Ages. Edited by Walter L. Wakefield and Austin P. Evans. New York: Columbia University Press, 1991.

BIBLIOGRAPHY

Hiestand, Rudolf. "Bernhard von Clairvaux, Norbert von Xanten und der lateinischen Osten." In *Vita religiosa im Mittelalter: Festchrift für Kaspar Elm zum 70. Geburtstag,* edited by Franz J. Felten and Nikolas Jaspert, 301–19. Berliner Historische Studien 31. Ordensstudien 13. Berlin: Duncker and Humblot, 1999.

Horstkötter, Ludger. "Die Prämonstratenser in Westfalen." In *Monastisches Westfalen: Klöster und Stifte,* edited by Géza Jászai. Münster: Westfälisches Landesmuseum für Kunst und Kulturgeschichte, 1982.

———. "Die Prämonstratenser und ihre Klöster am Niederrhein und in Westfalen." In *Norbert von Xanten,* 247–65.

Jaeger, C. Steven. "Cathedral Schools and Humanist Learning, 950–1150." *Deutsche Vierteljahrschrift für Literaturwissenschaft und Geistesgeschichte* 61 (1987): 569–616.

———. *The Envy of Angels: Cathedral Schools and Social Ideals in Medieval Europe, 950–1200.* Philadelphia: University of Pennsylvania Press, 1994.

———. *The Origins of Courtliness: Civilizing Trends and the Formation of Courtly Ideals, 939–1210.* Philadelphia: University of Pennsylvania Press, 1985.

Jones, David. *An Early Witness to the Nature of Canonical Order in the Twelfth Century: A Study in the Life and Writings of Adam Scot, with Particular Reference to His Understanding of the Rule of St. Augustine.* Analecta Cartusiana 151. Salzburg: Institut für Anglistik und Amerikanistik, 1999.

Kleinberg, Aviad M. "Hermannus Judaeus's *Opusculum:* In Defense of Its Authenticity." *Revue des études juives* 151 (1992): 337–53.

Krings, Bruno. *Das Prämonstratenserstift Arnstein a. d. Lahn im Mittelalter (1139–1527).* Wiesbaden: Selbstverlag der Historischen Kommission für Nassau, 1990.

———. "Die Prämonstratenser und ihr weiblicher Zweig." In *Studien zum Prämonstratenserorden,* 75–105.

Ladner, Gerhart B. *The Idea of Reform: Its Impact on Christian Thought and Action in the Age of the Fathers.* Rev. ed. New York: Harper and Row, 1967.

Landau, Peter. "Der Begriff *ordo* in der mittelalterlichen Kanonistik." In *Studien zum Prämonstratenserorden,* 185–99.

Lawless, George. *Augustine of Hippo and His Monastic Rule.* Oxford: Clarendon Press, 1987.

Leclercq, Jean. *The Love of Learning and the Desire for God: A Study of Monastic Culture.* Translated by Catharine Misrahi. New York: Fordham University Press, 1961.

Lees, Jay T. *Anselm of Havelberg: Deeds into Words in the Twelfth Century.* Studies in the History of Christian Thought 79. Leiden: Brill, 1998.

——. "Anselm of Havelberg's 'Banishment' to Havelberg." *AP* 63 (1986): 5–18.

——. "Charity and Enmity in the Writings of Anselm of Havelberg." *Viator: Medieval and Renaissance Studies* 25 (1994): 53–62.

Leistikow, Andreas. *Die Geschichte der Grafen von Cappenberg und ihrer Stiftsgründungen: Cappenberg, Varlar und Ilbenstadt.* Studien zur Geschichtsforschung des Mittelalters 10. Hamburg: Dr. Kovac, 2000.

Lentze, H. J. "Der Messritus des Prämonstratenser-ordens." *AP* 25 (1949): 129–70; *AP* 26 (1950): 7–40; 127–51; *AP* 27 (1951): 5–27.

Lexikon des Mittelalters. Edited by Robert Auty. 10 vols. Munich: Artemis, 1977–99.

Lexikon für Theologie und Kirche. Edited by Walter Kasper and Konrad Baumgartner. 3 vols. Freiburg: Herder, 1994.

Little, Lester. *Religious Poverty and the Profit Economy in Medieval Europe.* Ithaca, NY: Cornell University Press, 1978.

Lotter, Friedrich. "Ist Hermann von Schedas *Opusculum de conversione sua* eine Fälschung?" *Aschkenas: Zeitschrift für Geschichte und Kultur der Juden* 2 (1992): 207–18.

Lubac, Henri de. *Exégèse médiévale: les quatre sens de l'écriture.* 2 vols. in 4. Paris: Aubier: 1959–64.

Matter, E. Ann. *The Voice of My Beloved: The Song of Songs in Western Medieval Christianity.* Philadelphia: University of Pennsylvania Press, 1990.

McCormick, Michael, ed. *Index scriptorum operumque Latino-Belgicorum medii aevi. Nouveau répertoire des oeuvres médio-latines belges, Pt. III: XIIe siècle, 2: Oeuvres non hagiographiques.* Brussels: Académie royale de Belgique, 1979.

BIBLIOGRAPHY

McCulloch, Florence. *Medieval Latin and French Bestiaries.* University of North Carolina Studies in the Romance Languages and Literatures 33. Rev. ed. Chapel Hill: University of North Carolina Press, 1962.

McGinn, Bernard. *Visions of the End: Apocalyptic Traditions in the Middle Ages.* New York: Columbia University Press, 1979.

Melville, Gert. "Semantik von *ordo* im Religiosentum der ersten Hälfte des 12. Jahrhunderts. Lucius II., seine Bulle vom 19. Mai 1144, und der 'Orden' des Prämonstratenser." In *Studien zum Prämonstratenserorden,* 201–23.

————. "Zur Abgrenzung zwischen *Vita canonica* und *Vita monastica.* Das Übertrittsproblem in kanonistischer Behandlung von Gratian bis Hostiensis." In *Secundum regulam vivere,* 205–43.

Mois, Jakob. "Geist und Regel des hl. Augustinus in der Kanoniker-Reform des 11.-12. Jahrhunderts." In *In Unum Congregati* 6 (1959): 52–59.

Mollat, Michel. *The Poor in the Middle Ages.* Translated by Arthur Goldhammer. New Haven, CT: Yale University Press, 1986.

Momigliano, Arnaldo. "A Medieval Jewish Autobiography." In *History and Imagination: Essays in Honor of H. R. Trevor-Roper,* edited by Hugh Lloyd-Jones et al., 30–36. London: Duckworth, 1981.

Mooney, Catherine. "Voice, Gender, and the Portrayal of Sanctity." In *Gendered Voices: Medieval Saints and Their Interpreters,* edited by Catherine Mooney, 6–15. Philadelphia: University of Pennsylvania Press, 1999.

Morrison, Karl F. "Anselm of Havelberg: Play and the Dilemma of Historical Progress." In *Religion, Culture and Society in the Early Middle Ages: Studies in Honor of Richard E. Sullivan,* edited by Thomas F. X. Noble and John J. Contreni. Studies in Medieval Culture 23, 219–56. Kalamazoo, MI: Medieval Institute Publications, 1987.

————. *Conversion and Text: The Cases of Augustine of Hippo, Herman-Judah, and Constantine Tsatsos.* Charlottesville: University Press of Virginia, 1992.

————. *Understanding Conversion.* Charlottesville: University Press of Virginia, 1992.

Neel, Carol. "Origins of the Beguines." *SIGNS: A Journal of Women in Culture and Society* 14 (1989): 321–41.

———. "Philip of Harvengt and Anselm of Havelberg: The Premonstratensian Vision of Time." *Church History* 62 (1993): 483–93.

———. "Philip of Harvengt's *Vita augustini*: The Medieval Premonstratensians and the Patristic Model." *AP* 71 (1995): 300–311.

Newman, Martha G. *The Boundaries of Charity: Cistercian Culture and Ecclesiastical Reform, 1098–1180*. Stanford, CA: Stanford University Press, 1996.

Niemeyer, Gerlinde. "Die Miracula S. Mariae Laudunensis des Abtes Hermann von Tournai: Verfasser und Entstehungzeit." *Deutsches Archiv für Erforschung des Mittelalters* 27 (1971): 135–72.

———. "Die *Vitae Godefridi Cappenbergensis*." *Deutsches Archiv für Erforschung des Mittelalters* 23 (1967): 405–67.

Norbert von Xanten: Adliger, Ordenstrifter, Kirchenfürst. Edited by Kaspar Elm. Cologne: Wienand, 1984.

Oberste, Jörg. *Visitation und Ordensorganisation: Formen sozialer Normierung, Kontrolle und Kommunikation bei Cisterziensern, Prämonstratensern und Cluniacensern (12.- frühes 14. Jahrhundert). Vita regularis*, Studien 2. Münster: LIT-Verlag, 2002.

———. "Zwischen *uniformitas* and *diversitas*. Zentralität als Kernproblem des frühen Prämonstartenserordens (12./13. Jahrhundert)." In *Studien zum Prämonstratenserorden*, 225–50.

O'Donnell, James J. *Augustine: A New Biography*. New York: HarperCollins, 2005.

Peil, Dietmar. "On the Question of a *Physiologus* Tradition in Emblematic Art and Writing." In *Animals in the Middle Ages: A Book of Essays*, edited by Nona C. Flores, 103–30. New York: Garland, 1996.

Petit, François. *Norbert et l'origine des Prémontrés*. Paris: Editions du Cerf, 1981.

———. *La réforme des prêtres au moyen-age: pauvreté et vie commune*. Paris: Editions du Cerf, 1968.

BIBLIOGRAPHY

————. *La spiritualité des Prémontrés aux XIIe et XIIIe siècles.* Paris: J. Vrin, 1947.

Regula sancti Augustini: Normative Grundlage differenter Verbände im Mittelalter. Edited by Gert Melville and Anne Müller. Paring: Augustiner-Chorherren-Verlag-Paring, 2002.

Renaissance and Renewal in the Twelfth Century. Edited by Robert L. Benson and Giles Constable. Cambridge, MA: Harvard University Press, 1982.

Roby, Douglass. "Philip of Harvengt's Contribution to the Question of Passage from One Religious Order to Another." *AP* 59 (1979): 69–100.

Roisin, Simone. *L'hagiographie cistercienne dans le diocese de Liège au XIIIe siècle.* Recueil de travaux d'histoire et de philology. ser. 3, fasc. 27. Louvain: Bibliothèque de l'Université, 1947.

Rosenmund, Richard. *Die ältesten Biographieen des heiligen Norbert.* Berlin: Ernst Siegfried Mittler und Sohn, 1874.

Russell, Jeffrey Burton. *Dissent and Reform in the Early Middle Ages.* Berkeley and Los Angeles: University of California Press, 1965.

Saltman, Avrom. "Hermann's *Opusculum de conversione sua:* Truth or Fiction?" *Revue des études juives* 147 (1988): 31–56.

Schmitt, Jean-Claude. *La conversion d'Hermann le Juif: autobiographie, histoire et fiction.* Paris: Editions du Seuil, 2003.

Schopf, Hubert. "Augustiner Chorherren." In *Kulturgeschichte der christlichen Orden in Einzeldarstellungen,* edited by Peter Dinzelbacher and James Lester Hogg, 37–54. Stuttgart: Alfred Kröner Verlag, 1997.

Schulenberg, Jane Tibbetts. *Forgetful of Their Sex: Female Sanctity and Society, ca. 500–1100.* Chicago: University of Chicago Press, 1998.

————. "The Heroics of Virginity: Brides of Christ and Sacrificial Mutilation." In *Women in the Middle Ages and the Renaissance: Literary and Historical Perspectives,* edited by Mary Beth Rose, 29–72. Syracuse, NY: Syracuse University Press, 1986.

Secundum regulam vivere: Festschrift für P. Norbert Backmund O.Praem. Edited by Gert Melville. Windberg: Poppe-Verlag, 1978.

Severino, Gabriella. "La discussione degli 'Ordines' di Anselmo di Havelberg." *Bulletino dell'Istituto Storico Italiano per il Medio Evo e Archivo Muratoriano* 78 (1967): 75–122.

Sheehan, Michael M. "Choice of a Marriage Partner in the Middle Ages: Development and Mode of Application of a Theory of Marriage." *Studies in Medieval and Renaissance History* 1 (1978): 1–33; repr. in *Medieval Families: Perspectives on Household, Marriage, and Children*, edited by Carol Neel, 157–91. Toronto: University of Toronto Press, 2004.

Sijen, G. P. "Les oeuvres de Philippe de Harveng, abbé de Bonne Espérance." *AP* 15 (1939): 129–66.

———. "La passabilité de Christ chez Philippe de Harveng." *AP* 14 (1938): 189–208.

———. "Philippe de Harveng, abbé de Bonne Espérance." *AP* 14 (1938): 37–52.

Simons, Walter. *Cities of Ladies: Beguine Communities in the Medieval Low Countries, 1200–1565.* Philadelphia: University of Pennsylvania Press, 2001.

Smalley, Beryl. "Ecclesiastical Attitudes to Novelty c. 1100–1250." In *Church and Society*, edited by Derek Baker, 113–31. Oxford: Basil Blackwell, 1975.

———. *The Study of the Bible in the Middle Ages.* Notre Dame, IN: University of Notre Dame Press, 1964.

Sterre, Johannes Chrysostomus van der. *Vita S. Norberti canonicorum Praemonstratensium patriarchae, Aniverpiae apostoli, archiepiscopi Magdeburgensis ac totius Germaniae primatis.* Antwerp, 1622.

Studien zum Prämonstratenserorden. Edited by Irene Crusius and Helmut Flachenecker. Veröffentlichungen des Max-Planck-Instituts für Geschichte 185. Studien zur Germania Sacra 25. Göttingen: Vandenhoeck and Ruprecht, 2003.

Van den Gheyn, J., ed. *Catalogue des manuscripts de la bibliothèque royale de Belgique.* 9 vols. Brussels: Henri Lamertin, 1901–9.

Van Engen, John. *Rupert of Deutz.* Berkeley and Los Angeles: University of California Press, 1983.

Vauchez, André. "Lay People's Sanctity in Western Europe: Evolution of a Pattern (Twelfth and Thirteenth Centuries)." In *Images of Sainthood in Medieval Europe*, edited by Renate

Blumenfeld-Kosinski and Timea Szell, 21–32. Ithaca, NY: Cornell University Press, 1991.

———. *La sainteté en occident au derniers siècles de moyen age: d'après les procès de canonization et les documents hagiographiques.* Rome: Ecole française de Rome, 1981.

———. *The Spirituality of the Medieval West: From the Eighth to the Twelfth Century.* Translated by Colette Friedlander. Cistercian Studies 145. Kalamazoo, MI: Cistercian Publications, 1993.

Venarde, Bruce L. *Women's Monasticism and Medieval Society: Nunneries in France and England, 890–1215.* Ithaca, NY: Cornell University Press, 1997.

Waefelghem, Raphael van. *Répertoire des sources imprimées et manuscrites relatives à l'histoire et à la liturgie des monastères de l'ordre de Prémontré.* Brussels: A. Dewit, 1930.

Walther, Hans, ed. *Carmina medii aevi posterioris latina 2: Proverbia sententiaeque latinitatis medii aevi, Lateinischer Sprichwörter und Sentenzen des Mittelalters in alphabetischer Anordnung.* 9 vols. Göttingen: Vandenhoeck and Ruprecht, 1963–86.

Walther, Johannes von. *Die ersten Wanderprediger Frankreichs,* vol. 1, *Robert von Arbrissel* and vol. 2, *Bernhard von Thiron, Vitalis von Savigny, Girald von Salles, Bemerkungen zur Norbert von Xanten und Heinrich von Lausanne.* Leipzig: Dieterich, 1903–6.

Weinfürter, Stefan. "Norbert von Xanten als Reformkanoniker und Stifter des Prämonstratenerordens." In *Norbert von Xanten,* 159–85.

———. "Norbert von Xanten im Urteil seiner Zeitgenossen." *Xantener Vorträge zur Geschichte des Niederrheins 5.* Duisburg, 1992.

———. "Norbert von Xanten—Ordensstifter und 'Eigenkirchenherr.'" *Archiv für Kulturgeschichte* 59 (1977): 66–98.

———. "Reformkanoniker und Reichsepiskopat im Hochmittelalter." *Historisches Jahrbuch* 97–98 (1978): 158–93.

———. *Salzburger Bistumsreform und Bischofspolitik im 12. Jahrhundert. Der Erzbischof Konrad I von Salzburg (1106–1147) und die Regularkanoniker.* Cologne: Böhlau, 1974.

———. "Vita canonica und Eschatologie: Eine neue Quelle zum Selbstverständnis der Reformkanoniker des 12. Jahrhunderts aus dem Salzburger Reformkreis (mit Textedition)." In *Secundum regulam vivere*, 139–67.

Weinstein, Donald, and Rudolph M. Bell. *Saints and Society: The Two Worlds of Western Christendom, 1000–1700*. Chicago: University of Chicago Press, 1982.

Werner, Ernst. *Pauperes Christi: Studien zu sozial-religiösen Bewegungen im Zeitalter des Reformpapsttums*. Leipzig: Koehler and Amelang, 1956.

Westfälisches Klosterbuch: Lexikon der vor 1815 errichteten Stifte und Klöster von ihrer Gründung bis zur Aufhebung. Edited by Karl Hengst. Münster: Aschendorff, 1992.

Weyns, N. J. "A propos des *Instructions pour clercs (De institutione clericorum)* de Philippe de Harveng." *AP* 53 (1977): 71–79.

Winter, Franz. *Die Prämonstratenser des zwölften Jahrhunderts und ihre Bedeutung für das nordöstliche Deutschland*. Berlin, 1865; repr. Aalen: Scientia, 1966.

Wolbrink, Shelley Amiste. "Noble Pursuits: Family, Power, and Gender in the Premonstratensian Monasteries of Northwestern Germany, 1120–1250." PhD diss., University of Cincinnati, 1998.

———. "Women in the Premonstratensian Order of Northwestern Germany, 1120–1250." *Catholic Historical Review* 89 (2003): 387–408.

Wouters, Josef. "*Schola claustrum alterum dici debet*: Filip van Harveng raadgevingen an studenten." *AP* 76: 107–32.

Zöllner, Walter. "Ekbert von Huysburg und die Ordensbewegungen des 12. Jahrhunderts." *Forschungen und Fortschritte* 38 (1964): 25–28.

Zumkeller, Adolar. *Augustine's Ideal of the Religious Life*. Translated by Edmund Colledge. New York: Fordham University Press, 1986.

INDEX

A Life. See *Vita A*
Aachen, Rule of, 5, 6, 9
Aachen, Synod of (816), 5
Abel, 50
Abraham, 50–51
Adam of Dryburgh, 15
Alexander III, Pope, 13, 14
Altercatio monachi et clerici
   (Rupert of Deutz), 32–33
Ambrose, Saint, 43
Anacletus II (antipope), 11–12,
   166, 170–71
Anselm, bishop of Tournai, 64,
   65, 66
Anselm of Havelberg, 5, 16,
   17–18, 21–22; *Apologetic
   Letter*, 29–62, 193;
   canonical charism, 24, 26,
   199; education of clerics,
   19; as *pauper Christi*, 34
Antichrist, 4
Antikeimenon (Anselm of
   Havelberg), 30, 31, 36
Apocalypse, 4, 19, 37, 199
Apologetic Letter (Anselm of
   Havelburg), 29–37, 193;
   text, 38–62
Augustine, Saint, 32, 97, 173,
   188

Augustinian Rule, 1, 4, 7, 11, 12,
   17, 18, 24, 79, 89, 95, 96,
   147, 188, 197; forms of, 6
Augustinians, 15, 16, 19, 24,
   32, 33

B Life. See *Vita B*
Bartholomew, bishop of Laon,
   69, 77–78, 84; and Herbert
   of Tournai, 65, 67; and
   Norbert, 10, 11, 67, 68,
   71–75, 78, 81, 136, 138,
   149
Bell, Rudolph, 221
Benedict, Saint, 48
Benedictines, 4, 5, 33, 34, 46
Berman, Constance, 17
Bernard of Clairvaux, 2–3, 11,
   194; Antichrist, 4; on
   Norbert, 2, 7, 18; and
   Norbert compared, 2, 68,
   78–79; women's place in
   apostolic life, 26
"Blessed is Norbert," 125; text,
   191
Boethius, 226
Bomm, Werner, 18
Brandis, Tilo, 121
Burchard, bishop of Cambrai,
   10, 11, 80, 81, 131, 136

Bynum, Caroline, 16–17, 197, 221

Caccianemici, Gerard. *See* Lucius II, Pope
Caleb, 51
Callixtus II, Pope, 10, 71, 72, 135, 136
Canons, 4–6, 199; education of, 194–217; monasticism and, 4–5, 16–17, 31–62; private ownership, 5–6, 9; regular canons, 6–7, 42, 44, 49; secular canons, 6; wearing of cowl, 43; *see also* Premonstratensians
Capella, Martianus, 198
Celestine II, Pope, 13
Chamart, Nicholas, 195
Chrodegang, bishop of Metz, 5
Cistercians, 13, 14, 17, 18, 146, 197
Clerics. *See* Canons
Constable, Giles, 35
Contemplation, 34–37, 50–58, 199

Daniel, 52
David, 51–52, 202, 212, 217
Dereine, Charles, 63–64
Dialogues (Anselm of Havelburg), 16, 21–22
Dialogus (Idung of Prüfening), 33
Disciplina monasterii, 6
Donatists, 4

Egbert of Huysburg, 20, 31–35, 38, 193
Ehlers-Kisseler, Ingrid, 86
Eugenius III, Pope, 65, 116, 194
Evermode, bishop of Ratzeburg, 138
Ezekiel, 52, 204

Francis of Assisi, Saint, 34
Frederick I, archbishop of Cologne, 63, 130, 143–44; ordination of Norbert, 9, 127
Frederick of Arnsberg, 60, 88, 99–100, 105–7, 110–11, 119, 157
Fulton, Rachel, 22, 198, 219, 220, 222

Gelasius II, Pope, 9, 10, 43, 71, 130, 135
Geoffrey, bishop of Chartes, 82
Gerberga, abbess of Münster, 94–95, 114–15
Gilbert of Sempringham, 3–4, 34
Godfrey of Cappenberg, 19, 20, 85–119, 156–57, 186
Goodich, Michael, 21
Grauwen, Wilfried, 29, 66–67, 122
Grundmann, Herbert, 66, 86

Hadrian IV (antipope), 13
Harding, Stephen, 2
Henry V, Holy Roman Emperor, 8, 9, 63, 88, 93, 105, 109

Heresy, 4, 11
Herman-Judah. *See* Herman the
  Jew
Herman of Cologne, 64
Herman of Laon, 63–64. *See also*
  Herman of Tournai, 1–2,
  3, 11, 24; *Miracles of St.
  Mary of Laon*, 8, 15, 19,
  63–84, 124; *Restoration of
  the Monastery of St. Martin
  of Tournai*, 8, 9, 63, 64
Herman the Jew, 16, 20–21,
  86, 89
Honorius II, Pope, 158, 166
Hugh of Fosses, 66, 123, 125,
  136, 180–81; abbot of
  Prémontré, 12, 13, 77,
  80–81, 123; preaching, 10,
  132, 140

Idung of Prüfening, 7, 26, 33
Innocent II (Pope), 48, 166,
  170–71, 226
Institutio canonicorum. See
  Aachen, Rule of

Jacob, 51, 202
Jaeger, C. Steven, 30
Jeremiah, 197, 198, 204–5
Jerome, St., 38, 46–47
John, the Apostle, Saint, 36, 37,
  55, 199, 205, 206, 207–8
Joshua, 51
Judah ben David. *See* Herman
  the Jew

Lateran Council (4th), 17
Lees, Jay, 22, 30, 31, 33, 34

Leonius, abbot of St. Bertinus,
  75, 78
Libellus de diversis ordinibus, 33
*Life of Godfrey of Cappenberg,
  The*, 24, 64, 85–91, 124;
  text, 92–119
"Life of Lord Norbert,
  Archbishop of
  Magdeburg." *See Vita A*
Life of Oda (Philip of Harvengt),
  24, 219–23; text, 224–42
Lothair III, Holy Roman
  Emperor, 7, 11–12, 162,
  170, 171–72, 174, 190, 226
Lubac, Henri de, 196, 198
Lucius II, Pope, 162

Malachi, 211, 213
Manitius, Max, 63
Martha. *See* Mary and Martha
Mary, Blessed Virgin, 51;
  devotion to, 1, 19, 22, 23,
  198, 219, 220
Mary and Martha, of Bethany,
  24, 26, 35, 37, 53, 57
Matter, Ann, 221
McGinn, Bernard, 22
Migne, Jacques-Paul, 195
Miracles of St. Mary of Laon
  (Herman of Tournai), 8,
  15, 19, 63–68, 124; text,
  69–84
Monasticism: canons and, 4–5,
  16–17, 31–62;
  contemplation, 57, 58;
  wearing of cowl, 43
Mooney, Catherine, 220

Morrison, Karl, 16, 20–21
Moses, 51, 201–2, 203

Nicodemus, 205–6
Niemeyer, Gerlinde, 64, 65,
    86, 87
Noah, 50
Norbert of Gennep, 32
Norbert of Xanten, Saint, 1–5,
    7–10; archbishop of
    Magdeburg, 2, 7, 11, 12,
    67, 81–83, 162–64, 170;
    attempts on life of, 123,
    124, 164–65; birth and
    early life, 7, 126;
    conversion, 8–9, 63, 122,
    126–27; courtier, 7, 8;
    death, 12, 65–66, 124,
    173–74; founder of
    Premonstratensians, 1–2, 4,
    7, 11–15; healing of
    demoniac, 190–91;
    ordination, 9, 127; others'
    visions of, 183–85;
    preacher and reformer, 2,
    4, 7–10, 11, 24, 26,
    130–31, 138; prediction of
    famine, 186; prediction of
    warfare, 190; *see also*
    specific topics, e.g.:
    Premonstratensians; *Vita A*
Norbertines. *See*
    Premonstratensians

Oda of Rivreulle, 19, 23, 24,
    193, 200, 219–42

On the Education of Clerics (Philip
    of Harvengt), 195, 197–98,
    220
"On the Knowledge of Clerics"
    (Philip of Harvengt),
    194–200; text, 201–17
*Opusculum de conversione sua. See
    Short Account of His Own
    Conversion* (Herman the
    Jew)
Order of Prémontré. *See*
    Premonstratensians
Ordo antiquus, 6
Ordo monasterii, 6
Ordo novus, 4, 6, 7
"Origins and Spread of the
    Premonstratensians." *See*
    Vita B
Otto of Cappenberg, 85, 87–88,
    89, 97, 104, 113–14,
    116–19, 186

Paschal II, Pope, 9, 63, 71
Paul, Saint, 39, 84, 198;
    contemplation, 36–37, 55,
    56; education of clerics,
    208–9, 217
Paul of Thebes, 59–60
Pauper Christi, 34
Peter of Hamersleben, 33, 41
Pharisees, 205–6
Philip of Harvengt, 16–17, 26,
    27, 31, 32; as Augustinian
    canon, 17; *Life of Oda*, 24,
    219–242; "On the
    Knowledge of Clerics,"
    194–217; Song of Songs,

22–23, 26, 198, 219, 220, 223

Pierleoni, Petrus. *See* Anacletus II (antipope)

Praeceptum, 6

Premonstratensians, 1–3, 11–27; administrative development, 12, 13–14; Eastern and Western houses distinguished, 14, 17, 37; preaching, 1, 19, 25, 37; women's houses, 11, 19, 23, 25–26, 67, 79–80, 223; *see also* specific topics, e.g.: Augustinian Rule; Canons; Contemplation

Regula ad servos Dei, 6

Regula canonicorum, 5

Regula secunda, 6

Regula tertia, 6

Restoration of the Monastery of St. Martin of Tournai (Herman of Tournai), 8, 9, 63, 64

Robert of Arbrissel, 3–4, 26, 34

Robert of Molesme, 2

Rosenmund, Richard, 122

Rule of St. Augustine. *See* Augustinian Rule

Rupert of Deutz, 32–33

Sadducees, 205

Schmitt, Jean-Claude, 21, 86

Schism, 13–14, 170–72

Servatius, St., 188–89

Short Account of His Own Conversion (Herman the Jew), 16, 20–21, 86

Song of Songs, 22–23, 26, 198, 219, 220, 222, 223

Stracke, D. A., 64

Tanchelm, 4, 11, 123, 159–60

Theobald II, count of Champagne, 82, 157–58, 162

Urban II, Pope, 43

Victorines, 24

Virgin. *See* Mary, Blessed Virgin

Vita A, 8, 10, 15, 19, 63, 87, 121–25; text, 126–74

Vita α, 122

Vita B, 8, 10, 15, 19, 36, 63, 87, 121–25; text, 175–91

Walter, abbot of St. Martin, 76, 77

Weyns, Norbert, 195

Wilmans, Roger, 63, 121–22

Wolbrink, Shelley, 25

Women, 2, 11, 19, 23, 25–26, 67, 79–80, 223

Other Volumes in This Series

Abraham Isaac Kook • THE LIGHTS OF PENITENCE, LIGHTS OF HOLINESS, THE MORAL PRINCIPLES, ESSAYS, LETTERS, AND POEMS

Abraham Miguel Cardozo • SELECTED WRITINGS

Albert and Thomas • SELECTED WRITINGS

Alphonsus de Liguori • SELECTED WRITINGS

Anchoritic Spirituality •ANCRENE WISSE AND ASSOCIATED WORKS

Angela of Foligno • COMPLETE WORKS

Angelic Spirituality • MEDIEVAL PERSPECTIVES ON THE WAYS OF ANGELS

Angelus Silesius • THE CHERUBINIC WANDERER

Anglo-Saxon Spirituality • SELECTED WRITINGS

Apocalyptic Spirituality • TREATISES AND LETTERS OF LACTANTIUS, ADSO OF MONTIER-EN-DER, JOACHIM OF FIORE, THE FRANCISCAN SPIRITUALS, SAVONAROLA

Athanasius • THE LIFE OF ANTONY, AND THE LETTER TO MARCELLINUS

Augustine of Hippo • SELECTED WRITINGS

Bernard of Clairvaux • SELECTED WORKS

Bérulle and the French School • SELECTED WRITINGS

Birgitta of Sweden • LIFE AND SELECTED REVELATIONS

Bonaventure • THE SOUL'S JOURNEY INTO GOD, THE TREE OF LIFE, THE LIFE OF ST. FRANCIS

Cambridge Platonist Spirituality •

Carthusian Spirituality • THE WRITINGS OF HUGH OF BALMA AND GUIGO DE PONTE

Catherine of Genoa • PURGATION AND PURGATORY, THE SPIRITUAL DIALOGUE

Catherine of Siena • THE DIALOGUE

Celtic Spirituality •

Classic Midrash, The • TANNAITIC COMMENTARIES ON THE BIBLE

Cloud of Unknowing, The •

Devotio Moderna • BASIC WRITINGS

Dominican Penitent Women •

Early Anabaptist Spirituality • SELECTED WRITINGS

Early Dominicans • SELECTED WRITINGS

Early Islamic Mysticism • SUFI, QUR'AN, MI'RAJ, POETIC AND THEOLOGICAL WRITINGS

Early Kabbalah, The •

Elijah Benamozegh • ISRAEL AND HUMANITY

Elisabeth Leseur • SELECTED WRITINGS

Elisabeth of Schönau • THE COMPLETE WORKS

Emanuel Swedenborg • THE UNIVERSAL HUMAN AND SOUL-BODY INTERACTION

Other Volumes in This Series

Ephrem the Syrian • HYMNS
Fakhruddin 'Iraqi • DIVINE FLASHES
Fénelon • SELECTED WRITINGS
Francis and Clare • THE COMPLETE WORKS
Francis de Sales, Jane de Chantal • LETTERS OF SPIRITUAL DIRECTION
Francisco de Osuna • THE THIRD SPIRITUAL ALPHABET
George Herbert • THE COUNTRY PARSON, THE TEMPLE
Gertrude of Helfta • THE HERALD OF DIVINE LOVE
Gregory of Nyssa • THE LIFE OF MOSES
Gregory Palamas • THE TRIADS
Hadewijch • THE COMPLETE WORKS
Henry Suso • THE EXEMPLAR, WITH TWO GERMAN SERMONS
Hildegard of Bingen • SCIVIAS
Ibn 'Abbād of Ronda • LETTERS ON THE ṢŪFĪ PATH
Ibn Al'-Arabī • THE BEZELS OF WISDOM
Ibn 'Ata' Illah • THE BOOK OF WISDOM AND KWAJA ABDULLAH ANSARI: INTIMATE CONVERSATIONS
Ignatius of Loyola • SPIRITUAL EXERCISES AND SELECTED WORKS
Isaiah Horowitz • THE GENERATIONS OF ADAM
Jacob Boehme • THE WAY TO CHRIST
Jacopone da Todi • THE LAUDS
Jean Gerson • EARLY WORKS
Jeremy Taylor • SELECTED WORKS
Jewish Mystical Autobiographies • BOOK OF VISIONS AND BOOK OF SECRETS
Johann Arndt • TRUE CHRISTIANITY
Johannes Tauler • SERMONS
John Baptist de La Salle • THE SPIRITUALITY OF CHRISTIAN EDUCATION
John Calvin • WRITINGS ON PASTORAL PIETY
John Cassian • CONFERENCES
John and Charles Wesley • SELECTED WRITINGS AND HYMNS
John Climacus • THE LADDER OF DIVINE ASCENT
John Comenius • THE LABYRINTH OF THE WORLD AND THE PARADISE OF THE HEART
John of Avila • AUDI, FILIA—LISTEN, O DAUGHTER
John of the Cross • SELECTED WRITINGS
John Donne • SELECTIONS FROM DIVINE POEMS, SERMONS, DEVOTIONS AND PRAYERS
John Henry Newman • SELECTED SERMONS
John Ruusbroec • THE SPIRITUAL ESPOUSALS AND OTHER WORKS
Julian of Norwich • SHOWINGS

Other Volumes in This Series

Knowledge of God in Classical Sufism • FOUNDATIONS OF ISLAMIC MYSTICAL THEOLOGY

Luis de León • THE NAMES OF CHRIST

Luther's Spirituality •

Margaret Ebner • MAJOR WORKS

Marguerite Porete • THE MIRROR OF SIMPLE SOULS

Maria Maddalena de' Pazzi • SELECTED REVELATIONS

Martin Luther • THEOLOGIA GERMANICA

Maximus Confessor • SELECTED WRITINGS

Mechthild of Magdeburg • THE FLOWING LIGHT OF THE GODHEAD

Meister Eckhart • THE ESSENTIAL SERMONS, COMMENTARIES, TREATISES AND DEFENSE

Meister Eckhart • TEACHER AND PREACHER

Menahem Nahum of Chernobyl • UPRIGHT PRACTICES, THE LIGHT OF THE EYES

Nahman of Bratslav • THE TALES

Native Mesoamerican Spirituality • ANCIENT MYTHS, DISCOURSES, STORIES, DOCTRINES, HYMNS, POEMS FROM THE AZTEC, YUCATEC, QUICHE-MAYA AND OTHER SACRED TRADITIONS

Native North American Spirituality of the Eastern Woodlands • SACRED MYTHS, DREAMS, VISIONS, SPEECHES, HEALING FORMULAS, RITUALS AND CEREMONIALS

Nicholas of Cusa • SELECTED SPIRITUAL WRITINGS

Nicodemos of the Holy Mountain • A HANDBOOK OF SPIRITUAL COUNSEL

Nil Sorsky • THE COMPLETE WRITINGS

Nizam ad-din Awliya • MORALS FOR THE HEART

Origen • AN EXHORTATION TO MARTYRDOM, PRAYER AND SELECTED WORKS

Philo of Alexandria • THE CONTEMPLATIVE LIFE, THE GIANTS, AND SELECTIONS

Pietists • SELECTED WRITINGS

Pilgrim's Tale, The •

Pseudo-Dionysius • THE COMPLETE WORKS

Pseudo-Macarius • THE FIFTY SPIRITUAL HOMILIES AND THE GREAT LETTER

Pursuit of Wisdom, The • AND OTHER WORKS BY THE AUTHOR OF THE CLOUD OF UNKNOWING

Quaker Spirituality • SELECTED WRITINGS

Rabbinic Stories •

Richard Rolle • THE ENGLISH WRITINGS

Other Volumes in This Series

Richard of St. Victor • THE TWELVE PATRIARCHS, THE MYSTICAL ARK, BOOK THREE OF THE TRINITY

Robert Bellarmine • SPIRITUAL WRITINGS

Safed Spirituality • RULES OF MYSTICAL PIETY, THE BEGINNING OF WISDOM

Shakers, The • TWO CENTURIES OF SPIRITUAL REFLECTION

Sharafuddin Maneri • THE HUNDRED LETTERS

Sor Juana gnés de la Crug • SELECTED WRITINGS

Spirituality of the German Awakening, The •

Symeon the New Theologian • THE DISCOURSES

Talmud, The • SELECTED WRITINGS

Teresa of Avila • THE INTERIOR CASTLE

Theatine Spirituality • SELECTED WRITINGS

'Umar Ibn al-Fāriḍ • SUFI VERSE, SAINTLY LIFE

Valentin Weigel • SELECTED SPIRITUAL WRITINGS

Vincent de Paul and Louise de Marillac • RULES, CONFERENCES, AND WRITINGS

Walter Hilton • THE SCALE OF PERFECTION

William Law • A SERIOUS CALL TO A DEVOUT AND HOLY LIFE, THE SPIRIT OF LOVE

Zohar • THE BOOK OF ENLIGHTENMENT

The Classics of Western Spirituality is a ground-breaking collection of the original writings of more than 100 universally acknowledged teachers within the Catholic, Protestant, Eastern Orthodox, Jewish, Islamic, and Native American Indian traditions.

To order any title, or to request a complete catalog, contact Paulist Press at 800-218-1903 or visit us on the Web at www.paulistpress.com